SUSTAINABLE COMMUNITIES FOR A HEALTHY PLANET

Katharine Zywert

Sustainable Communities for a Healthy Planet presents an unconventional collection of ideas, practices, and ways of living together with the potential to enable long-term human and planetary health. Grounded in first-hand accounts from researchers, health practitioners, and social innovators across diverse fields, Katharine Zywert's book argues that the most promising approaches often depart substantially from the incentive structures, goals, and mindsets that define the status quo and do not necessarily align with mainstream sustainability discourses.

The book instead presents promising approaches that disrupt dominant ideas about mental health, ageing, and chronic illness; circumvent exploitative markets for medications, medical technologies, and professionalized care; attend not only to the health of individual human bodies, but to the health of internal ecologies, human populations, nonhuman species, and the planet as a whole; and embody alternative, more inclusive ways of practicing medicine within communities and ecosystems. The stories assembled in this book illustrate how human beings might live healthy lives, supported by health systems that are not dependent on perpetual economic growth.

Sustainable Communities for a Healthy Planet challenges conventional ways of thinking about the future of health systems and asks hard questions about what it takes to cultivate human and planetary health in a time of rapid ecological, economic, and social change.

KATHARINE ZYWERT is an independent researcher and writer working at the intersection of social-ecological systems change and health.

Sustainable Communities for a Healthy Planet

KATHARINE ZYWERT

UNIVERSITY OF TORONTO PRESS
Toronto Buffalo London

© University of Toronto Press 2024
Toronto Buffalo London
utorontopress.com
Printed and bound by CPI Group (UK) Ltd, Croydon, CR0 4YY

ISBN 978-1-4875-4803-2 (cloth)   ISBN 978-1-4875-5045-5 (EPUB)
ISBN 978-1-4875-4866-7 (paper)   ISBN 978-1-4875-4964-0 (PDF)

Library and Archives Canada Cataloguing in Publication

Title: Sustainable communities for a healthy planet / Katharine Zywert.
Names: Zywert, Katharine, 1986– author.
Description: Includes bibliographical references and index.
Identifiers: Canadiana (print) 20230591396 | Canadiana (ebook) 20230591485 | ISBN 9781487548032 (cloth) | ISBN 9781487548667 (paper) | ISBN 9781487549640 (PDF) | ISBN 9781487550455 (EPUB)
Subjects: LCSH: Medical care – Environmental aspects. | LCSH: Medical economics. | LCSH: Community life – Environmental aspects. | LCSH: Sustainability. | LCSH: Social ecology.
Classification: LCC RA394.Z99 2024 | DDC 338.4/73621–dc23

Cover design: Will Brown
Cover image: *Everybody's Cyclopedia* (New York, NY: Syndicate Publishing Company, 1912); B.P. Holst, *The Teachers' and Pupils' Cyclopaedia* (Kansas City: The Bufton Book Company, 1909); George Nicholson, *The Illustrated Dictionary of Gardening*, Div. VI (London, England: L. Upcott Gill, 1884).

We wish to acknowledge the land on which the University of Toronto Press operates. This land is the traditional territory of the Wendat, the Anishnaabeg, the Haudenosaunee, the Métis, and the Mississaugas of the Credit First Nation.

University of Toronto Press acknowledges the financial support of the Government of Canada, the Canada Council for the Arts, and the Ontario Arts Council, an agency of the Government of Ontario, for its publishing activities.

Canada Council for the Arts   Conseil des Arts du Canada

ONTARIO ARTS COUNCIL
CONSEIL DES ARTS DE L'ONTARIO
an Ontario government agency
un organisme du gouvernement de l'Ontario

Funded by the Government of Canada   Financé par le gouvernement du Canada

For Morgan and Virginia

Contents

List of Figures and Tables ix

Foreword xi

Acknowledgments xix

Introduction 3
A Note on the Meaning of "Health" 15

Part 1: The Ecological Foundations of Health 21

  1 Health in Deep Time 23
  2 Health across Nested Social-Ecological Scales 31
  3 Problems of Scale in Human and Planetary Health 51
  4 Soil Health 72
  5 Gardening for Health 81
  6 Care Farming 99

Part 2: A Political Economy for Health 117

  7 Political-Economic Transformation for Health 121
  8 Relocalization for Human and Planetary Health 143
  9 Community Organizing for Health and Well-Being in a Global Pandemic 167
10 Health and Care in Two Ecovillages 177
11 Community Nursing 187
12 Community Care for Severe Mental Illnesses in Geel, Belgium 194

Part 3: Social-Ecological Systems Change for Health   203

13 How Social-Ecological Systems Change Happens   205
14 Promising Systems Change Strategies for Cultivating Human and Planetary Health   217
15 The Midnight Kitchen   247
16 Complexity Medicine Group   259
17 Herbalism in a Post-Growth Transition   270

Conclusion: Cultivating Human and Planetary Health for a Sustainable Future   279

Appendix: Justification for Inclusion Criteria   295

References   299

Index   325

Figures and Tables

Figures

8.1 Drivers of relocalization in social and economic systems   163
13.1 The three basins of attraction of the global social-ecological system   214

Tables

8.1 Potential characteristics of an alternative modernity arising from key social-ecological drivers   155
8.2 Contrasts between ideal-type low-throughput and high-throughput societies   158
C.3 How prefigurative alternatives align with inclusion criteria   285

Foreword

It is difficult to come to terms with the fact that the very health systems we have built to care for each other are contributing to their own instability. Responsible for about 5 per cent of greenhouse gas emissions (Romanello et al. 2022) and substantial amounts of air pollution and chemical pollution that are harmful to both human and planetary health (Romanello et al. 2022; Eckelman, Sherman, and MacNeill 2018; Landrigan et al. 2023), our health care systems impose a heavy load on a planet whose climate regulatory system is approaching dangerous tipping points (Steffen et al. 2018).

As temperature records shatter and wildfires drive the evacuation of communities throughout Canada, sending smoke across international borders, I have been thinking that if the Earth were one of my ER patients I would move her into the trauma room for one-on-one nursing care and active management. Once physiologic instability is identified in acute care spaces, we act fast, propelled by embodied memories of times we were too slow. When one organ system starts to struggle, it puts pressure on the others, and it is all too easy to see a somewhat unstable patient suddenly spiral into multisystem dysfunction, to "crash" as we say. In an effort to prevent that, we monitor vital signs continuously in such patients, call for help, and treat aggressively, preparing resuscitation equipment in case we need it.

These crux points of team-based, time-sensitive work are often definitive in a patient's illness trajectory. I became an ER physician because I believe that treating acute, fast-moving reversible disease is one of the things that modern medicine does best. Building, staffing, and supplying emergency rooms capable of this demands a high level of societal complexity. Having spent six months resuscitating severely malnourished infants and children in a low-income health care setting, I am too familiar with the wrench of closing silken eyelids for the last time when ventilators are not available. My drive to keep the best of health care functioning is fierce, and has fuelled much of the fourteen years that I have been working to help deliver a healthy response to climate change.

Unfortunately, we have been sluggish in responding to the Earth's signs and symptoms. We must now both quickly reduce the load that we place on her and prepare in case she tips into severe dysfunction. How can we best support health and health care in a world of fiscal and ecological constraint? We must consider both how to volitionally refine our practices in order to deliver the best outcomes with the greatest degree of efficiency, and how to plan for a possible lack of resources resulting from a reduction in societal complexity. Humanity has always faced cycles of flourishing and collapse. However, global interconnectedness now increases the possibility that a problem in one location or one system can rapidly affect others. As Katharine Zywert says, "While crises have always visited human communities and ecosystems, past crises were better at staying put."

To have the opportunity to provide care we can be proud of for the rest of our practice lifetimes, and to hand over a system to the next generation of providers that allows us to keep the best of what we have had, we must choose wisely at hospital, community, health system, and planetary scales. We undergo this transition at a moment when the mainstream of medicine is only just being introduced to planetary health. Even now, the vast majority of medical students are not being taught about climate change and air pollution (Omrani 2020), and most practising physicians are aware of climate change as a health issue but are not sure how to respond (Kotcher 2021). Canada has committed to the WHO resilient, low-carbon health systems initiative but has just begun to develop a plan to deliver on our goals (WHO 2021). For the most part, members of the health and care sector have been in a state where they don't know what they don't know about the ecological crisis.

In essence, then, Katharine Zywert has written a book to help us address a confluence of challenges that is only just landing with many. She has had the tenacity to stick with difficult subject matter – to outline not only why we need to be concerned as the ecological foundations of health and health systems become destabilized in the Anthropocene, but to examine the behavioural, political, and social drivers for the ecological stressors as well as provide solutions and evidence-aligned mechanisms via which social-ecological systems systems change in service of health can be realized.

Is it depressing to think about this? Adjusting to new knowledge of challenges that affect not only our patients but ourselves and our loved ones requires emotional work. Readers may find that they have to take breaks, go for walks, go to bed early, and cuddle up to their kids. I invite you to give yourselves grace, to take your time – *and* to persist. We are alive at this crux moment in history –we have an opportunity to affect outcomes that no future humans will have. As Dr Zywert points out, knowing the worst-case scenario can compel action, as did the idea of "nuclear winter" in 1983. It can also inform policy interventions to improve resilience and help us weight the risks and benefits of emergency action (Kemp 2022). It is difficult to think strategically if every new data point feels like a punch to the gut. Just as "tactical breathing" is now encouraged to help trauma team leaders manage their own emotions in order to optimize their team's performance, health system leaders need to explicitly develop practices that allow them to work with the information presented here in a clear-headed manner. Given the magnitude of the challenge, this can be considered a goal in itself.

Katharine Zywert has provided a tremendous service by having done much heavy lifting in terms of research and analysis, and presented it here in a solutions-oriented manner. In sourcing and describing case studies of low-resource, good-outcome care models, Zywert grounds us to the reality that the polycrisis is the biggest reason we have ever had to do many of the things we always talk about:

- to harvest the health benefits of time in nature by tending to gardens in a manner that reduces chemical pollution and enhances soil health and local food security;
- to rediscover the power of herbs and traditional medicines to heal, tempering our cynical raised eyebrows with the knowledge that the wondrous ASA is found in willow bark and that game-changing curare comes from a tree;
- to create community support structures that invite neighbours to invest time in mutual aid, secure in the knowledge that they have 24/7 access to a network of professional nurses, reducing burnout amongst caregivers and overburdened health systems and offering our elders improved opportunities to age with dignity in the community;
- to build a society that recognizes that food, exercise, sleep, friendship, and nature time are all medicine, and to work those into every design feature, every program, every day.

Fundamentally, we need to invite our communities into the circle of care. This is a necessary part of adapting to the climate change we are already experiencing, and will become progressively more important. We are not at a new normal – under all feasible emissions scenarios we will continue to see changing temperature and precipitation in Canada until at least mid-century (Bush and Lemmen 2019). My disaster medicine specialist friends remind me that the definition of a disaster is "an event that overwhelms official local systems." That means that the people who will help us during floods, wildfires, and heat emergencies are most likely to be our family and neighbours. If we build networks of mutual care into our day-to-day lives, relationships and practices will be ready for the additional strain of climate-related dysfunction, whether it be acute, as during a wildfire, or long term, as in the case of a lasting reduction in societal complexity. Zywert states, "Perhaps one of the most promising ways to steward processes of social-ecological systems change is to contribute to building a 'back-up system' that operates in tandem with the dominant system and that can serve as a 'fallback' in the case of cascading failures." In case of systemic risk to the stability of the dominant paradigm of consumer capitalism, these alternatives become the ideas that are lying in reserve. Complexity science suggests that their existence makes it more likely that the system will flip not into a state of collapse but into the amplification and mainstreaming of such solutions.

The polycrisis is reason to reconsider the ideas that form the roots of our current system. Is it possible to achieve a good life for all within planetary limits while maintaining a growth-dependent economy? This year at Oxford I have had the privilege of being in many rooms with brilliant economists, and have listened intently for the answer to that question. There are reasonable, caring people who would say yes and offer a data-driven reply. Equally, there are evidence-driven practitioners who would say no. I have not, however, yet met an economist who has a strong understanding of planetary boundaries who is not questioning growth dependency. To be clear, this has not been a passing curiosity – I've made a point of sidling up to a lot of experts over both hot and cold beverages and asking them in private. I sometimes wait until after two or three cold beverages and ask them again, just to be sure.

All agree that there are currently structural growth dependencies within our economies. As Herman Daly has pointed out, "a steady-state economy is not a failed growth economy. An airplane is designed for forward motion. If it tries to hover it crashes. It is not fruitful to conceive of a helicopter as an airplane that fails to move forward. It is a different thing designed to hover. Likewise a SSE is not designed to grow" (Daly, 2008, **n.p.**). Humanity lived for most of its history in a state of negligible annual growth, but this has shifted over the past two hundred years, leaving us in a position where the Earth can no longer sustain the inputs and outputs of the economy. Daly quips, "Economists have focused too much on the economy's circulatory system and have neglected to study its digestive tract" (Daly, 2008, **n.p.**), leaving us now harmed by air pollution, chemical pollution, wildfires, heat, and severe weather resulting from the products of the economy's nether regions. We may very well need to figure out how to turn our airplane into a helicopter mid-flight.

Much like the health professions, the discipline of economics is evolving in its understanding of the intersection of its work and the demands of the ecological crisis, with many current students calling for change (e.g., Rethinking Economics Oxford 2023). We can expect that a heterogeneity in approach will continue, amplified as always by implicit and explicit pressures related to power and academic funding and research. We in the health sector, recognizing that many powerful economists are as yet under-briefed regarding linkages between ecological stability, economic stability, and health, ought to help make those connections and provide strong support for a transition towards an economy that is explicitly designed to optimize well-being – work that is already underway (Canadian Association of Physicians for the Environment 2022).

It is all scary until we ground ourselves in the moment, in our community. I know that a lot can be done when a small amount of material resource is paired with a large amount of social capital, human capital, and generations-old teachings: I know this from watching the response people in the North have to land-based initiatives at the Arctic Indigenous Wellness Foundation. I have visited there in the depths of the subarctic winter and noticed faces familiar from the ER enlivened by the swing of an axe in pursuit of firewood to contribute to the communal fire, and have seen the light in people's eyes as they share tea and food with friends.

Dene healer Be'sha Blondin once told me that one of the first questions she asks when people come to her for help with mental health troubles is, "What do you still need to contribute?" I compared this to the mandatory questions I ask in the ER – "Have you had thoughts of harming yourself? Do you have a plan? Do you have access to the tools required to carry out your plan?" – and was embarrassed by the degree to which my questions shamed and disabled, whereas hers contributed to vision and ability. On another occasion, when I had brought a Canadian Medical Association president to the camp, we were sitting in a woodstove-warmed canvas tent learning from Be'sha and Elder Francois Paulette when laughter burbled up outside our tent, rolling through the fabric in wave after wave. It happened so many times that we stopped and smiled, listening. In twenty years in the Canadian health care system I cannot remember a time when a conversation with other care providers was interrupted by the laughter of our patients in a situation where mirth was not only welcome, but had been purposefully kindled.

Work by the Arctic Indigenous Wellness Foundation intersects with our current mainstream system: when a patient of theirs became too ill, they accompanied him to the emergency room when I was working, resulting in one of the most humane handovers of care that I have ever participated in. We now offer psychiatry inpatients at the hospital transport to the camp several times a week.

There is healing in such communities that is wise and good, and that in the right circumstances, for the right people, is better than anything we can offer in the fluorescent-lit box that is our hospital. This healing is based on the understanding that we are all part of an interconnected ecosystem, that our contributions matter and are non-substitutable, and yet that none of us is responsible for the whole.

We all want to feel that our lives matter. We are living at a moment that is so close to tipping points both for good and for ill that every decision we take has the potential to impact health not only now but for all future generations. Our actions couldn't possibly matter more than they do right now. What a time to be alive.

In this book Katharine Zywert has laid out the beginnings of a treatment plan that can help us make the most of this opportunity that we have. We should honour this thinking in the best way we can – by threading it into our work in service of providing a good life for all within the limits of what the planet can support.

Will we rise to the occasion? The curious thing about humanity is that we are often at our best when things are at their worst. Fifteen years into life as an emergency physician I have learned an interesting truth: if a patient with a cold is in a room next to a patient with a heart attack, I know that I am very likely to see a patient who is brave, who is sensible, and who inspires me with their courage. It isn't the person with the cold.

Thank you, Katharine. *Bon courage, mes amis.*

Courtney Howard, MD
Oxford, UK
10 July 2023

REFERENCES

Bush, E., and D.S. Lemmen, D.S., eds. 2019. *Canada's Changing Climate Report*. Ottawa: Government of Canada.

Canadian Association of Physicians for the Environment. 2022. "Canadian Health Professionals Call On the Prime Minister and Premiers to Transition to a Society Focused on Well-Being for World Health Day." Press release. https://shorturl.at/frtMX.

Daly, Herman E. 2008. *Towards a Steady-State Economy*. Essay commissioned by the Sustainable Development Commission, UK (April 24, 2008). Available: https://is.muni.cz/el/fss/jaro2015/ENS242/um/55677449/3_Daly_2008_Towards_a_Steady_State_Economy.pdf

Eckelman Matthew J., Jodi D. Sherman, and Andrea J. MacNeill. 2018. "Life Cycle Environmental Emissions and Health Damages from the Canadian Healthcare System: An Economic-Environmental-Epidemiological Analysis." *PLoS Medicine* 15, no. 7: e1002623. https://doi.org/10.1371/journal.pmed.1002623.

Kemp L, Xu C, Depledge J, et al. Climate Endgame: Exploring catastrophic climate change scenarios. Proceedings of the National Academy of Science 2022; 119.

Kotcher, John, Edward Maibach, Jeni Miller, Eryn Campbell, Lujain Alqodmani, Marina Maiero, and Arthur Wyns. 2021. "Views of Health Professionals on Climate Change and Health: A Multinational Survey Study." *Lancet Planet Health* 5, no. 5: e316-e323. https://doi.org/10.1016/S2542-5196(21)00053-X.

Landrigan, Philip J., Hervé Raps, Maureen Cropper, Caroline Bald, Manuel Brunner, Elvia Maya Canonizado, Dominic Charles, et al. 2023. "The Minderoo-Monaco Commission on Plastics and Human Health." *Annals of Global Health* 89, no. 1: 23. https://doi.org/10.5334/aogh.4056.

Omrani, Omnia El, Alaa Dafallah, Blanca Paniello Castillo, Bianca Quintella Ribeiro Corrêa Amaro, Sanjana Taneja, Marouane Amzil, Md Refat Uz-Zaman Sajib, and Tarek Ezzine. 2020. "Envisioning Planetary Health in Every Medical Curriculum: An International Medical Student Organization's Perspective." *Medical Teacher* 42, no. 10: 1107–11. https://doi.org/10.1080/0142159X.2020.1796949.

Rethinking Economics Oxford. 2023. "Oxford Students Call for New Curricula This Year to Tackle Global Polycrisis." Press release. https://docs.google.com/document/d/1DmmlNdST-ZQ1FhqefvN2lADjPbBNcZzX3S-Zcx4rUeg/edit?usp=sharing

Romanello, Marina, Claudia Di Napoli, Paul Drummond, Carole Green, Harry Kennard, Pete Lampard, Daniel Scamman, et al. 2022. "The 2022 Report of the Lancet Countdown on Health and Climate Change: Health at the Mercy of Fossil Fuels." Lancet 400, no. 10363: 1619–54. https://doi.org/10.1016/S0140-6736(22)01540-9.

Steffen, Will, Johan Rockström, Katherine Richardson, Timothy M. Lenton, Carl Folke, Diana Liverman, Colin P. Summerhayes, et al. 2018. "Trajectories of the Earth System in the Anthropocene." *Proceedings of the National Academy of Science* 115, no. 33: 8252–9. https://doi.org/https://doi.org/10.1073/pnas.1810141115.

World Health Organization. 2021, 9 November. "Countries Commit to Develop Climate-Smart Health Care at COP26 UN Climate Conference" [Press release]. https://www.who.int/news/item/09-11-2021-countries-commit-to-develop-climate-smart-health-care-at-cop26-un-climate-conference.

Acknowledgments

I am incredibly grateful to all the researchers, doctors, and change makers who generously contributed their stories and wisdom to this book. Our conversations will stay with me always and have shaped my thinking not only about human and planetary health, but about what is most important in life. Extra thanks go to Didi Pershouse, Jane Myat, and William Sutherland for bringing me into your worlds, for many long conversations, and for reviewing multiple drafts. Your work energizes me and makes me hopeful about the future.

For your support, encouragement, and insight over many years, thank you to Stephen Quilley, Jennifer Lynes, Dan McCarthy, Craig Janes, Beth Conklin, Barb Davy, Katie Kish, Susan and Gerry Remers, Carole and Colin Zywert, and Tyson Remers.

Thank you to the team at University of Toronto Press for exceptional support, especially Meg Patterson, Jennifer DiDomenico, and Jodi Litvin.

For funding that made the original research for this book possible, thank you to Dr. Frances Westley, the Briarhurst Travel and Research Award, the Canadian Institutes of Health Research, the Government of Ontario, and the University of Waterloo.

This book was written in Waterloo, Ontario, which is located on the traditional territories of the Neutral, Anishinaabe, and Haudenosaunee peoples. Waterloo is part of the Haldimand Tract, six miles on either side of the Grand River that was promised to the Haudenosaunee Confederation in an agreement that settlers did not honour.

SUSTAINABLE COMMUNITIES FOR A HEALTHY PLANET

Introduction

This book is a collection of ideas, practices, and ways of living together that could make it possible for health systems in the world's wealthiest nations to step back from ecological overshoot and instead enable long-term human and planetary health. It aims to offer glimpses of the future of health and social inclusion on a rapidly changing planet, considering questions such as: What could a health system that meets population-level health and care needs without consuming unsustainable levels of resources and energy look like? What existing ideas, behaviours, structures, and relationships prefigure such a health system and how might they (purposefully or unintentionally) enable its emergence in high-income nations? How can we (interested health practitioners, researchers, leaders, social change makers, members of families and communities) nudge health systems towards greater long-term sustainability and resilience as broader social-ecological systems transformations (e.g., paradigm-level changes to the political economy, climate systems, governance structures) unfold in the coming decades?

These questions are complex, and so before I attempt to answer them, it is important to situate my perspective and approach both as a researcher and as a human being with a particular stake in the outcomes of systemic change. In doing so, I hope to demonstrate the value of the work I have done while at the same time acknowledging that there are innumerable ideas I did not include, places I did not investigate, and communities whose wisdom is not reflected in this book.

The principles that guide my work are grounded in a wide-ranging, transdisciplinary literature review (see appendix) and primary data collection in the form of conversations with academics, doctors, health practitioners, social change leaders, and participants in social innovations for health and care. Yet this book presents a niche perspective; for the most part, the future I want to consider resides beyond mainstream sustainability discourses. It inhabits a place that is more difficult to articulate, more shadowed in uncertainty, and more challenging to reconcile with widely held twenty-first-century values and expectations. I sometimes think of it as the difference between a somewhat untamed, overgrown medicine garden and a clean, bright, net zero hospital. In thinking about it this way, I am in no way trying to suggest that decarbonizing health care is not a worthy goal, especially if pursued alongside broader paradigm-level shifts in the way we think about health and structure health systems. Rather, I am stating upfront that the future envisioned through the lens of mainstream sustainability – a future much like the present except clean energy replaces dirty energy, green growth replaces ecologically corrosive growth, and cyclical supply chains enable mass consumption in perpetuity – is not the subject of this book.

I want to know what is growing in the garden. I want to learn about the cultivated patches of herbs and about the volunteer medicinals that so often get called "weeds." I want to know because it is very possible that eco-modernist visions of a high-tech, prosperous, progressive, *and* sustainable future (see Asafu-Adjaye et al. 2015) may be impossible to realize. More than that, I have profound doubts about whether a future rooted in the theories and practices of mainstream sustainability could achieve long-term human and planetary health even if the transition towards such a system was feasible (see chapters 7 and 8). When applied to health systems in high-income countries, mainstream sustainability initiatives tend to focus on lowering the ecological footprint of health care services in order to reduce waste, save money, and ensure that health care is not contributing to the very problems it is there to solve (e.g., reducing GHG emissions in an effort to curb the climate crisis and lower the health sector's direct contribution to respiratory illnesses – see Thiel et al. 2015). These initiatives are undoubtedly worth pursuing as a way of lowering the material and energetic intensity of modern health care. But as a framework for securing long-term human and planetary health at a global scale, mainstream sustainability approaches fall short because they do not adequately attend to

1. the existence of ecological limits to human activities, particularly to the scale of economic growth that is possible and desirable on a finite planet;
2. the extent to which transformations at the scale of the social-ecological regime[1] can cascade through other interconnected systems, rendering certain practices, approaches, and structures obsolete while creating opportunities for new, unexpected, and potentially uncomfortable patterns to emerge; and

3. the paradoxes, tensions, and trade-offs involved in simultaneously pursuing health and sustainability at scales ranging from individual human bodies to human communities, populations of non-human species, ecosystems, and planetary biophysical processes.

This book aims to show that the approaches that hold the greatest potential depart substantially from the incentive structures, power dynamics, goals, and mindsets that define the current social-ecological regime. Whether they disrupt dominant ideas about mental health, ageing, chronic illness, or death, circumvent exploitative markets for medications, medical technologies, or professionalized care, or embody alternative ways of practising medicine within communities and ecosystems, these approaches all have one foot in a very different kind of world. For this reason, they both offer glimpses of how a social-ecological system with the capacity to enable long-term human and planetary health might be structured and begin to clear a path towards this future.

The ideas, practices, and ways of living assembled in this book include care farming, the soil health movement, time banking, herbal medicine, complexity medicine, mutual aid, ecovillage health systems, community nursing, and doctors gardening with their patients. They all speak (some directly, others more implicitly) to how human beings might live healthy lives, supported by health systems that are not dependent on perpetual economic growth. Many represent new, unanticipated, and at times disconcerting patterns of thought and action while others are rooted in older ways of caring for one another that managed to survive the transition to capitalist modernity. Most of them provoke at least some tension because they take seriously not only the health of individual human bodies but the health of internal ecologies, non-human species, communities, the global human population, or the planet as a whole. By bringing these approaches together, I hope to challenge conventional ways of thinking about the future of health systems and to open up space to consider alternative meanings, practices, and strategies for change.

Investigating Planetary Health as a "Rush of Stories"

> It is in listening to that cacophony of troubled stories that we might encounter our best hopes for precarious survival ... To listen to and tell a rush of stories is a method. And why not make the strong claim and call it a science, an addition to knowledge? Its research object is contaminated diversity; its unit of analysis is the indeterminate encounter ... But we have a problem with scale. A rush of stories cannot be neatly summed up.

Its scales do not nest neatly; they draw attention to interrupting geographies and tempos. These interruptions elicit more stories. This is the rush of stories' power as a science. (Tsing 2015, 34–7)

This book aims to identify promising ideas and practices with the potential to cultivate long-term human and planetary health in the Anthropocene. My approach to primary research was inspired by two methodological developments that began in the field of anthropology and that have since spread across the social sciences: multisited ethnography to investigate global problems, and a multispecies lens that foregrounds non-human species as subjects on a changing planet (Crate 2011; Marcus 1995; Silvast and Virtanen 2019; Kirksey and Helmreich 2010; Tsing 2005; Kohn 2013). The questions I investigated for this book concern social-ecological systems changes that cross geographic, temporal, political, and sectoral boundaries. I could not adequately address these issues by limiting my search to any single group of health practitioners or researchers, or any single community. Instead, I chose to share what Anna Tsing describes as a "rush of stories" through which we may begin to unearth "our best hopes for precarious survival" (2015, 34).

I am also asking questions that are difficult to localize in time and space. I am concerned with long-term transformations of human society that occur within broader social-ecological systems of which our species is a small but increasingly influential part. To think about human and planetary health at this scale, and specifically to think about the future of health in an epoch when the trajectories of social-ecological systems cannot be taken for granted (Olsson et al. 2017; McMichael 2014), requires bringing together diverse perspectives. For this reason, I took a multisited ethnographic approach that allowed me to consider how the global challenges of environmental sustainability and human well-being are negotiated across varied local contexts. Multisited ethnography has been proposed as a useful methodology for studying the effects of the climate crisis, a global issue manifesting in a myriad of localities (Crate 2011; Marcus 1995; Silvast and Virtanen 2019). By drawing together multiple field sites and practitioner groups, I aim to convey the collective potential of a range of practices, social arrangements, and ways of thinking.

Because this book is fundamentally concerned with the embeddedness of human well-being within ecological systems, I also took a multispecies approach to the ethnographic accounts presented in this work. Multispecies approaches help to ground research activities in systemic, ecological ways of knowing. Ecological ways of knowing recognize the importance of relationships within complex adaptive systems, particularly how patterns of feedback between components in a system determine its structure, behaviours, and purpose (see Meadows 2008). Multispecies ethnography brings non-human beings such as animals and plants out of the background and onto centre stage in ethnographic writing (Kirksey and Helmreich 2010). For instance, increased attention to microbiota calls into question the assumption that humans are individual beings, repositioning the human as a site of complex ecology (Harraway 2008 as cited in Kirksey and Helmreich 2010). Multispecies approaches disrupt the dominance of rational, self-contained individual humans in anthropological research by devoting ethnographic space to multispecies "assemblages" that illustrate how "staying alive – for every species – requires liveable collaborations" (Tsing 2015, 22, 28). Taking a multispecies approach when researching alternative arrangements for health and care helped me to foreground the extent to which health is an emergent property of complex adaptive systems that cannot flourish apart from their ecological components.

The Potential of Diverse Prefigurative Initiatives

In deciding which ethnographic field sites to profile in this book, I chose to focus on natural experiments in health and care that are already occurring in high-income nations. Natural experiments informally test hypotheses by establishing new practices, behaviours, or social conditions that can be compared to the status quo (Bernard 2006). For instance, when Dr. Jane Myat decided to build a garden around the Caversham Group Practice in North London, she became engaged in a type of informal experiment that asked whether gardening can help to build health and social connectedness among her patients. Many of the sites I profile in this book can similarly be seen as natural experiments, for instance, family care for mental illness in Geel, Belgium; care farms in the Netherlands and in Canada; mutual aid during a global pandemic; health and care teams in intentional communities; and a weekly group that draws on the principles of complexity medicine. The primary focus of this book is not to formally evaluate the effectiveness of these approaches, but instead to assemble first-hand qualitative accounts from practitioners and/or participants. I complement this primary data with analyses of secondary data, including scientific research from diverse fields, grey literature from governments and non-governmental organizations, and news articles.

Many of the natural experiments that are discussed in this book represent prefigurative alternatives that could gain more traction if social-ecological systems tip in a direction that dramatically limits access to energy and resources, particularly in high-income contexts that have become accustomed to material abundance. When social movements adopt the ways of thinking and of structuring social relations that they hope to see in a transformed society, their approach can be seen as *prefigurative* in the sense that the models they enact could foreshadow future social arrangements (Leach 2013). Prefigurative alternatives work to draw aspects of adjacent possible systems into the present (see Kauffman 1999). For social movements working towards radical change, prefigurative politics is a way to live into new patterns of social relations that can be imagined from within the current system, but that diverge too much from the mainstream to gain widespread traction under existing conditions (Breines 1980, 1982 as cited in Cornish et al. 2016; Kauffman 1999). Prefigurative experiments are grounded in collective values. They do not necessarily seek change using the mechanisms of the existing system (e.g., multilateral agreements, government policy change), but find spaces within the current system to establish new modes of being in the world (Leach 2013).

The literature on social-ecological systems transformation suggests that prefigurative alternatives can help systems to avoid catastrophic collapse and enable catagenesis, a period of creative flourishing that can follow systemic breakdown (Homer-Dixon 2006). Building alternatives and generating social momentum around them before a crisis occurs can improve the chances that humane alternatives will take root after a period of creative destruction (Homer-Dixon 2006; Jackson 2009). Identifying "possible new trajectories" for systems before they cross thresholds therefore increases the chances of constructive transformations (Walker and Salt 2012, 21). Building energy around diverse and numerous adaptive solutions further strengthens the resilience of possible alternatives (Greer 2009; Westley 2013; also see section 13.2 for a more substantive discussion of the value of prefigurative movements in social-ecological systems change).

The prefigurative alternatives that I consider in this book exist across different communities, were developed by different sectors and practitioner groups, and seek to address diverse problems affecting human and planetary health. However, they all take seriously the context of the Anthropocene by offering up alternative practices, ideas, and structures that hold potential to "move the global trajectory" away from the dynamics that created the societal and environmental challenges before us (Olsson et al. 2017, 3). All are also grounded in a different underlying logic than the modern consumer capitalist regime and either intentionally or indirectly address both social and ecological outcomes in a way that could help humanity become a positive force for change on the planet that sustains us (see Olsson et al. 2017).

The stories I have chosen to tell in this book are further united by a set of four criteria that I see as essential to cultivating human and planetary health for a sustainable future. The appendix provides a justification for these criteria grounded in diverse disciplinary and multidisciplinary literatures (an earlier iteration of these ideas is also available in Zywert 2017).[2] In order to be included in this book, prefigurative ideas, practices, and approaches needed to have the potential to

1. generate synergistic benefits for human and planetary health across social-ecological scales;
2. embody ways of thinking and acting with the potential to disrupt the current trajectories of the Anthropocene by foregrounding alternative sources of meaning, social commitments, and connections to place;
3. achieve positive health outcomes at a low ecological and economic cost; and
4. re-embed aspects of health and care work in networks of family and community reciprocity.

Overview of the Book

This book draws together core theoretical and practical orientations that have built my understanding of what a sustainable health system is, how the transition towards such a system is likely to occur, and what role agents of change can play in making social-ecological systems change more equitable and healthful across scales. Yet as I note above, in the literature on sustainability and health my perspective is an uncommon one. And so before we go on, I want to say something about what I understand to be true about the world. Think of the themes below, each of which corresponds to one section of the book, as the foundational premises upon which my perspective is built. Or, think of them as stones set into the Earth, marking the entrance to an overgrown garden. Many of the theories and data that ground these positions are highly debated both within and across disciplines and fields of practice. In an ultimate sense, no one can know whose predictions will be borne out, or which future our descendants will inhabit. What we can know is that the positions we hold shape our analyses and decision making in the present. With that in mind, this book is organized into three parts, each of which considers a foundational premise about the nature of health in the Anthropocene:

Part 1: The Ecological Foundations of Health

Underlying Premise: Human Health Is Dependent on Planetary Health

Human activities (industrialization, consumption, pollution) have become a dominant driver of change at the scale of the planet's biophysical systems. Climate change, biodiversity loss, and soil degradation, among other processes, are destabilizing the planet's life-support systems and threatening its capacity to support thriving human civilizations. Although human health outcomes have risen throughout the period of industrial modernity, population health is ultimately dependent on the health of ecosystems across scales that range from the soil and gut microbiomes to local ecosystems and global biophysical processes (Whitmee et al. 2015; Cole 2019b; Myers and Frumkin 2020; Canadian Public Health Association [CPHA] 2015; Steffen et al. 2015b; Rockström et al. 2009; Pörtner et al. 2022).

Taking premise 1 seriously raises "wicked"[3] tensions associated with pursuing health at different scales simultaneously:

- Pursuing individual human health outcomes to the exclusion of planetary health (for instance, by devoting substantial amounts of resources and energy to extending the lifespan of individual humans regardless of the ecological cost) will result in declining population-level health outcomes.
- Transitioning towards health systems that prioritize population health over individual health requires adopting commitments, decision-making processes, strategies, and approaches that depart significantly from those of modern medicine.
- Securing planetary health is beyond the scope of health systems alone; it requires fundamental changes to political economies, social arrangements, cultural paradigms, and ecological practices.

To explore this premise, chapter 1 sets the stage for thinking about health over long time horizons and across social-ecological scales. It traces milestones in human and planetary health from the emergence of life through the development of complex human societies capable of altering planetary systems. Chapter 2 then explores key determinants of health. It outlines what planetary health is, how human health is affected by biomedical health care and the social and ecological determinants of health, and how the microbiome contributes to health. Chapter 3 considers how prioritizing human health and wellbeing over the health of the planet that sustains us has contributed to complex challenges, including climate change, biodiversity loss, antimicrobial resistance, and the COVID-19 pandemic. Next, three ethnographic examples illustrate the ecological foundations of health. Chapter 4 tells the story of Didi Perhouse's leadership in the soil health movement, which aims to build health at the microbial scale to have a global impact on the water cycle and the carbon cycle. Chapter 5, "Gardening for Health," considers how leveraging the shared work of growing a garden can enable community health, social inclusion, and ecological regeneration. Finally, chapter 6 discusses practices of care farming in the Netherlands and Canada. Care farming is a multifunctional approach to agriculture that combines health care and social care by providing opportunities for populations experiencing mental illnesses and disabilities to contribute to working farms (see part 1 introduction for further details).

Part 2: A Political Economy for Health

Underlying Premise: Economic Growth Undermines Planetary Health

There is sufficient evidence to conclude that it is exceedingly difficult, if not impossible, to decouple economic growth from environmental destruction. Although local examples of absolute decoupling do exist, at a global scale economic growth continues to be associated with greater consumption of materials and energy, and thus higher rates of pollution, waste, habitat destruction, and contribution to the climate crisis. A global-scale transition towards a post-growth political economy oriented around *sufficient* use of materials and energy would enable planetary health by creating the conditions to step back from ecological overshoot (Engelman, Bongaarts, and Patterson 2020; Ward et al. 2016; Meadows et al. 1972, 2004; Büchs and Koch 2019; Fanning and O'Neill 2019; Missoni and Morales Galindo 2020; Hensher and Zywert 2020).

Taking premise 2 seriously raises wicked tensions associated with the transition to a post-growth political economy:

- Downscaling human activities will require reducing the size of the economy across all industries. Economic contraction is likely to lower the scope of treatments, technologies, and professionalized care services available through health systems.
- Extracting health systems from their dependence on economic growth will require significant restructuring of national welfare states, which, since their emergence after the Second World War, have funded such services as health care, social security, education, and public health by taxing growth.

- Maintaining the health outcomes we have come to expect in modern society will require an expansion in the availability and adoption of low-cost and low-throughput approaches such as robust public health measures, preventative behavioural strategies, informal networks of care, appropriate technologies, and cultural meaning frameworks that support greater acceptance of illness and even death.

The chapters in part 2 consider these tensions and present ethnographic cases that offer potential solutions. Chapter 7 examines the complex relationship between economic growth and health, discussing how a post-growth transition is likely to affect the welfare state and what downscaling the economy could mean for future societies and cultures. Chapter 8 then explores relocalization as a response to a contracting economy. It considers what relocalization will mean for health and health systems and delves into some of the most wicked problems associated with returning to more place-bound ways of living, including the destabilization of taken-for-granted left-right political divides. Chapter 9 situates the mainstreaming of the mutual aid movement during the COVID-19 pandemic as part of a potential alternative political economy. It also discusses the development of the Canadian Principles for a Just Recovery, a campaign that aimed to gather political support for prioritizing principles of equity, sustainability, and health in the recovery from COVID-19. Chapter 10, "Health and Care in Two Ecovillages," illustrates how members of intentional, sustainable communities support one another's health and well-being by building support into the governance of community life. Chapter 11 then shares insights from interviews with members of Community Nurse Connection, a community-driven initiative in which residents secure funds to hire a nurse to care for elders who wish to age in place. To conclude, chapter 12 tells the story of Europe's first therapeutic community in Geel, Belgium, a seven-hundred-year-old family foster care model for serious mental illnesses rooted in Catholic traditions (see part 2 introduction for further details).

Part 3: Social-Ecological Systems Change for Health

Underlying Premise: We Can Steward Social-Ecological Systems Change Processes to Make Human and Planetary Health Possible over Long Time Horizons

In a complex social-ecological system, there is no single source of top-down control, and thus no simple way to change the rules, relationships, feedback patterns, or paradigms that govern the system as a whole. Systems change often occurs in response to crises, and the reorientation of the system into a new stable state can itself be destructive and abrupt. Because of their complexity, systems change processes are inherently unpredictable, and attempts to intervene are likely to generate unintended consequences and counter-intuitive results. However, as individuals, communities, and organizations, we are part of the self-organization of the complex systems in which we live, and therefore have some capacity to influence the course of systemic change. If we hope to effectively leverage this limited agency to enable long-term human and planetary health, we need to understand complexity and work with the dynamics of complex adaptive systems to steward, rather than direct, the process (Westley et al. 2011; Westley et al. 2013; Köhler et al. 2019; Homer-Dixon et al. 2015; Lovelock 2014; Hahn and Nykvist 2017; Westley, Zimmerman, and Patton 2007).

Taking premise 3 seriously raises wicked tensions associated with stewarding social-ecological change processes:

- Working in conditions of complexity involves learning through doing and embracing emergence, self-organization, and other complex systems dynamics to effect meaningful and lasting change.
- Building resilience can no longer be about shoring up the current system against disruption, but about building capacity to use crises as opportunities to nudge systems towards configurations that are better able to meet basic human needs without surpassing planetary boundaries.
- Transitioning towards a social-ecological regime that can uphold human and planetary health over the long term will involve negotiating a new balance between globalization and relocalization within health systems and in broader economic and cultural spheres.

Part 3 delves into the complex work of social-ecological systems change with two theoretical chapters and three ethnographic chapters. Chapter 13, "Social-Ecological Systems Change Processes," discusses how social-ecological systems transitions occur and how they can be stewarded to achieve desirable transformations for health, equity, and sustainability. Chapter 14 then brings together insights about what is needed to cultivate human and planetary health, including adopting new mindsets, building community capacity, and supporting the self-organization of innovative responses. Three ethnographic chapters follow to illustrate promising systems change strategies. Chapter 15 traces the emergence of a virtual kitchen table that helped to sustain change makers during the first wave of the COVID-19 pandemic. Chapter 16 explores participants' experiences in a co-created weekly group that approaches health and healing using insights from complexity science. Finally, chapter 17 considers how cultivating and using plant medicines can contribute to social-ecological change by enhancing preventative health and building community (see part 3 introduction for further details).

This book is an effort to unpack the three premises presented above and to more deeply consider the paradoxes and wicked tensions that they raise. It brings forward a diverse set of existing ideas, practices, and ways of living that offer meaningful responses to these tensions. The approaches it discusses operate across different scales and geographies and emerge from different positions both within and outside of health systems. Each was chosen for its insight into the kinds of systemic conditions that can support human and planetary health as our species navigates a time of unprecedented social, economic, and ecological change. Together, the stories assembled here begin to shed light on what a post-growth, sustainable health system might look like and what it could take to get there. The conclusions and hunches shared in this book are rooted in the voices of the people who generously gave their time and attention to thoughtfully answer my questions, questions that were often difficult due to the complex nature of the problems and solutions we discussed. Wherever I could, I included their own words and am grateful for each of their contributions to the theoretical analyses and the "rush of stories" (Tsing 2015, 34) that are presented in this book.

NOTES

1 A social-ecological "regime" is defined by Beddoe et al. (2009) as "a culture embedded in, and co-evolving with, its ecological context. 'Regime' suggests a complete, interacting set of cultural and environmental factors that operate as a whole" (p. 2483).
2 Table C.3 in the concluding chapter offers a comprehensive description of how each prefigurative alternative aligns with the inclusion criteria.
3 "Wicked" problems are inherently complex and do not have easy or obvious solutions. Addressing wicked problems is a process of engaging with paradox and potentially uncomfortable trade-offs (see Rittel and Webber 1973; Meadows 2008; also see chapter 3).

A Note on the Meaning of "Health"

"Health" is at the centre of this book, and so it is necessary to begin with a discussion of what I – and the health practitioners, researchers, and change leaders who helped to shape my thinking over the course of this work – mean when we talk about health. Dr. William Sutherland, physician and thought leader in the field of complexity medicine, describes the question "What is health?" as a koan, a paradoxical question or statement used by Zen Buddhists to expose the limitations of logical thought and inspire people to engage with uncertainty (Complexity Medicine, n.d.-a). Dr. Sutherland challenged me as I wrote this book to reflect on the question "What is health?" In turn, I incorporated this question into my conversations, asking doctors and social innovators to unpack an often taken-for-granted concept at the core of their work.

Understandings of health are context dependent, culturally constructed, and changeable over time (Baer, Singer, and Susser 2013; McElroy and Townsend 2014). What follows provides insight into how those whose voices informed this work understand the concept of health. The goal of sharing these reflections is to problematize preconceived and taken-for-granted understandings of health, including assumptions about what health is, where it resides, and how it emerges. This discussion aims to nudge readers to question what it means to either experience or not experience health. Perhaps most importantly, it is meant to challenge conventional thinking about what we can, should, and should not do in our pursuit of health, not only individually but as families and communities, as nations, and as a species living in the Anthropocene.

Health Can Co-exist with Long-Term Illness, Disability, or Frailty

The diverse health practitioners, researchers, and social innovators I spoke with emphasized that while disease can certainly affect health, experiencing chronic or acute illnesses and disabilities does not make a person "unhealthy." Conversely, the absence of illness does not equate directly to health, as many people may not experience themselves as "healthy" even if they do not have any diagnosable physical or mental health problems.

> I think health needs to be defined very carefully, particularly in the frail elderly. I certainly wouldn't define it just in terms of the presence of illness or not. To me it's more a quality-of-life issue. (Sarah Jo Brown, personal communication)

> [Health is] that people have the capacity and feel capable of living a good life. Even if you have an illness you can still feel healthy because you can cope with your illness ... I think it's important to first look at what are the objectives of each individual? And it has to be that people can participate, that they feel happy, that they have the idea that they have influence on their lives, that they are in contact with other people, have positive relationships with other people, of course also that they have physical health, but that they have a positive image of themselves. That they like to live. That they are happy with the life they are leading. (Jan Hassink, personal communication)

> I think health is probably what we need to adequately function. I think most people, including myself, don't have absolutely perfect health all the time. I think maybe certain people have unrealistic ideas about health. They may have a sore throat and they think they need to see the doctor about that, but really, having sore throats is part of being healthy in the sense that it's a part of normal life. (Peter Gray, personal communication)

Health Is Holistic and Includes Physical, Mental, Social, and Spiritual Aspects, as Well as Overall Sense of Well-Being and Quality of Life

In my conversations, I also heard that health is a multifaceted experience that incorporates diverse components of the self and one's interactions with the surrounding society and environment. Health was seen to be much more about a person's subjective experience of his or her life than it is about any objective measure.

> The idea that health is more than so-called biomedicine is very important. Health is to me about having a reasonably good level of function but it's not perfect ... So the WHO [definition is] a bit utopian. I think the idea that it includes some social factors that contribute to health and environmental factors, that's quite important ... To have a reasonable state of function, you don't just need to be free of diabetes or have a normal calcium level or something in your blood, you also need to have social connections. This

mental aspect to it, feeling good about yourself and the world, that's very important for health. And that's really hard to pick out through a blood test. (Colin Butler, personal communication)

Health means, it is wellness, actually. Wellness doesn't mean that physically you look like you have big muscles, and you have beautiful structure – this is physical health. Mental health is also very important, that we should be mentally strong, we should be mentally well-rounded, we should be mentally stable. Mental health is very important, because human beings are not like tables and chairs, but they have life and they have emotions, so we have to keep our emotions very steady and very stable. And then after that, there is spiritual health. So because of your cultivation, because of your healthiness, because of your job, because of your skill, because of your intellectual abilities, you are on a spiritual, energetic path, and this is like part of a light bulb. As you look at it, physical health, mental health, spiritual health go through and make this light bulb become shiny. And if the lightbulb is shiny there is illumination. The darkness goes away and everything is seen, and there is heat also. And everything becomes positive when this happens. So what is health? Health is the physical, mental, spiritual and social, nutritional, environmental well-being and improving the quality of life of humans. Physical, mental, and spiritual aspects of a person should be well aligned for optimal health and the organ systems to function harmoniously. This can be understood like the focus on a camera. A camera out of focus will not take good photos. A camera in focus is functioning optimally. So, a person that is healthy is like a camera that is in focus. If misalignment occurs, we become unhealthy due to imbalance and disharmonization of the energetic and organ systems. (Dr. Steven Aung, personal communication)

What I think of, in the context of my practice, and I work a lot with frail older people, [health] really means to provide an opportunity for people to have a level of satisfaction and a quality of life at the end of their lives that gives them stimulation, gives them a sense of well-being, and gives them a sense of community ... One of the things that's clear to me for older people, is it's not about people's blood pressure anymore or their A1Cs if they're a diabetic. It's really about what their sense of well-being happens to be in the moment. (Laurie Harding, personal communication)

The Health of Humans Depends on Conditions within Surrounding Ecological, Social, and Economic Systems

Discussions about what health is revealed that diverse human and non-human systems such as the political economy, local community networks, and ecosystems have a strong influence on health.

> I think it's about living in a world where you can breathe the air and drink the water and eat the food and you have shelter and you have access to everything that you need, including care when you are physically or mentally not well. You have community support, connection. You aren't worried about losing your livelihood when you're unwell. And you know your access to all of these things doesn't depend on your ability to contribute to the economy in a particular way. (Amara Possian, personal communication)
>
> To live in a way that the environment contributes to well-being, but also that one's own behaviour contributes to the well-being of the surroundings. So that it is a kind of give-and-take relationship to the environment. I would say that that is something that I would understand as health, as being healthy. (Thomas van Elsen, personal communication)
>
> I think that health is something that really can only be understood interdependently, meaning the well-being of all species. One individual cannot be well if the community is sick, and one species cannot be well if other species are suffering. I don't think that my paradigm on this is the dominant one, or even a popular one. But I think it's something about a bigger equilibrium where all species are able to flourish. (Hayley Lapalme, personal communication)

Healthy People and Systems Display Resilience

Resilience, the capacity of an individual or a system to respond to stress without changing its essential structure and function (Walker and Salt 2006), is perceived as a core component of health.

> [Health is] when a system has the freedom and flexibility to respond in a new way to each circumstance. I think the flip side of that is that sickness or a non-functioning system is not adaptive and not resilient in that way. (Didi Pershouse, personal communication)
>
> From the perspective of an individual, the ability to function effectively within society, not necessarily totally free, but free of unacceptable constraints due to pain, fatigue, physical or mental inability to meet the demands placed upon you. But from the point of view of society, it's perhaps more the ability to sustain yourself, to respond to challenge, respond to physical or mental insult as it were, and to come back out of it relatively untouched. (Don Spady, personal communication)
>
> I'm going to use Dan Seigel's work, the professor of psychiatry at UCLA. He has a lovely way of conceptualizing health and well-being and saying that it's being in the river of integration. So a place where you feel flexible, adaptable, where life has coherence, where you feel energized and stable

and where you're navigating the river between the banks of chaos on one side and rigidity on the other ... I guess my idea of health would be to find that place, which I think means looking after your physicality, but your interiority as well. Not splitting mind and body at all, but recognizing that they are completely integral. They are one thing. So getting away from the dualism. I guess it's mirroring broader ideas of psychological or societal health where you're holding tensions all the time, trying to hold contradictions. (Jane Myat, personal communication)

Questioning the Meaning of Health

When I asked researchers, health practitioners, and social innovators "What is health?" many found the question difficult to answer. Even among those working in health-related fields, the nature of health itself was not something they often considered directly. Nevertheless, their responses to the question were thoughtful and illuminating. The sense that health is not a simple or a singular "thing" that can be easily defined came through strongly. People reflected that health is multifaceted, context dependent, and entwined with the state of broader social, ecological, and economic systems. It is also affected by the unique, situated experiences that communities and individuals have within these systems, and is about much more than the presence or absence of illness. These insights about what health is significantly influenced the way I conceptualize the kinds of transformations that health systems may undergo in the age of human impact. I encourage readers to allow the ideas presented above to open up a space of questioning and unknowing about what health is, what it could be, and how it might be achieved. At this juncture, human societies are experiencing transformations at scales including planetary biophysical processes, the global political economy, and the social institutions that support health and well-being in our communities – processes that confound taken-for-granted understandings of health (see chapters 2 and 7). As such, it is useful to carry the question "What is health?" with us as we move through this book.

PART 1

The Ecological Foundations of Health

Part 1 demonstrates that human health is dependent upon ecological dynamics unfolding at diverse scales, from the microbial life that inhabits our guts and our soils to the self-regulating systems that maintain life on this planet. It then presents a set of practices that integrate and support health across social-ecological scales.

Chapter 1, "Health in Deep Time," introduces a deep-time perspective as an essential lens for understanding the relationships between human and planetary health. Rapidly tracing the evolution of the planet from the emergence of life through the Holocene epoch and into the Anthropocene, it argues that following the Great Acceleration in 1950, human and planetary health begin to display paradoxical outcomes. With the transition to modernity, human economic activities are responsible for both improving human health outcomes and destabilizing the planetary systems that secure the long-term health of our species. The chapter considers the challenges facing human and planetary health in the Anthropocene and establishes what it means to take a systems view of health.

Expanding on this theme, chapter 2, "Health across Nested Social-Ecological Scales," explores the ecological roots of health at the macro scale (planetary health), the meso scale (the interplay of health care, human behaviours, genetics, and the social and ecological determinants of health), and the micro scale (the ecosystems of microbial life within us). In each section, it traces the most significant influences on health, demonstrating the extent to which health is affected by a set of interconnected variables that cannot be easily disentangled. In doing so, the chapter sets the stage for envisioning a health system with the capacity to meet the urgent needs of individuals and communities in the present while also contributing to the long-term health of ecosystems across scales.

Chapter 3, "Problems of Scale in Human and Planetary Health," builds on the theoretical touchstones laid in opening chapters to examine the wicked problems associated with health across scales. It considers the climate crisis, biodiversity loss, antimicrobial resistance, and the COVID-19 pandemic as unintended consequences of human actions, actions that often aim – in the short term at least – to improve human well-being. This chapter argues that attempting to maximize the health of a single species, humanity, has resulted in the emergence of planetary health problems at higher scales that circle back through complex feedback patterns to undermine human health. Yet attending to health across scales is not a straightforward process and may require trade-offs that are difficult to contemplate, let alone activate within the current system.

The following three chapters illustrate a set of unexpected, creative solutions to the difficult questions raised in the previous three. Chapter 4, "Soil Health," introduces the soil health movement as a form of systems-based medicine that intervenes at the smallest scale – the microbes living in the soil – to effect planetary change. It describes how soil sponge strategist Didi Pershouse came to see the soil as a key leverage point for sustainability and health. In doing so, it demonstrates that human health depends on the work of countless living species of bacteria and fungi, and how learning to support the work of these living systems at the micro scale can build a world more conducive to all life on Earth.

Chapter 5, "Gardening for Health," then considers how the shared work of growing a garden can improve mental and physical health as well as community cohesion while making positive contributions to ecosystems by, for instance, moderating local temperature and increasing biodiversity. The chapter presents several examples, including The Listening Space garden, a community space founded by family physician Dr. Jane Myat at the Caversham Group Practice in London, England; the use of therapeutic landscape principles in health-care institutions; enabling gardens, spaces designed to be inclusive for people of all physical and cognitive abilities; and home gardening for health and sustainability.

Chapter 6, "Care Farming," concludes part 1. The practice of care farming brings together agricultural production, health care, and social supports. Care farmers engage participants, including people experiencing mental illnesses and long-term disabilities, to contribute to the essential daily tasks that take place on a working farm. Participants in turn become part of a strong community, do purposeful work that enhances their esteem and confidence, and enjoy the physical and mental health benefits of spending time outdoors. Some care farms also offer therapeutic experiences such as counselling in an agricultural setting. The chapter investigates the thriving care-farming sector in the Netherlands and describes four unique care-farming models in the Netherlands and Canada.

1 Health in Deep Time

To think about health not only at the scale of an individual human's life, but in the long stretch of time that characterizes human co-evolution with the Earth and other species, is an act of defiance. It defies some of the most salient preoccupations of modern consumer culture: preoccupations with what is new and immediate, with the nuances of individual choice, with the things that divide us from each other and the world. In the long stretch of time, each singular life recedes from focus. Species flow across the landscape. Communities of plants, people, animals, microbiota coalesce and break apart. Choices blend together into waves of human action. Consequences nest down with their causes. In the long stretch of time, there is no denying symbiosis or interdependence, or the constraints of place and context. To think about health over long time scales is to recognize the influence of one form of life on another. In the simplest terms, life is what makes life possible on this planet (see Lovelock, 1991).

But it can be hard to keep deep time's horizon in our minds. Modernity represents such a fissure of discontinuity between humanity's past and its present that for many of us living in modern, Westernized cultures in high-income countries, it is easy to overlook the interconnectedness of all life. In so doing, we also forget, or at least routinely think and act in ways that ignore, the extent to which the health of one living system affects the health of all other living systems. The goal of this chapter is to remind us of the ecological foundations of health. It begins by drawing together perspectives from Earth systems sciences, global health, and the rapidly expanding transdisciplinary field of planetary health so that we can more easily understand health in the long stretch of time.

In *Healing Gaia: Practical Medicine for the Planet*, James Lovelock (1991) turns to Gaia, the living planet Earth, as though he were a planetary physician. He traces Earth's history with a lens that sees great "disturbances" such as collisions with planetesimals, the shift to an oxygen-dominated atmosphere, and rising human impact on the environment as states of "disease" within a living system (12). In Lovelock's model, the rock strata that form the Earth's geological record are its "medical record" (32). This record shows how dramatically the Earth's "anatomy" has changed over time from its beginnings as a lifeless rock to a planet populated by oceans and bacteria to a green Earth rich in biodiversity and now into the age of human impact and an uncertain future (56).

The Earth was formed 4.6 billion years ago in the wake of an exploding supernova that also created the sun and the other planets in our solar system. The earliest evidence for life on Earth has been dated to 4.4–4.2 billion years ago (Hedges 2009). Although scientists cannot be sure why life emerged or precisely what kind of life came first, during the Archean period (3.7–2.5 billion years ago), the Earth came to be inhabited by bacteria – photosynthesizers that converted carbon dioxide and sunlight into simple sugars, and fermenters that converted the waste products and dead bodies of other bacteria into methane and carbon dioxide (Lovelock 1991). The balance between the chemical reactions created by these two early forms of life maintained the greenhouse effect within the Earth's atmosphere (Lovelock 1991). In so doing, bacteria ensured that conditions remained favourable for their continued existence; life held open the "'window' for life" that otherwise might have appeared and then quickly vanished (83). Lovelock describes the period in which the evolution of bacteria and changes to the Earth's atmosphere and surface "ceased to be two separate and independent processes" as "the birth of Gaia" as a living, self-regulating system (84).

For over a billion years, single-celled bacterial life flourished, expanding into each inhabitable niche the Earth had to offer. Eukaryote cells (cells with a nucleus – the building blocks of animal and plant life) most likely arose through a symbiotic merger between archaebacteria and eubacteria, and are thought to have emerged between 2.7 and 2 billion years ago (Hedges 2009). With the appearance of eukaryotes, the tree of life began to diversify more rapidly. Plants appeared around 1.4 billion years ago, fungi 1.2 billion years ago, and the first animals 1.1 billion years ago (Hedges et al. 2015; Kumar et al. 2017). Evidence of the first vertebrates can be traced back to 615 million years ago, the first mammals to 177 million years ago, the first primates to 74 million years ago. The evolutionary line of *Homo sapiens* diverged from chimpanzees, their closest living primate relative, around 7 million years ago (Hedges et al. 2015; Kumar et al. 2017). *Homo sapiens*, anatomically modern humans, did not step into the long stretch of time until 200,000 years ago, in the Pleistocene epoch (McMichael, 2014).

It can be helpful to think this timeline through in more tangible terms. If you turn the Earth's history into a 4.6-kilometre walk that represents the 4.6 billion years since the formation of the Earth, each metre you traverse is a million years. You will walk almost to the very end before human beings even exist. On a 4.6-kilometre walk, *Homo sapiens* diverges from its ancestor species 20 centimetres before the finish line. The end of the last ice age is 13 millimetres before the finish line. The Industrial Revolution occurs one-fifth of a millimetre before the finish line (Deep Time Walk, n.d.). And yet it is in that span of time – in the last fifth of a millimetre of a 4.6-kilometre-long walk – that human activities began to disrupt ecological processes and so threaten the long-term prospects for human health on this planet. But before we consider these escalating risks, let us back up to the twenty-centimetre mark, returning to the Pleistocene, the place and time in which the first human beings were born.

The Pleistocene epoch was a time of climate instability that placed significant environmental stresses on hominid populations (McMichael 2014). Environmental fluctuations including changing food sources and cycles of glaciation put evolutionary pressures on hominid brain and cultural capacities. Larger brains, greater dexterity, the ability to communicate, and general "intellectual flexibility" were associated with reproductive success (46). Fossil evidence suggests that our earliest ancestors ate well and grew strong, reproduced in their teens, and lived on average to the age of thirty. Likely sources of disease and death for early humans included injuries, predation, occasional infectious diseases, intestinal and liver diseases, and extreme weather events. By around 17,000 years ago, the climate was beginning to stabilize and warm following the most recent ice age. *Homo sapiens* expanded their geographic range and genetic diversity increased as local ecologies exerted evolutionary pressures that account for much of humanity's current phylogenetic differences (e.g., stature, skin colour, presence or absence of metabolic enzymes) (McMichael 2014).

Around 11,000 years ago, the Pleistocene gave way to the Holocene epoch, a time of extended climate stability. Temperatures, freshwater availability, and flows of essential chemical compounds like nitrogen and phosphorus remained within a "narrow range" well suited to human flourishing (Rockström et al. 2009, 472). Around this time, humans began to systematically cultivate the land and settled in the first agricultural communities. In the self-regulating, stable ecological conditions of the Holocene, farming became a successful subsistence strategy. Agriculture enabled societies to grow more socially and technologically complex, which in turn made them more dependent on climate stability. Periods of drought, for instance, could now decimate crops and along with them the health of the community (McMichael 2014). There is ample evidence in the fossil record that the transition away from hunting and gathering to farming was associated with lower health outcomes: nutrition decreased as diets became less diverse and more dependent on a successful harvest; rates of infectious disease increased due to dense living arrangements, fecal contamination, and close proximity to domesticated animals; social stratification and specialization increased, resulting in the first systematic wealth- and status-related health disparities (McMichael 2014; Armelagos, Brown, and Turner 2005; Barrett et al. 1998). The advent of agriculture also represented a significant shift in the dynamics of human evolution. As populations rose and early agriculturalists harnessed new energy sources from wind, water, and domesticated animals, social complexity expanded further (McElroy and Townsend 2014; Tainter 1988) and the ecological evolutionary pressures that had shaped hominid evolution for over six million years were "overshadowed by faster-moving human-directed cultural evolution" (McMichael 2014, 47).

During the Holocene epoch, *Homo sapiens* transitioned from an entirely hunting and gathering species with little global-scale ecological significance through early agriculture to urbanization and industrialization. At each stage, humanity's population and its influence on surrounding ecosystems grew (Zalasiewicz et al. 2019). The Industrial Revolution, beginning in Europe in the late eighteenth century, rapidly increased the scale of human impacts on the environment and once again shifted patterns of health and disease (McMichael 2014; Barrett et al. 1998; Harrison 2004). Early industrial cities were ridden with infectious diseases like measles, smallpox, and whooping cough that thrived in overcrowded, unsanitary slums. Pollution and exposure to the toxic substances that fuelled industrialization became core drivers of disease and death (McMichael 2014; Barrett et al. 1998). Yet industrial modernization also improved human health outcomes by enabling higher food yields, increasing understanding of the germ theory of disease, and bringing about the discovery of antibiotics, enhanced surgical capacities, eventual improvements in hygiene, and the establishment of coordinated public health measures including vaccination programs (Barrett et al. 1998; Harrison 2004).

By the twentieth century, developments in public health and biomedical knowledge and the institutionalization of formal health care systems had together increased lifespans, dramatically reduced deaths due to infectious disease, and improved child survival rates (McMichael 2014; Harrison 2004). As people began to live longer lives in environments that departed more radically from those of our ancestors, non-communicable diseases like heart disease, respiratory illnesses, diabetes, cancer, and mental health issues became dominant causes of illness and death (McMichael 2014; Horton 2012; Barret et al. 1998; Hidaka 2012). Low- and middle-income nations began to suffer from a double burden of disease due to the resurgence of new and previously under control infectious diseases (often due to human encroachment on animal habitats and other ecological disruptions) and the emergence of antimicrobial-resistant pathogens alongside high rates of chronic conditions (Zuckerman 2014; Barrett et al. 1998). Inequities associated with income, level of education, race, gender, employment status, physical environment, social networks, and other aspects of life circumstances became crucial determinants of health (see WHO, n.d.-a).

Until the first half of the twentieth century, the Earth's biophysical systems operated relatively independently of humanity's socio-economic systems (Steffen et al. 2015a). The global spread of industrial modernization, powered by the extraction and combustion of vast quantities of fossil fuels, significantly increased the scale of human impacts on the biosphere, but it was not until the year 1950 that we can see "fundamental shifts in the state and functioning of Earth systems" (Steffen et al. 2015a, 93). Will Steffen and colleagues describe 1950 as the beginning of the "Great Acceleration," a period in which rapid growth in human population, GDP, and energy use began to closely mirror rises in atmospheric carbon dioxide, surface temperature, and ocean acidification. With the Great Acceleration, human socio-economic activities became, for the first time, drivers of Earth systems trends. As the human population and its rate of consumption rose, human-induced planetary changes began to push the Earth out of its stable Holocene state (Steffen et al., 2015a). The Earth's oceans, land, atmosphere, climate, biosphere, and cryosphere now display patterns that depart so significantly from Holocene conditions that Earth system scientists propose that we have entered a new geological period, the Anthropocene epoch (Zalasiewicz et al. 2010, 2019). The Anthropocene marks a profound and permanent reorientation of planetary dynamics; humanity's impact on the Earth's biophysical systems is now visible in the geological record (Zalasiewicz et al. 2019).

In the Anthropocene, the health of the human population and the integrity of the planet display paradoxical outcomes. In 1950, at the start of the Great Acceleration, 63 per cent of the world's population lived in extreme poverty, global life expectancy was forty-six years, and the child mortality rate was 225 per 1,000 births. Sixty five years later in 2015, the global population was three times what it was in 1950, yet only 10 per cent of the population lived in extreme poverty, life expectancy had risen to seventy-two, and the child mortality rate had fallen to 45 per 1,000 births (Roser and Ortiz-Ospina 2017; Roser, n.d., and Roser and Ritchie, n.d., as cited in Myers and Frumkin 2020). When we consider human health in the context of deep time, these outcomes rest uneasily, as the same drivers that made such impressive advancements in health possible have simultaneously caused a significant expansion in the ecological footprint of human activities, to the point that in 2018 human civilization was consuming 1.7 Earths' worth of resources each year (Myers and Frumkin 2020; Global Footprint Network 2019 as cited in Evison and Bickersteth, 2020).

Humanity is well adapted to the ecological conditions of the Holocene, but in the Anthropocene human activities are likely to cause Earth systems to flip into novel states that could depart significantly from the environments in which our species evolved (Rockström et al. 2009; Steffen et al. 2015b). Johan Rockström and colleagues (2009) propose that there are nine "planetary boundaries," biophysical systems that must remain within specific parameters to maintain a Holocene-like environment. For these nine systems, surpassing the boundary could result in rapid, non-linear, and potentially "irreversible" changes if key variables surpass thresholds associated with stable Holocene states (472). Many of the nine planetary boundaries are also "tightly coupled," meaning that changes in one system could feed back in ways that contribute to surpassing the thresholds of other, interconnected systems (474). The inherent complexity of the Earth's biophysical processes (e.g., self-regulation of temperature, climate, atmospheric composition, nutrient cycling) and the connections between processes mean that we cannot know in advance exactly what the world will be like if key systems reconfigure themselves into novel states. However, the most advanced scientific models suggest that new stable states are not likely to be as "hospitable to the development of human societies" as the states experienced over the past ten thousand years (Steffen et al. 2015b, 1259855–1).

And so, in the long stretch of time, our species returns to a period of global-scale ecological instability. Much like our ancestors navigating cycles of glaciation in the Pleistocene, human lives are increasingly defined by rapid, unpredictable, non-linear transformations at the scale of the Earth's biophysical systems. The primary drivers of ecological change are already directing human health outcomes. Climate change, biodiversity loss, resource availability, land-use changes, pollution, and altered biogeochemical cycles affect our air quality, food production, exposure to infectious disease, access to fresh water, and vulnerability to natural disasters and extreme weather events. In turn, these variables shape global patterns of malnutrition, infectious disease, noncommunicable disease, mental health, migration, and conflict (Myers and Frumkin 2020; Field et al. 2020; Butler 2014). Even more concerning are the ways in which the ecological foundations of human health, the self-regulating biophysical systems of the Earth, are being systematically disrupted, eroded, and dismantled, opening up a gulf of uncertainty about the future prospects for human health, or even human life (McMichael 2014; Myers and Frumkin 2020; Whitmee et al. 2015). Future generations carry the greatest burden of risk, with the impacts of ecological disruptions like the climate crisis likely to become more severe, not less, even if human societies make swift changes to alter our current course (Frumkin 2020; Butler 2014; CPHA 2015).

1.1 Taking a Deep Time Perspective

In briefly tracing the formation of the Earth through the origins of life into the unprecedented destabilizations of the Anthropocene, and in outlining the ways in which human health has been shaped by ecological conditions since our time as Pleistocene hunter-gatherers, we can make a number of connections. These connections defy common assumptions about what will enable human beings to live healthy lives on a changing planet. When we consider the linked trajectories of planetary change and human health, for instance, it becomes clear that human health cannot be meaningfully separated from the integrity of other living systems. Human health is entwined with, for example, the health of microbial species and the regulation of the Earth's climate. Taking a deep time perspective demonstrates how crucial it is to attend to health at different scales rather than attempting to maximize outcomes for individual humans in the present.

The deep time trajectory also draws attention to the extent to which, since the first bacterial species arose billions of years ago, life has contributed to creating the conditions that allow life to come into being and flourish. This connection suggests that biodiverse plant and animal life (soil bacteria, trees, pollinators, grazing animals, crop plants) could make a significant contribution to preventing planetary boundaries from being crossed or to improving human health through more direct pathways such as enhancing nutrition, increasing physical activity, and strengthening mental health outcomes (see chapters 2 and 4). Viewing human and planetary health in deep time can also remind us that planetary processes and states such as temperature regulation, carbon dioxide concentration in the atmosphere, levels of pollution, ocean acidification, and nutrient cycling are the ultimate arbiters of human flourishing. In addition, they have direct health implications: air pollution contributes to non-communicable diseases; encroachment on animal habitats contributes to the spread of new infectious diseases; the climate crisis contributes to famine and migration (see chapter 2). Given these facts, reducing humanity's impact on the Earth and bolstering ecological resilience in the face of human activities can simultaneously improve human and planetary health. These connections have only begun to be intimated by thinking about the ecological foundations of health across long time scales. Their implications will be developed further in chapter 2, which considers health in the context of nested social-ecological systems.

2 Health across Nested Social-Ecological Scales

> Health care, if we do it right, will have gone full circle – from early healers practicing in isolated locales, to specialists practicing high-tech medicine on a global scale, to a new era in which we are called to practice collaborative, whole-systems care – taking into account local communities and global concerns, while welcoming the perspectives that come from the microscope, the telescope, the curious child, and communion with the world itself. (Pershouse 2016, 287)

The conditions of the Anthropocene call for a transition towards what Didi Pershouse describes as "whole-systems care" (2016, 287). Our well-being seems increasingly to depend on our capacity to approach healing and care in ways that take into account diverse drivers of health outcomes – not only human health outcomes, but those experienced by the multitude of living systems that make up the ecological whole of the Earth. The boundaries between these living systems at different scales are hazy at best. An individual human being is home to a complex ecology of microbial life, is part of a social community, resides within a local ecosystem, and participates in activities that aggregate to influence planetary processes. By the same token, the climate is a self-regulating system in its own right and is shaped by systemic processes as far ranging as the chemical reactions of countless bacteria, the burning of millions of barrels of oil each day, and the in- and out-breaths of trees. Given how difficult it is to draw firm boundaries around scales of influence, I find it helpful to think about the social-ecological systems that affect health as nested within one another. This framing offers enough conceptual clarity to discuss the salient patterns, relationships, and experiences that define particular systems while continuing to hold complexity close and to recognize the dynamic interactions between scales.

To think through the ecological roots of health, this chapter will first consider how planetary health affects the health of human populations, discussing how equity figures into a planetary health paradigm. Next it will move to the meso scale, to the interplay of health care, human behaviours, social and ecological determinants of health, and genetics, outlining the ways in which each contributes to population-level health outcomes. It will then consider the ecosystems of microbial life that reside within human beings and that act as conduits between inner and outer ecologies. The goals of drawing out the connections between human health outcomes and the resilience of nested social-ecological systems are to once again highlight the extent to which human health is inseparable from ecological integrity, and to further uncover the ways in which feedback patterns within and between social-ecological systems can improve health outcomes across scales. This discussion lays the groundwork for considering some of the tensions that arise when individual health outcomes are prioritized over the health of populations or of the planet as a whole.

2.1 The Macro Scale: Planetary Health

> The notion of a planet visiting the doctor is odd. It assumes for a start that the planet – in this case the Earth – is capable of feeling ill, and so is in some sense alive. It also assumes that there is a suitable doctor to visit – one with the knowledge and experience of planetary maladies to give sound advice. (Lovelock 1991, 9)

Planetary health is at once a transdisciplinary academic field, a movement of grass-roots action, and a "lens" through which to understand the connections between ecological change and human health (Cole 2019a, xii; Horton et al. 2014). At its core, planetary health is intended to be "an acknowledgement that human health depends on the integrity of natural systems ... it is a broad definition which encompasses the interrelationship between human health and the health of civilization, and the state of the natural systems on which that health ultimately depends" (Andy Haines, personal communication; see also Whitmee et al. 2015, 1978). Planetary health is distinct from other environmental approaches to health in that it focuses on how global patterns of ecological change will affect future generations, rather than on how current environmental states influence human health in the present (Cole 2019b). Grounded in the concepts of the Anthropocene, the Great Acceleration, limits to growth, planetary boundaries, Gaia theory, and a deep time perspective (Cole 2019c), planetary health seeks not only to understand but to address the greatest risks to human health and society posed by human-induced ecological disruptions (Horton et al. 2014). In a sense, the field seems to be working to realize Lovelock's (1991) image of a planetary physician capable of both understanding the illnesses of the Earth and offering up meaningful remedies.

As a field of study and practice, planetary health emphasizes the urgency with which we need to act to secure the functioning of Earth systems into the future (Cole 2019a; Whitmee et al. 2015; Myers and Frumkin 2020; Whitmee, personal communication). The goal is to find strategies that will work, that will be broadly acceptable to leaders and citizens, and perhaps most important, that will improve health, well-being, and equity while at the same time shifting the trajectory of global-scale environmental trends (Engelman, Bongaarts, and Patterson 2020; Whitmee, personal communication). Researchers have begun cataloguing robust examples of initiatives worldwide (see Duff et al. 2020) that can generate "win-wins" for human and planetary health. Doing so is part of the field's commitment to honestly communicate the seriousness of the issues we are facing while creating space to talk about how we can have a "good Anthropocene" (Whitmee, personal communication).

Keeping the Earth healthy will require rapid, paradigmatic societal change. Planetary health researchers recognize, for instance, that focusing on short-term economic growth and development compromises the health and well-being of future generations and undermines the stability of the planetary systems that enable human societies to flourish (Whitmee et al. 2015). As a result, a wholesale "redefinition of prosperity" is key to improving planetary health, alongside transformative changes to the ways in which people (especially those of us living in high-income contexts) consume resources, reproduce, and make strategic use of technology (Whitmee et al. 2015, 1974). Given the scale of the ecological changes already in motion since the Great Acceleration, we can only achieve planetary health if we are willing to reimagine most of the systems that define modern human societies, including how we grow our food; manufacture our clothing and other material goods; build, heat, and occupy our homes; care for our children, our elders, and those among us who experience illnesses; think about medicine and structure health systems; and choose to spend our time (Myers and Frumkin 2020).

Because the planetary health field is concerned with transforming not only health systems but the fundamental relationships between human societies and their surrounding ecosystems, planetary health approaches see the biomedical view of health as only part of the picture, with other dimensions of well-being and quality of life taking on greater significance (Myers and Frumkin 2020). When I spoke with Sarah Whitmee, one of the lead authors of the Rockefeller-Lancet Commission's inaugural planetary health publication "Safeguarding Human Health in the Anthropocene Epoch," she said that it is not always clear whether the longer lives made possible through advances in personalized medicine are in fact "better-quality lives" (Whitmee, personal communication). This question speaks to an underlying tension between the biomedical paradigm, which is focused on curing and extending the lives of individual humans often regardless of the ecological cost, and the planetary health paradigm, which is focused on securing population health and improving human well-being without transgressing planetary boundaries. To gain some insight into this tension, I asked Sir Andy Haines, professor of environmental change and public health at the London School of Hygiene and Tropical Medicine and chair of the Rockefeller-Lancet Commission on Planetary Health, what it would take for planetary health to become a guiding paradigm for health systems around the world. Haines reflected that such a transition would require

> increasing understanding that the biomedical model can obviously deliver some important advances, and most of us want to partake in those, where they are effective. But at the same time it's becoming apparent that many of the diseases and health problems we're struggling with and that health systems are struggling with are in part related to the way in which we live, the lifestyles and consumption patterns that we're following, which are responsible for transforming the global environment in many ways, some of which are going to be very negative. (personal communication)

Haines is concerned that the global health community may not fully recognize the implications of the Anthropocene for human health. He said that many people do not yet understand how "completely unprecedented" the new geological epoch is; they assume that the future will be "an extension of the past, whereas our analysis is that there will be many discontinuities, potentially, between the past and the future of health" (personal communication). Planetary health aims to draw attention to these discontinuities. Research in planetary health shows the extent to which high growth rates in human populations, per capita consumption, and technological development have contributed to ecological overshoot (Myers and Frumkin 2020). As human activities surpass the Earth's available stocks of resources and sinks for pollution and waste, we are creating "disruptions [that] interact with each other in complex ways to alter the fundamental conditions for human health and wellbeing and, ultimately, affect nearly every dimension of human health" (7).

Focusing on the scale of Earth systems, planetary health maps the connections between

- human-induced ecological disruptions (e.g., the climate crisis, biodiversity loss, ozone depletion, forest clearance, land degradation);
- direct human health effects (resulting from floods, droughts, exposure to pollution);
- environmentally mediated health effects (caused by changes to patterns of infectious disease risk, under-nutrition, reduced access to natural medicines); and
- indirect health effects (influenced by migration, conflict, and loss of livelihoods). (Whitmee et al. 2015)

One of the principal challenges for planetary health is to find accessible and persuasive ways of talking about the pathways between Earth systems and human health outcomes. Whitmee notes that for many people, planetary ecological change and human health appear to be two or three steps removed from one another, especially because the field is new and the evidence base is still growing. In this context, trying to get individuals or governments to actively preserve planetary health can be like asking them to act on the precautionary principle. Yet while the precautionary principle is a difficult sell psychologically, many of the strategies proposed by planetary health researchers have the advantage of being simple and mutually beneficial. For example, improving diets can significantly reduce the ecological footprint of food systems while at the same time increasing nutrition and lowering the health care costs associated with treating diet-related illnesses (Whitmee, personal communication).

Conceptualizing health on a planetary scale is also deepening conversations about equity in relation to ecological change and sustainability transitions. The planetary boundaries framework developed by Johan Rockström and colleagues proposes that we should do all we can to avoid pushing Earth systems out of their stable Holocene states. Without escalating human influence on the biosphere, a Holocene state would have been expected to persist for several thousand years into the future (Rockström et al. 2009). More importantly, the Holocene state of the Earth system "is the only one that we know for certain can support complex human societies" (Steffen and Stafford-Smith 2013, 404). Starting in the Industrial Revolution and through the Great Acceleration, some communities and industries have contributed significantly more to transgressing planetary boundaries than others. In doing so, they have also benefitted more from disproportionate access to energy, resources, and wealth (Steffen et al. 2015b). As a result, the worst effects of ecological disruptions like the climate crisis are felt by populations that are already vulnerable, such as those living in poverty (Field et al. 2020; Frumkin 2020; Pörtner et al. 2022). Remaining within planetary boundaries while achieving an equitable distribution of the Earth's limited resources will require high-income regions to downscale their impact on the planet so that lower-income areas can increase their material standards of living and enhance their resilience to ecological disruptions (Steffen et al. 2015b).

Downscaling economic activity in high-income countries will inevitably reduce *material* standards of living (see chapters 7 and 8). However, Steffen and Stafford Smith argue that moving towards a more equitable distribution of resource use between high-, low-, and middle-income countries could ultimately improve well-being at the global scale and is *"in the self-interest of wealthy nations"* (2013, 403, emphasis in original). Although low-income regions usually experience more severe direct impacts of ecological disruptions, wealthy populations are also negatively affected by things like natural disasters and mounting tensions related to resource access (Steffen and Stafford Smith 2013). Also, well-being and material standards of living are not as connected as one might think (Steffen and Stafford Smith 2013; also see chapter 7). Greater income equality has been associated with increased well-being for individuals and communities, measured in outcomes as diverse as life expectancy, rates of mental illness, obesity, and homicide (Wilkinson and Pickett 2009 and de Maio 2009 as cited in Steffen and Stafford Smith 2013). Wealthy people within more equal nations have better social outcomes than those in less equal nations, benefitting personally from a society-wide commitment to equity (Wilkinson and Pickett 2009 as cited in Steffen and Stafford Smith 2013). Evidence suggests that coupled equity and well-being gains could be "an emerging property at the global level" due to rising social, cultural, and economic integration (406).

Despite these linkages between equity and well-being, the planetary boundaries framework raises serious questions about how we can collectively step back from ecological overshoot without losing ground when it comes to health and social justice. Economist Kate Raworth sought to conceptualize this balance by adding a "social foundation" to the planetary boundaries framework (Raworth 2012, 2017). Raworth's model, called "The Doughnut," illustrates the extent to which both ecological and social boundaries are essential for human well-being. We need to avoid crossing ecological thresholds at all costs, but must also find ways to ensure that we create conditions for all humans to live healthy and satisfying lives (Raworth 2017). Raworth describes the space between the social foundation and the ecological ceiling as "an ecologically safe and socially just space in which all of humanity has the chance to thrive" (E48). The components of the social foundation are adapted from the sustainable development goals and include adequate energy, water, food, health, education, income and work, peace and justice, political voice, social equity, gender equality, housing, and social networks. At a global scale, there is currently a significant shortfall in meeting the social foundation; millions of people worldwide do not have access to basic necessities (Raworth 2017). There is also a dangerous overshoot of five planetary boundaries, leaving all of humanity vulnerable to potentially devastating ecological changes (Persson et al. 2022).

Seeking to understand whether it was in fact possible to meet basic human needs without exceeding planetary boundaries, Dan O'Neill and colleagues (2018) studied data from 150 countries, tracking eleven social outcomes against seven indicators of national ecological impact. They found that not a single one of the 150 countries met the social foundation without exceeding the ecological ceiling. There is a definitive trend in the data: "the more social thresholds a country achieves, the more biophysical boundaries it transgresses" (90). The countries that meet more social needs have higher rates of life satisfaction and healthy life expectancy, but they also breach more planetary boundaries. High-income countries do well on the social indicators but consume resources at rates that greatly exceed equitable per capita limits. Further, the boundaries for climate change and material consumption are most tightly coupled to positive social outcomes. It does appear that there are diminishing social returns to increased resource use beyond a certain threshold, a relationship that holds true for all social outcomes except equality. Equality remains linearly related to resource use, meaning that greater equality is associated with greater consumption of resources (O'Neill et al., 2018).

O'Neill et al.'s study (2018) also found that the qualitative aspects of well-being (democratic quality, social support, equality, secondary education) were associated with higher rates of resource use than basic needs (nutrition, sanitation, access to energy, income). For this reason, they suggest it would be possible to meet these four basic needs for everyone on the planet without crossing biophysical boundaries. They also found that some countries managed to attain certain social thresholds with a much lower level of resource consumption than other countries, meaning that the ways in which these needs are met – the provisioning systems for health care, education, and state social safety nets – represent key leverage points for change. Although no single country can be seen as a model that meets *all* social needs without crossing *any* ecological boundary, different countries demonstrate that it is possible to meet *different* social goals while remaining within *certain* ecological boundaries. O'Neill and colleagues propose that one of the highest-impact actions high-income countries could take towards reducing their environmental impact without falling behind on social outcomes would be to accept "sufficiency" of resource use, an approach that recognizes that overuse of resources creates its own problems, both social and ecological (92).

When we consider health at the macro scale, it becomes clear that human-induced ecological change is rapidly decimating planetary health, threatening the health and survival of future generations. Paradoxically, the same activities that have enabled gains in human health and well-being since the Industrial Revolution (e.g., rising resource consumption, energy use, water use, pollution) are also the root causes of planetary ecological disruption, suggesting the need for wholesale transformation of human societies to achieve planetary health (Whitmee et al. 2015; Cole 2019b). Specific strategies for improving planetary health very often have clear mutual gains for human health (e.g., eating healthier, more sustainable diets). However, a key dilemma at the intersection of human and planetary health is the fact that no country in the world currently meets basic human needs without surpassing planetary boundaries (O'Neill et al. 2018). It remains unclear whether modern conceptions of health and well-being are compatible with living within the planet's means given current levels of population, societal complexity, and cultural expectations (see chapter 7).

2.2 The Meso Scale: Health Care, Social and Ecological Determinants of Health, and Social Genomics

From a social-ecological systems perspective, human health resides at the meso scale. Research overwhelmingly demonstrates that social, environmental, genetic, and behavioural factors intersect in complex and dynamic ways to affect individual and community health (see Hancock 2017; Woolf 2019; CPHA 2015; Mikkonen and Raphael 2010; WHO, n.d.-a). Although biomedical health care is widely considered to be one of humanity's most significant accomplishments, health care has been shown to account for only between 5 and 20 per cent of health outcomes (Kaplan and Milstein 2019 as cited in Woolf 2019; Hancock 2017). Health-related behaviours are thought to be responsible for 30 to

50 per cent of health outcomes, social conditions for 15 to 40 per cent, physical environments for 3 to 20 per cent, and genetics for 20 to 30 per cent (Hancock 2017). These ratios are further complicated by the extent to which social and environmental factors influence the behavioural options available to individuals, the expression of their genes, and their access to health care (Hancock 2017; Woolf 2019; Cole 2014; Woolf and Purnell 2016).

Social-ecological models of health are relatively recent developments in medicine, gaining traction in the late twentieth and early twenty-first centuries (see Del Bianco et al. 2020; Fitzgibbon et al. 2018). For most of modernity, biomedicine has been the dominant paradigm structuring professional understandings of health and illness as well as the delivery of health care services around the world (Baer, Singer, and Susser 2013; Lock and Nguyen 2010). Embedded within the Western scientific tradition, biomedicine tends to conceptualize illness from a naturalistic perspective, focusing on removing pathogens and other isolatable causes of disease with pharmaceutical treatments or surgical interventions (Foucault 1994; Harrison 2004; Lock and Nguyen 2010). Grounded in mechanistic views of the human body, biomedicine has historically taken a reductionistic view of human health and is oriented towards curing disease (Foucault 1994; Harrison 2004; Schepper-Hughes and Lock 1987). Processes of individualization that deepened with the transition to modernity also shaped medicine throughout its development as a scientific field and continue to influence the extent to which people see individuals as responsible for their own health and their own illnesses (Giddens 1990; Polanyi 1944; Beck and Beck-Gernsheim 2002).

As noted above, behaviour does account for a significant proportion (30–50 per cent) of human health outcomes (Hancock, 2017), but contrary to what one might assume, behaviour is governed less by individual choice than it is by social context (Woolf and Purnell 2016; Woolf 2019). Behaviours including getting physical exercise, eating healthy food, not smoking tobacco, consuming alcohol in moderation, sleeping well, avoiding injuries, and limiting exposure to damaging UV rays are all shown to enhance "health, longevity, and quality of life" (Hilliard et al. 2018, xvii). Smoking, poor nutrition, and physical inactivity are particularly damaging and have been found to have the greatest influence on mortality (McGinnis and Foege 1993 and Mokdad et al. 2004 as cited in Puterman et al., 2020). Yet despite these strong associations and the apparent simplicity of behavioural solutions (e.g., eating a healthy diet, getting enough exercise), health researchers and practitioners struggle to understand the factors that influence behaviour change as well as how new behaviours can best be maintained over time. Changing health-related behaviours has turned out to be exceptionally difficult despite rising knowledge of behavioural risks. These difficulties are believed to arise due to the immense complexity and interactivity of factors at play, including individual characteristics (attitudes, beliefs, personality traits, perceptions of self-efficacy) and community-level variables (social, economic, cultural, and ecological influences on behaviour) (Janevic and Connell 2018; Fitzgibbon et al. 2018).

Systems approaches to health recognize that health outcomes cannot be attributed to individuals alone, but emerge at the intersection of health care infrastructure, individual health-related behaviours, physical and social environments, socio-economic circumstances, and the policy landscape (Woolf and Purnell 2016; Woolf 2019). Social determinants of health frameworks, for example, demonstrate the extent to which inequitable living conditions affect health and well-being. The social determinants include demographic factors such as race, gender, Indigenous status, and disability as well as social circumstances such as early life experiences, education, employment and working conditions, food insecurity, income, and social exclusion. Social determinants act on health in part when poor living conditions cause prolonged physiological and psychological stress, deepening vulnerability to physical and mental illnesses, increasing the likelihood that people will use unhealthy behaviours to cope with difficult situations, and limiting people's capacity to engage in healthy behaviours (Mikkonen and Raphael 2010).

Insight into the pervasive influence of the social determinants of health has profound implications for how governments, health systems, and communities can best prevent illness and promote population health. Woolf et al. (2007) conducted a study to determine which would save more lives, investments in social change or in medical advancement. Using US data, they estimated how many deaths between 1996 and 2002 were averted as a result of medical innovations, comparing this figure to how many deaths would have been avoided if everyone in the United States had the same mortality rate as college-educated people. They found that closing the mortality gap between those with less formal education and those with more would avert eight times as many deaths as continuing to invest in medical advancement, saving approximately 1,370,000 lives instead of 178,000. Even though education affects mortality rates through complex social, economic, and environmental pathways, these striking results suggest that supporting meaningful social change holds significantly higher potential to improve human health than developing new medical technologies. Similarly, investing in closing the mortality gap between white and Black people in the United States, which research has found to be rooted in inequitable access to health care, income disparities, and differential educational outcomes among other social and environmental factors, would avert five times as many deaths as investing in medical innovation (Woolf et al. 2004 as cited in Woolf et al. 2007).

Woolf and colleagues recognize that the systems change work needed to enable more equitable health outcomes is extensive, requiring action across all social determinants of health as well as across sectors. It would entail grass-roots action to strengthen community supports as well as changes to funding regimes, government safety nets, cultural paradigms, and economic policies (Woolf et al. 2007; Woolf 2019). However, the level of effort required to pursue this course of action does not discount the value of the approach, which would generate multiple benefits for individuals, families, communities, and even health systems. Ensuring that people live in affordable housing, for instance, has been shown to reduce emergency room visits as well as admissions to hospital (Woolf 2019). Finding effective ways to address the social determinants of health is becoming increasingly critical in the context of widening wealth inequality. Over the past two decades, health inequities have deepened significantly in the United States, with the gap in life expectancy between the wealthiest one per cent and poorest one per cent rising to 14.6 years (Chetty et al., 2016 as cited in Woolf and Purnell 2016). Again in a US context, the pandemic has highlighted how economic and racial inequity affect vulnerability to contracting coronavirus. Although African Americans represent 13 per cent of the US population, one-third of first-wave COVID-19 cases were among African Americans, who were also twice as likely to die from the virus (Brown et al. 2020). The social determinants of health are at the heart of these stark discrepancies; Black Americans are over-represented in front-line health care support work, as well as in low-paid food service and manufacturing jobs, the overcrowded prison system, areas with inadequate housing, and other life circumstances that make self-isolation, social distancing, and accessing government supports more difficult (Brown et al. 2020). Richard Horton (2020), editor-in-chief of *The Lancet*, suggests that COVID-19 is not really a "pandemic" at all, but a "syndemic," a synergistic epidemic in which a novel coronavirus engages with human hosts living in conditions of profound inequity, conditions that affect the transmission and severity of the disease.

In addition to the social determinants of health, physical environments exert a strong influence on human health outcomes. The WHO estimates that 23 per cent of deaths and 22 per cent of the global burden of disease are caused by environmental factors, including occupational conditions; air pollution (ambient and within households); exposure to toxins including tobacco smoke, radon, and lead; and water and sanitation infrastructure and practices (Prüss-Üstün et al. 2016). Diseases most likely to be affected by environmental conditions include stroke (42 per cent), ischaemic heart disease (35 per cent), diarrhoeal diseases (57 per cent), lower respiratory infections (35 per cent), and cancers (20 per cent) (Prüss-Üstün et al. 2016). Air pollution was responsible for 4.2 million deaths in 2016, mostly as a result of its contribution to non-communicable diseases, and the WHO estimates that more than 90 per cent of the world's population breathes in unhealthy levels of pollution every day (WHO 2019a). Environmental factors disproportionately affect low- and middle-income countries, raising serious concerns about inequity in global patterns of disease (Prüss-Üstün et al. 2016), especially given that high-income nations have contributed most to the ecological changes now threatening population health on a planetary scale (Steffen et al. 2015b).

In Canada, public health practitioners are calling for greater recognition of the ecological determinants of health in research, practice, and policy (CPHA 2015). Ecological determinants of health are the essential functions that humans require from ecosystems in order to live healthy lives. They include having enough oxygen, water, and food; the effective functioning of the ozone layer, the nitrogen and phosphorous cycles, and the planet's detoxification systems; and the presence of healthy soils, fresh water systems, and oceans. To sustain complex societies, humans also require access to resources to make shelters and tools, sufficient energy, and a climate whose stability and temperature range support human life and essential biodiversity (see CPHA 2015, 3). At the most basic level, the Earth must be able to sustain life in order for humans to be healthy (CPHA 2015). Yet human activities are currently eroding all the ecological determinants of health, with potentially devastating consequences: "When ecosystems decline or collapse, the communities and societies embedded within and dependent on them also decline and may collapse (Diamond, 2005). The decline in ecosystem functioning at a global and regional scale represents perhaps the greatest threat to the stability of our societies and thus to health in the 21st century" (Hancock 2015, e253). As described when we discussed planetary health, the primary drivers of ecological destruction are human population growth, increasing wealth (particularly its association with rising expectations for material consumption), and the expansion of technology (Hancock 2015; CPHA 2015; Myers and Frumkin 2020). Underpinning these trends is the continued commitment to modernization as a paradigm for thought and action (Hancock 2015; CPHA 2015).

The ecological determinants of health framework acknowledges that "human evolution takes place within ecosystems, and there are deep psychological, social and cultural connections to ecosystems that go well beyond mere physiological needs" (CPHA 2015, 1). As such, the framework is inherently relational, drawing attention to the primacy of relationships between ecological and social systems, and the degree to which the well-being of human and non-human communities "are inextricably interwoven" (Parkes et al. 2019, n.p.). Because ecological systems are so closely coupled to social and economic systems, the ecological and the social determinants of health should be considered together as mutual influences on population health (CPHA 2015). In a Canadian context, for instance, social determinants of health such as access to health services, geographic location, and degree of influence over decision-making processes make the country's marginalized populations, including Indigenous people, youth, and those living with low-income, more vulnerable to the negative health effects of the climate crisis (Clean Air Partnership 2011 and Kumar 2018 as cited in CPHA 2019).

A systems view of the meso scale would be incomplete without considering how genetics influences human health outcomes. While genetic factors are thought to account for between 20 and 30 per cent of health outcomes (Hancock 2017), human genetics are not static. Rather, the expression of genes responsible for disease can be influenced by "physicochemical processes" initiated when toxins, certain microbes, or pollutants are present in the environment (Cole 2014, 2). Gene expression can also be influenced by "psychological processes" that occur when people feel threatened or uncertain (2). Either or both processes can begin a chain reaction through which neural or endocrine responses result in certain genes being activated or repressed. In other words, the social and environmental stressors that humans are exposed to alter which genes are expressed, making people who live in adverse conditions more vulnerable to a host of diseases. In particular, difficult social environments such as low socio-economic status, chronic stress, and bereavement tend to activate pro-inflammatory genes and decrease the activation of genes responsible for antiviral and antibody responses. This process is known as the conserved transcriptional response to adversity (CTRA), and genomic research has found that CTRA occurs in response to diverse forms of social and environmental stress (Cole 2014). Social genomics research has also produced evidence to suggest that individualism is bad for health. Frederickson and colleagues found that people who report higher levels of hedonistic well-being (pursuit of positive emotions and self-focused gratification) show more CTRA gene expression than those who report higher levels of eudaemonic well-being (the longer-term satisfaction that comes from contributing to a purpose beyond oneself) (Frederickson et al. 2013 as cited in Cole 2014). These findings suggest that approaching well-being in ways that transcend self-interest and finding meaning in collective purpose may contribute to health at the genetic level (Cole 2014, 4).

Considering human health outcomes from a systemic perspective reveals that variables across the domains of health care, social circumstances, environmental conditions, and genetics interact in complex ways to affect health. This section began by discussing the comparatively small influence of biomedical health care in comparison to other domains. As Trevor Hancock points out, health care is more accurately an "illness care system" that can effectively treat disease and injury, but that makes little contribution to addressing the other determinants of health (Hancock 2017, E1571). Although there is a substantial body of evidence to support Hancock's conclusion, biomedicine nonetheless does play an essential role in human well-being. Given the choice, few people would want to live without access to pain killers, life-saving surgeries in the event of an accident, modern dentistry, or antibiotics. Yet some of these capacities are being undermined by dynamics at higher and lower scales. For instance, it remains to be seen what level of technological development will be possible in a world experiencing tightening ecological constraints on human action (see chapter 8). Antimicrobial resistance could also render antibiotics ineffective as a result of inappropriate overuse of antibiotics in agriculture and medicine in conjunction with the rapid pace of microbial evolution (WHO 2020, 2021; also see chapter 3). In addition to describing how systemic influences on health play out at the meso scale, this section suggests that even in a future in which doctors are more limited in their capacity to treat illness and disease, our knowledge of the social and ecological determinants of health, as well as how life circumstances influence genetics, offer new pathways for improving health outcomes by embracing approaches beyond the scope of biomedicine. Potential applications of these insights can be seen in the soil health movement, therapeutic gardening, and care farming, among other prefigurative movements discussed in this book.

2.3 The Micro Scale: Inner Ecologies

> The realization that humans are not merely "individuals," but rather complex ecosystems may be one of the major advances in our understanding of human health in recent years, with significant implications for both ecology and human health. (WHO 2015, 8)

Individualism is pervasive in modern, Westernized societies, determining how we experience our personal autonomy and agency, directing much of biomedicine's approach to diagnosis and treatment, and fundamentally shaping the psychology of modern people (Beck and Beck-Gernsheim 2002; Bauman 2012; Lock and Nguyen 2010). Yet in the same way that the dynamics of planetary ecological processes are clinically relevant to our health, humans harbour complex inner ecologies whose implications we are only beginning to comprehend (Prescott et al. 2016; Schnorr 2015). The human microbiome is made up of between five hundred and one thousand species of bacteria, as well as fungi, other microbes, and viruses that together form "complex commensal communities" (Eisenstein 2020, S6). The bacterial species residing in the human gut possess 150 times more genetic material than the human genome (Savage 2020). Sheltering this diversity within us, humans may more accurately be seen as "multispecies organisms" than as atomistic individuals (Prescott et al. 2016, 2). In a biological sense, we are not separate from the ecosystems in which we live; instead, every person is a complex ecosystem in his or her own right (Prescott et al. 2016).

The microbiome is a "human co-evolutionary partner" with a role in nutrition, immunity, and protection from environmental exposures (Rampelli et al. 2015, 1682). It conveys information between our inner and outer environments, is a crucial component of human biological function, and contributes to maintaining health (Schnorr 2015). It is widely accepted that disrupting microbial ecosystems is a causal factor in many disease processes (Eisenstein 2020, S6). The microbiome is now directly implicated in the aetiologies of illnesses as diverse as schizophrenia and depression (Kelly et al. 2016 as cited in Savage 2020), anxiety (Schnorr and Bachner 2016), autism, gastric ulcers, cancer (Pepper and Rosenfeld 2012), diabetes, obesity, allergies, other inflammatory respiratory conditions, and a general inflammatory state seen to contribute to a host of other illnesses (Eisenstein 2020). Indeed, it appears that the microbiome could play a role in most non-communicable diseases (Prescott et al. 2016). Researchers studying the causal relationships between the microbiome and mental health, for instance, now think in terms of a "gut-brain-axis," a model in which the brain, the central nervous system, and the gut are believed to be in constant communication with one another through the enteric nervous system (Schnorr and Bachner 2016, 398). The gut-brain-axis plays a regulatory role within the body, influencing both mental health and behaviour (Schnorr and Bachner 2016). Stephanie Schnorr and Harriet Bachner (2016) explain that dramatic increases in anxiety and depression in high-income, Westernized societies are occurring alongside rises in autoimmune and metabolic illnesses. They suggest that these trends are likely connected, and that although mental health, autoimmune, and metabolic illnesses each have multiple complex causes, most can be traced to unhealthy or even "toxic changes" within modern industrial societies (398), such as consumption of processed, sugary foods and too little sleep.

Because the microbiome provides a mechanism through which human beings can biologically adapt to changes in social arrangements, diet, and lifestyle, it is highly sensitive to such changes. This dynamic creates unintended consequences for human health as our lifestyles depart more and more substantially from the conditions in which our species lived for many thousands of years. Microbial adaptations are extremely fast in comparison to the evolution of our species (Goodrich et al. 2016 as cited in Eisenstein 2020). At a population level and even within individual households, the microbiome is shaped by human subsistence patterns and key lifestyle factors. In populations that eat large quantities of unprocessed plant foods, for example, the microbiome is made up of bacteria that help extract micronutrients and metabolites from a range of raw plants; in contrast, the gut bacteria of people consuming Westernized diets provide enzymes designed to break down foods high in protein, simple sugars, and fats (Rampelli et al. 2015).

Studies of contemporary hunter-gatherer populations show us how the microbiome might have functioned for the greater part of human evolutionary history (Schnorr 2015). Schnorr (2015) found that the microbiomes of the Hadza in Tanzania, for instance, display some significant differences from the microbiomes of populations living modern, urban lifestyles. The bacteria in Hadza guts are highly diverse, creating a stable and adaptable inner ecology that makes it possible for them to deal with endemic pathogens in their environment as well as seasonal fluctuations in diet. Among the Hadza, gender roles are pervasive, resulting in distinct gut microbiomes. Women and men consume more of the foods they are differentially responsible for gathering, meaning that women end up with a higher abundance of bacteria suited to digesting the tubers and other plants that make up most of their diets. This adaptation of the microbiome could be what makes it possible for Hadza women to obtain enough nutrition to reproduce, even in an environment in which food availability is inherently unpredictable and often limited. As such, Schnorr's study suggests that the microbiome may have been integral to human survival and reproduction when our capacity to obtain the basic necessities of life was much more uncertain (Schnorr 2015, S15).

In contrast, modern life can negatively affect the microbiome by preventing essential early exposures to beneficial bacteria and increasing exposure to factors that create "dysbiotic drift," literally "difficult living," or disruptions to microbial communities (Prescott et al. 2016, 3, 2). These factors include the presence of environmental toxins, eating processed foods and high-sugar, high-fat diets, lack of sleep, and sedentary behaviours (Prescott et al. 2016). Other modern ways of life that could negatively affect the microbiome include keeping houses too clean, living in urban rather than rural environments, and taking pharmaceuticals that have intentional or unanticipated antibiotic effects (Eisenstein 2020; Savage 2020). Even the ways in which we construct modern homes could be reducing our exposure to beneficial airborne microbes (Ruiz-Calderon et al. 2016 as cited in Prescott et al. 2016). Lifestyle factors are one of the strongest influences on the microbiome, and studies suggest that modernity and urbanization are "highly disruptive to the tight-knit relationship that has evolved between humans and their microbes" (Eisenstein 2020, S7).

The environments in which humanity evolved, which entailed close interactions with outer ecosystems through foraging and hunting and spending most of our days outside, established a microbiome tailored to the local environment and capable of providing specific, targeted protection and assistance (Rampelli et al. 2015). Modern society, on the other hand, "deprives us of the necessary environmental interaction to acquire a diverse ecosystem as is our ancestral legacy" (Rampelli et al. 2015, 1689). Taken together, modern lifestyle factors result in gut microbiomes that are less diverse than those of our ancestors or of living hunter-gatherer populations (Schnorr 2015). Biological anthropologist Stephanie Schnorr and I discussed whether this loss of diversity means that Westernized microbiomes lack resiliency and functionality for modern people. Schnorr reflected that from a scientific perspective

> we still know very little about the limitations and stressors that can topple a Westernized microbiome ... but it does seem as though the diversity that we see with more traditional communities lends a sort of robusticity to the environment, and by contrast that Western, urban, industrial populations do retain communities that are much more fragile. (Schnorr, personal communication)

Schnorr emphasized that Westernized microbiomes are not less adapted to the environment, but rather are adapted to the environments we currently live in, environments that are characterized by a reliance on technology, medicine, and sanitation (personal communication). In modern societies, interventions like sanitation, industrial food production, and antibiotic use have taken on the role once performed by the microbiome, so that our guts are no longer as responsible for fighting disease or helping us digest unprocessed, fibrous foods (Schnorr 2015). She explained that this process represents a trade-off in which we are substituting "biological and evolutionary adaptation for technological adaptive traits." For example, "in a sanitized world, we remove the threat of everyday pathogens with our technology, with sanitation. That means that that function, that defence system, does not need to come from our biology itself, from the commensal organisms that live within us" (personal communication). Similar kinds of trade-offs have been made throughout our evolutionary history:

> The ability to make tools, the ability to use fire, these compensate for biological traits that our ancestors may have had, such as really thick enamel on the teeth to be able to chew very tough food, or immunity for pathogens for eating raw meat. Cooking provides us with a way to sterilize and prevent parasites from infecting us. So we use these tools to compensate, and I think this is also something that could be going on in the microbiome, where our everyday lives now in this built, human-made environment, are doing things to our biology, while our biology is responding by shedding unnecessary traits, or shedding organisms in the microbiome that are no longer needed, that don't provide a necessary function because it's already being taken care of.

As Schnorr notes above, scientific knowledge of the microbiome remains limited; researchers do not yet have a strong mechanistic knowledge of all the functions the microbiome provides for humans. Accordingly, it is hard to say what we have lost in the course of these microbial trade-offs, whether we have lost anything irretrievably, or whether interventions like fecal transplants or dietary and lifestyle changes could return functions such as the ability to break down certain polysaccharides in the gut (Schnorr, personal communication).

One thing that is clear is that although there is no single healthy gut microbiome to aspire to (Eisenstein 2020), the implications of microbiome research for personalized medicine are immense. The microbiome is established early on, during infancy, and the microbes children come in contact with early in life can prime them to become vulnerable or resilient to diverse health conditions throughout their lifetime (Eisenstein 2020). Microbial exposure during infancy could have a strong influence on immune system function, allergic responses, mental health, and gastrointestinal diseases (Prescott et al. 2016). Medical interventions like caesarean sections, for instance, have been shown to limit a newborn's exposure to the beneficial bacteria present in the mother's birth canal.

However, simple practices like swabbing the birth canal can improve outcomes for babies born through C-section (Eisenstein 2020). And, because infancy is the time during which the microbial community is being established, there is great potential to direct therapeutic interventions at this window of the life course in order to influence a host of non-communicable disease processes later in life (Prescott et al. 2016).

Focusing on the microbial scale could also provide new pathways for treating anxiety and depression using "inexpensive and non-invasive" strategies such as changes to diet (e.g., reducing processed foods or consuming more probiotic and fermented foods) (Schnorr and Bachner 2016, 407). Other similar interventions include taking probiotic or prebiotic supplements, modifying bile acid, and conducting fecal transplants (Prescott et al. 2016). However, substantive and long-lasting changes to the microbiome can only be sustained if the underlying causes of microbial disruption are also addressed (Prescott et al. 2016). For instance, biodiversity loss, loss of time spent in nature, the prevalence of processed foods and other unhealthy dietary patterns, the way we construct our homes, and our obsession with cleanliness will continue to exert pressures on our inner ecologies unless we intentionally shift both our behaviours and the ways in which modern lifestyles impact ecological dynamics at higher scales (Prescott et al. 2016).

For these reasons, emerging knowledge of the microbiome could contribute to making reductionist approaches to health untenable. If we acknowledge the sheer scale of complex interactions occurring between gut bacteria themselves, at the "gut-brain-axis," and between the microbiome and outer ecologies (local ecosystems as well as the broader biosphere), a systems view is clearly required to account for the health effects of inner ecosystems (Pepper and Rosenfeld 2012; Maier and al'Absi 2017). With increasing understanding of how the microbiome affects health, ecological and complex systems paradigms take on greater relevance for medical science and systems-based approaches are drawn further into standard medical models and innovations in personalized care (Pepper and Rosenfeld 2012; Prescott et al. 2016).

2.4 Embedding Multiscale Approaches to Health in Thought and Practice

A significant paradigm change in modern health systems could be on the horizon as more people recognize that health emerges due to the interactions of biological, social, and environmental factors at different scales (see Maier and al'Absi 2017; Prescott et al. 2016). An effective health system for a sustainable future must be able to meet the urgent needs of individuals, families, and communities in the present while also contributing to the long-term health of ecosystems, from the microbial scale to that of the planet. This chapter has introduced some of the concepts that could contribute to such paradigmatic change, including planetary health, the social and ecological determinants of health, and insights about the microbiome. Together, these frameworks demonstrate the extent to which health is affected by the dynamics of nested complex systems at various scales. If a synthesis of these diverse perspectives can be increasingly embedded in thought and practice, it also has the potential to overcome our cultural fixation with individual health outcomes, instead promoting ecological, systems-based approaches to health. Chapter 3 will build on these ideas by considering what is lost when societies prioritize one scale – the human scale – over all others. The three stories in part 1 – soil health, gardening for health, and care farming – then illustrate what might be possible for health systems that meaningfully attend to health across social-ecological scales.

3 Problems of Scale in Human and Planetary Health

We are in a tight bind in the early decades of the twenty-first century. We know that to sustain flourishing human civilizations, Earth systems must remain within narrow parameters, many of which we have already breached (Rockström et al. 2009; Steffen et al. 2015b). We also know that no country in the world secures basic human needs, let alone social justice for all, without crossing planetary boundaries (O'Neill et al. 2018). The need for systems change is urgent, and the problems before us are "wicked" (see Rittel and Webber 1973; Meadows 2008). There are no obvious or simple solutions. Working through a wicked problem is a process of negotiating uncomfortable trade-offs, contending with paradox, and even entering into unexpected alliances (Rittel and Webber 1973; Meadows 2008). When it comes to health in the Anthropocene, the wicked problems we face are complex, global in scope, and unfolding across long time horizons. They also manifest within our bodies, our communities, and our local ecosystems. On the one hand, global measures of human health like life expectancy and child mortality are better than they ever have been (Myers and Frumkin 2020). On the other, the Earth has been profoundly altered, depleted, and polluted by the growth of human economic activity. Planetary health researchers warn that "we have been mortgaging the health of future generations to realise economic and development gains in the present" (Whitmee et al. 2015, 1973). This paradox is rooted in a well-documented dynamic within complex systems: intervening to solve a problem at one scale can generate unintended consequences at higher scales. Often, this dynamic arises due to feedback processes involving geographically and temporally distant effects that cannot be anticipated in advance (Rogers 1983; Holling, Gunderson, and Peterson 2002; Meadows 2008). Paradox is daunting on its own. Combined with the very real risk of severe unintended consequences, it can be difficult to know where to begin.

The purpose of this chapter is to open up a conversation about wicked problems of scale, a conversation that I will return to throughout this book. I will begin by discussing how the climate crisis, biodiversity loss, antimicrobial resistance, and the COVID-19 pandemic represent aggregate unintended consequences of human actions at more localized scales, actions that are often (though not always) intended to *improve* human well-being. I will also consider some of the implications for health systems of moving away from individualism – an integral part of modern culture – towards greater recognition of health as a property of interconnected social-ecological systems.

A central argument of this book is that securing long-term health, equity, and sustainability at a global level requires us to attend to the ecological foundations of health across scales. As discussed in chapter 2, the health of the microbiome is a form of ecological integrity, a population-level resilience of diverse bacterial species and other microscopic life. Within human populations, social, economic, and environmental circumstances shape health outcomes more profoundly than access to health care; they even affect the expression of our genes. At the planetary scale, the self-regulating processes of the Earth's climate, its nutrient and chemical cycles, and the extent to which its lands and waters sustain biodiverse life are both signs and determinants of health (see CPHA 2015; Lovelock 1991). Yet within modern societies, human development and well-being tend to be pursued in ways that erode rather than reinforce the ecological foundations of health, often due to the rampant individualism that pervades modern life (see Beck and Beck-Gernsheim 2002; Zywert and Quilley 2017). Moving away from individualism in the ways in which we think about and structure health systems will not be a straightforward process. The potential for mutually reinforcing gains across social-ecological systems is significant, but so too is the need to confront difficult trade-offs. By beginning to delve into these wicked problems of scale, this chapter sets the stage to discuss a set of practices, ideas, and structures that hold promise for improving human health by directing our attention towards the health of whole, nested, social-ecological systems.

3.1 The Climate Crisis

> I think there are trade-offs [between human health and environmental outcomes]. We should ask ourselves, "How much of that human health benefit is occurring, especially at a very big population level, at the cost of environmental degradation?" ... Climate change is a classic example of ecosystem failure. Our environment has been so degraded that our Earth

can no longer maintain its proper thermal regulation. And in the process of that happening, by burning all those fuels and using those fuels to create a fantastic civilization and society, we have improved our health dramatically. But maybe that's not the right thing to do. I mean, that would be a tough one to argue, but I think maybe one has to look at that. (Dr. Don Spady, epidemiologist, personal communication)

Climate change increases the risk of almost every form of human suffering: infectious diseases, chronic diseases, poor mental health, injuries, disrupted lives. (Frumkin 2020, 253)

The climate crisis is primarily a direct, though unintended, consequence of fossil fuel combustion. The world burns 186,000 litres of oil, 116,000,000 litres of gas, and 171,000 kilograms of coal every second to fuel human economic activities. In 2018 human activities were responsible for releasing 33.1 gigatons of CO_2 into the atmosphere (Cooper and Johnson 2018, IEA 2017, EIA 2018 as cited in Watts et al. 2019). As a consequence of rising greenhouse gas emissions, the Earth has warmed by around 1 degree Celsius since 1900 (Field et al. 2020; Watts et al. 2019). If we continue on a high-emissions (business-as-usual) trajectory, we will reach 3 degrees of warming by 2100, creating unprecedented risks to human health and civilization (Field et al. 2020; Watts et al. 2019). To keep warming to 1.5 degrees Celsius, a range that has been determined to incur an acceptable degree of risk, would require reaching net zero emissions by 2050 (Watts et al. 2019). Unfortunately, since 1990 the carbon intensity of our energy systems has remained constant, and carbon dioxide emissions on a global scale have continued to rise following a brief period of stability between 2014 and 2016 (Watts et al. 2019). While fossil fuel combustion is the primary direct driver of increased CO_2 in the atmosphere, human energy use is currently coupled with the size of the human economy. This coupling means that increases in GDP continue to be associated with increases in material resource and energy consumption, generating negative ecological consequences including pushing past the planetary boundary for climate change (Steffen et al. 2015b). To the degree that economic growth remains coupled to GHG emissions, efforts that seek to improve human well-being by expanding the formal economy are unintentionally undermining the ecological foundations of health by creating conditions that perpetuate the climate crisis (see chapter 7 for a more detailed discussion about the relationship between economic growth and health).

As an emergent effect of economic development, climate change is responsible for a myriad of health conditions that could reverse the well-being gains associated with global modernization. The climate crisis affects human health through "complex and multilevel pathways" that are both direct and indirect (Frumkin 2020, 246; see also WHO 2019a; IPCC 2022; Pörtner et al. 2022). For instance, more frequent extreme weather and natural disasters, lower air quality, increased risks related to infectious disease, a shift in patterns of migration and conflict, declining crop yields and nutrition, intensification of allergies, and greater mental health problems have all been tied to climate change (Frumkin 2020; Field et al. 2020; WHO 2019a; IPCC 2022; Pörtner et al. 2022). Increased heat alone has already been associated with:

- A rise in rates of heat rash and heat stroke
- More cases of kidney stones and renal disease
- Sleep disruptions
- Interpersonal violence and suicides
- More emergency room visits, hospitalizations, and mortality from existing non-communicable diseases (cardiovascular deaths, for instance, tend to increase during heat waves) (Frumkin 2020; Smith et al. 2014 as cited in Frumkin and Haines 2020)

Higher frequency of severe weather and natural disasters due to climate change has also been shown to negatively affect health by causing:

- Serious injuries
- Reduced air quality
- Droughts and flooding
- Destruction of homes
- Mental illnesses, including the impact of trauma on mental health
- Increased substance abuse and domestic violence (Frumkin 2020; IPCC 2022; Pörtner et al. 2022)

Extreme weather events caused by climate change can also disrupt health care continuity. Following disasters such as floods and storms, for example, people with chronic conditions such as cardiovascular diseases, diabetes, and cancer tend to experience worsening health due to power outages, breakdowns in transportation systems, and interrupted supply chains (Ryan et al. 2015 as cited in Frumkin and Haines 2020). The health effects of the climate crisis are felt most strongly among those who are already vulnerable for other reasons, including the young and old, people who are ill, people of colour, and those living in poverty or in vulnerable regions (Field et al. 2020; Frumkin 2020; IPCC 2022; Pörtner et al. 2022).

When it comes to infectious disease, the climate crisis intensifies risks associated with vector-borne, waterborne, and foodborne illnesses (Frumkin 2020; WHO 2019a; IPCC 2022; Pörtner et al. 2022). Climate change alters conditions within the habitats of common disease vectors, pathogens, and host organisms and influences their behaviour (Ostfeld and Keesing 2020). As regions warm, for example, disease vectors and host populations can spread to higher latitudes, expanding their typical ranges. Cold-blooded organisms reproduce more quickly and feed more in hotter environments, potentially increasing rates of disease transmission (Ostfeld and Keesing 2020). The spread of Lyme disease throughout North America between 2001 and 2017 can be attributed in part to warmer temperatures that made it possible for ticks to become endemic in regions that would have previously been too cold for the vector to thrive (Ostfeld and Keesing 2020). Increased rain and flooding coupled with rising temperatures has also led to higher incidence of diarrhoeal diseases (e.g., cholera) and other gastrointestinal illnesses (IPCC 2022; Pörtner et al. 2022). It is as yet unclear whether climate change will make some regions too hot for certain pathogens, resulting in an overall shift as opposed to an increase in the global burden of disease (Ostfeld and Keesing 2020). So far, however, trends indicate that warmer temperatures equate to an expansion of the geographical range and the virulence of many infectious diseases (Alley and Sommerfeld 2014; IPCC 2022; Pörtner et al. 2022). For instance, dengue risk is expected to increase substantially due to longer seasons and an expanding geographic range, potentially exposing billions more people to the disease this century (IPCC 2022; Pörtner et al. 2022).

The climate crisis is also a central component of what Swinburn and colleagues call the Global Syndemic, a "synergy of epidemics" that coexist in time and place, interact in complex ways, and emerge from the same root causes (2019,791). The Global Syndemic describes the interconnected effects of obesity, undernutrition, and climate change, and is currently seen to be one of the most significant threats to human health in the world (Swinburn et al. 2019). The negative health effects of the Global Syndemic arise where feedback patterns between biological, behavioural, and environmental variables common to all three pandemics converge. Malnutrition (both undernutrition and obesity), for instance, is a primary contributor to poor health outcomes at a global scale, increasing vulnerability to almost all categories of disease. Nutrition is in turn highly vulnerable to the effects of climate change, which reduces agricultural capacities and threatens food security due to increased heat; greater frequency and severity of storms, droughts and flooding; reduced nutrient content of crops; increased presence of pests and weeds; and worsening working conditions for farmers (Swinburn et al. 2019; Frumkin 2020). Undernutrition and obesity are also connected, with lack of nutrients in utero and infancy increasing the risk of becoming obese later in life. Moderate levels of food insecurity are also associated with greater rates of obesity (Swinburn et al. 2019). Further, as low- and middle-income countries develop and populations become more affluent, rates of obesity rise and people contribute more GHG emissions through their dietary habits as they begin to eat greater quantities of highly processed foods and animal products (Swinburn et al. 2019). Through complex feedback loops, the climate crisis contributes to undernutrition and obesity, undernutrition contributes to obesity, and obesity circles back to contribute to the climate crisis. In this way, the Global Syndemic is perpetuated and deepened.

The Global Syndemic is a strong illustration of the kinds of unknowable health effects that are likely to continue arising as the climate crisis inevitably intensifies over the coming decades. Even if we transitioned to a fully carbon-neutral society today, the ecological consequences of past human activities would continue to exacerbate climate change for many, many years (CPHA 2015). And as described above, we are nowhere close to achieving net zero emissions. Although there are indicators of progress that suggest it might still be possible to meet the 2050 target, currently emissions remain on an upward trajectory (Watts et al. 2019). In 2018, the IPCC warned that we may only have eleven more years in which to act before we are guaranteed to exceed 1.5 degrees of warming, a threshold beyond which we can anticipate even more profound health effects than have already been documented (IPCC 2018 as cited in Harmer et al. 2020).

The climate crisis has the potential to negatively impact almost every aspect of human health as well as the ultimate survival of our species on this planet (Frumkin 2020; Rockström et al. 2009). As such, addressing the climate crisis holds unprecedented possibilities for improving health and well-being (Frumkin 2020; CPHA 2015; WHO 2019a). The Canadian Public Health Association calls climate change "the greatest health threat" *and* "the greatest health opportunity of this century" (CPHA 2019, 3). In public health terms, mitigating climate change is a form of "primary prevention," while adaptation builds "disaster preparedness and resilience" (Field et al. 2020, 73–4). Some solutions are simple in theory and generate clear win-wins across domains such as soil life, human population health, and ecosystem restoration. For instance, the negative health effects of the Global Syndemic could be substantially reduced by widespread dietary shifts towards healthier, more plant-based diets upheld by more sustainable agricultural practices that improve food security, nutrition, and agricultural resilience while also lowering GHG emissions and consumption of highly processed foods (Swinburn et al. 2019). Multilateral organizations like the WHO recognize and advocate for such opportunities as key leverage points in global health, emphasizing that enabling these changes will require collaboration with and action across sectors as diverse as industry, housing, transportation, health, energy, agriculture, and labour (WHO 2019a). What remains to be seen is whether attention to individual health can be reconciled with effective climate action given the high and rising contribution of the health care sector to GHG emissions (Eckelman, Sherman, and MacNeill 2018). A further barrier is the deep cultural entanglements within modern society between status, well-being, and ecologically corrosive conspicuous consumption (see Solomon, Greenberg, and Pyszczynski 2015; Davy 2020). These wicked tensions will be discussed further in chapters 7 and 8.

3.2 Biodiversity Loss

> My inclination is to say that the trade-off [between human health and environmental outcomes] is an illusion and that what we have gained or appear to have gained in global health statistics are going to come at a cost that's going to be precipitous and catastrophic. So we've bought a little bit of good health at the cost of future generations, in other words. And it's worth maybe settling for two years less average lifespan if it means that our grandchildren and their grandchildren can actually survive. And that other creatures on the planet can share the space with us. (Jessica Pierce, bioethicist, personal communication)

> The ongoing sixth mass extinction may be the most serious environmental threat to the persistence of civilization, because it is irreversible. (Ceballos, Ehrlich, and Raven 2020, 13596)

Human health depends on thriving, biodiverse living systems (Prescott et al. 2016; WHO 2015; Field et al. 2020; Ceballos, Ehrlich, and Raven 2020). Biodiversity refers to the number of species as well as to the genetic variation that exists within and between those species and the ecosystems they inhabit (WHO 2015; Field et al. 2020). Biodiversity has been identified as one of the nine planetary boundaries that should not be crossed if we hope to maintain Holocene-like conditions; it is also one of five boundaries (including recent evidence on novel entities) that have already been breached (Steffen et al. 2015b; Rockström et al. 2009; Persson et al. 2022). The core drivers of extinction include:

- Climate change
- Loss of habitats due to the expansion and intensification of agriculture
- The introduction of invasive species
- Overexploitation of species through unsustainable hunting, fishing, and harvesting (Field et al. 2020; WHO 2015)

Much like the climate crisis, all of these drivers are in turn rooted in the rapid growth of the human population and its rate of consumption, both of which are projected to continue increasing into the indeterminate future (Ceballos, Ehrlich, and Raven 2020).

Homo sapiens evolved at a time in the Earth's history when global levels of biodiversity were higher than ever before (Ceballos, Ehrlich, and Raven 2020). Now, as a result of human impacts on the biosphere, biodiversity is falling at an unprecedented rate (Field et al. 2020; Ceballos, Ehrlich, and Raven 2020). Approximately one million species face extinction within a matter of decades, and the current extinction rate is one thousand times higher than would be expected to occur without human influence (IPBES 2019 and Pimm et al. 2014 as cited in Field et al. 2020). Scientists warn that human activities have pushed the Earth into a sixth mass extinction, a global die-off of species akin to the extinction of the dinosaurs (Field et al. 2020; Ceballos, Ehrlich, and Raven 2020). The IPCC estimates that 3 to 14 per cent of assessed terrestrial species will be at "very high risk of extinction" in a 1.5-degree global warming scenario; at 3 degrees, the high-end estimate increases to 29 per cent, and at 5 degrees it increases to 48 per cent (2022,14). Within declining ecosystems, extinction begets extinction and species that are closely connected in ecological niches often succumb together to the pressures of inhospitable living conditions (Ceballos, Ehrlich, and Raven 2020). It is becoming increasingly clear that biodiversity loss is a threat to human society on par with the climate crisis, though its effects on the capacity of ecosystems to meet human needs are both "more immediate" and less understood by decision makers across sectors (13601).

Biodiversity has been linked to human health through multiple, interconnected pathways, affecting human psychology, physiology and nutrition, air and water quality, and patterns of infectious disease transmission (WHO 2015). At an ecosystem level, loss of biodiversity is one of the most influential variables contributing to broader ecological changes and thus declining health outcomes (Field et al. 2020; Hooper et al. 2012 as cited in WHO 2015). In the most basic sense, biodiversity upholds an ecosystem's ability to provide the goods and services that enable human health and well-being (Field et al. 2020; Ceballos, Ehrlich, and Raven 2020; WHO 2015). Complex interactions between pollinators, pathogens, herbivores, carnivores, and primary producer species are necessary to maintain a range of ecosystem functions, including the capacity to mitigate excess heat and reduce air pollution (WHO 2015; Aerts et al. 2018). Declining biodiversity has also been shown to increase the transmission and severity of infectious diseases by bringing species into contact in new ways (see section 3.4 on COVID-19 below) and by disrupting the regulation of the human immune system, a process that depends on exposure to diverse antigens (Field et al. 2020).

Biodiverse life is also the primary source of traditional and modern medicines that sustain the health of billions of people around the world. Plant and animal species contain essential nutrients and chemical compounds that humans may not be able to access in any other way. Medicines to relieve pain, nine out of the thirteen classes of antibiotics, and countless preventative tonics and healthful foods are all sourced from biodiverse ecosystems (WHO 2015; Beresford-Kroeger 2013). The WHO reports that one in five wild plant species are endangered, with medicinal plants more likely to be vulnerable due to overharvesting, climate change, and habitat destruction (WHO 2015; Susan Leopold, personal communication). Declining diversity and quantity of pollinators in an ecosystem can also reduce food security and lower agricultural yields, and could undermine human nutrition, especially for populations that are already vulnerable to nutritional deficiencies (WHO 2015). The crops that are most essential to the "planetary health diet" – vegetable, legume, fruit, seed, and nut crops that are not only less intensive to cultivate but are preventative for a host of non-communicable diseases – are particularly vulnerable to the decline of pollinator species (Willet et al. 2019). For these reasons, loss of biodiversity undermines the capacity of health systems to prevent and treat disease as well as the ability of agricultural systems to provide healthy and sustainable diets to a growing population (WHO 2015; Whitmee et al. 2015).

In a cultural sense, relationships to biodiverse life are at the centre of Indigenous and traditional worldviews, influencing the development of languages; traditions of music, art, and craft; local medical knowledge; foodways; and social arrangements (WHO 2015). In cultures that remain connected to traditional landscapes, loss of local biodiversity can significantly reduce community well-being, decrease physical and mental health, and weaken social support networks (WHO 2015). Even in mainstream Westernized communities that are less place based and arguably more culturally disconnected from local biodiversity, contact with nature delivers a host of physiological and psychological health benefits. Well-documented benefits of being in nature include reduced anxiety and depression, lower blood pressure, fewer headaches, decreased obesity, increased levels of anti-cancer proteins, greater reported quality of life, increased capacity to overcome addictions, and stronger social connectedness (Sandifer, Sutton-Grier, and Ward 2015). Biodiversity in particular has been shown to be inherently appealing to humans due to an embedded biophilia, an "intrinsic affinity to other species and nature" that is thought to have emerged as a result of human co-evolution within diverse ecosystems (Aerts et al. 2018, 8). The biophilia hypothesis may account for many of the health benefits of being in nature, including nature's ability to restore mental attention, reduce mental fatigue, and enhance recovery from physiological stress (Aerts et al. 2018).

Research into the workings of the human microbiome puts forward another explanation for the health benefits of being in nature. The human colon has been described as one of "the most densely populated and biodiverse ecosystems on Earth" (Quercia et al. 2014, 1). This biodiversity is seeded at birth and during infancy, then is built throughout the life course through contact with microbes in the air, on the land, and on the bodies of other animals, plants, and humans (WHO 2015; von Hertzen et al. 2015 as cited in Prescott et al. 2016). As a result, living near green spaces may improve health partly because it provides an opportunity for people to encounter beneficial microbes living in the soil or, for instance, on the leaves and bark of trees (WHO 2015; Aerts et al. 2018; Prescott et al. 2016). One study found that when neighbourhoods lost trees due to infestations of the invasive emerald ash borer, they experienced a simultaneous rise in illnesses such as respiratory infections and cardiovascular disease (Donovan et al. 2013, 2015 as cited in Prescott et al. 2016). Researchers found evidence that the microbiome played a role in these illnesses, as loss of neighbourhood trees limited people's exposure to helpful microbes in their environment and led them to spend less time outside overall (Jones 2016 as cited in Prescott et al. 2016).

Biodiversity therefore affects human health through reciprocal relationships between outer and inner ecosystems, with the biodiversity that is present in our external environments shaping the biodiversity that makes up our bodies (Prescott et al. 2016). For this reason, the microbiome represents a central conduit through which global-scale ecological changes influence the health of individuals and communities (WHO 2015). The climate crisis and other planetary ecological disruptions could dramatically reduce the quantity and diversity of the microbiota that we find on our lands, in our oceans, and on our food crops (Liddicoat, Waycott, and Weinstein 2016 and Scheffers et al. 2016 as cited in Maier and al'Absi 2017). This loss of diversity poses risks to human health such as higher likelihood of contracting infectious diseases because interactions between pathogens and the microbes in our guts contribute immensely to whether or not a pathogen can take hold and make us ill, or whether it is neutralized by the body's immune response (Costello et al. 2012 and Pedersen and Fenton 2007 as cited in Maier and al'Absi 2017). Loss of microbial biodiversity has also been shown to contribute to autoimmune disorders in which the body mounts an immune response against its own cells, allergic reactions to particular foods or environmental inputs like pollen, and a range of chronic inflammatory illnesses (WHO 2015).

In an evolutionary sense, genetic diversity in the microbiome is an essential determinant of future adaptive capacity, making it possible for the microbes in our guts to evolve in response to changing environmental conditions (WHO 2015). Given that we are only beginning to understand the connections between the biodiversity of outer and inner ecosystems, the extent to which microbial diversity is declining as plant and animal species succumb to the sixth mass extinction represents a significant but likely unquantifiable loss. What is clear is that since the Industrial Revolution, optimizing for the short-term health and development gains of a single species, *Homo sapiens*, has resulted in the loss of an inordinate number of species already, with countless others to follow before the end of the century. Plummeting biodiversity weakens the capacity of ecosystems to function in ways that meet basic human needs in the present, let alone support thriving human civilizations into the future. Many of the ideas and practices discussed in later chapters, including the soil health movement, care farming, and gardening for health, among others, make meaningful contributions to rectifying this problem of scale, restoring biodiversity while at the same time creating favourable conditions for human health.

3.3 Antimicrobial and Antibiotic Resistance

> Antibiotic resistance is putting the achievements of modern medicine at risk. Organ transplantations, chemotherapy and surgeries such as caesarean sections become much more dangerous without effective antibiotics for the prevention and treatment of infections. (WHO 2020, n.p.)

Antibiotics are without a doubt one of biomedicine's most impactful innovations. The development of antibiotics revolutionized modern medicine's ability to cure infectious diseases. It also led to a massive expansion of surgical capacities by substantially reducing rates of fatal post-operative infections (Harrison 2004). The first antibiotic, sulfa, was developed in a German lab in the mid-1930s, followed by penicillin in the 1940s, which was even more effective against a wider variety of harmful bacteria (Hager 2019). Both sulpha and penicillin were used generously during the Second World War, significantly reducing the number of soldiers who died from infected wounds and lowering rates of gonorrhoea and other communicable diseases (Hager 2019). In the mid-twentieth century, new antibiotics proliferated quickly and were prescribed at every turn, reducing deaths from common childhood diseases by over 90 per cent in the United States (Hager 2019). It is estimated that antibiotics alone are responsible for adding ten years to the average American lifespan (Hager 2019).

Yet misuse and overuse of antibiotics and other antimicrobials (antifungals, antivirals, and antiparasitics) have bred resistant pathogens (Søgaard Jørgensen et al. 2017; WHO 2020, 2021). Antimicrobial resistance develops because microbes evolve at an incredibly rapid pace, generating potentially adaptive genetic mutations in the course of mere hours (Pray 2008; WHO 2021). The bacteria *Staphylococcus aureus*, for instance, which causes many common skin infections, divides twice every hour; in twelve hours, a single *Staphylococcus aureus* bacterium can become a population of one million cells. In little more than a day, each nucleotide base pair in the bacteria's genome will have mutated thirty times, meaning that every potential genetic mutation that is possible for the species could exist in the population that resides within your body (Pray 2008).

Antibiotic resistance is not a new phenomenon. By the end of the Second World War, sulfa was already noticeably less effective in treating gonorrhoea than it was at the beginning of the war (Hager 2019). Alexander Fleming, who won the Nobel Prize in 1945 for his discovery of penicillin, warned in his Nobel lecture that taking doses of the drug that were insufficient to kill the entire population of bacteria had been shown to breed resistant microbes (Fleming 1945 as cited in Søgaard Jørgensen et al. 2017). Today, the WHO classifies antibiotic resistance as "one of the biggest threats to global health, food security, and development" (WHO 2020a, n.p.). Antimicrobial resistance is considered to be one of the top ten global threats to public health (WHO 2021). Drug-resistant HIV strains threaten the long-term effectiveness of antiretroviral therapies (WHO 2021), and antibiotic resistance makes common bacterial infections like pneumonia, tuberculosis, and gonorrhoea more difficult to treat. More intractable infections lengthen hospital stays, leading to escalating health care costs (WHO 2020). Antibiotic resistance also undermines basic health care capacities like curing blood and wound infections, threatens child and maternal health by limiting options for preterm babies and complicated deliveries, and makes routine and major surgeries as well as cancer treatments more dangerous (Søgaard Jørgensen et al. 2017). In some regions, *K. pneumoniae*, bacteria responsible for many hospital-acquired infections such as pneumonia among ICU patients and newborns, is now resistant to last-resort antibiotics about half of the time (WHO 2021). High rates of bacterial resistance to common ailments like urinary tract infections and some STIs have led the WHO to conclude that we are "running out of effective antibiotics" (n.p.). To date, no new antibiotics have proven effective against the most resistant bacterial strains (WHO 2021).

As Alexander Fleming recognized in 1945, antimicrobial resistance is affected by human behaviours. While antibiotic resistance is a natural evolutionary response on the part of microbes, the process has been accelerated by human tendencies to overprescribe and overuse antimicrobials (WHO 2021). It is also affected by poor sanitation infrastructures and practices that enable person-to-person transmission of resistant microbes, as well as by lack of access to other preventative measures like vaccines (WHO 2021). In many parts of the world, antibiotics are available without a prescription, leading to frequent misuse, including failure to take the full course of treatment (WHO 2020). In agriculture, antibiotics are often administered even when herds are healthy as a preventative measure or to increase growth rates, another leading cause of resistance (WHO 2020). Use of antibiotics in intensive agriculture not only breeds resistant pathogens but can also disrupt the beneficial microbial communities in the human gut (WHO 2015).

Antibiotic-resistant bacteria now inhabit every country on Earth, spread as people and goods travel through our globalized world (WHO 2020). The proliferation of antimicrobial resistance more generally represents a significant shift in "the global microbiome" and is not only a medical issue, but an ecological challenge with implications for planetary sustainability (Søgaard Jørgensen et al. 2017, 66). Since the discovery of antibiotics in the 1930s, humans have employed these miracle drugs to increase individual health, using them to cure diseases and improve agricultural outcomes without attending sufficiently to the broader ecological consequences of these actions (Søgaard Jørgensen et al. 2017; Zywert and Sutherland 2020). In this way, an intervention that is effective at the individual level is responsible for the emergence of more virulent infectious diseases that now constitute a major threat to population health (Zywert and Sutherland 2020). That being said, prioritizing ecological health by refusing to administer antibiotics to someone presenting in hospital with pneumonia would be seen as cruel and unacceptable by most doctors, policy makers, and community members. Negotiating our way through this wicked problem of scale asks us to learn to attend to multiple disease processes simultaneously, those unfolding before us in individual patients as well as those presenting at the population and planetary scale. Working to achieve a global sustainability transition towards a "pro-microbial planet" could involve leveraging microbial diversity and evolution to improve human and ecological health while leaving space to use antibiotics appropriately at local levels (Søgaard Jørgensen et al. 2017, 66). Chapter 4 on the soil health movement will suggest further promising avenues towards such a "pro-microbial" world.

3.4 The COVID-19 Pandemic

> Seen together, climate change and the pandemic suggest that there is *a pattern* that is *characteristic of the Anthropocene*, namely, that certain, apparently harmless, local activities turn out to have unexpected, inequitably distributed, problematic effects globally. (Heyd 2020, 4)

The COVID-19 pandemic is widely acknowledged to have begun in December 2019 when a cluster of pneumonia cases were diagnosed in Wuhan, China (Hu et al. 2021). In early January 2020 scientists in China identified a novel virus as the cause of the unexplained outbreak. Occurring around the lunar New Year in China, a time of festivity and travel, the novel virus outbreak spread quickly, and by the end of the month cases could be found throughout China's thirty-four provinces. In early February the International Committee on Taxonomy of Viruses named the new pathogen SARS-CoV-2 due to its relation to severe acute respiratory syndrome coronavirus (SARS-CoV) and Middle East respiratory syndrome coronavirus (MERS-CoV) (Hu et al. 2021). On 11 March global spread of the new coronavirus was on the rise and the WHO declared COVID-19, the disease resulting from SARS-CoV-2 infection, to be a global pandemic (Hu et al. 2021). By November 2022 approximately 634 million cases of COVID-19 had been reported to the WHO, including around 6.6 million deaths (WHO, n.d.-b).

Most researchers agree that COVID-19, like the majority of emerging infectious diseases, has a zoonotic origin (Hu et al. 2021; Frumkin and Myers 2020; Maxmen and Mallapaty 2021). Microbiological studies of the COVID-19 genetic code have found that the pathogen is most closely related to coronaviruses found in bats in Southern China, though an exact genome match has not yet been identified (Hu et al. 2021; Lytras et al. 2021 as cited in Maxmen and Mallapaty 2021). Some researchers argue that it is worth considering the possibility that the COVID-19 pandemic originated due to an accidental lab leak from the Wuhan Institute of Virology. Still others believe that the pandemic may have been created by a bioengineered virus that was intentionally released into the human population. Ongoing investigations continue to seek evidence to answer this crucial question (see Maxmen and Mallapaty 2021; Horton 2021).

Assuming COVID-19 does indeed have a zoonotic origin, the interspecies jump was likely spurred on by planetary ecological changes as well as economic pressures. Forest loss and other forms of habitat destruction, altered rainfall patterns, declining biodiversity, and increased contact between human and animal populations due to more intensive agriculture and logging practices are well-known causal factors in the emergence of novel viruses (Frumkin and Myers 2020; Ceballos, Ehrlich, and Raven 2020; WHO 2015; Asayama et al. 2020). The growing wildlife trade, which is gaining momentum in areas where poverty prompts rural populations to turn to wild animals for nutrition and income, is also known to enable the spread of viruses from animal to human hosts (Ceballos, Ehrlich, and Raven 2020; Spinney 2020 as cited in Heyd 2020). Affected by these intersecting ecological, economic, and cultural influences, COVID-19 has been described as a "quintessential planetary health problem," the kind of "predictable surprise" that, while foreseen decades ago by public health experts, has nonetheless been experienced as "rapid … sudden and shocking" (Frumkin and Myers 2020, 489–90).

Thomas Heyd (2020) proposes that the coronavirus pandemic is part of a discernible pattern of phenomena that characterize the Anthropocene: natural processes that occur at local scales (in this case, zoonotic transmission of pathogens to humans) are mediated and amplified by human activities (such as encroaching on wildlife habitats, consuming bushmeat, and living in crowded cities), then transmitted around the world by hyper-mobile modern citizens, becoming global in scope and disproportionately affecting vulnerable people and systems. Globalization is a key variable in this pattern: without it, emerging infectious diseases would be more likely to cause local outbreaks than to become global pandemics (Zhu et al. 2020 as cited in Asayama et al. 2020; Heyd 2020). Climate change, Heyd (2020) argues, follows a similar pattern. A natural process (the carbon cycle) is amplified by human economic activities (principally the expansion of industrialization and dependence on fossil fuels). It is then transmitted around the world through atmospheric air circulation, undermining the prospects for health and quality of life, with the most acute effects clustered among impoverished populations.

This shared problem of scale is one of a number of convergences between the climate crisis and the pandemic that have been widely recognized in academic circles (Belesova, Heymann, and Haines 2020; Asayama et al. 2020; Heyd 2020), in the mainstream media (Basu 2020; Vidal 2020), and among health practitioners and non-profits (Karliner 2020; Howard 2020). Josh Karliner (2020), international director for program and strategy at Health Care Without Harm, notes that climate change has an exacerbating effect on pandemics. For instance, air pollution from fossil fuel combustion causes respiratory health problems that can make people less resilient when they encounter respiratory viruses like SARS Co-V-2. Food scarcity and malnutrition, both growing in response to changing climatic patterns, can also compromise the immune system, leaving people more susceptible to disease as well as more likely to seek out novel sources of food like bushmeat that accelerate the emergence of new viruses.

The COVID-19 pandemic is also opening up space within environmental politics to make stronger connections between ecological change and health. Scientists, practitioners working at the nexus of health and sustainability, and climate justice activists are becoming more vocal about the need to adopt shared solutions that reduce the risks of both crises (Basu 2020; Karliner 2020; Asayama et al. 2020; Belesova, Heymann, and Haines 2020; Edger et al. 2020; Howard 2020). The COVID-19 pandemic exposes the extent to which preventing future pandemics depends on mitigating the climate crisis and stepping back from other forms of ecological overshoot. Halting biodiversity loss, restoring degraded habitats, and creating policies that disincentivize the bushmeat trade (and that work to build more sustainable livelihood opportunities), for instance, could serve climate goals while protecting against zoonotic transmission of more novel infectious diseases (Karliner 2020; Vidal 2020; Ceballos, Ehrlich, and Raven 2020). Writing about how declining biodiversity affects human health, Gerardo Ceballos and colleagues conclude:

> There is no doubt … that there will be more pandemics if we continue destroying habitats and trading wildlife for human consumption as food and traditional medicines. It is something that humanity cannot permit, as it may be a tipping point for the collapse of civilization. What is at stake is the fate of humanity and most living species. (2020, 13601)

COVID-19 is also bringing to light the health effects of pre-existing inequities at global and local scales. There is increasing media attention to the ways in which "protecting public health from climate change is a climate justice issue, and climate justice is a health equity issue" (Karliner 2020, n.p.). Those with the least political power and wealth tend to suffer the most from the effects of both climate change and infectious disease (Heyd 2020). Numerous campaigns for a just recovery from COVID-19 urge governments to adopt strategies that will put the health of people first while building community resilience and supporting the transition to a post-carbon future ("Open Letter," n.d.; Edger et al. 2020; also see www.thepeoplesbailout.org; chapter 9, section 1). There is also growing recognition that the same inequities that reduce the health outcomes of marginalized, impoverished, and systemically disenfranchised people not only limit the life prospects of individuals within these groups but impact population health (Howard 2020; Guterres 2020). Writing in the *Guardian* in early April 2020, the UN secretary general warned that lack of capacity in the health systems of the global south could be disastrous not only for local populations in the developing world but for the entirety of our species (Guterres 2020). High rates of overcrowding, poverty, and lack of basic sanitation and hygiene infrastructure in southern countries renders public health measures like social distancing and frequent hand washing more difficult or, in some cases, impossible (Guterres 2020). We have since seen these conditions, combined with lack of access to affordable vaccines in the global south, enable the emergence of viral mutations like the Delta and Omicron variants that have gone on to re-infect other regions. "In our interconnected world," Guterres says, "we are only as strong as the weakest health systems" (2020, n.p.).

In the global north, attempts to curb the spread of the virus also made it increasingly impossible to ignore the profound socio-economic inequities that shape patterns of health and disease in wealthy countries. The public health measures designed to keep everyone safe – especially those most likely to experience the worst outcomes of COVID-19 – have paradoxically had a disproportionately negative impact on the health and livelihoods of the most socio-economically vulnerable people (Frohlich and Potvin 2008, Lancet 2020, Newland 2020 as cited in Asayama et al. 2020). The economic losses and additional psychological distress caused by COVID-19 therefore represent another tier of risks associated with the pandemic (Asayama et al. 2020). During lockdowns and other staged openings, for instance, low-paid workers such as those working at pharmacies and grocery stores, in retail, and in homes for the elderly were reclassified as "essential workers," while higher-income earners were able to isolate themselves by working from home. Social distancing has proven to be much easier for those with wealth and good, stable jobs and unattainable for many low-wage earners (Weill et al. 2020 and Bonaccorsi et al. 2020 as cited in Asayama et al. 2020). As a result, various forms of social marginalization among communities of colour, migrant workers, people in the prison system, sex workers, low-income people, and people experiencing homelessness overlap with increased rates of infection from COVID-19 (Asayama et al. 2020).

Woolf and colleagues (2020) found that US data from March and April 2020 also demonstrate that while 95 per cent of deaths reported during the first two months of the pandemic were "excess deaths" (deaths above average rates), only 65 per cent were attributable to COVID-19 (510). The remaining 30 per cent of excess deaths were attributed to other underlying causes including heart disease, diabetes, cerebrovascular disease, and Alzheimer's. In fourteen states, over 50 per cent of the excess deaths reported in March and April were not COVID related. Although these data remain provisional and are based on a short time period, the study's authors suggest that many of the excess deaths represent "secondary pandemic mortality" caused in part by reduced access to health care as well as by the effects of social determinants of health such as loss of employment and/or increased social isolation (512).

Yet at the same time as the social determinants of health were being felt more strongly than ever, the pandemic gave us "glimpses of how a post-carbon future might look" (Roberts 2020 as cited in Frumkin and Myers 2020, 494). The economic closures associated with the pandemic led to demonstrable, though temporary, reductions in air pollution due to lower CO_2 and nitrous oxide emissions from industry and travel, as well as reduced global demand for and use of fossil fuels (Zowalaty et al. 2020). It is estimated that GHGs fell by 17 per cent in April 2020 from 2019 levels (Le Quéré et al. 2020 as cited in Belesova, Heymann, and Haines 2020). Researchers estimate that the direct effects of the pandemic response on the climate crisis will be negligible, with the economic slow-down projected to reduce our current trajectory of warming by only 0.01 degrees Celsius by 2030 (Forster et al. 2020 as cited in Belesova, Heymann, and Haines 2020). However, COVID-19 has resulted in rapid adoption of new behaviours across society, such as telecommuting, reducing reliance on cars in favour of cycling and walking, and creating more public spaces for outdoor recreation in some areas, all of which improve health while reducing GHG emissions. There is an opportunity as societies learn from the pandemic to institutionalize many of these behaviour changes to achieve (potentially) lasting gains for planetary and human health (Belesova, Heymann, and Haines 2020). By binding together the narratives around the climate crisis, health, and inequity, COVID-19 also opens up space to think differently about what we need to do to secure health into the long-term future. Engaging policy makers, health practitioners, and grass-roots community organizers, these messages could support the emergence and institutionalization of more long-term, social-ecological approaches to health (see "Open Letter," n.d.; Edger et al. 2020; also see www.thepeoplesbailout.org). The potential of such responses is discussed further in chapter 9.

3.5 Enabling Health within Social-Ecological Wholes

In a state of health, the vital systems of a human body – our circulatory, respiratory, immune, and nervous systems, for instance – operate without conscious control. We do not need to think about pumping blood throughout the body, or make sure that our lungs extract the right amount of oxygen from the air we breathe. When our body systems lose the capacity for self-regulation – if our kidneys no longer filter blood, or if our endocrine system does not release hormones the way it should – we may experience disease. In modern society, health systems can step in to compensate. A medical professional can diagnose the problem and intentionally manage a body system that has lost the capacity to regulate itself. Depending on the nature of the problem, health systems may offer pharmaceutical treatment or a surgical intervention, or recommend changes to diets or behaviours. They may also work to prevent similar problems from occurring at a population level by gaining traction over the social and/or the ecological determinants of health. In some cases, these interventions will restore self-regulation to the altered body system, and in other cases they will not. When the latter happens, management will become a long-term process.

In the case of planetary health, there is scientific consensus that the Earth's biophysical systems are rapidly losing their capacity for self-regulation (Myers and Frumkin 2020; Whitmee et al. 2015; Steffen et al. 2015a; Cole 2019b). The planetary ailments that result have been discussed in this and previous chapters: the climate crisis, biodiversity loss, ocean acidification, changes to the nitrogen and phosphorus cycles (Rockström et al. 2009; Steffen et al. 2015a; also see Lovelock 1991). Yet while human beings experiencing illness can turn to the formal and informal networks of support that constitute modern health systems, there is no concomitant "planetary health system" to step in as the Earth loses ground. And, as James Lovelock (1991) warned in the early 1990s, the task of managing the Earth's biophysical systems could easily become relentless and all-consuming for humankind. In the same way that long-term medical management of human disease is often time- and resource-intensive for individuals and their caregivers, preventing the breakdown of ecological integrity is preferable to long-term treatment (Lovelock 1991).

But what, exactly, does prevention entail at the planetary scale, given that the ecological changes currently unfolding have emerged as a result of the escalating impact of human activities? There is no doubt that expansive global development has improved human well-being substantially. Since 1950, literacy doubled, the percentage of the world's population living in extreme poverty fell by more than 50 per cent, life expectancy rose by twenty-six years, and infant mortality rates plummeted (Myers and Frumkin 2020). During the same time period, humanity's ecological footprint also expanded so rapidly that our activities now threaten the ecological foundations of human *and* planetary health (Steffen et al. 2015a; Myers and Frumkin 2020; Whitmee et al. 2015).

This chapter has brought together evidence that suggests there is an inherent tension between maximizing the health of a single species over the health of the planet and its biodiverse populations and ecosystems as an integrated whole. Attending to the human scale over all others has enabled the emergence of ecological problems at higher scales, each of which circles back to undermine human health outcomes. The climate crisis, biodiversity loss, antimicrobial and antibiotic resistance, and the COVID-19 pandemic all display this dynamic:

- The climate crisis not only threatens the long-term survival of our species, but has direct and indirect effects on health, such as changing patterns of infectious disease, injuries and death caused by extreme weather, increased violence and non-communicable disease deaths during heatwaves, greater food insecurity and malnutrition, rising incidence of syndemics, and mental health issues.
- Biodiversity loss undermines essential ecosystem functions, reduces agricultural yields, negatively impacts the diversity of the human microbiome, can limit the availability of traditional and modern medicines, and accelerates the emergence of new infectious diseases.
- Antibiotic and antimicrobial resistance, caused by human misuse of antibiotics and antimicrobials in medicine and agriculture, could make many infectious diseases untreatable; it also heightens the risks of routine surgical interventions, potentially reversing one of modern medicine's most impactful advances.
- Ecological changes and globalization together enable the emergence of new infectious disease pandemics that have devastating health and socio-economic consequences, including deepening existing health inequities.

These paradoxical problems of scale raise important questions about the future of human society, and about the overall purpose and structure of modern health systems. For instance, would prioritizing planetary health necessarily be good for human health, everywhere and in all ways? Or will there be trade-offs to negotiate? Who is likely to benefit, and will others be left behind? Will humankind need to relinquish some gains in life expectancy or infant mortality to ensure that our activities remain within planetary boundaries? If we lower our ecological footprint enough to meet climate targets and mitigate the worst effects of planetary ecological change, how will the socio-economic transition affect human health? If we take the scientific evidence presented above to heart, these open questions, confounding paradoxes, and the potential for trade-offs should not stop us from shifting our attention away from optimizing individual health outcomes towards supporting the health of social-ecological wholes (see Zywert and Sutherland 2020). Instead, we must extend our search for promising ways forward, seeking not only within but also outside and at the margins of health systems. The next three stories introduce ideas and practices that attend to health across social-ecological scales and offer insight into the complex relationships between human and planetary health.

4 Soil Health

> Plants, soil microbes, and all other species do work to build the soil sponge matrix that makes life on land possible, by influencing flows of water, carbon, and nutrients; creating and defining the structure and function of every landscape; and regulating the temperatures and weather patterns on Earth. (Pershouse 2020b, 266)

I first spoke with Didi Pershouse, acupuncturist and holistic health practitioner turned author, educator, and soil sponge strategist, in the summer of 2017. I reached out to Didi to learn more about what she called "systems-based ecological medicine," a "practice and theoretical framework" she developed "to restore health to people as well as the environmental and social systems around them" (see https://www.didipershouse.com/didi-bios.html). I was particularly curious about what made her decide to reorient her career from treating individuals to seeing soil health as a primary leverage point for public health. For twenty-two years, Didi did clinical work with clients. She founded the Center for Sustainable Medicine and practised out of her home in Thetford, Vermont. Didi's work as a "body fixer" (Pershouse 2011, n.p.) was always about more than correctly positioning needles or recommending a supplement; she was engaged in "treating wholes" (Pershouse, personal communication). Her practice invariably involved listening deeply to her patients for root causes of their symptoms (her intake process ranged from 1.5 to 3 hours on average) (Pershouse 2011), offering dietary advice, and prescribing time outdoors. Increasingly she also found herself building connections between the people who came to her practice seeking healing and the local farmers she knew who were growing healthful food. As she worked with her clients, a strong network of relationships began to knit itself together around her (Pershouse 2016; Pershouse, personal communication).

Then in 2011, tropical storm Irene devastated Didi's community. In a single night of severe rain and flooding, Vermont lost five hundred miles of roads and two hundred bridges (Pershouse 2016). In the fallout from the storm, Didi began to think differently about the connections between the water cycle, unusual weather events, global climate change, and public health. She noticed that in areas where the soil biology was intact, the landscape held together and the damage caused by flooding was minimal. In contrast, the "places where soil biology was not very active were washed away entirely" (Pershouse 2017a, viii). Struck by the power of living systems to protect the land from destruction, Didi soon discovered that the concept of soil health tied together the various threads of her work: her interest in sustainable health care, her growing unease about biomedical health care's dependence on oil, and the role of microbes in human health and the health of the land.

With this new understanding, the nature of Didi's work changed almost overnight. As she learned more about the living soil, the water cycle, and the relationship between biological work and health, she focused her work on supporting the soil health and regenerative agriculture movements. She explains, "I shifted to working on that level thinking that it was going to impact public health more than treating patients one at a time"[1] (personal communication). Instead of seeing clients in her home, Didi now worked with farmers to help them see opportunities to build healthy soils, reduce flooding and drought, improve wildfire resilience, and contribute to local and regional cooling (see Regeneration International 2017). She developed curriculum and wrote a teaching manual called *Understanding Soil Health and Watershed Function* (Pershouse 2017a), facilitated soil health workshops, and spoke at conferences. She taught policy makers, farmers and ranchers, students, and scientists more about soil health and "living-systems thinking" (see https://www.didipershouse.com/didi-bios.html). Health, Didi came to realize, is above all dependent on the soil. Soil is the starting place, quite literally where the roots of all other forms of health reside.

Diana Wall and colleagues, writing in *Nature*, insist on the importance of soil biodiversity to the health and integrity of all living systems:

> It is time to recognize and manage soil biodiversity as an underutilized resource for achieving long-term sustainability goals related to global human health, not only for improving soils, food security, disease control, water and air quality, but because biodiversity in soils is connected to all life. (Wall, Uffe, and Six 2015, 74)

Yet the average person living in a modern, urban context may not think much about the soil or how it relates to health. Unless one is a farmer or has a personal interest in gardening, it would be easy to *never* think about the soil, or about the life and work involved in building this essential aspect of the Earth system. Many of us probably do not even know what soil really is. Soil is composed of tiny particles of rocks that have eroded over thousands of years, the broken-down dead bodies and wastes of plants and animals, and countless living organisms, mostly bacteria and fungi (Pershouse 2016, 2017a). Without life, soil is nothing more than sand, silt, or clay. It is the living things in the soil – the root hairs, fungal hyphae, and the slimes and glues excreted by microbial beings – that bind the soil together and allow it to perform indispensable functions in the landscape. Didi describes how "over time, the relationship between lifeless minerals and living organisms creates living soil, or a soil carbon sponge. This soil carbon sponge is a living ecosystem, with many processes going on all at once, similar to the living tissue of animals" (2017a, 14).

Didi uses a simple illustration when she teaches people about the soil carbon sponge or, as she now calls it more simply, the soil sponge. First, she brings out two plates, one that holds a mound of loose flour and the other a piece of bread. To demonstrate how depleted soil reacts to rain, she pours a cup of water over the loose flour. When the water hits the flour, it moves sideways across the plate and some of the particles dissolve into the water, which soon becomes white and murky. In the same way, unaggregated soil particles move sideways across the landscape, creating runoff that carries away topsoil, draws chemical pollutants into water systems, and causes flooding. Without the soil sponge, water is not absorbed by soils or held underground. Dusty soils fed only with chemical fertilizers and dosed with pesticides and herbicides have no structural integrity to hold them together when the wind blows or water moves across them. They contribute to poor air and water quality and, because of the lack of a biological workforce to source nutrients for plants, poor food quality as well.

Didi then pours a cup of water over the piece of bread, which – like healthy soil – has structural and functional integrity created by biology. The water is absorbed by the bread and when it is saturated, it filters down to provide a reservoir of water for plants, refill groundwater supplies, and seep slowly out into clean springs. In this way, the soil sponge reduces the risk of flooding, drought, and wildfire. Plant leaves use the water for transpiration, dramatically cooling the air around them through latent heat flux and releasing water vapour that recondenses into clouds and will later return to the land as rain. The difference between the flour (unaggregated soil) and the bread (the soil sponge), Didi explains, is "biological work" (personal communication; Pershouse and The Regenerative Economy Collaborative, 2020).

One of Didi's core teachings is that the soil sponge emerges from the diligent and often overlooked work of other species, primarily the bacteria and fungi that reside within the soil. If we notice this work and respect it in the ways in which we manage land, we can work *with* living systems to create a world more conducive to *all* life (Pershouse 2016, 2017a, 2020b). Didi's socialist leanings led her to develop a strong metaphor of soil microbes as invisible workers, as members of the working class trying to make a life for themselves under untenable conditions within a capitalist regime of intensive industrial agriculture (see Pershouse and The Regenerative Economy Collaborative 2020). Likewise, the microbes within human bodies are ignored or attacked by industrial medical regimes. Inside and outside of our bodies, we have degraded the working conditions of the essential microbes that support our health. We have been working within a "sterile" model of care that kills off what doesn't fit with pesticides and antibiotics, rather than a "fertile" model of care:

> The fertile model of care recognizes the work that other species are doing. It's not just microbes, it's earthworms, it's wolves, it's the whole system. If we recognize that and we don't try to kill off what doesn't fit, then we're working in a worker's cooperative. We then see ourselves at the right level. We are part of that system. We can't just step in and say "do all this for us, it doesn't matter what your working conditions are." (Pershouse, personal communication)

In a *Medium* article published in 2020, Didi discusses the implications of moving away from the "fertile" model in both agriculture and medicine:

> Both agriculture and medicine shifted away from what I would call a "fertile" model, and towards a more "sterile" one, that competed with, or killed off, what was not wanted. We turned away from stewardship, collaboration, and cooperatives, and towards competition, profits and patenting. We used pesticides and herbicides, rubber gloves and antibiotics, and turned away from compost and manure, human touch and probiotics. Both agriculture and medicine shifted from seeing things in the context of whole integrated systems, focusing instead on individual parts. We moved away from diversification and focused instead on specialization, we abandoned small-scale localized infrastructure and invested in

large-scale corporations. In the process, we lost touch with traditional knowledge that works with natural patterns and cycles, and rushed instead into chemical and high-tech manipulation of nature. This left us with a planet swimming in industrial waste and struggling to adapt to an entirely new climate – all in the guise of feeding ourselves and keeping ourselves healthy. (Pershouse 2020a)

As Didi describes above, we are now "suffering the effects" of having allowed the sterile model of care to dominate global land management and medical regimes for decades, evidenced in the breakdown of our internal microbial communities and in the loss of much of the planet's soils (Pershouse, personal communication; also see Pershouse 2016, 2020b). Soil loss has been a factor in the collapse of multiple agricultural civilizations around the world, and has significant ramifications for human and planetary health in the Anthropocene (Field et al. 2020). Research conducted by the UN found that land degradation including soil loss currently reduces the well-being of 3.2 billion people (Scholes et al. 2018 as cited in Field et al. 2020). Soil loss is influenced by dynamics occurring at the planetary scale, including climate change, which disrupts soil biodiversity through altered patterns of precipitation, extreme temperatures, and other disaster events (Field et al. 2020; Wall, Uffe, and Six 2015). Urbanization, deforestation, pollution, and the growing prevalence of intensive agricultural practices accelerate erosion, reduce the organic content of the soil, kill off healthy soil microbes, and decimate soil biodiversity (Field et al. 2020; Wall, Uffe, and Six 2015). Affected by these global trends, soil loss then becomes part of a pattern of feedback that perpetuates the climate crisis by reducing the soil's capacity to act as a carbon sink. Soil is one of the most significant stores of carbon on Earth, retaining 2,500 billion tons of carbon (compared to 780 billion tons in the atmosphere and 560 billion tons in plants) (Rattan 2010 as cited in Pershouse 2016). As a result of ecological destruction, the soil is thought to have lost between 50 and 70 per cent of its carbon storage capacity (Rattan 2010 as cited in Pershouse 2016).

But since Didi published her book *The Ecology of Care* in 2016, she has moved away from the narrative of carbon sequestration to focus on a feedback loop that she considers to be much more instrumental to the health of the land and people: the relationship between soil health and the water cycle. When there is soil loss and degradation, it dramatically affects the incidence and severity of flooding, drought, and wildfires. It also raises surface temperatures due to the loss of plant transpiration, which has been shown to cool the land (Pershouse, personal communication; Pershouse and The Regenerative Economy Collaborative 2020).

(For example, a study in Turkey found that the air above a green transpiring landscape is on average 5.3 degrees Celsius cooler than bare soil, and 11.79 degrees Celsius cooler than pavement; Yilmaz et al. 2008.) The connections between soil health and the water cycle receive less research and media attention than the narrative about carbon sequestration. However, Didi argues that restoring the water cycle could make a much faster contribution to mitigating the climate crisis than focusing solely on drawing down carbon. It could also be less amenable to co-optation by investors and corporations trying to make a profit from the carbon derivatives market (personal communication).

At best, the soil health and regenerative agriculture movements aim to restore the soil's vital planetary functions by working with – rather than against – the self-organizing capacities of living systems. Cultivating soil biodiversity can rebuild ecosystem functions like water infiltration, pest and pathogen control, and resilience to erosion (Wall, Uffe, and Six 2015; Pershouse 2017a). Re-establishing diverse plant cover on bare soils and regenerating the soil sponge can not only draw down carbon into plants, soil biology, and longer-term soil carbon, it can also improve human health and make communities more resilient to the climate crisis by enabling the soil to effectively absorb and filter water, refilling the water table, reducing the negative impact of floods and droughts, reducing surface temperatures, and increasing the availability of clean drinking water (Pershouse, personal communication; Pershouse 2016, 2017a). The soil sponge is built by plants and microbial life, by the glues and slimes exuded by microorganisms and by the root hairs of plants and the mycelial threads of fungi (Pershouse 2016). As a result, nurturing life at the microbial scale can benefit the health of the planet as a whole.

Farmers, ranchers, governments, and nearly anyone who has a bit of land to work can employ the "principles of soil health" (see textbox on following page) to "manage land in ways that support the plant, microbial, and other biological processes that create the fundamental infrastructure of life: the soil aggregate" (Pershouse 2017a, ix). Applying the soil health principles has been shown to improve plant and animal health, make crops and livestock more resistant to disease and insect pressures, increase the nutrient content of foods, and enhance the resilience of the land to flooding, drought, runoff, and wind and water erosion (Pershouse 2017a). One principle is to leave the soil undisturbed by tillage. No-till agriculture, when combined with approaches such as using diverse, continual cover crops and animal grazing to terminate crops could have substantial benefits across ecological scales.[2] It has been found, for instance, that when farmers grow crops without tilling

> **Soil health principles**
>
> - Much of soil life is fed by liquid carbon compounds produced by plant photosynthesis, exuded through plant roots. Keep living roots in the ground as much of the year as possible.
> - Soil life is hard at work building underground structures that form a porous, strong "soil sponge," the foundation of life on land. Allow the structure of the soil sponge to grow deeper and stronger by minimizing soil disturbance.
> - Soil life needs protection from heat, pounding rain, and wind. Keep soil covered year-round (preferably with living plants, dead plant litter, or mulch).
> - A diverse system is more resilient than a monoculture. Increase the diversity of plants growing together, to provide food and habitat for diverse soil microorganisms, beneficial insects, birds, and other species.
> - Like any other living system, soil ecology will succumb to overwhelming stresses (such as excessive use of pesticides, chemical fertilizers, compaction, undergrazing, overgrazing, etc.). Minimize chemical, physical, and biological stresses.
> - A healthy landscape soaks up, stores and filters water, cools the surrounding atmosphere, creates mist and clouds, and is more resilient to flooding and drought. Natural communities involving all kingdoms of life are responsible for the water cycle on land. Plan, monitor, and adapt your management with the whole water cycle in mind.
> - Nature never farms without animals. Animals move nutrients, create small and large pores in soil, manage flows of water, pollinate crops, balance predator/prey relationships, and replenish soil microbes. Find ways to integrate and welcome a diversity of animals, birds, and insects into the system.
> - Every place has a history, and unique strengths and vulnerabilities. Get to know the context of the land.
>
> © 2020 Didi Pershouse, Land and Leadership Initiative, www.landandleadership.org

the soil, soil erosion occurs at rates that are close to the rate of soil production. Tillage, on the other hand, creates rates of soil erosion that are ten to one hundred times faster than those of soil production, degrading ecosystems more quickly and incurring costly problems for farmers (Montgomery 2007 as cited in Field et al. 2020). Untilled soils allow vast mycorrhizal fungal networks to develop, effectively extending plant root systems in ways that not only improve the structure and function of the soil itself, but also improve the health and nutritional integrity of crops, grazing animals, and the entire food web. Food that is grown in living, microbially diverse ecosystems is higher in essential nutrients and lower in toxic compounds. In an intact soil sponge, fungi and other microbes act as "intelligent filters," absorbing nutrients from the surrounding soil in appropriate quantities and forms, then delivering them to plant roots (Pershouse 2016, 24). Heavily tilled industrial soils, doused in human-made fertilizers and pesticides, cannot develop or sustain these fungal networks, and in contrast do not benefit from the work of these intelligent membranes. Without help from microbes, plants are unable to effectively filter what they absorb from the soil, and tend to take in larger quantities of easily soluble ions like nitrates and phosphates, as well as naturally occurring toxins like lead and uranium (Pershouse 2016). Crops grown in tilled fields where the mycelial network is perpetually disturbed have less capacity to find essential micronutrients like selenium and zinc that enable plants and animals to build the enzymes they need to maintain their health and ward off disease. Living, undisturbed soils with diverse mycorrhizal relationships therefore enable the growth of more nutritious foods that are better for human health (Pershouse 2016). They also tend to reduce crop loss to insect pressures, increase agricultural yields, require fewer inputs, prevent erosion and land degradation, and generate longer-term economic prosperity for farmers (Wall, Uffe, and Six 2015; Scholes et al. 2018 and Sanchez 2002 as cited in Field et al. 2020).

Although the soil health principles go against many of the tenets of mainstream land management, Didi hopes that one day if "most of our food is grown using those soil health principles, that will lead to really abundant human health, both mental health and physical health. That then becomes the feedback loop that is creating more and more healthy societies and people who can think better about each other" (personal communication). The approach also holds value in that it disrupts dominant narratives about what needs to be done to reverse current climate trends, offering something tangible and impactful that is not about consumerism or constraining one's behaviour. Instead, it is about creating and sustaining *life*. Didi describes how within conventional climate narratives

> we've only ever been offered opportunities to stop doing something or to buy something. And that's just reinforcing the educational system of "sit still and let us tell you what to do." And capitalism – if you buy the right thing, everything will be better. It's not empowering in any way. Whereas the farmers that have created landscapes that work, when you walk there, it's so beautiful.

There are all these flowers and insects and wildlife that comes back, and the soil smells good and the food tastes good. You're seeing life in action. I think we just intrinsically know that's good. It's like when you're falling in love, it's like "oh, this is good, this is life!" Whereas a Prius might be fun to have and you feel less guilty about driving, but it's not life. (personal communication)

4.1 Improving the Health of Microbial Communities to Heal the Planet

Regeneration of soil structure and function is an under-utilized and highly relational approach to cultivating health within nested social-ecological systems. Building a biodiverse, living soil sponge can benefit health by strengthening the resilience of local landscapes to climate change, increasing human nutrition, sequestering atmospheric carbon, improving the water cycle, and cooling the land. Implementing the soil health principles can also increase yields for farmers, regenerate agricultural landscapes, and improve the economic viability of family farms and other small-scale agricultural operations (also see section 8.2). While the soil health movement can generate multiple benefits for the health of diverse living systems, these benefits can only be realized by attending to health not only at the scale of individual human beings or even human populations, but also at the landscape scale of plants and microscopic communities of bacteria and fungi. This work is not usually done by doctors and other health practitioners, but by farmers, ranchers, urban planners, and gardeners. As such, the approach demonstrates the importance of considering leverage points for health that reside outside of formal health systems. By nurturing the smallest scale – what Didi Pershouse calls the invisible microbial workers in the landscape (Pershouse 2016, 2020b; Pershouse and the Regenerative Economy Collective 2020) – improving soil health builds planetary health from the ground up.

NOTES

1 Didi occasionally returns to one-on-one work and finds that these "individual relationships of caring" represent another entry point into large-scale systemic change (Pershouse, personal communication).
2 Didi argues that no-till approaches are only effective if they incorporate other regenerative techniques such as continuous cover crops and animal grazing. Industrial agriculture approaches can be technically "no till" but nonetheless erode human and planetary health by relying heavily on fertilizers and herbicides such as glyphosate (Pershouse, personal communication).

5 Gardening for Health

> There is one prescription in medicine, a medicine that I actually believe is universal, and it's the only one that I prescribe over and over again. There's a little caveat, because everyone does it differently every time they do it ... Planting a garden is that medicine ... You will be surprised by the wonderment. You will be surprised by how it changes you on every level. Exercise. Nutrition. The diversity in your yard. You will see bugs you've never seen, you will see birds you've never seen, you will taste tastes you've never tasted. You will stretch and move in ways your body has not stretched and moved perhaps in decades ... Garden for the rest of your life. (Dr. William Sutherland, co-host, Complexity Medicine, n.d.-b)

I did not set out to write a book so centred on gardening. The first people I spoke to as part of this research were academics interested in limits to growth and health care, or peak oil and health care. I talked to doctors concerned about the ecological footprint of medicine, and doctors integrating systems thinking and complexity into their work. I spoke to degrowth scholars and planetary health researchers, and academics studying relocalization. I wanted to understand how we could transition from the political economy we have today to one that has the potential to uphold long-term human and planetary health. In particular, I wanted to know how health systems could contribute to this transition and what might be in store for them as we move into a post-growth, post-carbon future. My take on these issues, shaped by having studied and worked in the fields of medical anthropology, social innovation, and community-based research, was that stepping back from ecological overshoot in a healthful and equitable way would require fine-tuning the balance between (and addressing wicked problems related to) high-tech, globally connected, biomedical health care upheld by systems of global economic integration and governance, on the one hand, and place-based, context-specific, ecologically attuned and people-centric approaches to health that meet the needs of local communities and ecosystems on the other. Soon enough, I found myself talking to gardeners.

I have called this chapter "Gardening for Health" because all the approaches profiled here leverage the shared work of growing a garden to improve health, often within communities experiencing marginalization and socio-economic vulnerabilities. Home gardens and community-based urban agriculture initiatives can have ecosystem-level impacts, contributing to building a healthy soil sponge, moderating the microclimate around the home, improving the water cycle, and enhancing biodiversity by creating habitat and food for native species (Lal 2020; Buck 2016). They can also generate demonstrable economic value, saving households money on their food bills, creating green jobs, providing medicinal herbs that can reduce reliance on expensive health care services, and enhancing food security by improving access to fresh, nutritionally dense foods (Lal 2020).

There is ample evidence that people turn to gardening during economic crises, and that in difficult times gardens can support health and resilience across social-ecological scales (Lal 2020; Montefrio 2020). During Cuba's special period, for instance, when the country was suddenly cut off from imported Soviet fossil fuels, agricultural machinery, and commercial pesticides and fertilizers, there was a rapid, national transition from industrial agriculture to organic farming (Borowy 2013). As part of this shift, people living in cities quickly adopted urban agriculture to increase their food security (Borowy 2013). Gardens bloomed in vacant land and were eventually sanctioned and resourced by the state (Borowy 2013). These initiatives had multiple co-benefits for individuals, communities, and local ecologies. Cuba's gardens provided food, employment, a sense of social cohesion, and improved mental health for communities while also restoring local ecosystem functions and lowering the carbon cost of high-quality food (Borowy 2013). Cuba's experience speaks to the potential of gardening to contribute to social-ecological resilience in a context of declining access to global supply chains.

Gardening also grew in popularity starting in 2020 when COVID-19 lockdowns slowed the global transportation of goods, creating real concerns about food security around the world (Lal 2020; Montefrio 2020; MacDonald 2020; Mejia et al. 2020). In Canada, one in five people started a home food garden for the first time during the pandemic, with two-thirds of new gardeners reporting that the COVID-19 pandemic significantly influenced their decision to begin (Mullins, Charlebois, and Music

2020). The pandemic seemed to create just the right conditions to encourage an interest in gardening: people were socially isolated and craving things to do with others at a safe distance; they were worried about continued access to healthy food; they had less money for groceries; they were stressed and mentally exhausted; many people were also temporarily unemployed or had their work hours reduced, leaving them with time to spare (Mejia et al. 2020; MacDonald 2020; Montefrio 2020).

In Ontario, Canada, there was an outpouring of public interest in community gardening in the spring of 2020 (MacDonald 2020). The provincial government responded to petitions launched by community gardening groups, declaring community gardens to be essential services that could remain open despite sweeping economic closures. The move was made not only because community gardens supplement the diets of many community members without access to private gardens, but because community gardens were seen to be a safe way of sustaining mental health during the pandemic (MacDonald 2020). The Village, a community garden in Rochester, Minnesota, that primarily serves growers from marginalized communities that do not have access to land around their homes (90 per cent non-Anglophone, non-European groups) saw the usage of their space rise from 65 per cent pre-pandemic to 100 per cent with a waitlist in the spring of 2020 (Mejia et al. 2020). Growers reported that amid pandemic restrictions, the community garden became an important source of food for their families and provided access to cultural foods that were no longer easily imported (Mejia et al. 2020). Gardeners at The Village said that the aesthetic appeal of the garden increased during the pandemic growing season and found that spending time in the garden made the chaos of the pandemic more manageable (Mejia et al. 2020). Interviews with gardeners found that "ownership of plots has provided social and emotional support during the pandemic" (5). The garden also offered "much-needed space for well-being during great stress" and "allowed for the strengthening of social relationships between new and existing gardeners" (5).

These examples suggest that people can use private and community gardens to meet their needs for healthy food, herbal medicines, social connection, mental health, physical activity, and meaning, especially amid uncertainty. In this chapter, I discuss a number of initiatives that deepen the conversation about how gardening can generate health outcomes across social-ecological scales. It is not meant to imply that any one of these approaches is enough, on its own, to ground a transition away from an industrial food system, an industrial medical system, or a culture preoccupied with consumerism and individualism. Every gardener knows that gardening is a long-term endeavour. As I write this, the sunflowers in my yard are bowing their heads as their blooms turn to seed. Carrots are pushing further into the soil. The green and purple pole beans that swelled through the summer are beginning to dry out in the sun. Next year, my garden will be home to the descendants of these plants. I am already collecting the seeds and planning for the next iteration. In the same way, this discussion is meant to be a kind of seed-gathering. It aims to show where gardening is already contributing to community health, social inclusion, and ecological regeneration, and where existing initiatives are holding space for what might one day grow in the more place-bound societies of the future.

5.1 The Listening Space

Dr. Jane Myat has been a family physician at the Caversham Group Practice in North London for twenty-two years. Founded by a group of communist doctors, Caversham Group Practice opened its doors on the very same day the NHS was established in 1948 (Barnett and Foot 2018). As one of the first practices to bring a group of physicians, nurses, health visitors, and social workers together under one roof, the Caversham Group Practice has always had a strong community orientation. Jane has continued this legacy, working with patients to co-create a community kitchen, craft space, and a garden where patients and health practitioners can engage with one another as full people, a rarity within modern health care systems.

Before transforming the disused lot surrounding the practice into a vibrant urban garden, Jane had become increasingly dissatisfied with the status quo in medicine. Faced with the imperative to see thirty-six patients a day, to monitor and track ever-expanding reams of patient data, and to keep up with prescriptions, telephone calls, and emails on top of everything else, Jane was profoundly concerned about the state of care she was able to give her patients. She worried that

> it was really the poor and the vulnerable, people who usually get marginalized, who were getting the short end of the stick. And it just feels really, really hard when it's people who you know. I chose general practice because I wanted the relationship, I like the continuity, I like knowing families, I like being part of a community. So I found it very difficult to disengage and say I'm sorry, we can't do that for you. The way I practice, I often will think "what would I want for myself, what would I want for my friends, what would I want for my family?" I knew that the things on offer weren't things I would choose for myself or those I care for. So it didn't feel right to offer those things for my patients. (Myat, personal communication)

To ensure that she could work in a way that aligned with her values, Jane reduced her paid hours. She began to work at the clinic half days, and in her "off" time she did home visits. Recognizing that doctors are well paid compared to others in society who are just as hard working, and knowing that her family would have enough to live on at a half salary, Jane thought of her unpaid time as pro bono work. She was just as busy as ever, perhaps working even longer hours than before. The difference was that she was now able to spend the time she needed to listen to her patients and to provide a level of care she could feel good about. She gave many of her patients her mobile phone number and her email address, something that most doctors do not do. While many health practitioners would perceive that level of personal connection to their patients to be draining, Jane reflected that "actually what I realized was that it was easier working like that" (personal communication).

Then in 2016, Jane began work on the community garden that became The Listening Space. The whole thing, she recalls, seemed to "materialize without a plan" (personal communication). Jane and her family had experience tending an allotment garden. She had grown up gardening with her grandfather and her parents, and she knew that gardening was restorative for her personally. There was a vacant green space at the practice, and Jane had hoped for years to set it up so that people who didn't have access to a garden could have somewhere to enjoy working with the earth, growing food, and being in nature together. Jane took a "friends and family approach" to the garden, once again standing partially outside of the formal health care system. She said that this approach was liberating – a way to circumvent all the rules and regulations that could stop anyone from even getting started trying to do something different in medicine. Because of her involvement with Transition Kentish Town, Jane and the community of volunteers that grew up around the garden used the principles of the transition movement to guide their work (see Transition Network 2020). At The Listening Space garden, the

> aim is to work as staff and patients, side by side, with positivity, creativity and imagination towards better health for ourselves, each other and our wider world. Our project and garden are run completely by volunteers: patients, practice staff and others who wish to contribute to our community-building efforts. The garden and, at times, our waiting room are used for small groups, community celebrations, a place of rest for the staff and as an outdoor consulting room. (www.thelisteningspace.uk)

Jane explained that "the main idea with the garden wasn't just gardening" (personal communication). It was about creating the conditions in which people can participate in a "complex activity"; more than growing plants, gardening is grounded in "where we come from as human beings and what we used to do together." Because of its deep connections to survival and community, Jane felt that gardening could be a way to heal some of the ruptures that exist between the natural environments in which humanity evolved and the economic, social, and technological conditions of modern society. She reflected that "maybe it's something that we've maintained through all the changes because it gives us that link with where we've come from."

The Listening Space was also intended to be a "hosting space ... where we could come together differently as a community." Jane described how "because of the position you hold as a doctor, you know a lot of people and you hold a lot of stories, and therefore you can look out for people quietly, and they know you're looking out for them, whilst introducing them to other people" (personal communication).

Seasonal celebrations in the garden were opportunities for people to meet one another, deepening community relationships in an area of London with stark income disparities and significant cultural diversity. Jane describes the garden as "a slightly protective environment and a safe environment":

> We've all become so fragmented and disconnected, and actually as a physician within a community, you know so many people. And the inspiration for the garden, the Listening Space, was to facilitate relational possibilities. It is important to attend to the ground (the culture and the roots) to create a safe, trusting and inviting space and then to act as a connector or a bridge between people in a community. (personal communication)

Since The Listening Space broke ground several years ago, various initiatives have gathered momentum according to the interests and energies of participants. Next came crafternoons, a space where patients could gather in the practice's large, warm waiting room to sew, knit, embroider, or work on their favourite craft. The space has proven particularly useful for people facing fuel poverty and isolation during the winter months. It also facilitates conversations in a different way than people might be used to when visiting the doctor: "You have very interesting conversations in groups when you don't have that eye-to-eye kind of contact. They can be quite honest conversations." Jane described these sessions as creating a vibrant and inclusive atmosphere at the practice:

> Our Friday crafternoons every week, it's joyous. I used to get to Friday afternoon, couldn't wait to get out of the practice. Now I can't wait to

stay in the practice ... We have three or four people with significant schizophrenia who come to the group with people who are upper middle class, we've got men now who are coming. We have people from our Bangladeshi community, people from the Somali community. Just to see the commonality in a community ... within those small groups, there are lots of shared interests, and people can navigate those difficulties. Not to say it's always – sometimes there are quite big tensions, but we always have worked them through. That's where I think the therapeutic part is important. I see myself as a facilitator in those groups. Usually I'm trying to do a bit of sewing or something but usually I'm not getting very much done, I'm chatting to people and making the tea and doing everything else. I think it's seeing people getting better, seeing them getting their own power and agency back. And recognizing in themselves that they've got strengths that they didn't know they had. (personal communication)

Part of Jane's motivation in creating the garden and finding space to come together around the essential activities of growing, cooking, and making at the practice has been to help shift behaviours in a tangible way. As a physician, she said, "I knew that people don't listen if you just tell them what to do, but I knew that people do things differently if you do things with them. It's not traditional to do that as a doctor. There are lots of things that I think set us apart (personal communication). Gardening with her patients, cooking food with them, sitting in the waiting room with knitting needles and a ball of yarn creates new kinds of relationships between doctors and patients, and new ways of being in community. Jane described how

the whole thing has been very energizing for me, even though I've spent more time at the practice than I did when things were difficult. I think because I feel like it's coherent with my ideas and values – it feels like it's according to the oath that we took, that then you realize that when you're working in that way it doesn't feel like work, it just feels like being. Properly being part of that community, which is what I always wanted and what it's supposed to be. And then it gives permission to everybody else to be part of it as well. (personal communication)

5.2 Gardening and Nature in Health Care Institutions

Jane Myat's work with The Listening Space can be seen as part of a burgeoning movement across the health care sector to incorporate gardening and access to green spaces into patient care. This work is grounded in the recognition that the design of health care facilities, particularly the ways in which they incorporate access to nature (or even views of nature) can affect patient healing (Sachs 2017). I spoke with Dr. Naomi Sachs, assistant professor in the Department of Plant Science and Landscape Architecture at the University of Maryland and founding director of the Therapeutic Landscapes Network, to learn more about how the health care sector is embracing the health benefits of gardens and gardening. Naomi has worked in the health care design field, focusing on how health care institutions incorporate access to nature, for over twenty years (Sachs 2020). During this time, there has been extensive research conducted on the health benefits of nature (see review by Frumkin et al. 2017), and specifically on how these benefits play out in health care settings (see Sachs 2019). A range of academic studies, for instance, have found that exposure to nature can reduce stress, improve mental health (e.g., by reducing depression, anxiety, and ADHD symptoms), create greater well-being and life satisfaction, improve immune function, lower blood pressure, reduce aggression, and enhance recovery from surgery (Frumkin et al. 2017). One particularly influential study published in 1984 found that patients with a window facing trees recovered more quickly from surgery, were able to leave hospital sooner, required less pain medication, and experienced fewer post-operative complications than those whose window faced a brick wall (Ulrich 1984 as cited in Cooper Marcus and Sachs 2014). The study has since been replicated in various contexts to similar effect (Marberry 2010 as cited in Cooper Marcus and Sachs 2014). It has also been shown that connection with nature "mak[es] people more pro-social, so more likely to engage with each other and their fellow human beings" (Naomi Sachs, personal communication; also see Frey and Meier 2004; Weinstein, Przybylski, and Ryan 2009; Frumkin et al. 2017).

Naomi noted that "whether it's a general acute care hospital or a psychiatric hospital or a paediatric hospital or an outpatient clinic, it's one of the most stressful things we go through when we're a patient and we're not well, or when we are a family member, taking care of someone and worrying about them, worrying about money, and trying to make these very tough decisions" (personal communication).

While patients and caregivers are often experiencing stress when they visit health care facilities, doctors, nurses, and other health care providers also have "very demanding and stressful jobs" (Sachs, personal communication). Naomi reflected that modern hospitals and health care facilities

> have a tradition of being very alien, antiseptic, sort of inhuman environments. They're not home-like at all. So in addition to this association we

have of hospitals with sickness and death, there's also this association with bright walls and bad acoustics and squeaky floors and fluorescent lights and just not a home-like, familiar place that anyone would want to be if they were healthy. A garden provides a break from that, and especially in that environment because it's so alien and sterile and because people are under so much stress, it's literally and figuratively a breath of fresh air and a place where people can escape. Even if it's just visually by looking out from their hospital room window or from the waiting room while they're waiting for a procedure or a test result or while they're working at the nurse station. (personal communication)

Gardens offer the opportunity for patients and health care workers alike to "look outside or know that you can go outside and interact with something that *is* life, and that is life-affirming and hopeful." In a health care setting, nature can encourage "a sense of hope and a sense of normality in a place and a situation that is anything but normal." Sachs has conducted numerous qualitative studies of people's reactions to being in gardens in health care facilities, and has found that people report that being in nature helps them to connect to something greater, to "the rest of the world," "other life ... people and the universe," as well as to their "deeper self." When gardens are part of health care, it can help people

to get beyond the day-to-day "oh, I've got this meeting and that meeting, and I'm worried about this, etc." It's, "okay, let's take a step back and a step deeper into life's purpose and what am I really here for and what are my greater values in life?" And I think that there's a lot of symbolism about gardens and plants and it's really interesting in qualitative research to hear people talking about the cycle of life and death and seeing plants go through that life cycle. Often in horticultural therapy they'll do things like grow radishes, which grow really fast, so you can actually go from planting a seed to eating a radish in a matter of weeks. Being part of that physical growing process then leads them to think about their own emotional or sometimes spiritual growth process. For people who are spiritual or religious there is also a connection with something greater than them, or god, or god that is represented by nature and plants and trees and animals like squirrels and birds. Birds are really important to people, and it may be that especially in health care, seeing healthy life, and birds that are flying in the garden and then get to fly away, I think that's really important to people. (personal communication)

Hospitals and other health care facilities are increasingly realizing these benefits and are investing in their gardens not only for their aesthetic value, but for their potential role in therapy. The Therapeutic Landscapes Network maintains an online directory of close to 250 gardens in health care and related facilities, most of them in the United States, Canada, and the United Kingdom. These gardens are designed for various purposes, including encouraging older adults to be more physically active, providing a space for children to play, helping people learn how to use a wheelchair outdoors, or simply offering places for people to sit alone or meet with their families (Therapeutic Landscapes Network, n.d.; Naomi Sachs, personal communication). Trained in landscape architecture, Sachs said that there are clear design principles that can be used to ensure that gardens become useful, multifunctional spaces that facilitate healing and connection to nature in health care settings (Naomi Sachs, personal communication; also see Cooper-Markus and Sachs 2014). These design principles are mostly simple things like offering a variety of comfortable places to sit that can be easily rearranged to serve groups of different sizes, or providing different options to be in the sun or in the shade. In health care settings, patients tend to get stripped of choice and agency, and even the opportunity to choose to go outside can be meaningful (Naomi Sachs, personal communication). Gardens can be further designed to increase sense of control by providing people with a choice of where to sit, what to look at, or what path to take (Cooper Marcus and Sachs 2014).

Some health care institutions hire a horticultural therapist who engages patients to work in the garden, to do deadheading or weeding, water plants, or do other tasks according to their capacities and interests (Naomi Sachs, personal communication). Naomi noted that the health care gardens with a practising horticultural therapist tend to be the ones that are best maintained and that become the most meaningful therapeutic spaces. To learn more about what horticultural therapy is and what it entails, I spoke with Christina Klein, a horticultural therapist working in a long-term care home in Ontario, and then-chair of the Canadian Horticultural Therapy Association. Christina said that the elder care sector is beginning to realize that when people go into long-term care, they can become disconnected from nature, which can in turn contribute to mental health issues. In long-term care settings, some residents will not go outside for months at a time. As a horticultural therapist, one of Christina's primary goals was to get elderly residents "outside as much as possible" to plant, weed, or simply enjoy being in the garden. Even though many residents have significant mobility issues, Christina would

> encourage them to do as much as possible, even if it's putting your hands on the lavender. I try to have a variety of smells and tastes so that everyone

can be part of that. A lot of people have this idea that they need to go digging, and they certainly don't. A lot of times it's the social aspect that is just as important, being in my program. I always say, just come, just come. And a lot of people just sit there. Sit outside, see the birds, and the butterflies, and we're across from the pond … A lot of people who have advanced Alzheimer's, they can't participate as much, so I try to do a lot of things that they can touch, things that they can smell. (Klein, personal communication)

Christina said that it can be easy for residents to become bored in long-term care. Boredom has been shown to be associated with depression, which is further linked to conditions like Alzheimer's (Christina Klein, personal communication; Ross, Gliebus, and Van Bockstaele 2018). While many activities are offered to long-term care residents to stave off boredom, stimulate the mind, and forge social bonds, things like colouring hold no appeal to many residents because they have never done those activities before and they do not create feelings of accomplishment. Gardening is perceived by many residents to be more meaningful than other activities. Keeping the mind active with the need to plan, adjust one's planning, and devote sustained attention to a task over time, gardening is "not just busywork" (Christina Klein, personal communication). I asked Christina why she thought gardening felt more meaningful than other activities for long-term care residents, and she said:

You're planning, you've got the seeds, you look at them sprout, you eat the food. And that's what makes it meaningful … They can see that this has gone from this process to this process, and it's something really healthful, you can eat it and you can help other people. That's what a meaningful activity is for me. It's not just keeping them busy.

5.3 Enabling Gardens

Health care institutions are not the only actors embracing gardens for their healing and community-building potential. Enabling gardens, gardens designed to be inclusive for people of all physical and cognitive abilities, are rising in popularity within public parks and botanical gardens. In November 2017 I visited an enabling garden in Ontario, Canada. The day was unusually warm and hazy for November. Tall pines moved in a strong wind and crisp brown maple leaves skittered across the wide trail where people walked their dogs and pushed strollers. I had come there to meet the resident horticultural therapist and coordinator of the enabling garden. As I approached the garden, I could see people working in the tall, raised beds. I later learned that they were recovering from strokes; "bending to place tools on milk crates and planting and pulling things out of the garden encourages flexibility and movement and can aid in recovery," the horticultural therapist explained.

After I interviewed her the week before, the horticultural therapist had invited me to join her weekly session with a group of three regular clients, all of whom had developmental delays and were non-verbal. The group had been coming to the garden every week for the past several years. When I got there, the three men and their support workers were already busy cleaning up the garden for the winter. Their first job that day was to install a snow fence around one of the garden beds. The horticultural therapist said, "They like the physical work and know the garden better than anyone who visits." Some of the work they do, like hammering in stakes, fixing ladders, and putting up the protective barriers around the garden beds, contributes to strengthening short- and long-term memory. Other tasks help them to build new skills while accomplishing essential work around the garden that has value in its own right. For instance, the group had planted several trees that would most likely stand in the garden for decades to come. When I first spoke with the horticultural therapist, she told me about one of the men in the group, reflecting that although he is non-verbal and cannot directly tell her what he is experiencing, she had observed significant gains in his abilities over time, as well as positive effects on his mood and demeanour when he worked in the garden:

> I have one client who's been coming since the start of the garden, every week for five years. This is a big man who is almost totally non-verbal. The difference in him from when I first saw him, where he was very restrained, and he couldn't understand how to push a wheelbarrow because that cognitive pathway of picking up and pushing forward just wasn't connecting. Now he actually runs down the path toward the garden, a big smile on his face. He is our top wheelbarrow pusher. But just the energy that he's giving and the smile on his face and the light in his eyes, that tells me that there's something else happening than just he's physically able to do more, or it's a nice day. This garden is affecting him on some level that we may not be able to categorize.

The enabling garden is intended to send the message "you belong here." As I observed the group that day, working to prepare the land they knew so well and had cared for over many years, the message shone through clearly. The enabling garden was "specifically designed for people with all abilities, not just people who are particularly mobile or have access to all of their limbs." The horticultural therapist said:

One of the huge goals of any enabling garden, but mine in particular, is that we have to be inclusive, and inclusive of people with all abilities. This is not just about how we're using the land, this is about how we view people. If we view people with any kind of a disability or perceived disability as other than, they are marginalized and not included. That is a societal problem. What an enabling garden does, is it unifies everybody. It makes working with the land possible for everybody. Many people think, well it's just an offshoot, it's not mainstream, or it's not central to all of our major concerns. But it is actually central, because it has to do with a civilization issue. A huge civilization issue. How we treat people ... You can take that overarching idea of civilization and take it right down to "who gets to work in the garden?" That's the level that I can work at and that individuals can work at. We are connecting everybody, and we're also training people to look at each of us differently, in a much more compassionate way.

The enabling garden provides a space for school groups, adults with developmental delays or mental health issues, people recovering from strokes or cancer, and women who have experienced trauma, "all of whom benefit from working directly with the soil." The horticultural therapist explained that the "overarching aim of the enabling garden is to connect people with nature so that they are able to implement their own self-healing and their own connection with nature." The model departs significantly from a traditional counselling or psychiatric approach, and is rooted in the idea that much of what people need to be healthy "can be right outside their back door."

The horticultural therapist tailored each of her programs to the needs of the individuals in the group. Her programs also offered ways of interacting with the garden that were seasonally appropriate and grounded in what needed to be done in the garden at any given time. As a result, her sessions often incorporated education on what nature needs in each season. In the fall, for instance, school programs might focus on taking up some of the dead annuals, looking for the last vegetables in the garden, pulling a carrot and eating it, or making a kale pesto together. For high-needs groups with low cognitive abilities, the programs were oriented towards building sensory connections. The horticultural therapist would take a group out to a large old maple standing by the river so that people could "taste the maple syrup and touch the tree bark and see the maple leaf on the tree."

For children, the focus was often on shifting unhelpful perceptions of nature. Children who don't know where their food comes from, for instance, can think that the soil is dirty, whereas interacting with soil can actually improve the immune system. By teaching children about gardening, the horticultural therapist also encouraged them to learn to nurture something: "If you have a garden or you've got the land, there's responsibilities, you have to take care of it. And I think giving young people that opportunity to take care of something, to plan, and to nurture, that's doing their well-being a huge service. Not just their well-being, but their humanness."

The horticultural therapist has also observed a wide range of other benefits for children attending programs at the enabling garden. For instance, she said that children with ADHD often become more focused in the garden:

> Even though there's a lot of external stimuli, we often find that the opposite happens, that they actually become more focused in the garden than they might be in the classroom with less stimuli ... Those who are on the autism spectrum who may be agitated very easily, we find they calm down a lot more with their connection to being in nature. It doesn't matter what they're doing, they may be standing in the garden, but that passive connection to nature seems to help calm whatever those nerve fibers are doing.

At the end of our interview, I asked the horticultural therapist whether she thought enabling gardens could help to support health in a context of declining economic growth, and specifically whether the model depends on growth to operate, or if it could be useful in a time of economic contraction. She said:

> Everyone, if you have even a yogurt container, can grow something. You don't need acres and acres of farmland to do that. If everybody starts to grow one seed, it can start the ball rolling. Seeds are easy to come by, they're not expensive, and you can collect them year after year. We have the ability to take care of ourselves if we use the land properly and respectfully. If we don't, then we won't be able to feed ourselves. I really think it's as simple and as fundamental as that.

5.4 Home Gardening for Health and Sustainability

Private and community gardens also have a role to play in supporting human and planetary health. The yards and gardens surrounding people's private homes are thought to account for between 25 per cent (Thompson and Head, n.d., as cited in Buck 2016) and 36 per cent (Cameron et al. 2012 as cited in Mahmoudi, Maller, and Phelan 2018) of the total urban land area. Private gardens represent a particularly high proportion of total green space in low-density cities and suburban areas (Cameron et al. 2012 as cited in Mahmoudi, Maller, and Phelan 2018). As a result, private gardens could make a meaningful contribution to increasing tree cover and biodiversity within cities and well as reducing the urban heat island effect by cooling the land, with knock-on effects for the provision of ecosystem services (Lin et al. 2015 as cited in Mahmoudi, Maller, and Phelan 2018). Private gardens have been associated with the same health benefits as public green spaces, including increased opportunities for social interactions, stronger social cohesion, and better mental and physical health. There is also evidence that people who spend more time gardening feel a strong sense of attachment to their home and the land around it (Mahmoudi, Maller, and Phelan 2018). These findings imply that encouraging gardening could become an important pathway for building felt connections to place and building social-ecological resilience at the community level.

Crystal Bradford and Liam Kijewski run Wildlife Gardening, a landscaping business aimed at "inspiring and educating people about the natural world and healthy ecosystems" (Liam Kijewski, personal communication). Some of the goals of their work include "encouraging and strengthening ecosystem biodiversity, increasing the amount of natural areas, giving back to wildlife by restoring and maintaining habitat, helping to preserve nature for future generations … [and] connecting people with the natural environment" (Wildlife Gardening, https://www.wildlifegardening.ca/about-us-1). Through Wildlife Gardening, Crystal and Liam design gardens using native and edible plants, sell perennials, and incorporate techniques like hügelkultur beds that make use of old wood, finding a place to store carbon in the garden instead of releasing it into the atmosphere. They also run workshops that teach skills related to foraging, gardening with native plants, and how to choose a native tree to plant in your yard. The core of their business is "providing for wildlife, not just any wildlife, but the wildlife that historically had a developed and connected ecosystem and relationships with each other" (Liam Kijewski, personal communication). Crystal explained:

> Our aim is to make little gas stations all over town for the pollinators to stop and refuel. When we teach kids, we say, you wouldn't drive to Florida with one tank of gas and one lunch, you'd have to have many stops. So if we can create these little gas stations to recharge all over the city, or encourage people to do that in their backyard by using plants that actually feed and aren't creating sterile ecosystems, or creating deserts, that's huge. (personal communication)

Wildlife Gardening has worked in partnership with a local sustainability organization in Waterloo Region, Reep Green Solutions (www.reepgreen.ca), to implement a rain garden program. Rain gardens have deep, absorbent soil and feature drought and flood-resistant native plants. They use the living systems around people's homes to absorb and filter rainwater, preventing excess runoff from entering the storm water system or helping to retain water in a dry area. Rain gardens can also help to prevent mouldy basements, and by incorporating more plants and trees into a yard, can have a cooling effect on the microclimate around a home (Reep, 2021). Through their work with Reep and their other garden landscaping projects, Crystal and Liam have observed the influence of culture on the kinds of gardens that are acceptable within a neighbourhood. For instance, some neighbourhoods value perfectly manicured lawns over providing food for pollinators and habitat for species of insects and other wildlife, while in other neighbourhoods front-yard gardens and raised beds are commonplace. In Kitchener, neighbourhoods that were involved in Reep's rain garden rebate program saw a rapid expansion in the adoption of front-yard rain gardens. Liam said that "the neighbourhood became a living laboratory" and reflected that offering the program at a neighbourhood scale allowed it to grow and expand rapidly (personal communication). As neighbours saw rain gardens being put in and became familiar with what they were, the concept became normalized on a hyper-local scale and took on momentum. In addition to greater awareness of rain gardens in southern Ontario, over the past several years Liam and Crystal have noticed increased interest in courses like wild edibles, more public knowledge about native plants, and a higher number of nurseries and conventional garden centres advertising native plant sections (personal communication).

Crystal and Liam work in a way that recognizes the extent to which looking after wildlife then "takes care of people" (Bradford, personal communication). Helping people to grow food plants on their own property, for instance, has an effect on food security and can also reduce reliance on agricultural systems that exploit people by offering extremely low pay and terrible working conditions. Crystal and Liam help to show people that it is easy to grow things like berries in your own yard without any pesticides, and with very little maintenance. A key branch of their work also involves teaching young children to love the magic of nature, as a way to "change our mindsets and create more compassion in the younger generation to keep going and keep caring." When I asked Crystal what impact she thought their work might have on human health, she said, "Just think about a kid walking home and seeing magic." When neighbourhoods are havens for biodiversity, when they support local plant and animal life and create places for people to gather and play, it is easier to connect to nature in a personal and immediate way. Gardens make it possible to watch things change throughout the seasons, as flowers come up and turn to seed, then fall and begin the cycle again (Bradford, personal communication).

5.5 Leveraging the Shared Practice of Gardening to Build Health

Governments and health systems are beginning to grasp the potential benefits of gardening for human and planetary health. A research report funded by the King's Fund, a charitable organization that aims to improve health and care in England, for instance, recommends that the NHS, Public Health England, local governments, and partnered social service providers take gardening seriously as a strategy for improving population health (Buck 2016). The report brings together research to build a business case for the relationship between gardening and health; it found that providing greater access to parks and green spaces could save the NHS two billion pounds in obesity-related health care costs alone (Groundwork, n.d., as cited in Buck 2016). The New Economics Foundation similarly evaluated the economic value of the Ecomind program, an initiative that creates outdoor experiences including gardening for people experiencing mental illness, and found that it saved the government around seven thousand pounds per person by lowering NHS costs, reducing the need for welfare payments, and increasing income tax revenues (New Economics Foundation 2014 as cited in Buck 2016).

This chapter has shown that leveraging the shared practice of growing a garden can improve health. For example:

- Therapeutic gardens in local GP practices, health care institutions, and retirement homes can become places for community members to gather, share food, connect with nature, and collectively provide for each other's basic needs.
- Enabling gardens can offer inclusive spaces where people of all abilities can belong and contribute to their communities.
- Home and community gardens can have ecosystem-level impacts by building a healthy soil sponge, moderating the microclimate around the site, improving the water cycle, and enhancing biodiversity.
- Gardens can improve food security, create sustainable livelihood activities (see chapter 8), and provide medicinal herbs that strengthen preventative health (see chapter 17).

However, one of the challenges to realizing these benefits at a societal scale is that relevant stakeholders and leaders across public health, environment, health care, horticulture, and sustainability and civil society organizations are not necessarily connected in ways that enable coordinated, strategic action (see Buck 2016). Building stronger relationships between diverse businesses, organizations, and community leaders with an interest in gardening to improve human and planetary health could reveal innovative systems-level approaches for securing health, social inclusion, and ecological regeneration. Loosely knitting together the various pieces of work taking place in local GP offices, health care facilities and long-term care, enabling gardens, and social enterprises, for instance, could begin to shift local practices and norms related to gardening while creating new ways for such initiatives to influence and coordinate their activities with health and social welfare systems.

6 Care Farming

Care farming is a multifunctional approach to agriculture that combines food production with health and social care. The practice takes diverse forms, but usually involves farmers inviting people with disabilities or people experiencing mental health issues or social marginalization onto the farm to become part of the farming team. Some care farms offer therapeutic programming for particular client populations (see Fiddlehead Care Farm, section 6.5), while others find that the daily work of nurturing crops, tending animals, and maintaining the farm itself improves the physical, mental, and social health of participants (see examples from the Netherlands, sections 6.1 to 6.4). Most care farms are working farms that yield plant crops and animal products by incorporating the labour and skills of community members with diverse health and care needs. Spending time on a care farm has been found to achieve measurable health benefits for youth with behavioural problems, children with ADHD, people with drug and alcohol addictions, people with learning disabilities, elders experiencing dementia, and adults living with long-term psychiatric illnesses such as schizophrenia and personality disorders (Elings 2012, 2020; Hassink, Hulsink, and Grin 2014; Hassink et al. 2020). Evaluations of care farming programs in the Netherlands have found, for instance, that youth with behavioural issues benefit from the daily structure of farm work, along with opportunities to take responsibility, make their own decisions, build positive social relationships, and focus on providing for their basic needs (Elings 2012). Adults living with psychiatric illnesses or experiencing drug or alcohol addiction say that they feel more useful and physically healthy after working on the farm and report greater life satisfaction and higher self-esteem (Elings 2012). They also find that they are more productive and engaged in other parts of their lives and tend to adopt more pro-social behaviours (Elings 2012).

Over the past several decades, the care farming movement has expanded rapidly across Europe and North America, and has taken hold particularly strongly in the Netherlands (Hassink et al. 2020; see also Elings 2020; Hassink and Elings 2006; Buist 2016). As a growing movement, care farming holds great potential to generate health across social-ecological scales. It has been shown to improve the physical and mental health of individuals by getting people outside onto the land to do things with their hands, by facilitating social connections, and by creating opportunities to contribute in a meaningful way to the essential work of a farm (Elings 2012, 2020). At the same time, the approach enhances the economic viability of local agricultural systems by creating a new societal role for small-scale farms, bringing novel sources of income to farming families, and integrating agriculture into the life of the community (Elings 2020; Hassink et al. 2020). Care farming can also regenerate local ecosystems by bringing hand work to the rural landscape and encouraging more widespread adoption of organic farming methods (Thomas van Elsen, personal communication; van Elsen, Günther, and Pedroli 2006; Hassink et al. 2020). With such a strong convergence of outcomes at the interconnected scales of individual health, community inclusion, local economic development, and ecological integrity, care farming holds significant transformative potential for communities seeking to contribute to healthy and equitable sustainability transitions in the Anthropocene. To understand more about how care farming can support human and planetary health, I spoke with several practising care farmers in the Netherlands and two researchers with extensive experience evaluating Dutch care farming interventions. I also visited and interviewed the owners of a care farm in Ontario, Canada, in the fall of 2018. This chapter brings together insights from my conversations with care farmers about the purpose, structure, and future possibilities of care farming.

6.1 Care Farming in the Netherlands

The Netherlands is a global leader in the care farming movement. Home to an estimated 1,250 care farms in 2018, the sector is highly developed and well networked, with strong professional organizations and communities of practice that support care farmers to learn, collaborate, and make the most of new opportunities (Hassink et al. 2020; Marjolein Elings, personal communication). Across the country, care farms have become "structurally embedded in society in general and in the health care and social care sectors in particular" (Hassink et al. 2020, 2). Although modernization resulted in the separation of agriculture, health, and social care into distinct, highly rationalized sectors in the Netherlands – as it did across Europe and around the world – care farming has since achieved a substantial reintegration of these domains (Hassink et al. 2020). As a result, care farming is a disruptive and unexpected innovation (Hassink et al. 2020) with the potential to reinvigorate some of the structural connections between social-ecological systems domains that affect health and well-being (e.g., agriculture; care for the mentally ill, the elderly, and communities that experience marginalization) that were eroded during modernization processes.

Jan Hassink, a researcher at Wageningen University who did his PhD on the developing field of care farming (Hassink 2017) and who is a care farmer in his own right, describes some of the factors that created an enabling environment for the care farming sector in the Netherlands:

1. the dedicated work of pioneering social innovators beginning in the 1960s and 1970s, who began experimenting with care farming models and approaches;
2. alignment between the goals of relevant sectors (the mental health care field was looking for ways to deinstitutionalize services and integrate people into community while the agricultural sector was simultaneously trying to address declining profits by creating more opportunities for multifunctional farms);
3. the development of the National Support Centre for Agriculture and Care, which "stimulated networking" (Hassink et al. 2020, 5) between groups of care farmers and between farmers and care institutions, building credibility over time;
4. a policy change that institutionalized "personal budgets for participants" (Hassink et al. 2020, 6), which allowed individuals to choose the programs they wanted to attend, made it possible for care farms to make agreements directly with their clients, and prompted new actors to enter the sector, such as care workers who were unhappy with aspects of the status quo in mental health services;
5. economic liberalizations within the health care sector, which made it possible for local associations of care farms to become accredited care organizations that could bill health insurance companies. (Jan Hassink, personal communication; Hassink 2017; Hassink et al. 2020)

Within this particular economic, policy, and cultural context, care farming emerged as a viable solution to a range of problems faced by stakeholders in different sectors. Farming families seeking to avoid agricultural intensification, care workers wanting to spend more time with their clients, and potential participants looking for effective services all found ways to meet their needs through care farming (Hassink et al. 2020; Jan Hassink, personal communication). In this way, care farming has become an effective "informal, non-care context" that can support the mental and physical health and social well-being of marginalized and vulnerable populations (Hassink 2010 as cited in Elings 2020).

Marjolein Elings, also a researcher at Wageningen University, has studied and evaluated care farming programs in the Netherlands for close to twenty years to better understand their associated outcomes, as well as why and how these outcomes arise. She says that one of the central benefits of care farms is providing a sense of "meaningful" purpose, activities, and relationships to orient a participant's life. This sense of meaning can be especially critical for people who have experienced exclusion from the labour market due to long-term disabilities or mental illnesses (Elings, personal communication). Elings' outcome evaluation studies have also found that people with dementia eat and drink more when they participate in care farming, and that youth with behavioural issues experience many positive changes in their lives such as better relationships with their parents and reduced interaction with the police (personal communication; Elings 2012). She suggests that across diverse participant groups, working on a care farm confers a sense of "meaningfulness" and the opportunity to "accomplish something" that has tangible value. For instance, after "putting seeds in the ground, you see that you get from your activity such a big pumpkin, and that gives you such a boost to your self-esteem." These experiences make participants feel "useful and respected," in contrast to conventional institutional settings that can be associated with a loss of dignity, purpose, and control. Elings has found that while being in nature is undoubtedly an important contributor to the success of care farming programs, "being part of the social community" of the farm is just as important. Elings reflects, "I think people are not here in the world to be alone" (personal communication). On a care farm, participants who return over long stretches of time form meaningful relationships with the farming family and with other participants, often referred to as "co-workers" (Elings 2020, 229). They also interact with nature in ways that are decidedly social – caring for animals through the seasons and tending plants from seed to harvest (personal communication). As a result, Elings and Hassink propose that care farming generates positive outcomes due to a number of "qualities" that care farms possess, including a "green environment," a "social community," "useful and diverse activities," and the "personal engagement" of the farming family (Hassink 2010 as cited in Elings, 2020, 232–3).

6.2 A Village Farm

Jan Hassink and his wife are founders of what he calls a "village farm," a care farm in an urban area that aims to engage neighbours and the general public in the life of the farm, thereby integrating people with disabilities into the community (Hassink, personal communication). The farm serves diverse participant groups, including "people with dementia, children, people with autism, adults with intellectual disabilities, and adults with psychiatric challenges." At the village farm, participants are able to choose from a variety of workplaces, including working in a restaurant that was established onsite, helping in the garden or in the fields growing vegetables, or working with animals. Jan has found that for some participant groups, such as people with dementia, the value of the farm comes from simply "being there, being outside, being active, also meeting other people." The length of time that a participant will work on the farm depends on his or her needs. Some individuals with intellectual disabilities will continue attending for five years or longer, while others, for instance people with dementia, will come for a shorter time depending on the progress of their illness (Hassink, personal communication).

For many participants, working on the farm has been shown to be more beneficial than other kinds of day programs. Jan explained that when people come to the farm they

> become more active, they spend more time outdoors, they have a different role, they feel more like they are a volunteer or even a worker on the farm instead of a client going to a day activity. They meet other people, I think that's important. And it's also important for the partners, the care giver at home. Because the people with dementia, they still live at home, and an important objective is to unburden the partner so that the person with dementia can stay at home longer. What you see is that the people who come to the farm, they appreciate the farm so much. It's much easier for the partner to ask the person with dementia to go to the care farm, because the person comes home happy instead of having to send your partner to a day activity centre that they don't like to go to because they don't have a choice of what they like to do there, and they have to sit inside. Especially a lot of men don't like those more traditional day activity centres. So they are much more active still in everyday life instead of going to the day activity centres where the activities are much more artificial, or we have to create activities for people. Here at the farm it's more like a normal life and normal activities, and people experience the difference. (personal communication)

In addition to more "normal," engaging activities, the relationships that people develop on the farm can be rich and genuine. Jan described how often

> there is a very close relationship between the farmers and the participants. There's also an equal relationship because you work together instead of having the kind of patient-treater, professional relationship. People on the farm are very good at looking at the possibilities of people instead of limitations. For children for instance, the farmer and the farmer's family can be kind of role models. Especially when they come from families with a lot of problems.

Many youth with behavioural issues, for instance,

> can see the farmer as a role model. You can imagine that when you go to an institution it's a different atmosphere than when you go to the farm ... They get responsibilities on the farm, that's what is important. They develop self-esteem because they get a positive response from the farmer. They feel they are important on the farm, they feel they are useful ... They experience that they really contribute to the work that needs to be done on the farm and that they are appreciated for what they are doing.

For people with psychiatric problems, the relationships they develop on the farm are of central importance. Working on the farm provides an opportunity to build relationships in a context where participants are not just talking to other participants about their illness all the time, but are discussing their shared interests on the farm and the work that needs to be done (personal communication). The farm also provides "the kind of workplace where, if they have a bad day, the farmer knows this and the work is adapted to the personal situation. They can learn to develop new contacts and also maybe by contact with the animals they learn how to develop trust for other living beings." Overall, Jan noted that one of the central benefits of the care farming model is that it "offers a very rich environment. It's a green environment with a lot of space, less stress. You have all these very practical concrete activities with plants and animals in real life that's useful work that has to be done. It's also very diverse."

6.3 Youth in Amsterdam

Wouter Joop operates a care farm in the heart of a large urban green space in Amsterdam. In the Netherlands, care farmers are provided with a government stipend that is paid per person according to the extent of care required by each individual (Joop, personal communication). The money comes from the unemployment benefit budget and can represent the majority of a care farm's income. On Wouter's farm, for instance, 20–30 per cent of their income comes from farming activities, and 60–70 per cent comes from the grants they receive for providing a workplace for people with special needs. Wouter described his farm as "built around the needs of our participants," who are mostly youth (personal communication). He explained:

> It is a productive farm, and that production is a very important instrument for development ... We operate about 40 acres of land, we have a herd of 30–35 beef cattle, 5–10 pigs, 150 hens, not really on a hobby level, but also not industrial scale. Everything has to be taken care of quite seriously, so the people that we receive on the farm, they are mostly youngsters with special needs as well as some behavioural problems. They come on the farm in so-called apprenticeship. They are in the last phase of their school every year, or they might have recently left school. They enter adult life on the farm.

Over time, Wouter has noticed that the young people who come to work at the farm experience outcomes such as fewer behavioural issues and reduced reliance on medications, but that these outcomes depend on their ongoing engagement on the farm. Care farming does not provide a cure for mental or physical illnesses. Rather, it is the process of doing the work on a regular basis that generates results. Many of the people who work on the farm will need support for their entire lives, while a smaller proportion, perhaps a third of people, Wouter estimates, are able to move towards "more demanding" or "less embedded" working situations (personal communication).

When I asked Wouter what he thinks it is about the farm environment that is so beneficial for participants, he said:

> It's a real working atmosphere. There's a very strong social community which we also actively take care of. We really focus on [ensuring that] people respect each other's shortcomings and possibilities even when it comes to use of language and bullying. So in a way we're quite nice to each other ... We use the farm in the broad sense as an instrument for development, as a laboratory where people can practice and make mistakes. That is with animals, that's with food, that's with relating to others, so there's a lot of diversity in things that you can try and taste and make mistakes ... Feeling that you are the one deciding and you are the one being confronted with your mistakes is really a healthy thing.

Wouter and his colleagues refer to participants as "assistant farmers" in recognition of their meaningful contribution to the operation of the farm (personal communication). Their goal is to focus on people's potential and to "waken up their initiative and their ability to make choices, to decide for themselves, to find something that they're good at." At the beginning of each workday, participants are asked what they would like to do, and farmers discuss what tasks must be completed. Wouter says, "I think our participants in a very healthy way can relate to their own needs as well as what the farm needs. This is a very social process." By learning to balance individual needs and desires with the needs of the farm and the many options that "life is offering" on any given day, participants build skills they can apply in their everyday lives beyond the farm. For instance, he says, they are able to "grow in their resilience to cope with things that happen without losing what they want themselves."

Wouter believes that care farming should not be limited to people with disabilities, as it can also have value for the general population. He suggests: "You don't need to be [someone with a mental illness or disability] in order to have the need to be part of a work community in which you learn to deal with resistance, how to work together with people, how to use your creativity, how to relate to other people, how to put your ideas in practice." For this reason, the farm also engages young people looking to do professional practicums in the care sector. Wouter notes that the farm offers a chance for young people to do something meaningful that makes a real difference in their local community.

> It is really empowering for our participants, also really empowering for young people who do a practicum. There are many young people who really want to do something, you know, to improve the world, and they think, "oh I have to go to Africa," or "how do we get rid of the plastic in the ocean?" These are big issues that are really serious, but in a way they're also paralysing problems. And it's fairly liberating and inspiring in a way for young people to come to a place where they can put their ideals in practice, but they can also come to a realistic view of what they really want to do or what they want to achieve.

6.4 A Working Dairy Farm

Floor de Kanter runs a working dairy farm with her husband. Together, they engage up to ten people with psychiatric problems to work on the farm. All their participants want to work but are not able to have a conventional job, often because of the psychological pressures and stress associated with regular work. On the farm, Floor and her husband try to remove as much of the pressure associated with work as they can, giving people meaningful and significant responsibilities while also making it clear that at the end of the day, the farmers are responsible and will deal with any mistakes or issues that arise (de Kanter, personal communication). Floor explained that for people with psychiatric problems, working on the farm can help build mental and physical resilience by providing real-world contexts in which to contribute, learn, and make mistakes:

> We give them back the feeling that everybody is useful, everybody can do something, and your challenge is bigger, and you have to deal with it, other people can help, but nobody's going to do it for you. It's a very important thing, you learn what your possibilities are and what your limit is. What you can do, what you can't do, when you have to stop, what you have to take care of. And I think that's something that they learn here, because they do work. I think when you put them at home, they don't have any experiences anymore. Everything happens at home with people with the same kind of problems and it's not real life. We try to put them back into real life and just learn the same way that we do, by working, and making mistakes, and having problems with other people, and just talking about it. So we try to bring that back again, to give them a feeling of being useful and just being human again, just with a bigger challenge. And that's different than having the feeling that you're just taken off the list, you're not useful anymore, you're only sick. I think that for them, it does a lot for their self-esteem. And because of that, they become stronger. Physically, but also mentally they become stronger. They have a better defence against the problems that they have to cope with.

Floor said that as a farmer, she also benefits from the connections to people with psychiatric illnesses. She described how being a care farm "puts us [farmers] back into society" (personal communication). Caring for people with diverse needs gives the farm a meaningful role outside of agricultural production, while also offering an opportunity to earn income. Floor characterized care farming as an inexpensive model, one that takes pressure off of other day centres, institutions, and professional services like psychiatric care, all of which are resource intensive for governments. By bringing people with disabilities onto the farm and bringing farmers back into society, Floor said, care farming makes communities "more complete and healthier."

On her farm, people work according to their abilities and interests. Some people like to do the same task everyday – often people with autism or participants who have experienced brain damage. She noted that "some of them are only able to do hand work, and really small [tasks]. We have one guy who feeds the cows ... it takes him four hours to spread the grass in front of the fence so that when they come in they can eat." Others like to do a variety of tasks that change each day: "for most people with a psychiatric background, they really need the change, they need new things and challenges all the time." The most important thing is that

> it's just the normal work. Feed the cows, work on the land. If we have to take out some weeds or repair the fences or feed the calves, clean the boxes. Everything, but also paint work, garden work, and we try to adjust it to the person. Sometimes we let people work together, if someone is very good with his head, he can still remember everything, but he's very bad with his hands, and the other one is not able to remember one thing, but he is able to work, we put them together, and they can manage.

Floor said that when people work on the farm, they work alongside the farmers in an equitable relationship based on mutual trust: "They don't feel like a client or sick person, they just work with us – we take care of them, but they do the work. And that's the unspoken agreement that we have. They do the work for us and we take care of them."

This relationship with the farming family creates a sense of personal investment in and responsibility for all that happens on the farm. For Floor, the extent to which farming returns people to what is most essential in life is part of the effectiveness of the approach. She explained:

> I think a farm, a running farm, is the basis of it all. We produce food. I worked in an office before and there I talked about the height of roofs and the kinds of tiles you can use, etc., and I felt very ... not useful. What am I doing? What is this contributing to the world? And now I'm producing milk ... I'm producing food and that's basic, everybody understands it. I think that's what makes a farm so special, that they bring someone back to the beginning, and it gives you a lot of peace.

6.5 Fiddlehead Care Farm, Ontario, Canada

Fiddlehead Care Farm is located close to Orangeville, Ontario. I visited the fifty-acre farm run by Stephanie Deaken and Breanne Mathers in the fall of 2018. When I arrived, Breanne took me on a tour of the property, which is home to cows, pigs, and chickens, has a series of nature trails through the forest, a sensory garden, a pond, and raised beds for growing vegetables. Breanne and Stephanie work mostly with children and youth with disabilities and special needs, taking "a play-based, exploratory approach" to therapy (Mathers, personal communication). They believe that providing active things for children with special needs to do while working towards therapeutic goals can generate better results than sitting in an office under fluorescent lights. As we walked past a large open field where cows were grazing, Breanne described some of the reactions they have received from their clients:

> Families will say, we've been doing this [counselling] for two years elsewhere and it's been ok, but the kids just get so much more joy out of what's happening here ... They enjoy coming here. A lot of times parents say they're fighting to get their kids to go see whoever. Because if it's not fun, it's not active, you're not hitting their interests, then they don't have the motivation to go. Whereas Steph and I do things in a very play-based way. It is definitely very goal oriented, but they don't really realize how much they're learning while they're doing it. The key message is that we're walking with them on this journey, there isn't this hierarchy of counsellor and patient. We try and build a good therapeutic relationship and friendship with them, and we're really working on this together. And with our experience and what we know from other kids we give them lots of suggestions and they work on things and they're happy to do homework and bring it back to us because it's a fun way to try things out ... I think we get a lot more done than in a conventional therapy setting. (personal communication)

Breanne and Stephanie describe themselves as "therapists first, farmers second." Stephanie's husband, Darryl Deaken, is a farmer and teacher and also plays a vital role in the working-farm aspect of the business. Stephanie is a certified social worker and Breanne is a certified child life specialist and a therapeutic recreation specialist. The two met when they worked together in the complex care unit of a downtown Toronto children's rehabilitation hospital, supporting children facing debilitating conditions who were often ventilator dependent, in palliative care, or experiencing multi-organ illnesses. Breanne and Stephanie's specialized training and experience is at the core of their approach to care farming; together, they provide nature-based programming and high-skilled therapy to people with often long-term, complex needs.

One of the unique features of Fiddlehead Care Farm is that it is fully accessible for people with disabilities. Breanne explained that this is extremely uncommon for natural areas: "We've had kids who have never been able to go into a forest setting because it's not accessible.

They're getting better, but a lot of walking trails have stairs on them, or don't have accessible washroom facilities, or there are so many barriers to participation. This is the first time they've been in a full forest, with trees all around them." Fiddlehead's trails are working towards full wheelchair accessibility. There is even a washroom with an adult-sized change table to ensure that everyone can be comfortable participating in their programs. Unlike some of the care farms in the Netherlands, Fiddlehead is less about providing opportunities to work on the farm and much more about "providing a whole complement of care farming services with therapeutic benefit" (Mathers, personal communication). Breanne and Stephanie offer individual and family counselling, special events for young people and their families, a low-ratio therapeutic summer camp for children with unique physical and psychosocial needs, and animal-assisted therapy. They have an adopt-a-plot program where families or organizations can grow a vegetable garden for the season, and create opportunities to build life skills, for instance through the Co-Care Farmers program, in which young adults contribute to the work of the farm and develop tangible skills that foster responsibility and independence. Fiddlehead is a registered non-profit, and charges for their services, but is open to doing what needs to be done so that finances are not a barrier for participants. Much of the therapeutic work they do is funded through the government's passport program, or through programs like "special services at home" for children with special needs, which allows families to be reimbursed for the cost of therapy. As a result, their funding is a mixture of government grants, fee for service, and "creative negotiation" (Mathers, personal communication).

The natural environment plays a key role in all that they do at Fiddlehead Care Farm. Breanne said that "so much of this is just about getting kids back out to nature ... more and more the research is showing especially for kids, that exposure to nature and those great nature experiences in early childhood can help in almost every domain of development." Breanne sees the farm as a unique environment with fewer boundaries and restrictions than children typically experience in the city. The landscape at Fiddlehead is designed to provide opportunities to explore safely so that children can have more "free rein" than they might be used to; this experience is particularly important for children with special needs, whose lives can be highly controlled and programmed: "So many kids are not allowed to do those things like climb trees or just have that real free play to learn their own strengths and abilities, and especially kids with special needs are often even more programmed and watched over than the average child. Unlike conventional therapeutic settings, nature also offers a "sensory experience" that benefits young people with special needs. Breanne reflected that many of their participants have "sensory needs" and that "nature is the ultimate sensory experience."

Breanne and Stephanie see nature as something that "grounds everybody" and is "the root of all of us" (Deaken, personal communication). Their goals are to help people learn to connect with nature while at the same time acting as guides in the process. They believe that nature has inherent benefits for mental and physical health, and so their programs incorporate

> that focus on getting back to nature, period. But the benefit of it being a care farm is that you have experienced individuals who can help facilitate that experience ... There's just something about having someone else walk with you on that journey. And realizing that we're teaching kids how to play, but we have to teach their parents how to play too, because a lot of parents in our generation or a little bit older were in that generation that didn't learn. (Mathers, personal communication)

Breanne said, for instance, that a lot of people

> don't know how to interact with nature, or they're so obsessed with washing their hands that they would never stick their hands in dirt, or they're worried because their feet get dirty. So it's getting everyone back to that. We often run family events, and we include families in the therapy in some way because we're also modelling to them. We're hoping that this is the beginning of a connection to nature and that they'll be able to incorporate it into their day-to day-life."

One way they approach building this connection to nature is by using the resources on the farm to teach children where their food comes from. For instance, when interacting with the chickens, they will encourage children to look for an egg. When a child finds a warm one, it "is like a treasure, and they take it home and they're more likely to eat it" (Mathers, personal communication). The other animals at Fiddlehead are also highly valued by young people, especially children who have experienced trauma or who are on the autism spectrum. Luna the pig, for instance, has helped children to open up about their feelings and experiences. Stephanie and Breanne have found that children will often talk to Luna about what's going on in their lives, even when they are reluctant to talk to a human about it. They have also used caring for Luna to teach children about hygiene practices and about the need to look after oneself and others. Breanne might ask a child what

Luna needs to be happy and healthy, and together they will discuss things like love and food and water and brushing, drawing connections between the care needs of the animal and one's own and other people's need for care. Luna has also helped children to begin to interact socially. Breanne described how they had

> a little girl, three years old, with autism, who was non-verbal. At the beginning she was in a stroller, wasn't interacting with anyone, she had never done any sort of social interaction or initiating activities. So we just had her sitting in front of Luna's pen and hanging out, and then she got out of the stroller and got a little closer. I offered, "Let's go in there, go inside her pen and then if she does want to interact she can." Well, next thing we know she's picked up some balls, and she's initiating throwing balls at Luna, and she's approximating words. We don't know what she's saying, but although her parents had heard her babble, she had never actually directed it at anyone before. Here she was not only trying to interact, but she was actually talking to the piggy.

While most of Fiddlehead's clients are children, youth, and their families, Fiddlehead has hosted people of all ages, from six-month-old babies to Alzheimer's patients in their nineties. Breanne said that spending time on the farm can benefit older people who may not be interested in conventional day activities, discussing the experience of a man with Alzheimer's who had recently visited the farm:

> For a gentleman like that, a courtyard [in his retirement home] is not the same. He used to farm 200 acres at one point and he started talking about all the different crops he grew ... It's those sensory things that sometimes really evoke those memories, and he was just so happy. Like he said, it's sometimes hard to get him out of his room. You could tell, he was a farm man, he worked hard, and he didn't want to get out to do beanbag toss or something. To him, he was just like, "why am I doing this?"

Stephanie and Breanne also rent the farm to other therapists who see the benefit of working in nature. One occupational therapist, for instance, found that nature can inspire people to push their limits and learn in a way they might otherwise resist. Breanne said that the occupational therapist used blackberry picking to encourage a client to strengthen her pincer grasp:

> She had been working for almost two years on a variety of fine motor stuff with one client, and she saw more improvement in her pincer grasp in one

session here than in the whole time they had been working in the office. It was because all she had to work on [in the office] were things like beads, whereas when this girl saw the blackberries, she was like, "I want to eat that!" Intrinsic motivation to want to take that off and eat it, and to put some in a bag to bring home to her family. It's incredible what kids will do to get to the places they want to. And I think maybe underneath, that girl could see the functional value of that, where she might be like, "how often am I going to be picking up beads?" Especially with a child who was very concrete. She had a variety of special needs and she was very concrete, so she probably was like, "I don't see the benefit of this," whereas she tasted the benefit of the blackberries!

6.6 Landscapes and Hand Work

In addition to improving the mental and physical health of participants and building community inclusion, care farms can make a meaningful contribution to actively developing biodiversity and ecological inclusion (van Elsen, personal communication; van Elsen, Günther, and Pedroli 2006). Thomas van Elsen's work has demonstrated the value of bringing more hand work back to agricultural systems. He noted that "the integration of people with special needs allows for activities related to caring for the landscape or development of the landscape and biodiversity" (personal communication). Van Elsen thinks about care farming as a form of "agri-culture" in which "landscapes are created through hand work and represent important cultural spaces while at the same time promoting health and biodiversity." Care farming practices make hand work more readily available within rural landscapes. Hand work allows for the continuation of traditional farming techniques that tend to be more self-sustaining because they make full use of materials found in the immediate environment. For instance, using the branches of shrubs to feed animals over the winter takes time and is not generally done anymore on industrial farms, but plays an important role in maintaining historical landscapes. However, the aim of care farming is not to return to the practices of former times, but to move forward together into a future that takes into account the value of nature as well as the value of caring for people with special needs in order to facilitate both social inclusion and ecological inclusion (van Elsen, personal communication).

In our interview, Thomas reflected on a visit he made to a Camphill Farm in the United Kingdom that changed the way he thought about the ecological value of care farming:

> About thirty years ago I did a farm visit at the Scottish-English border and there was a Camphill Farm that integrates people with mental disabilities,

it's a kind of living and working community. And the farmland of this farm, the landscape looked totally different than the surrounding landscape. For example, there were many walls built out of stones because it was a landscape rich with stony pastures and the stones were collected and used to build walls. All these walls in the surrounding landscape were destroyed because they weren't used anymore, electro-sensors were used and so on, and so the whole farmland looked totally different because they really cared for the historical landscape elements and also planted new hedgerows. The farmer who was asked then by the group of visitors why it is like that, he said, "We can do this because we have more helping hands."

Having more "helping hands" on the farm allows care farmers to use agricultural techniques that do not depend on industrial farming methods or chemical fertilizers. For this reason, care farms can lower the ecological footprint of agriculture using approaches that have local cultural meaning. Wouter Joop explains:

Ninety-nine per cent of the ecological value or the biodiversity in the Netherlands has a relation with human influence. So many places that people consider as valuable landscapes or worthwhile keeping is not something that you leave to the wild, but is a result of human interaction. In the past, this was on a small scale, all done by hand, it was a local cycle, and many of the interesting landscapes which people like to be in during their holidays just disappear because the way of life or the way of farming that created it is not viable or profitable anymore. So there's a big loss of landscape, and you just need people to work it. In terms of landscape conservation or biodiversity, there's really a relation between human interaction like we do it [on the care farm] and the quality of the landscape. (personal communication)

When I spoke with Jan Hassink, he also discussed the extent to which care farming can produce ecological benefits. Because care farms integrate multiple participants, "they have a lot of labour on the farm, so they have more time to take care of the landscape and to, let's say, regenerate the hedges on the farm, or to pay attention to biodiversity, to introduce new, traditional species."

The care farming model also encourages the use of organic growing methods. Since people are working in such close proximity to the soil and to animals, and because the goal is to protect and nurture their health, chemical inputs are undesirable and are limited or non-existent (van Elsen, personal communication). Instead of using pesticides and herbicides, for instance, care farmers can control insects and weeds by hand. By providing salutogenic opportunities – the chance "to experience the seasons in the landscape or on the farm and to be in contact with the plants and animals and the soil" (van Elsen, personal communication) – care farming generates outcomes for human and planetary health that are only beginning to be realized.

6.7 Care Farming on a Finite Planet

In my interview with Marjolein Elings, I asked her whether she thought care farming would be a viable model in a world facing significant economic contraction and resource limits. She reflected that care farming could deliver multiple benefits in such a context, such as strengthening preventative health and building inclusive communities that value the skills, strengths, and contributions of people experiencing disabilities and mental illnesses. Asked the same question, Breanne Mathers reflected that although care farming may not be carbon intensive,

> taking care of the land and animals at Fiddlehead is a life-long commitment of the Deaken family that requires much experience. We truly believe that it is necessary to have a farmer involved in the care farming process to ensure its credibility and the safety of the animals and clients. This expertise is essential and requires a significant commitment of time and energy on the part of care farmers.

Care farming requires expertise and experience to do it right, as well as a long-term commitment to the farm and its participants. This commitment is at the heart of the model's ability to generate meaningful outcomes for participants. It is also what makes it a promising prefigurative practice for a more place-bound future in which greater ecological constraints exert pressures on communities and ecosystems to meet more of their basic needs for food, health, and care using locally available resources (see chapter 8).

The stories shared in this chapter illustrate the extent to which care farming could contribute to human and planetary health during the transition towards more sustainable health systems. The care farms profiled above support participants to build strong, often long-lasting relationships grounded in mutual respect and support. Care farms provide a diverse and engaging environment, a place that feels like "real life" (de Kanter, personal communication) where participants can spend their days building tangible skills and competences while contributing to the essential productive activities of a working farm. Outcomes associated with the model include increased physical and mental health as well as greater social connectedness for vulnerable populations such as people experiencing long-term disabilities, mental illnesses, addictions, behavioural issues, and dementia (Elings 2012, 2020; Marjolein Elings, personal communication). In some circumstances, care farming can even enable people who have been excluded from the labour market to earn a modest living or to meet some of their basic needs by producing their own food on a hyper-local scale (Elings, personal communication). Insights from my conversations with Thomas van Elsen, Wouter Joop, and Jan Hassink further reveal how care farming could become part of a regenerative economy, contributing to ecological restoration and the maintenance or development of culturally valuable landscapes.

PART 2

A Political Economy for Health

Part 2 makes the case that over long time horizons, growth economics is incompatible with planetary health. It considers the wicked dilemmas that arise as societies transition away from growth as an organizing principle and presents a set of ideas and practices that could uphold positive human and planetary health outcomes in a post-growth political economy.

Chapter 7, "Political-Economic Transformation for Health," aims to disentangle the relationship between economic growth and health to understand whether desirable health outcomes can be expected to be maintained in a world experiencing prolonged economic contraction. It discusses how a shrinking economy could affect the welfare state, suggesting that declining government capacity to invest in health care requires rethinking state approaches to policy making, corporate regulation, and the social economy. Presenting evidence from relevant examples such as Cuba's "special period," the chapter argues that health is not fundamentally dependent upon growth and that a degrowth society could be more healthful for people and the planet. This transition, however, cannot be taken for granted and will not proceed without significant challenges. Realizing the potential health benefits of downscaling economic activity will depend, for instance, on our capacity to embrace a more place-bound existence while maintaining sufficient global connectedness.

Chapter 8, "Relocalization for Human and Planetary Health," considers how the return to more place-bound ways of life could affect sustainability and health. Relocalization has been at the heart of green visions of a sustainable future for decades, but the potential trade-offs of relocalization (for instance, how losses of social complexity could affect technological innovation, ways of thinking, and political life) are not always clear. This chapter aims to bring to light the wicked tensions of relocalization. It considers the potential role of technology in a relocalizing world, as well as the ways in which drivers of relocalization are destabilizing taken for granted divides in environmental politics. It argues that it makes good sense to look to the past to consider what a relocalized world could look like in the future. At the same time, it recognizes that *re*-localization will not be a straightforward process of modernization in reverse, and that new and unexpected social configurations and political alignments are already emerging.

Four ethnographic chapters follow to illustrate what a political economy for human and planetary health could look like in a sustainable future. First, chapter 9, "Community Organizing for Health and Well-Being in a Global Pandemic," considers two movements that arose in the early months of the COVID-19 pandemic in Canada, the articulation of "Principles for a Just Recovery" and mutual aid. These movements are discussed as facets of an adjacent possible political economy taking shape in response to the pressures and gaps revealed by the pandemic. It considers how both movements prioritize alternative forms of value beyond the exchange of capital and how they contributed to deepening community relationships and strengthening networks across Canada.

Chapter 10, "Health and Care in Two Ecovillages," investigates how intentional sustainable communities organize health and care activities. It begins by considering how ecovillages enable health by structuring life around principles of sustainable agriculture, healthy eating, shared work, and community care. It then explores the structures that ecovillages develop to support the health of their residents, including health/care teams that convene to provide wrap-around supports during times of illness, crisis, or end of life. Finally, it discusses the ways in which ecovillages interact with formal health care systems beyond their communities, integrating biomedical and alternative medicines to support resident health.

Chapter 11, "Community Nursing," then tells the story of Community Nurse Connection, an initiative that makes it possible for elders in small New England towns to maintain a high quality of life and remain in their homes as they age. Based on the parish nursing model, community nursing is funded by the local community. Community nurses act as care managers, supporting elders who are experiencing frailty but are not in acute distress, filling an essential gap in health care services. At the same time, they support the networks of informal caregivers who assist seniors aging at home. The model demonstrates how professional medical care can be effectively integrated into informal networks of family and friends in a cost-effective way that embodies the principles of "slow medicine."

The concluding chapter in part 2 describes the enduring effectiveness of the oldest therapeutic community in Europe. Chapter 12, "Community Care for Severe Mental Illnesses in Geel, Belgium," describes a seven-hundred-year-old family foster care model for mental health care rooted in Catholic traditions. In Geel, families make lifelong commitments to care for people with psychiatric disabilities and severe mental illnesses by taking them into their homes and integrating them into family and community life. Geel's unique approach is decidedly non-medical, though families are supported by wrap-around services that cost the state substantially less than other models of care. Family foster care in Geel reveals a set of principles that might guide the design of other community-based approaches to health in the Anthropocene, including using resources that are already available in the community and leveraging non-rational drivers of behaviour.

7 Political-Economic Transformation for Health

> Dogmatically sticking with economic tools designed in a previous age to address a different set of problems presents a very real threat to planetary health. (Evison and Bickersteth 2020, 391)

Health systems are shaped by political-economic forces. The political economy has a pervasive influence on, for instance:

- The way health care and community services are structured, funded, and delivered
- The balance between professionalized and informal care
- How health practitioners are trained
- How illnesses are diagnosed and experienced
- How prevention and treatment are approached
- How medicines are developed and administered
- The relationships between health practitioners and community members (Missoni and Morales Galindo 2020; Baer, Singer, and Susser 2013; Lock and Nguyen 2010; Zywert 2017)

For this reason, paradigmatic changes to the political economy can also be expected to cascade through health systems. Political-economic transformations affect the professional infrastructures and informal networks that support health. They fundamentally alter the ways in which health systems are conceptualized and how they operate. Ultimately, changes to the political economy can determine the capacity of health systems to enable human and planetary health (Missoni and Morales Galindo 2020; Hensher and Zywert 2020; Zywert 2017).

We currently live in a growth-centric political economy. In a growth economy, expansion is the rule. At a rate of 3 per cent growth per annum, the economy would double in size in twenty-three years and would be sixteen times larger in 2100 than it was in 2017 (Engelman, Bongaarts, and Patterson 2020). Given the already massive and unsustainable levels of resource extraction, pollution, and energy demand associated with the current economy, future growth could only be reconciled with environmental sustainability if it were possible to achieve absolute decoupling of economic growth and environmental harm at a scale sufficient to bring our societies back within planetary boundaries (see Hensher and Zywert 2020). Decoupling can be either relative (GDP grows faster than resource and energy use) or absolute (GDP grows while material and energy use and the resulting environmental impacts decrease) (Ward et al. 2016). There is ample evidence that relative decoupling is occurring around the world; in other words, our economies are becoming more resource and energy efficient over time (Ward et al. 2016; Hickel and Kallis 2019; Kovacic et al. 2018). On a global scale, however, there has been no absolute decoupling of growth from material and energy use, nor is there likely to be any in future (Ward et al. 2016; Daly 2019). Robust modelling indicates that "growth in GDP ultimately cannot plausibly be decoupled from growth in material and energy use, demonstrating categorically that GDP growth cannot be sustained indefinitely" (Ward et al. 2016, 10).

Although researchers have foreseen the "limits to growth" since the early 1970s, growth continues to be a prominent societal goal. Growth is used by governments around the world as a proxy for multiple social goods, including health and well-being (Meadows et al. 1972; Meadows, Randers, and Meadows 2004; Ward et al. 2016; Missoni and Morales Galindo 2020). Yet as ecological destabilizations become more severe and more frequent, pursuing social goods by growing the economy is not only increasingly ineffective, but poses serious risks to health. Because sufficient absolute decoupling has been shown to be impossible (Ward et al. 2016; Meadows, Randers, and Meadows 2004), any form of economic growth will continue to contribute to planetary ecological changes that undermine health across social-ecological scales (see chapters 2 and 3). Health systems that remain dependent upon growth will also be vulnerable to shocks and crises unfolding in the political economy, as we have already seen during the COVID-19 pandemic (Hensher and Zywert 2020; Kish et al. 2021). Transitioning away from a growth-centric towards a post-growth political economy is necessary if we hope to secure human and planetary health into the long-term future. But given the extent to which modern health systems have co-evolved within modern growth economies, the process of disentangling health and social welfare systems from growth will not be simple. It will require significant reorientations of worldview and practice that are likely to be experienced as difficult and demanding (Hensher and Zywert 2020; Zywert and Quilley 2017). This chapter will consider how post-growth transformations at the level of the political economy could affect health systems, focusing on the implications for high-income countries with high-overhead, materially and energetically intensive, largely professionalized health systems (see Zywert 2017). It will also raise some wicked tensions we may face along the way and set the stage to discuss several promising prefigurative practices, elements of which could become more prominent within the post-growth health systems of the future.

7.1 Disentangling Economic Growth and Health

To identify the kinds of ideas, practices, and structures that could support health within a post-growth political economy, it is important to first understand the relationships between growth and health within the existing growth economy. For instance, to what extent has economic growth itself been responsible for gains in human health and well-being within industrial capitalist economies? How might we expect human and planetary health outcomes to be affected by economic contraction? What lessons have communities around the world learned about how to navigate degrowth scenarios, and can we apply any of these insights to broader systemic transitions away from growth? Mainstream economics operates under the assumption that GDP growth and growth in human health and welfare outcomes are causally linked (Daly 2019). Most governments and the general public also think and act in ways that assume economic growth is necessary to maintain high standards of health and well-being (Büchs and Koch 2019; Fanning and O'Neill 2019). There are good reasons why these beliefs and assumptions persist within capitalist political economies. For the past two centuries of economic modernization, growth has been responsible for increasing standards of living for billions of people around the world. It has enabled improvements in housing, nutrition, medical capacities, and health infrastructures, as well as reductions in world hunger and extreme poverty (Borowy and Aillon 2017; Evison and Bickersteth 2020). Yet multiple studies spanning different nations, time periods, and economic scenarios demonstrate that the causal connections between human and planetary health, well-being, and growth are anything but straightforward (Granados and Roux 2009; Borowy 2013; Fanning and O'Neill 2019).

A study by Granados and Roux (2009), for instance, found that contrary to what one might expect, during the Great Depression in the United States population health did not fall, but rather improved.

Mortality decreased across age cohorts, genders, and racial groups, and life expectancy rose between 1930 and 1933. The periods of growth that preceded and followed the Great Depression, in contrast, were characterized by rising mortality and declining life expectancy. The authors suggest that this pattern could be attributable to increases in traffic accidents, workplace injuries, and exposure to pollution that tend to accompany phases of growth, as well as to shifts in behaviour that favour greater risk taking. Times of growth are associated with higher rates of alcohol and cigarette consumption, less sleep, and increased stress due to difficult physical labour and longer working hours. Data suggest that people are more socially isolated and receive less social support from informal networks during periods of growth. This dynamic is thought to arise because the more people are employed full time outside the home, the less time they have available to care for one another. Taken together, the social and workplace conditions that characterize periods of growth can reduce health outcomes for otherwise healthy people and exacerbate chronic illnesses, which increases mortality rates from existing conditions. In addition to the unexpectedly positive health implications of the Great Depression, there is evidence that economic recession more generally can increase life expectancy and health outcomes (Büchs and Koch 2019; Borowy and Aillon 2017). These effects could arise due to decreases in air pollution associated with less economic activity, as well as reduced traffic and workplace accidents (Granados and Ionides 2017 as cited in Büchs and Koch 2019). The positive health outcomes observed during recessions could also be partially explained by the "counter-cyclical" nature of health-care spending, wherein governments tend to invest more heavily in health services during recessions and reduce spending during times of growth (Stevens et al. 2015 as cited in Büchs and Koch 2019, 158).

Cuba's "special period" – a time of rapid economic contraction beginning in 1989 with the dissolution of the Soviet Bloc and the imposition of increasingly tight US trade embargoes – also problematizes common assumptions about the relationship between growth and health (Borowy 2013). During Cuba's special period, international trade ground to a halt and Cubans had no choice but to consume less, meet basic needs locally, exchange energy-intensive for labour-intensive production systems, and live more simply. Some immediate negative health impacts were experienced early on, such as a rise in malnutrition and vitamin deficiencies as well as a resurgence of infectious diseases due to food shortages, reduced availability of clean water, and lack of access to vaccines. However, infant and child mortality rates remained constant and even saw some improvement during the crisis, and maternal mortality and undernutrition fell quickly after the crisis peaked (Meso-Lago 2005, Nayeri and López-Pardo 2005, and UNDP 2005 as cited in Borowy 2013). Obesity rates dropped rapidly, reducing deaths from diabetes by 51 per cent and stroke by 35 per cent (Franco et al. 2007 as cited in Borowy 2013). Life expectancy climbed throughout the special period, largely due to population-level reductions in cardiovascular diseases, which are responsible for a significant proportion of deaths from non-communicable disease (PAHO 1998 as cited in Borowy 2013). Borowy (2013) concludes that "overall, it seems that several years of living a life of economic decline and changed life-styles left people similarly healthy or healthier than before" (19).

In Cuba, several cultural and political factors made it possible to achieve positive gains in health outcomes in a time of unprecedented economic decline. The Cuban government made extensive investments in health care and health system design, putting in place a high-density network of primary care doctors and nurses at the local scale and enhancing secondary care capacities. They also implemented strategic public health measures including immunization and maternal and prenatal care programs (Borowy 2013). The special period was characterized by extremely limited access to medical technologies, pharmaceuticals, and basic supplies such as soap, running water, and consistent electricity. The lack of basic amenities was offset by increasing the number of trained medical personnel. Between 1990 and 2003, the number of health care professionals in Cuba rose by 36 per cent, the number of doctors increased by 76 per cent, and the number of clinics, hospitals, medical research facilities, and elder care facilities also rose (Borowy 2013). As well, 99.8 per cent of children received early medical care, a key factor in lowering infant and child mortality (WHO 2008 as cited in Borowy 2013). A large corps of volunteers was also mobilized to support health and well-being within communities (Nayeri and López-Pardo 2005 as cited in Borowy 2013). Borowy (2013) reflects that Cuba was well positioned to realize these health system changes quickly and successfully due to:

- Pre-existing commitments to universal health care and public health
- A culturally homogenous population with a high degree of cohesion and a community-centric culture accustomed to significant social control
- Agreement that external factors had caused the crisis and that there was no way to cope but to implement profound changes

It is important to note that while Cuba's experience may appear inspiring and hopeful from the outside, strategies such as urban agriculture "were adopted not out of a sense of ecological responsibility but as a matter of despair. The Special Period was not meant to be, nor was it primarily perceived as the beginning of a new era but as a time of exceptional hardship" (Borowy 2013, 24).

These examples nonetheless demonstrate that economic growth is not necessarily an essential ingredient for health, and that economic recession and even depression *can* lead to rising health outcomes. However, recessions can also negatively affect health, especially for those directly experiencing stressful life events like loss of employment (McKee-Ryan et al. 2005 as cited in Büchs and Koch 2019). Recessions have been associated with an increase in mental health issues, smoking and alcohol consumption, and suicide, which can lower life expectancies (Gavrilova et al. 2000 and Breuer 2015 as cited in Büchs and Koch 2019). Economic contraction can also be experienced as difficult, reducing people's sense of life satisfaction. National comparisons continue to show, for instance, that countries in which individuals have higher average incomes report higher levels of subjective well-being (Fritz and Koch 2016 and Koch et al. 2017 as cited in Büchs and Koch 2019; Fanning and O'Neill 2019). Comparative data also show that when people's capacity to consume is reduced due to economic hardship, they tend to report losses in subjective well-being. This finding was documented in Greece, Syria, Egypt, Germany, the United Kingdom, Central Asia, and Eastern European nations following the economic crash of 2008 (Diener and Tay 2015, Mertens and Beblo 2016, and Habibov and Afandi 2015 as cited in Büchs and Koch 2019). The effect has been attributed to a psychological phenomenon known as "loss aversion" (Tversky and Kahneman 1991 as cited in Büchs and Koch 2019; Fanning and O'Neill 2019), whereby people find it difficult to psychologically adapt to losses, but quickly become accustomed to gains. The theory of loss aversion also helps to explain why reductions in GDP are associated with declining subjective well-being, while increases in GDP do not create significant well-being gains (Fanning 2016 as cited in Büchs and Koch 2019; Fanning and O'Neill 2019). From a psychological perspective, economic losses seem to impact people more negatively than economic growth affects them positively (Büchs and Koch 2019; Fanning and O'Neill 2019).

A study by Fanning and O'Neill (2019) reveals further paradoxes in the relationship between economic growth, ecological damage, health, and well-being. In a sample of 120 countries over a ten-year period between 2005 and 2015, they found that life expectancy increased across all countries, and that this rise in life expectancy was *not* related to consumption. In 2015, achieving life expectancies of seventy-five years required 25 per cent less income and 35 per cent less carbon to maintain than it did in 2005. And in countries that experienced stagnated or falling consumption, life expectancy remained constant. Self-reported happiness, in contrast, fell in countries where consumption did not increase or where it decreased. However, consuming more did not make people happier; in counties with rising rates of consumption, happiness did not increase. And in 2015, slightly more income and carbon were required to reach a life satisfaction of 6 out of 10 than were required to achieve the same ratings in 2005. These results largely confirm the Easterlin paradox, which proposes that although consumption and well-being appear to rise together up to a certain point, beyond that point more income and carbon expenditure do not generate greater happiness (Fanning and O'Neill 2019).

Although happiness continues to be affected by levels of consumption, especially when losses are experienced, significant relative decoupling seems to have occurred in the relationship between health (as measured by life expectancy) and growth (Fanning and O'Neill 2019). These results are both encouraging and problematic. They suggest on the one hand that transitioning to a post-growth economy with reduced consumption, contracted formal markets, and lower carbon footprints could be achieved without reductions in life expectancy. On the other hand, such a transition is not likely to occur without negatively affecting self-reported happiness (Fanning and O'Neill 2019). Still, because growth was found not to increase happiness, "the pursuit of economic growth appears to be a dangerously inefficient strategy to increase well-being in a climate-constrained world" (818). Further, expectations and values do play a role, suggesting that cultural changes could help to make happiness more resilient to economic decline. People who place less value on consumption tend to be less affected by reductions in material standards of living than those who value it more highly (Matthey 2010 as cited in Fanning and O'Neill 2019). These insights uphold the important role of strategies aimed at reducing the extent to which people in modern society rely on consumption to demonstrate social status and protect against existential fears (see Becker 1973; Dickinson 2009; Solomon, Greenberg, and Pysczcynski 2015).

The studies discussed above call into question the common assumption that growth is necessary to secure human health and well-being. But are there ways in which growth is actively *bad* for health? Degrowth scholars argue that growth in GDP without adequate redistribution to ensure equity across society has no positive effects on health (Aillon and D'Alisa 2020; CSDH 2008 as cited in Missoni and Morales Galindo 2020). Moreover, when health systems are not intentionally designed with the specific cultural and socio-economic realities of local communities in mind, "they tend to reflect instead the needs of the market" (Missoni and Morales Galindo 2020, 85). By serving capitalist markets instead of local communities, health systems within growth economies perpetuate inequities in access to care (Missoni and Morales Galindo 2020). They also become caught in cycles of buying and disposing of medical equipment and technology. Driven by the corporate profit motive, new technologies increase the resource- and energy-intensity of health systems but often contribute little to health outcomes (Missoni and Morales Galindo 2020; also see section 8.1). Economic growth can also undermine population health at the community level by weakening non-market sources of welfare (Daly 2019). The individualism associated with a growth-centric political economy has, for instance, been demonstrated to erode family and community relationships and social capital (Douthwaite 1999, Daly and Cobb 1989, and Hirsch 1976 as cited in Büchs and Koch 2019). The growth paradigm has also been associated with negative mental health outcomes due to its emphasis on competition, status, and productivity (James 2007, Kasser 2002, and Offer 2006 as cited in Büchs and Koch 2019).

Degrowth scholar and medical doctor Eduardo Missoni explains that many of the conditions that burden current health systems arise from an economic model oriented towards consumption, waste, and pollution. If you consume too much sugar and unhealthy fats, for example, you can get diabetes and several other chronic health conditions. At the same time, the industrial consumption model is polluting the food chain and the atmosphere, leading to an increase in cancers and immune system diseases, along with other conditions whose aetiologies we don't yet fully understand, but that are undoubtedly linked to changes in the environment (Missoni, personal communication). Growth economies, argue Missoni and Morales Galindo, do not promote the development of health systems *"for* health" (2020, 92). The authors argue that such a system would depart quite significantly from the kinds of hospital-based institutions that arise within growth economies. A system *for* health, they argue, would instead:

- Be designed to meet the specific needs of local people and communities
- Offer universal access with no point-of delivery costs
- Make strategic use of financial, energetic, and material resources
- Measure success by tracking health outcomes
- Emphasize primary prevention over treatment
- Be integrated with social services so that health can be addressed by improving working conditions, housing, transportation systems, physical environments, etc.

- Involve community members and all local stakeholders in the development of sustainable approaches
- Engage community networks of reciprocal care such as extended families, grassroots organizations, and self-help supports
- Integrate traditional and complementary medicine to enable local relevance and empowerment (Missoni and Morales-Galindo 2020, 92)

From a planetary health perspective, growth economies are inherently destructive and untenable over the long term (also see chapters 2 and 3). Although growth may be able to achieve some societal goals in the present, it also entrenches approaches to health and care that depend on "living beyond our environmental means" (Evison and Bickerseth 2020, 389). This dynamic has been perpetuated partly because mainstream economic models tend to ignore or significantly downplay the important role of *throughput* in the economy (Daly 2019). Throughput is the full cycle of resource and energy use required to support economic activity. This cycle includes resource extraction, the production and consumption of goods and services, and any resulting pollution (Daly 2019). As discussed above, research in ecological economics demonstrates that throughput will always be coupled to GDP (Daly 2019; Ward et al. 2016). In other words, the more that GDPs around the world increase, the more resources are being depleted and the higher the rates of pollution, waste, and environmental damage we will experience globally. Ecological economists do not argue that there is no flexibility whatsoever in the relationship between growth and throughput, but rather have found that it is not possible to completely dematerialize the economy (Daly 2019; Ward et al. 2016). While energy use per dollar has decreased in recent decades, population growth combined with increases in consumption mean that throughput continues to rise on a global scale (Engelman, Bongaarts, and Patterson 2020). Increases in absolute wealth have been found to contribute more than any other variable to absolute environmental impact (other significant variables include population and governance capacity) (Bradshaw et al. 2010 as cited in Whitmee et al. 2015). GDP, it turns out, cannot grow forever without continuing to cause environmental harm (Daly 2019; Ward et al. 2016). Those who take a thermodynamic approach to economics argue that degrowth is unavoidable; as a process involving finite quantities of materials and energy circulating in a closed system, it is impossible for the economy to grow both indefinitely and exponentially (Morgan, n.d.; Odum 2007). Socio-economic systems therefore have a biophysical basis that must be considered as we think about the viability of current economic models as well as the transition to an alternative political economy (Melgar-Melgar and Hall 2020; Meadows, Randers, and Meadows 2004).

Recognizing the biophysical basis of our economy has profound implications for the ways in which we secure social goods like health at local, national, and global scales. If we hope to maintain Holocene-like conditions into the future, it will not be possible, for instance, for low- and middle-income nations to pursue development using the same energy sources, technologies, and patterns of material consumption that were harnessed by high-income nations in the twentieth and early twenty-first centuries, as doing so would lead us to transgress too many planetary boundaries. Any gains won through such an approach to development would be overshadowed by the long-term negative implications for human well-being created by accelerating ecological destruction (Steffen and Stafford Smith 2013). Degrowth scholars argue that economic growth is socially and ecologically corrosive and that although the global south clearly requires ecological room to expand in order to meet basic needs, the poverty of the global south is not caused by the absence of growth but is an insidious unintended consequence of growth in wealthy nations (Demaria, Kallis and Bakker 2019). Some degrowth theorists propose that the term "sustainable development" is an "oxymoron"; growth cannot be sustained over the long term, but is in fact constrained by ecological limits (Missoni and Morales Galindo 2020, 84; Missoni, personal communication). Although there are parts of the world, such as the Sahel in Africa and other impoverished areas, where improving quality of life would create growth "as a consequence," growth in and of itself "should not be our objective" if our goal is to secure long-term human and planetary health (Missoni, personal communication).

When I spoke with Andy Haines, chair of the Rockefeller-Lancet Commission on Planetary Health, I asked him whether he thought it was a contradiction that a lot of planetary health work takes a very traditional sustainable development approach even though growth is one of the reasons we are increasingly surpassing planetary boundaries. He reflected that early in the movement, much of the empirical research being conducted was focused on the impacts of environmental change on vulnerable populations, which likely accounted for the movement's emphasis on sustainable development. He noted that to date, there had been

> less [work] that focuses on how we reduce the environmental footprint of high-income and emerging economies and at the same time protect health. Obviously that's a politically difficult debate to have, but it seems to me to be absolutely essential. And I think there is a danger of ignoring those key

issues about how those of us who live in high-income or emerging economies can transform our economies to make them much lower environmental footprint but at the same time healthy economies, health-promoting economies ... And that requires different types of research, really, with a particular focus on solution-focused research. (personal communication)

Haines identified the desire for "a high consumption society in which our economic model is based on high levels of throughput of raw materials and energy use" as the most profound challenge facing human health today. He emphasized:

We need to find new economic approaches, some people call them the circular economy, which really emphasize re-use, remanufacturing, recycling, and shared use ... I think one of our conclusions was that we need to explore these different economic models and their implications for human health and well-being and for the sustainability of human society. And I see that as being the major challenge. (personal communication)

Some suggest that to create a functional political economy in a constrained world, we need a wholesale reorientation of economic activity away from the goal of growth towards the goal of increasing happiness, because many of the "key determinants of happiness draw little or nothing from the planet's carrying capacity" (Helliwell and Hall 2020, 261). Repositioning the goal of the political economy around increasing happiness would also be a way of prioritizing mental and physical health, creating virtuous circles in which happiness improves health and health improves happiness. This positive feedback loop could have the knock-on effect of increasing society's capacity to cope with and mitigate ecological change (Helliwell and Hall 2020). A happiness-oriented economy could also reduce the resource intensity of health systems by centring preventative approaches and health promotion strategies that are cheaper economically and ecologically than curative health care institutions focused on treating disease (Helliwell and Hall 2020). Novel measurement frameworks like Bhutan's Gross National Happiness demonstrate how this kind of economic reorientation can be achieved in practice, as well as how it can shape a nation's approach to health (Sithey, Li, and Thow 2018). Within Bhutan's framework, health is seen to be essential to achieving happiness. Citizens report that, for instance, experiencing the effects of chronic non-communicable diseases reduces their happiness, creating policy incentives to prevent non-communicable diseases and to develop health-promoting social environments (Sithey, Li, and Thow 2018). When happiness is measured rather than growth, prevention is preferable to treatment because it helps to avoid suffering and increase well-being. When economic growth serves as a proxy for social goods, perverse incentives can lock health systems into dynamics that perpetuate ill health. For instance, in cases where prescription drugs have negative instead of positive outcomes (e.g., iatrogenic illnesses, illnesses caused by pharmaceuticals and other treatments), prescribing less medication can improve health but will lower GDP (Grady and Redberg 2010 and Pallante 2011 as cited in Borowy and Aillon 2017).

Others argue that post-growth political economies should be grounded in needs-based approaches to social good instead of subjective measures of well-being such as happiness (Büchs and Koch 2019). Aside from the psychological adaptation processes discussed above that lead people to become accustomed to gains more quickly and easily than they do to losses, there are cultural differences in the ways in which people report well-being. For instance, East Asian countries tend to display a "modesty bias," reporting lower average levels of happiness because individual "happiness" as such is not generally seen to be a central goal in life (Gough 2015 as cited in Büchs and Koch 2019, 158). These and other issues can skew results when subjective well-being data are compared across regions and time periods (Büchs and Koch 2019). Within needs-based models, basic human needs are seen as universal, while the ways in which these needs can be met can be highly local and culturally determined (Max-Neef 1991 as cited in Büchs and Koch 2019). For this reason, basic needs approaches may be more suited to the pursuit of global equity. Basic human needs are seen to be both "non-substitutable" in that all are necessary for well-being and "satiable" in the sense that a threshold can be identified beyond which further inputs of material and energetic resources will not increase the satisfaction of the need (Gough 2017 as cited in Büchs and Koch 2019). In contrast, subjective well-being is inherently insatiable, as the next technological advance or increase in consumptive capacity can indefinitely create new longings for more and better (Büchs and Koch 2019). Needs-based approaches align with eudaemonic theories that see happiness as contingent on opportunities to, for instance, exert personal autonomy, form meaningful relationships, participate in political decision making, work, and enjoy good health (Ryff and Singer 2008 as cited in Fanning and O'Neill 2019; Büchs and Koch 2019). Kate Raworth's doughnut model is an example of such a needs-based approach, envisioning a transition away from a goal of growth towards a target of living between the social foundation (basic human needs) and the ecological ceiling (planetary boundaries) (Raworth 2017; Evison and Bickersteth

2020; also see section 2.1). The goal of the doughnut, Raworth argues, is to inspire a "deep renewal of economic theory and policymaking" that replaces the focus on economic growth with an imperative to "transform economies, from local to global, so that they become regenerative and distributive by design" (Raworth 2017, E49).

7.2 The Welfare State in a Contracting Economy

Evidence shows that economic growth is not – as many within capitalist societies assume – a prerequisite for human health. Cross-country comparisons and in-depth studies of rapid economic contraction suggest that growth on its own contributes little to a country's capacity to achieve desirable health outcomes like long life or low infant mortality rates. Growth does not protect people from experiencing chronic or acute diseases, and it does not make people "happy." Moreover, economic growth can actively undermine the health of individuals, communities, and the planet that all of us call home. Despite these findings, the transition to a post-growth political economy will not be simple or proceed without distress. Even the most vocal supporters of planned degrowth policies recognize the enormity of the cultural and political work involved in the transition to a post-growth economy (see Büchs and Koch 2019; Buch Hanson 2018). Aside from the forces that may actively work to maintain the status quo (including the vested interests of some of the world's most powerful and well-resourced individuals and industries), there are wicked, systemic problems with which to contend (Zywert and Quilley 2017; Zywert 2017; Kish and Quilley 2017). These wicked problems arise from the extent to which the worldviews and institutions that co-evolved alongside market economies since the nineteenth century remain thoroughly dependent upon growth for legitimacy and funding (Quilley 2012, 2013; Büchs and Koch 2019). Growth economics is "tightly coupled," for instance, to the role of the nation state, the purpose and structure of national health and welfare systems, taxation as a primary strategy for funding public goods, progressive legal regimes, public education systems, technologies and technology development, scientific practice and science-based worldviews, the ways in which we create and shift our identities over time, and mainstream cultural beliefs and practices, especially individualism (Büchs and Koch 2019, 160; Quilley 2013; Kish and Quilley 2017).

When one considers how political-economic change could transform health systems, the welfare state is a site of significant paradox and tension. National health care systems arose as part of the institutionalization of state welfare services following the Second World War (Hanlon et al. 2011). Modern health care regimes, workplace legislation, social welfare services, and universal education were established in direct response to rapid modernization processes, which left people socially dislocated and unmoored from the support of place-based networks of family and neighbours (Polanyi 1944; Quilley 2013). As part of the creation of the welfare state, modern health care played a role in the formalization of what Polanyi called the "double movement" (1944, 79). As the expansion of market society into every domain of life disrupted the informal economies of home- and community-based care and production, nation states offered protection from the unpredictability of market forces to maintain social control and appease those left behind in the rapid transition to an unfamiliar new political economy (Polanyi 1944; Quilley 2012; Dale 2010; Zywert and Quilley 2017). An unintended consequence of the development of the welfare state was that it enabled consumer society to penetrate even further into the realms of family life and personal identity. Positioning the nation state as the central authority in control of resource redistribution rendered networks of community reciprocity no longer necessary for survival, and old obligations were relinquished (Quilley 2012; Beck and Beck-Gernsheim 2002; Zywert and Quilley 2017). Individuals were free for the first time to leave behind traditional identities, roles, and responsibilities (at least to a certain extent), becoming mobile, modern citizens and workers within capitalist nation states (Quilley 2012; Beck and Beck-Gernsheim 2002).

Economic growth was a central driver of this process, making it possible to fund welfare state services through income-dependent individual taxation and social security contributions (Büchs and Koch 2019). Most progressive political positions since the Second World War have continued to see the welfare state as the central mechanism through which to redistribute wealth and achieve social goods (Bailey 2015; Quilley 2012). Yet welfare states continue to reinforce the paradigm of economic growth in subtle and not so subtle ways. For instance, by providing income for those out of work and by offering free health care and education, they reduce social and class conflict, shore up consumption capacity, and enhance the productivity of the population, all of which contribute to growth (Büchs and Koch 2019; Gellner 1998). One of the central challenges high-income nations currently face is developing new funding and operating models for welfare states so that they can contribute to facilitating social equity and securing population-level health outcomes, and do so in environmentally sustainable ways within contracting economies (Bailey 2015). If growth and environmental sustainability are indeed incompatible (Ward et al. 2016), the transition to a post-growth scenario will place significant pressures on welfare states already attempting to cope with the fiscal challenges of demographic change as large aging populations live longer, supported by smaller populations of working-aged people (Bailey 2015). Welfare states are also already burdened by the extent to which individualism is eroding the sense of collective social responsibility that originally upheld systems of state redistribution (Beck and Beck-Gernsheim 2002).

I spoke with Dr. Daniel Bailey, author of "The Environmental Paradox of the Welfare State" (2015) about some of the wicked tensions associated with decarbonization and welfare capitalism. His article draws attention to the fact that the role of the welfare state in furthering green agendas is inherently paradoxical. The end of growth would seem to imply the need for smaller, more fiscally conservative welfare states as taxation-based state revenues decline. However, welfare states can also help societies progress towards environmental, health, and social equity goals through strategic governance and policy responses (Bailey, personal communication; Bailey 2015). Bailey argues that to address these wicked problems, there is a need for

> what you might call the social economy and a different kind of state, one which intervenes in the private sector to tackle the causes of ill health rather than being entirely defensive in its approach, which is what we have now. We pay for employment insurance and health care and income support, whereas actually we could raise the minimum wage and put caps on rent and that would certainly control housing support and income support and a few other things. And you know, facilitating the social economy could really help in the areas of social care, elder care, and childcare. (personal communication)

Although ecological limits may mean that welfare states need to reduce the amount that they dole out, Bailey suggests that there is "a limit on the amount we can roll [state services] back. We just have to reallocate responsibility to society, by which I mean the social economy, and to the private sector to make the welfare state less necessary than it currently is."

Enhancing controls on the private sector and creating a more enabling environment within which the social economy could flourish might help address some of the social and political consequences of reduced welfare state capacity that are already emerging. For instance, there is evidence that welfare state retrenchment in the poorest areas can lead to the rise of populism, and support for figures like Trump and Marine Le Pen (Halikiopoulou 2015; Bailey, personal communication). This dynamic is not well recognized within the degrowth movement (Bailey, personal communication; Quilley 2013). Bailey notes that some degrowth or post-growth advocates can be "utopian and naive in underestimating the extent to which we would need an institutional redesign of both the private and the public sectors in such a context" (personal communication). For instance, shifting to a preventative approach to health care can be more or less radical. At its most conservative end, it could come down to "challenging the twin burdens of overwork and underwork." By implementing policies and programs to address this single social determinant of health, governments could "do an awful lot, not only for physical health, but mental health, which isn't really taken very seriously right now in this country." More radical and comprehensive approaches would go further to meaningfully tackle inequity. Bailey explains:

> We don't really know what the welfare state beyond growth would look like, and the welfare of a lot of the very poorest people in our society is predicated upon growth. That's not to say they benefit from economic growth – they don't. Their wages don't tend to go up even if economic growth is 3 per cent or 4 per cent a year, their wages tend to stagnate, but they do certainly suffer when there is no growth, when we have a financial crash.

The transition away from economic growth, no matter how necessary, is likely to spark political tensions and could have wide-ranging unintended consequences for human and planetary health.

> We're seeing now in a way what happens when we don't have growth. There's an awful lot of communities already, the very poorest communities in the rustbelt of America or northern England who are voting for Brexit, voting for Trump, they're lining up behind these sort of anti-establishment figures that are not really anti-establishment at all. These are communities that have lived without growth for a long, long time. They haven't been included in the economic recovery, so called, since 2009. And they are pissed off. In that context it's so hard to see how a government could do anything about economic growth without provoking these tensions further, without making life worse for these people. And actually the democratic repercussions of that is that they're going to vote for even nastier far-right figures who are less likely to do anything about the environmental crisis at all. So it's a hell of a bind we find ourselves in. I almost think that we can't have any transition toward environmental sustainability unless we have a more inclusive economy, and that's just not where we are right now. We're trapped in growing inequality.

Asked what it would take to escape from this trap, Bailey reflected that it would likely "involve a massive program of decommodification of the labour market" to protect people from economic forces like low pay, unemployment, and "the volatility that will occur in the economy as a result of both climate change and the transition to environmental sustainability. Greater institutional forms of protection than they've probably ever experienced ... And that is utterly unforeseeable right now."

As my conversation with Daniel Bailey illustrates, welfare states in post-growth political economies will need to rethink the balance between preventative and proactive policymaking to address the social determinants of health while increasing corporate regulation and creating an enabling environment in which the social economy can thrive. Such an approach could, again paradoxically, begin to repair some of the place-based networks of mutual obligation that lost their power during modernization processes, re-entrenching more ecologically and socially sustainable ways of living (see Zywert and Quilley 2017). Unsurprisingly, however, this could create its own set of wicked tensions that will be considered in chapter 8.

7.3 Downscaling Economic Activities

If shoring up growth economies is no longer compatible with "living well on a finite planet" (see Zywert and Quilley 2020b), it is time to turn our energies to stewarding as healthful and equitable a transition towards a post-growth political economy as possible. Lovelock insists that at this point in the life course of our planet, the "best course of action may not be sustainable development, but a sustainable retreat" (2014, 3). A "sustainable retreat" could involve intentionally downscaling economic life in high-income countries, before contraction is forced upon us (Borowy and Aillon 2017; Missoni and Morales-Galindo 2020). Many of the academics, health practitioners, and people involved in grass-roots movements with whom I spoke as part of this research think that we are already "in the very early stages of the contraction process" (Peter Gray, personal communication). A smaller economy is inherently an economy that is less complex (Morgan, n.d.). The process of economic decomplexification will reduce the scale of some sectors while making other business activities, even ones that are quite lucrative within a growth economy, obsolete (Morgan, n.d.). Economic decomplexification has profound implications for hospital-based, technologically intensive, specialist-oriented, curative biomedical health systems. Given the high throughput associated with health systems in growth economies, what would a sustainable retreat really mean for health systems in high-income nations?

For one, we might expect some of the most expensive, highly technological medical interventions to become less available in a degrowth society. As epidemiologist Donald Spady and I discussed, the infrastructures associated with health systems will be affected by declining resource and energy availability, as will all other societal infrastructures. Health systems may "have to work out how they're going to meet the needs of society in a context where their own infrastructure is failing as well" (Spady, personal communication). But will this necessarily be bad for health? Many working at the crossroads of degrowth theory and health insist that a contracting economy can preserve the health and well-being gains won through the course of capitalist modernization, while also making life easier and better in multiple ways, especially for those who suffer most from the inequities perpetuated within capitalist economies (see Borrowy and Aillon 2017; D'Alisa, Demaria, and Kallis 2015; Aillon and D'Alisa 2020; Missoni and Morales Galindo 2020; Büchs and Koch 2019). Degrowth as a concept has even been described as the "equitable downscaling of production and consumption that increases human wellbeing and enhances ecological conditions at the local and global level, in the short and long term" (Schneider et al. 2010, 511, as cited in Büchs and Koch 2019). Within a degrowth political economy, there is the potential to reposition health and well-being as the central aim and purpose of the economy (Borowy and Aillon 2017).

The data on global health spending clearly demonstrates that aspirational population-level health outcomes can be achieved at a much lower price tag than they are currently. The WHO, for instance, has found that similar life expectancies can be obtained for investments of $4k per capita as opposed to the $10k per capita spent in many high-income nations. The WHO also reports that 20–40 per cent of health-related expenses do not contribute much to health outcomes (WHO 2014 as cited in Borowy and Aillon 2017). High life expectancies are mostly a factor of modest investments in population-level health infrastructures, vaccination programs, and education (Büchs and Koch 2019). In addition, the 2012 Global Energy Assessment concluded that "if policies to meet targets for energy use, climate change, air quality and health were made together rather than separately, 40% of total costs could be *saved*" (WHO 2019a, emphasis in original). So while austerity measures are usually implemented in ways that gut health systems and reduce their capacity, there is scope to reimagine health care delivery models and otherwise reinvent health systems to achieve positive population-level health outcomes for a much lower price (Borowy and Aillon 2017). This could involve, for instance, a transition towards more social approaches to health that promote healthy behaviours, emphasize primary care, and seek to meet local, contextual needs arising within specific communities (Borowy and Aillon 2017; Missoni and Morales Galindo 2020).

Yet to a certain extent, it remains difficult to anticipate the full impact of downscaling economic activity on health and well-being. Although many of the studies discussed above suggest that economic growth can certainly be disentangled from health, "degrowth" as such has never been purposefully undertaken at a national, let alone a global, scale. And, as degrowth scholars emphasize, degrowth is not the same as recession or depression and may not generate the same results (Büchs and Koch 2019; D'Alisa, Demaria, and Kallis 2015). Ultimately, any transformation away from a growth-centric political economy entails parallel transformations of culture, governance, social institutions, and provisioning systems for health and welfare (Büchs and Koch 2019). These paradigmatic changes call into question the entire "logic" of growth that is embedded within our social-ecological system and within our "minds, bodies, and identities" (Büchs and Koch 2019, 160). Political-economic changes of this magnitude have certainly happened in the past (for instance, in the transition to modernity) and are likely to occur again in future. However, they are unlikely to proceed in linear or rational ways (Kish et al. 2021).

So far, the degrowth movement, while presenting a strong vision of a well-being-centric economy, has struggled to make systemic change. Degrowth approaches have gained some traction at the local level but encounter significant resistance at higher scales (Buch-Hansen 2018). This result is largely because the degrowth paradigm lacks popular appeal. In the absence of public support or even "passive consent" of the general population, it is exceedingly unlikely that degrowth will be formally institutionalized, at least not any time soon (Buch-Hansen 2018, 161). And people who have experienced losses during economic crises can become *more* averse to perspectives like degrowth that advocate for voluntary reductions of material well-being (Matthey 2010 as cited in Borowy 2013). While degrowth offers tangible solutions to crises like rising inequality and environmental destruction that are associated with capitalism, degrowth policies are not likely to be adopted democratically (Buch-Hansen 2018). Widespread resistance, lack of understanding, and the resilience of the growth paradigm could mean that high-income nations will only shift towards a degrowth or postgrowth policy space if it is imposed by external crises (Borowy 2013). Although such crises are becoming more apparent within growth-centric economies, "the vast majority of people find it almost impossible to conceive of a world without capitalism" (Buch-Hansen 2018, 161). Any meaningful transition away from a life of easy and cheap consumption will be perceived as undesirable and indeed profoundly threatening to many who have grown up not only with expectations related to expanding material consumption, but with values that make them feel as though any reduction in their consumptive capacity must represent a personal failing (Buch-Hansen 2018; Solomon, Greenberg, and Pyszczynski 2015).

Missoni admits that degrowth remains a "niche" or "marginal way of thinking" (personal communication). But he insists that part of its value, and what is needed, is enabling people to see "concrete examples of how we can modify lifestyles" to live with sufficiency as a core value. Embracing sufficiency is about reimagining what we need to be healthy and re-examining our societal and individual commitments to health and care (Hensher and Zywert 2020). For instance, Didi Pershouse suggests:

> As we start to understand the challenges of a failing growth economy, dwindling natural resources, supply-chain interruptions, and increasing numbers of expensive natural disasters, we might want to start looking at health care the other way around: to understand that there are limits to certain material resources but plenty of untapped skills, knowledge, caring, and other social resources that we can access. (2016, 252)

We also have an unprecedented opportunity to draw on all that we have learned over the past hundred years about what really matters when it comes to living healthy lives to make strategic investments to achieve impact for human and planetary health. Epidemiologist Hank Weiss, for instance, notes that we know enough about diet, exercise, and things like reducing exposure to environmental toxins that most people could conceivably live into their seventies and eighties even in a context of economic decline and encroaching material and energetic limits (personal communication). Colin Butler similarly explains: "I think we actually know a great deal about how to get really good health for a large number of people with really good diet, exercise, social connections, contact with nature – there's a whole lot of things and they don't actually require a lot of money" (personal communication).

There is also a sense in which economic decomplexification could be good for us mentally, though the transition period may be difficult. Peter Gray, a family physician, reflects:

> I like to think that if our society decomplexifies itself, which it's going to have to do, then mental health would improve. Because the largest single part of my workload as a physician is low-level mental health problems. Anxiety, depression, stress. And I simply can't believe that as a species we evolved to be like that. I'm sure that the amount of depression and anxiety

I'm seeing must have environmental causes, it must be coming from the society that people find themselves in. I don't think enough attention is paid to that. The problem is of course, if we're going through a very messy transition period, that itself is going to cause a lot of stress. (personal communication)

The negative psychological impacts of downscaling economic activities could potentially be mitigated to the extent that societies could ensure that everyone's basic needs are met in times of economic upheaval, an achievement that is plausible, even if it is not currently occurring (e.g., see Raworth 2017; O'Neill et al. 2018). Dr. Jane Myat notes that in health care in particular, there is a huge amount of waste and ineffective, expensive ways of working that could be rethought not only to reduce the resources consumed by health systems but to improve patient care and well-being. She says, "I think I know now – really know from the lived experience of our projects – that you need a little bit of money for some things, but you don't need a lot" (personal communication). Perhaps more important than money at this stage in the transition towards a viable post-growth economy is, as Missoni implies above, our capacity to model, experiment with, and share new approaches that can show people how things could be done differently, before the harder constraints of forced degrowth take hold.[1] It would seem that the issue is not that we do not know what to do, but that we do not know how to shift conditions within social-ecological systems so that they can create space for promising initiatives to take on more foundational roles within the health systems of high-income nations.

7.4 Challenging Assumptions about Economic Growth and Health

High-income nations have pursued economic growth as a primary strategy for securing human health and well-being since industrial modernization. However, the ecologically destructive impacts of growth on planetary health make the transition to a post-growth political economy necessary and urgent. The turn away from economic growth as an organizing principle for society has profound implications for the ways in which nations structure and provision health systems. High-throughput health care may be increasingly de-emphasized, with initiatives that currently exist on the margins of formal health systems taking on greater prominence in more place-bound, ecologically constrained societies (see chapter 8). Investigations of the relationship between human health, well-being, and growth reveal important tensions that will need to be negotiated in the transition towards a post-growth political economy. It is exceptionally hopeful that health indicators like life expectancy have been decoupled from growth since the turn of the twenty-first century (Fanning and O'Neill 2019). Happiness, however, remains oversensitive to reductions in material consumption (Fanning and O'Neill 2019). This psychological dynamic will require attention and action as post-growth transitions unfold. Welfare states will also face increasing pressures and are likely to require significant transformation if they hope to continue provisioning coordinated universal health care services and social safety nets for vulnerable members of society as resources become increasingly limited. Any global transition towards a smaller economy is likely to force health systems to shed layers of complexity in order to operate within planetary boundaries or local resource constraints. There are a range of approaches that can lessen the negative implications of such economic downscaling, such as addressing the social and ecological determinants of health (see chapter 2), invigorating the social economy (see above), and pursuing strategies that secure human and planetary health at the same time as they increase community inclusion and well-being for marginalized groups (see, for instance, chapters 5 and 6). Yet the success of these strategies depends on our collective capacity to embrace more place-bound lives while maintaining a level of global connectedness that is sufficient to allow people around the world to address common challenges and pursue shared goals. Finding this "sweet spot" will require high-income countries to contend with multiple wicked problems associated with relocalization, problems to which I turn next.

NOTE

1 Chapter 13 considers the role of prefigurative alternatives in social-ecological systems change in greater depth.

8 Relocalization for Human and Planetary Health

Relocalization, by which I mean a return to living more place-bound lives that can meet basic needs without exceeding the biophysical limits of local ecosystems, is at the heart of many green visions for a sustainable future (Schumacher 1973; Hopkins 2008; Chamberlin 2018). Raymond De Young, associate professor of environmental psychology and planning and editor of *The Localization Reader: Adapting to the Coming Downshift*, sees relocalization as one "plausible response" to interconnected crises including the end of economic growth, energy descent, and ecological overshoot (personal communication). Ideally, De Young says, relocalization would be a process of shifting the centre of gravity of society away from globalization and towards local systems of food production, material provisioning, and cultural meaning making. The goal is to do so strategically, while retaining some degree of regional, national, and global interconnectedness through ongoing flows of information, people, and resources (personal communication; De Young and Princen 2012). De Young sees relocalization as inevitable, at least to a certain extent, as societies are confronted with the effects of climate disruption, resource limits, and economic contraction (personal communication; De Young and Princen 2012). He explains: "I think we're going to be forced to worry about how we provision ourselves over the rest of this century. I think that once you've become convinced about energy descent and limits to growth, you realize that we really have no choice. We are going to have to accept the limits of the biophysical basis of existence."

As a result, De Young argues that it would be a "good idea to begin preparing ourselves for localization, rather than just waiting for it to happen" (personal communication). Key to such preparations is the ongoing process of conducting many small experiments and seeing how they play out (De Young 2014). Multiple community-based initiatives should be put in motion "while we still have time, while we still have social capital and financial capital and physical capital to run the experiments" (personal communication; see also De Young and Princen 2012; De Young 2014). This approach could help societies avoid what De Young calls "negative localization," or a fast and uncontrolled decline towards a "hyperlocal existence" in which we lose many of the benefits of global connectivity (De Young and Princen 2012, xxi). Framed as such, localization is not an end in itself, but a strategy for bringing human activities back within the limits of the ecosystems that support human life and well-being (De Young and Princen 2012).

This chapter will consider what relocalization might mean for human and planetary health. It will pay particular attention to the systemic dynamics that could unintentionally couple processes of economic contraction and relocalization to the loss of cherished values and capacities that currently uphold modern notions of liberty, personal autonomy, and social justice (Quilley 2013, 2020b; Kish and Quilley 2017; De Young 2014). The goal is to demonstrate that while relocalization holds significant potential to *improve* human and planetary health, it is also likely to require people in high-income countries to think differently and make very different kinds of social commitments that could very well change what we mean by health and how we structure health systems (Zywert and Quilley 2017, 2019a). Some of these commitments could resemble those of our place-bound ancestors more than they do those of contemporary urban citizens living within individualistic consumer cultures (Zywert and Quilley 2017; Quilley and Zywert 2019b). Moving away from individualism could open up space to prioritize population health or even planetary health as a key function of health systems (Quilley and Zywert 2019b). Yet as we are already seeing in the political landscape, the drivers of relocalization and associated calls to shift away from unsustainable levels of individualism and consumerism are coming from both the "left" and "right" of the political spectrum, and in many cases are entirely defying taken-for-granted political divides (Quilley 2020a, 2020b; Kish et al. 2021). Relocalization as a response to linked ecological, social, and economic crises thus suggests the emergence of a new environmental politics that can sit uneasily with mainstream sustainability agendas (Kish and Quilley 2017; Quilley 2019, 2020a). Reconciling the wicked tensions inherent in this new political space will be crucial if we hope to secure long-term human and planetary health in a way that preserves the best of modern medicine within reinvigorated, more place-bound communities while making it possible for health systems to operate within the ecological limits of a post-growth political economy.

8.1 Health, Health Systems, and Appropriate Medical Technology for a Relocalizing World

In my conversations with physicians and researchers, many said they believe that overall, relocalizing life would be likely to have a positive effect on health, especially mental health. Raymond De Young, whose work is grounded in the fields of environmental and conservation psychology, suggested that "humans evolved to be more in touch with a local place, with the biophysical reality around them." People are primed to approach life through a lens of frugality and to make choices in contexts where our actions make an "immediate difference":

> I don't think we're well adapted, well evolved to handle affluence or globalization. We can probably do it, but at some considerable psychological cost … The uncertainty, the angst, the anxiety that people feel may be a result of them having to cope with global interactions and relationships at a distance, and extremely abstract kinds of concepts, whereas we evolved to deal with more tangible things, more immediate relationships. And so in some ways I think what we're going to see if localization occurs, if energy descent and resource descent occurs, if limits to growth and climate disruption kick in, is that people are going to find themselves well suited to living locally and helping one another. (personal communication)

De Young concedes that the transition from highly globalized to much more localized societies may very well involve periods of significant stress and collective grief as people in high-income countries deal with the loss of things like cheap, fast consumption and personal mobility (personal communication; De Young, 2014). However, once we have made the shift towards a more local existence, we may find that the helplessness, anxiety, and uncertainty that characterize life in the modern globalized world recede, with positive implications for mental health and well-being:

> Our ability to cope, our ability to share, our ability to be creative, probably means people would suddenly feel like their individual choices truly matter, that they can make a genuine difference. And so the sense of agency, the sense of accomplishment, the sense that their lives actually matter may increase as life becomes more materially and energetically constrained. (personal communication)

This effect is borne out by research investigating older people's experiences of previous decades when material goods were less abundant and daily life was economically and physically more challenging. De Young describes how

> whenever we're doing interviews with older folks about what life was like years ago, they always describe it as both harder and more meaningful. Harder, more difficult, and yet more rewarding. And so, out of that comes the idea that actually, people may find the absolute necessity to be frugal as very intrinsically rewarding. It's quite the opposite of what many people assume. (personal communication)

While relocalization is likely to decrease people's opportunities for hedonic well-being, "long-term purpose and meaning in our choices and behaviours are going to be much more available" (De Young, personal communication). For example, Don Spady says that "because we won't have the ability to have as much waste and consumption as we do today, we will develop much better community resources and community entertainment and community cultures that will give people motivation and hope, and a structure to their lives" (personal communication). Research suggests that a population-level shift in the ways in which people seek out well-being could enhance mental and physical health. For instance, studies in social genomics have found that pursuing eudaemonic well-being is associated with stronger immune responses and a down-regulation of genes responsible for pro-inflammatory responses compared to pursuing hedonic well-being (Frederickson et al. 2013; also see section 2.2).

In terms of implementing experiments in relocalization, De Young argues that we might look to the past to understand what a more constrained future might be like. Relocalization could see people spending more of their day engaging with the biophysical bases of life, regardless of their other professional or family obligations. People would spend time every day growing and preparing food, providing heat for homes, and making clothing and other material goods, all activities that provide opportunities for meaning making and community contribution. Within more place-bound communities, ideally "the intent is not just to feed yourself, but to see that others are well-fed" (De Young, personal communication). Taking a "well-fed neighbour" approach could be at the centre of a community's efforts to address social issues. In communities with more local networks of dependence and obligation, it can be easier to recognize that if one's neighbours don't have enough, in either resources or well-being, it poses a risk to one's own resources and well-being. Looking after others becomes important not only intrinsically, but also from the perspective of one's own self-interest (De Young, personal communication).

> Relocalization would affect not only the rhythms of daily life and how these influence health, but also the ways in which we structure and direct resources within health systems. Don Spady explains: "Right now health is a national or international industry. We get drugs from all over the world, we get supplies from all over the world, and we don't think locally. It's Canadian health care, not Edmonton health care ... We're going to have to start to think more narrowly, because we may not have as much. We will have some communications, we will have some links, but they won't be as fluid as they are today" (personal communication).

As Spady describes, economic downscaling is likely to reduce the "fluidity" of the linkages across national and geographic divides. It is unclear how much fluidity will remain in a post-growth political economy, as this will depend on the pace of economic contraction and the social and political contexts in which it occurs. But Spady concludes that although some integration is likely to endure, "I really don't see as time goes on how we're going to have all the just-in-time infrastructure and availability of drugs and chemicals and all the instruments and all the plastics and everything that is used in a hospital or a health care situation, just at the snap of a finger."

The decline of mass consumption would limit the material and technological resources available to health systems, which could have several systemic effects, including encouraging communities to turn to the untapped potential of social innovation to meet many of their needs for health and care (Zywert 2017; Zywert and Quilley 2020a; Kish et al. 2021). Strengthening social networks by spending time fostering diverse kinds of relationships within communities, for instance, would consume little in terms of material and energetic resources while providing a high return for health and well-being (Helliwell and Hall 2020). Provisioning health systems through more local supply chains and open-source production methods could also help to build resilience to shocks that affect remaining global trade, while ensuring that indispensable material goods like PPE, surgical supplies, parts to repair medical equipment, and essential drugs remain as abundantly available as possible (see Kish et al. 2021; Hensher et al. 2020).

Relocalization at the level of the political economy could also open up novel innovation space for health systems at the crossroads of historical and modern social arrangements and technologies (Zywert and Quilley 2017). For example, components of post-growth health systems may draw on past modes of resourcing to deliver equitable care to hyperlocal populations. Peter Gray, for instance, recalls:

> My father tells me before the birth of the national health service in England, that the way it was done was the doctor had an assistant, maybe a teenager, who would go round to all the families in his roster once a week and collect a pound from each of them by way of a subscription. And if they were paid up and one of them got sick, he would do a house call and he wouldn't charge at the point of service. And I think we're probably going to have to move back to something like that kind of a model. I think in the days before publicly funded health services, doctors knew that it was their duty that if a patient didn't have any money and needed medical treatment, they would do pro bono work and as long as that didn't take up more than 10 per cent of the practice and the other 90 per cent were paying patients, they could carry that. (personal communication)

Such affordable subscription/insurance models could be taken up by social enterprises for health and care in a post-growth world. They could be particularly useful for care workers supporting older people or individuals with special needs or mental illnesses, as well as non-biomedical health practitioners like massage therapists and counsellors, community herbalists, acupuncturists, and traditional healers. Other historical models along similar lines include guilds, friendly societies, and voluntary fraternities (Quilley 2012; Quilley and Zywert 2019a).

Relocalization may also inspire an unexpected (perhaps even unimaginable) bricolage of existing technologies, historical technologies, and new improvisations aimed at salvaging and repurposing components and functions in ways that shorten supply chains and build local production capacity within ecological limits (Kish 2018; Greer 2009; Carson 2010; Thomson and Jakubowski 2012). Many ecological modernists, mainstream sustainability researchers, corporate leaders, and members of the general public continue to argue that technology will eventually eliminate resource and energy constraints and enable economic growth in perpetuity (see Asafu-Adjaye et al. 2015; Dryzek 2013). The potential for absolute decoupling of growth from environmental harm has already been discussed in chapter 7. Here it will suffice to say that the transition to a post-growth political economy, if it entails a global-scale process of relocalization, could curtail certain kinds of technological innovation such as profit-motivated technological innovation that depends upon continual cycles of mass consumption and complex global supply chains. Instead, relocalization could enable other forms of continued technological advancement such as peer-to-peer innovation through distributed production technologies (Quilley, Hawreliak, and Kish 2016; Quilley 2013). The prospect of losing any technological capacity in health care may sound disastrous to those of us accustomed to the high-tech health systems of affluent nations, but the role of technology in generating positive health outcomes in high-income contexts is more ambiguous than many assume. Don Spady reflects:

> Most technology actually demands more in terms of resources than it saves. In other words, the promise is greater than the product. And it's also sexy, it's very appealing. Unfortunately, that makes people think that technology will be the answer and I strongly think that it will not be the answer. I think that we need to get back to thinking a little bit more with our heads and less with Google ... We have to get simpler rather than more advanced. I'm not the kind of person who wants to go back to the 1800s or 1900s, but in the 1800s a lot of things were done that were really very ingenious, and it worked. It was superseded because it became cheaper or easier with some energy product or machine to do it, but it doesn't mean you can't do it in another way. And I don't think that we necessarily should go back to those levels, but we shouldn't discount them out of hand and we most certainly should not lose knowledge of past technologies. We may want to go back to them and think, well how did they do that then? An awful lot of medicine is a bit like that too. We go for the newer drugs when the older drugs are really very good. The newer ones are maybe a *little* better, and of course they cost a lot more money. The drug companies push that to the doctors, and the doctors use it because it's the expectation. I think that sort of idea translates to other professions and specialties as well. What we used 30 years ago was actually pretty good, and probably a lot simpler, and close to being as effective. Maybe not quite, but close to it. (personal communication)

Research in the field of industrial ecology, which considers the material and energy flows and resulting environmental impact of production and other industrial processes, bears out Spady's insight. Higher-tech approaches like laparoscopic and robotic surgery, for example, are designed to be less invasive for patients and can result in less pain and faster recovery times than traditional surgeries. However, they use significantly more resources and produce more waste, including disposable electronics and greenhouse gases (Thiel et al. 2015). In a comparison of four different surgical techniques used to perform hysterectomies, one of the most frequent major surgeries for women in the United States, industrial ecologist Cassandra Thiel and colleagues found that robotic surgery had the highest ecological footprint across all metrics, followed by laparoscopic and then abdominal and vaginal techniques (Thiel et al. 2015). A similar trend was found in a study of cataract surgery. Phacoemulsification, a more technological approach conducted by machine, carried a significantly higher carbon cost than the older manual small-incision approach (Somner et al. 2009 as cited in Venkatesh et al. 2016). Although it is easy in high-resource settings to say that even minimal improvements in patient outcomes are worth the ecological costs of technological advancements, future resource constraints could renew the relevance of lower-intensity options. And, given the incredibly high carbon cost of surgery compared to other forms of health care and the need to expand surgical capacity throughout middle- and lower-income countries, it would be wise to begin factoring in the ecological costs of different surgical techniques sooner rather than later (see Roa et al. 2020). To offer a sense of what is at stake, one type of minimally invasive day surgery – cataract surgery – in England, was estimated to release approximately 63,000 tonnes of CO_2eq into the atmosphere in 2011 (Morris et al. 2013). At the time, the average annual carbon footprint of a UK citizen was 10 tonnes of CO_2eq, meaning that the carbon burden of all cataract surgeries conducted in England in one year was equivalent to that of *6,300 people* living in a high-income nation (Morris et al. 2013). These findings are significant considering that surgery in well-resourced settings is trending decisively away from "larger incisions and small tools held in the surgeon's hand to smaller incisions requiring more sophisticated technology" (Thiel et al. 2015, 1780).

Beyond the surgical specialties, the increased use of existing technologies in health care is a primary reason for rising costs, though little research effectively investigates whether the benefits justify the expense (Bryan, Mitton, and Donaldson 2014). A study of the English National Chlamydia Screening Programme, for instance, found through mathematical modelling that a simple partner notification approach (a social strategy) would be cheaper than expanding screening capacity (a technological approach) while generating comparable results (Turner et al. 2011 as cited in Bryan, Mitton, and Donaldson 2014). Overall, it has been estimated that 20–50 per cent of high-tech imaging in health care does not yield usable data (Rao and Levin 2012 as cited in Borowy and Aillon 2017). These findings suggest that employing high-tech approaches merely because they are available may not be the most strategic use of resources (see Bryan, Mitton, and Donaldson 2014). Degrowth scholars Missoni and Morales Galindo (2020) go so far as to argue that at this stage in the development of modern health care, incorporating more technology does *not* deliver any substantive benefits for health. They insist that because medical technology companies are fundamentally motivated to increase profit over all other considerations, they frequently introduce improvements such as a new way of turning on and off a machine that have little real value for health outcomes (Missoni and Morales Galindo 2020; Missoni, personal communication). Businesses may also incorporate "planned obsolescence" into their equipment, trapping health care facilities in rapid cycles of consumption and disposal of goods (Rosenthal 2014 as cited in Missoni and Morales Galindo 2020).

However, these considerations are not meant to suggest that technology does not have an essential role to play within post-growth health systems. Technologies like telemedicine, predictive algorithms, and smartphone-based monitoring and tracking, for instance, have the potential to revolutionize primary care (Cameron Chiarot, personal communication). By providing constant feedback that empowers people to adjust their behaviours, these accessible technologies could reduce the demand on physicians, help keep people out of hospitals, and be part of a societal shift towards greater emphasis on prevention and health promotion (Cameron Chiarot, personal communication). As Spady notes above, most of us would hope that living within ecological limits doesn't mean that we will need to return to the technologies of the 1800s. Rather, the goal in a post-growth world could be to make more strategic use of existing and new technologies that genuinely increase our capacity to prevent, diagnose, and treat disease, while more actively rejecting technologies that fuel growth without improving well-being (Missoni, personal communication). Making this shift in thought and practice would involve emphasizing *sufficiency* in our use of technology within health systems (see Hensher and Zywert 2020). But determining what "sufficiency" means at different scales is a complex process that can be difficult to negotiate across multiple stakeholder groups. Missoni reflects that on a personal level, he has been engaged in a lifelong search for "what is essential." For individuals, this search often proceeds as a personal struggle against a pervasive system aimed at making us "consume more and more and consequently produce more waste in order to promote production and economic growth" (personal communication). Yet what is sufficient may not even be agreed upon by all the members of a single household, let alone within a primary care practice, hospital, or entire national health care sector. As a result, finding an agreed-upon understanding of sufficiency is not only a societal problem, but an issue that we need to engage with at the level of families and local communities (personal communication).

Dr. Steven Aung, a traditional Chinese medical doctor in Edmonton, Alberta, whose career has been dedicated to bringing together traditional

Chinese and Western medical systems, says that it is useful to think about technology in medicine like a seesaw on a playground. If technology is too dominant, something is lost. However, rejecting technology altogether would be just as profound a loss. Dr. Aung suggests that seeking balance between technology and human connection is part of a broader project of rebalancing scientific and artistic or aesthetic approaches to healing:

> We need to train our next generation not only telling them that science is the best thing, because science is not the only thing. We should also be artistic in healing. In the olden days when [traditional Chinese] physicians touched your hand, they could tell which organ was having trouble. Those sorts of skills no longer exist, they exist only in history. We should study science, do scientific theory, and at the same time we should not lose our skills ... I would like to see balance. If you don't balance, then you stop being healthy. If my blood pressure is very high, that's not good, I'm going to get a stroke. Or if my blood pressure is so low that I keep fainting on the ground, that is also not good. So what is good? Having normal blood pressure. The next generation should also be aware of the many resources provided by Mother Nature. Only through balance of science, technology, the artistry of healing, and Mother Nature, can the next generation create a self-healing paradise. This is our human responsibility to make this a reality. (personal communication)

In addition to seeking greater balance between the technological and aesthetic aspects of medicine, Dr. James Truong maintains it is essential to ensure that medical professionals in high-income countries retain the knowledge of how to provide basic medical care without the bells and whistles of high-tech medicine (personal communication). Truong, a medical doctor practising in a small community in northern Ontario, notes that unexpected events like natural disasters can instantly make technological solutions obsolete in the short term, while resource and energy constraints are likely to make them less available over the long term. Truong and I spoke shortly after Hurricane Harvey swept through Houston in 2017. He sees these kinds of natural disasters – crises that are only becoming more frequent and severe due to climate change – as important learning experiences for doctors about the realities of working with limited access to technology:

> It's all fine and good to say that we can discover cancers using MRI's, but you know what? Every MRI in Houston just shorted out ... Right now, they're better off paying attention to Third World techniques of applying medicine rather than First World ones. All the MRI scanners and all the chief surgeons aside, they can't do their work.

In the search for strategies that could make it possible to maintain the most impactful modern health care technologies in a more localized, ecologically constrained world, we can draw on insights from the "appropriate technology" movement inspired by Schumacher, Gandhi, Illich, and radical place-based innovations like China's "barefoot doctors" (Shumacher 1973; Illich 1973; CHF-BRI 1983; Hazeltine and Bull 2003; Zhang, Kleinman, and Tu 2011). An appropriate technology is a technology that suits the needs, means, and capacities of the people who will use it (Fleming, n.d.). The concept arose as a critique of twentieth-century international development approaches that imposed high-tech solutions in resource-constrained, low-income settings that did not have the infrastructures, wealth, or skilled labour needed to maintain them over time (Schumacher 1973; Fleming, n.d.; Zywert and Quilley 2020c). Grass-roots movements and limits-to-growth theorists have since seen appropriate technology as a cornerstone of diverse visions for an "alternative modernity," a modern life for a much lower economic and ecological cost (Zywert and Quilley 2020c, 9). It is important to note that even the early theorists on this topic recognized that the kinds of appropriate technologies that could become foundational within an alternative, place-bound, and post-growth modernity are much more likely to arise where resources are already limited as opposed to where high-throughput approaches are still the norm (Zywert and Quilley 2020c). Today, thousands of health care facilities in low- and middle-income countries lack basic water, sanitation, energy, and waste management systems, making it exceedingly difficult for them to provide hygienic environments or to deliver even routine procedures (WHO 2019a). In eleven Sub-Saharan African countries, for example, 25 per cent of health care centres do not have access to electricity (WHO 2019a). In a study of 125 low- and middle-income countries, 43 per cent of health care facilities did not have hand-washing stations, 26 per cent did not have access to clean water, and 21 per cent did not have adequate sanitation (WHO 2019a). In health care facilities like these, developing energy-efficient medical devices and processes is an urgent priority (WHO 2019a) and "frugal innovations" frequently arise to meet local needs (Tran and Ravaud 2016, 1).

Frugal innovations developed in low-income, resource-limited contexts fall into several categories (Tran and Ravaud 2016). "Lean tools and techniques" are simplified versions of existing technologies from high-income settings, such as ECG or CPAP machines designed to be mobile, long lasting, and easy to repair (Tran and Ravaud 2016, 1). The WHO keeps a compendium of such technologies that is updated regularly and that includes products like a low-cost, portable anaesthesia machine, disinfecting equipment, mobile phone platforms for health care, and a "virtual midwife" (WHO 2018b). "Opportunistic solutions" use technologies like smartphones that are readily available to improve long-standing problems like treatment adherence (Tran and Ravaud 2016, 1). The use of 3D printed prosthetics is an opportunistic solution because the technology could be made available at a relatively low cost to non-specialists. "Contextualized adaptations" leverage available materials or techniques for new purposes (Tran and Ravaud 2016, 2), for instance, building incubators out of motorcycle parts to ensure that local people have the skills and materials needed to maintain the machines (Johnson 2010). "Local bottom-up innovations" are unique, often simple but ingenious strategies that serve local needs in highly constrained contexts (Tran and Ravaud 2016, 2). An example would be Kangaroo Care, the practice of carrying preterm infants skin-to-skin in the absence of more advanced neonatal care (2). Appropriate technologies for post-growth health systems would likely consist of all these categories of frugal innovation, many of them filtering back to high-resource areas after having been developed in low-resource contexts (see Tran and Ravaud 2016).

8.2 Wicked Problems of Relocalization and the Destabilization of Environmental Politics

A number of drivers currently exerting pressure on the political economy make the prospect of a relocalized future that is at once communitarian, green, high-tech, equitable, and healthful more possible than ever. Such an alternative modernity was first envisioned in the 1930s by Lewis Mumford, who described a "neotechnic" society grounded in a "decentralised, autonomous, and clean regime of high-tech but community-based production" (Quilley 2020a, n.p.). Table 8.1 presents some of the contradictory ways in which diverse drivers could potentially influence the characteristics of an alternative modern society that could remain within planetary boundaries while also enabling human health and well-being. However, the transition towards such a future is by no means guaranteed, as these drivers are highly ambiguous and often contradictory in their effects, creating opportunities for health at the same time as they erect new barriers (Quilley 2020a; Kish et al. 2021). At the very least, realizing the health benefits of economic contraction and relocalization will require actors across the breadth of society – entrepreneurs, non-profit staff and leaders, educators, health professionals, parents, farmers, caregivers, green activists, and politicians, to name a few – to confront paradoxical challenges, embrace

Table 8.1. Potential characteristics of an alternative modernity arising from key social-ecological drivers

Drivers	Societal domain	Potential characteristics of a livelihood-based, post-growth alternative modernity
• Limits to growth • The climate crisis and other ecological crises • Distributed production technologies • Disenchantment and the need for meaning • Economic crises • Social and political implications of inequity • Left/right political realignments	Global economy	Reduced global trade, focused on raw materials; more limited trade in commercial goods and food; local production where feasible
	Nation state	Greater regulatory powers related to global economy and corporations; less regulatory power related to communities and households
	Welfare state	Smaller welfare state with lower cost, stripped-down safety net; window of opportunity for universal basic income
	Community-level governance	Greater powers of self-governance for regions, communities, and households
	Compensating survival units	Re-emergence of extended families as sources of care and security; religious or community forms of association; guilds, friendly societies, voluntary networks as primary sources of physical and economic security
	Technology and production	Distributed production through disruptive maker technologies (see Kish 2018)
	Health systems	Universal health care focused on primary care, public health, health promotion and a smaller secondary/tertiary care sector; cross-sector focus on addressing the social determinants of health; less professionalized approaches to care in which elders, children, and people experiencing mental illnesses, chronic health conditions, and disabilities are supported within extended families and community mutual aid networks
	I/we balance	Shift away from individualism towards more embedded, place-bound social roles and identities; less individualistic, more communitarian forms of civil society

Source: Adapted from Table 1 in Quilley and Zywert 2019a.

unexpected opportunities, and engage in at times unsettling conversations and collaborations (Quilley 2020a, 2020b; Kish et al. 2021). Those inclined to notice and reflect upon how the systems around them are shifting may find it necessary to entirely reimagine *why* they do what they do in their lives and work and *how* to approach their goals given the changing landscape. But regardless of whether one is engaged in an intentional process of alignment with emerging system dynamics, all will be swept along in the current of a political-economic transition that is bringing to light many wicked questions. These paradoxical problems centre around the following domains (see Quilley 2013, 2017; Kish and Quilley 2017; Zywert and Quilley 2020b):

1. *Technology:* What level of technological complexity and innovation is possible within an economy that is small enough to maintain the integrity of the biosphere?
2. *Social Complexity:*
    a. What level of social complexity (e.g., in our institutions, division of labour) is possible within a small-enough economy?
    b. Will this level of social complexity be sufficient to maintain cherished modern values like equity, individual rights, and cosmopolitanism, or will place-bound life result in the formation of new value configurations that depart substantively from those that currently uphold modern liberal democracies?
3. *Politics:*
    a. How might actors across the political spectrum respond to, support, oppose, benefit from, or stand to lose in the transition towards a more relocalized world?
    b. What political realignments may occur as various drivers of relocalization intersect, and how might the left and right achieve cross-cutting goals, by working either together or in parallel with one another?

This section will elaborate on how and why these wicked dilemmas need to be considered by those concerned about the long-term prospects for human and planetary health in a post-growth world.

The wicked questions outlined above hinge on the relationship between different forms of complexity within social-ecological systems. Modern globalized societies are characterized by an exceptionally high degree of social and technological complexity. As a result, they exist "far from thermodynamic equilibrium," which means that they require continual, massive throughputs of energy to maintain (Homer-Dixon 2006, 40). From a thermodynamic perspective, high levels of complexity tend to become more ecologically, economically, and energetically expensive over time. As societies experience a declining energy return on investment, they become vulnerable to shocks that threaten to push the entire system back towards equilibrium (in other words, towards reduced complexity) (Tainter 1988, 2014; Homer-Dixon 2006; Morgan 2016). A largely relocalized, post-growth political economy would be comparatively less complex and would require lower levels of energy to maintain. It would therefore be more ecologically and economically sustainable, and potentially less vulnerable to external shocks. However, a decomplexified economy would also inevitably entail parallel reductions in social complexity, which would in turn influence the kinds of ideas, values, and even personality structures that would be able to take root (Quilley 2013; Odum 2007; Elias 2011). This dynamic is rarely accounted for by environmentalists, many of whom do not recognize the extent to which their values are premised upon high levels of resource and energy consumption within growth-centric economies (Kish 2018). What they fail to see is that not only products but also social processes, institutions, and ideas have what Odum refers to as a "transformity cost" or "emergy" (embodied energy) (2007, 69). Cosmopolitanism, for example – the idea that all people are part of a single global community – arose in a systemic context in which people and things could circulate rapidly within a highly globalized, networked world with access to cheap and abundant energy (Quilley 2013; Kish and Quilley 2017). It is difficult to know whether cosmopolitan values can survive a long-term economic contraction involving less mobility, shorter supply chains, comparatively less global connectivity, and reduced reliance on fossil fuels.

Individualism as a value and way of being in the world also shows signs of being sensitive to levels of social complexity. It is very likely, given the historical development of individualism, that an economy with a lower throughput of energy and materials would as a result generate less individuated personality structures, or a population-level relinquishment of the strong, separate self-sense that co-evolved alongside the development of the nation state and capitalist modernity (Quilley 2020b; Elias 2011). Polanyi argues that when the fictitious commodities of land (nature) and labour (people) were incorporated into formal markets, the result "was to annihilate all organic forms of existence and to replace them by a different type of organization, an atomistic and individualistic one" (1944, 171). Marx, Weber, Durkheim, Foucault, and Elias also argue that individualism can only emerge within highly complex societies with extended socialization processes (Beck and Beck-Gernsheim 2002). If individualism is a function of market penetration

Table 8.2. Contrasts between ideal-type low-throughput and high-throughput societies

Domain	Low-throughput societies	High-throughput societies
Values	Communitarian	Cosmopolitan
Identity	Ascription	Achievement
Social role	Status	Contract
Worldview	Enchanted	Disenchanted
Economy	Embedded	Disembedded
Survival unit	Family/clan	Citizen
Social arrangements	*Gemeinschaft* (community)	*Gesellschaft* (society)
Sense of self	"We"	"I"

Note: This table is not meant to suggest that all low-throughput or all high-throughput societies follow this exact pattern in every domain, but to identify broad binaries within ideal-type societies in order to consider the implications of reduced social complexity.

Source: Adapted from Zywert and Quilley 2017.

into all spheres of life and if it depends on high levels of social complexity to arise and be maintained, it follows that economic contraction could cause the pendulum to swing in the other direction (Zywert and Quilley 2017). Taken to its logical conclusion, the implication is that a post-growth society could resemble the past in many essential ways (Zywert and Quilley 2017; Quilley 2013). For example, in a more relocalized future, we might expect to see a shift towards more communitarian social arrangements and personality structures, a greater embeddedness of economics within place-bound communities, and perhaps also the reemergence of more ascriptive identities and/or a renewed societal commitment to traditional family structures (Quilley 2013; Elias 2011; Zywert and Quilley 2017). Contrasts between ideal-type low-throughput (e.g., premodern, traditional) and high-throughput (e.g., modern industrial capitalist) societies are summarized in table 8.2.

The potential for the future to resemble the past is recognized by environmentalists like Shaun Chamberlin, activist and co-founder of the transition movement, who reminds us that "most of human history had been bred, fed and watered by another sort of economy, but the market has replaced, as far as possible, the social capital of reciprocal obligation, loyalties, authority structures, culture and traditions with exchange, price and the impersonal principles of economics … The New Economy that we need is, in many ways, the Old Economy" (2018, n.p.). The trouble with this prospect is that modern people may not be prepared for what the Old

Economy could mean in terms of their personal liberty and autonomy, or their perceptions of the value of different kinds of social diversity (cultural, sexual, religious, etc.) (see Kish and Quilley 2017). More place-bound futures, even the most healthful ones we can imagine, would undoubtedly entail at least some degree of restriction in the choices available to people (e.g., choice of profession, social roles within extended family groups, choice of material goods available). Many social theorists argue that the endless choices on offer within modern societies create psychological insecurities, anxiety, and other mental health issues (see Bauman 2012; Beck and Beck-Gernsheim 2002). However, any restriction in the choices available to those of us alive today is very likely to be perceived as a regression, an imposition on autonomy, and a curtailment of liberties (Quilley 2013, 2017; Kish and Quilley 2017; Zywert and Quilley 2017). And, due to the psychological phenomenon of "loss aversion" (see Fanning and O'Neill 2019), such restrictions could result in widespread declines in happiness and subjective well-being, at least during the period of transition.

Another essential dynamic to contend with is the extent to which the well-worn tracks of inequity that pervade modern societies will be exacerbated by economic contraction, and whether relocalization can become a force for greater equity or will be a driver of resurgent ethnocentrism, racism, ablism, and patriarchy. The COVID-19 pandemic shined a light on the health effects of inequity among, for instance, racialized communities, people with low incomes, and women (Brown et al. 2020; Gravlee 2020; Maroko, Nash, and Pavilonis 2020; Kish et al. 2021). In the case of gender equity during the pandemic, there has been a disproportionate effect on women's participation in the market economy. As women continue to perform the majority of care work and tend to earn less income than their male partners, many have had to leave the workforce to care for children and elders, or else perform untenable juggling acts to meet all of their obligations while being entirely cut off from the in-person support of their families and communities (Kish et al. 2021; Canadian Women's Foundation 2022; Sultana and Ravanera 2020). As the pandemic has made clear, we might expect any sustained contraction of the economy to equate to at least some degree of retreat of women from the workforce, but this does not *necessarily* need to result in a cultural abandonment of the gender equity gains experienced in the course of modernization (Kish 2018). Avoiding such a slide, however, would require the emergence of new cultural meaning frameworks that attribute value to unpaid care work and, more generally, to the economic work of sustaining a home and a community (Kish 2018; Kish et al. 2021). Stewarding relocalization processes so that they support equity is certainly possible, but positive outcomes are by no means inevitable. Further, we might anticipate new cultural understandings of equity in a relocalizing world to be shaped by many of the context-specific characteristics of relocalizing communities, such as their unique governance systems, production processes, available housing options, and dominant technologies. Understandings of equity would also be shaped by contextual factors like the availability of energy, the size and capacity of the welfare state, the ongoing commitment (or lack of commitment) of local community actors to equity in various forms, and pre-existing levels of social, racial, economic, and other forms of diversity within communities.

One path by which relocalization could become a force for greater equity would be if it enabled a proliferation of context-specific, hyper-local, whole-person-centred approaches to health and care within a reinvigorated domain of livelihood activities. Livelihood, as understood by Polanyi, is the economic space of the household, the informal/DIY economy, and reciprocal networks of mutual support (Polanyi 1944; Quilley and Zywert 2019a, 2019b). Some contemporary livelihood-based approaches to health and care echo historical modes of social organization. Mutual aid networks, community nursing, and home-based care for people with mental illness (all discussed in subsequent chapters), for instance, display elements of historical livelihood-based support structures for vulnerable community members and could become the cornerstones of post-growth, equitable health systems. But to activate this potential, it will be essential to expand the role of the livelihood economy throughout society while at the same time balancing this re-emerging domain with policies and practices that ensure limited welfare state resources are directed more strategically to support those who need them most and corporate regulations that uphold sustainability and decent work across market-based industries (see Quilley and Zywert 2019a). Livelihood is the often-overlooked key to realizing visions of a low-throughput modernity with computers, the Internet, modern dentistry, and antibiotics (Quilley and Zywert 2019a). Recentring livelihood within a post-growth political economy would shift the balance of the standard modern "survival unit" away from the state and market and towards the domain of family, community, and place (Quilley and Zywert 2019a). Table 8.1 above presents a high-level summary of what such a livelihood-based, post-growth political economy might look like across various societal domains.

While healthful, relocalized, post-growth futures could conceivably be grounded in a radical expansion of livelihood-based economic activity, disruptive appropriate technologies and production processes will be necessary to ensure that an alternative modernity operating within ecological limits can furnish modern conveniences like effective painkillers, dentistry, antibiotics, vaccines, personal computers, and digital devices. Environmentalists, degrowth theorists, and other green activists often underestimate the extent to which technological complexity and innovation could be curtailed across all sectors in a post-growth future (Quilley 2013). We cannot assume that reserving technological capacities for certain parts of the economy like the innovation of vaccines or smartphones will be possible, let alone straightforward as societies shed layers of social complexity (Quilley 2013, 2017; Dartnell 2014). The rapid development of the COVID-19 vaccine, for example, was possible due to pre-existing highly complex and interconnected networks of multinational biotech companies, universities, research laboratories, government and private funders, production facilities, and global transportation systems, each of which has its own highly specialized, trained workforce as well as highly regulated procedures and quality standards (see, for instance, Lurie et al. 2020). On a smaller scale, one dose of the antibiotic penicillin requires processing two thousand litres of "mould juice." Even though the raw materials (penicillium fungi) could be cultivated locally without much trouble, producing antibiotics at a population level would always depend upon a fairly high degree of social and technological complexity (Dartnell 2014, 163). As noted in table 8.1, the emergence of disruptive technologies that enable peer-to-peer, distributed production (things like 3D printing, accessible renewable energy technologies, and open-source knowledge and innovation processes) is one of the primary reasons that a high-tech alternative modernity is now conceivable (Quilley, Hawreliak, and Kish 2016; Kish 2018; Quilley 2020a). While these approaches would not entirely eliminate the dependence of more place-bound communities on global supply chains for raw materials, they do have the potential to

1. return ownership over the production of essential goods to communities, reducing reliance on corporations and governments;
2. incentivize cooperation and pro-social approaches to provisioning material and public goods;
3. strip out layers of complexity that cause significant ecological damage within industrial capitalist regimes; and
4. create new opportunities for creativity, meaning, and life satisfaction that could reduce psychological dependence on mass consumption, easing the transition to a post-growth political economy (Quilley, Hawreliak, and Kish 2016; Hensher et al. 2020).

Yet the opportunities afforded by such disruptive technologies are also implicated in the destabilization of taken-for-granted left-right political alignments, which in turn has repercussions for long-term sustainability (Quilley 2020a). Aspects of the "fourth Industrial Revolution" (Schwab 2017) naturally appeal to greens for their capacity to make more comfortable, connected, high-tech localism possible. But by enabling the proliferation of small and medium enterprises operating with greater freedom from state regulation, peer-to-peer and distributive production approaches may also appeal to conservatives and working-class rural people interested in renationalizing production, increasing national self-sufficiency, and returning jobs to their communities (Quilley 2020a). A livelihood-based economy energized by fourth–Industrial Revolution technologies may also find support among libertarians because it would open up space for more informal production activities to occur within households and small businesses that would be less amenable to state oversight and less curtailed by corporate monopolies (Quilley 2020a).

The return of status and pride to local cultural landscapes, farming traditions, and ecosystems could also appeal to both greens and conservatives, with greens grounded in the values of social equity and environmental justice and conservatives grounded in the values of national heritage and religion (Quilley 2020a, 2020b; Kish et al. 2021). Figure 8.1 highlights some of the common ground for sustainability that could be realized at the local, national, and global scales regardless of whether green or conservative relocalization projects take root. The figure aims to demonstrate that despite pursuing relocalization for different reasons and despite employing very different mechanisms (e.g., Green New Deal, nationalism), either pathway could potentially enhance long-term sustainability by reinvigorating place-based economic activity, reducing the ecological footprint of high-income nations, and increasing the resilience of global social-ecological systems. However, the route we take towards localization could generate divergent outcomes when it comes to equity. And, as Quilley explains, achieving common goals will require communication, engagement, and negotiation among all involved:

> Greens will leap at the chance of low-overhead localist production systems with orders of magnitude reductions in the ecological footprint. But politically, this means working with conservatives and nationalists to advance an agenda that is post-liberal and anti-globalization. If greens are involved, there is certainly a better chance that the "imagined community" animating this movement is civic, rather than ethnic or religious, in character. Conservatives will likewise have to accept that political success may well involve a much greater emphasis on drivers such as climate change and ecological integrity – in relation to which they have accrued a significant residue of ideological scepticism. (2020a, n.p.)

Figure 8.1. Drivers of relocalization in social and economic systems

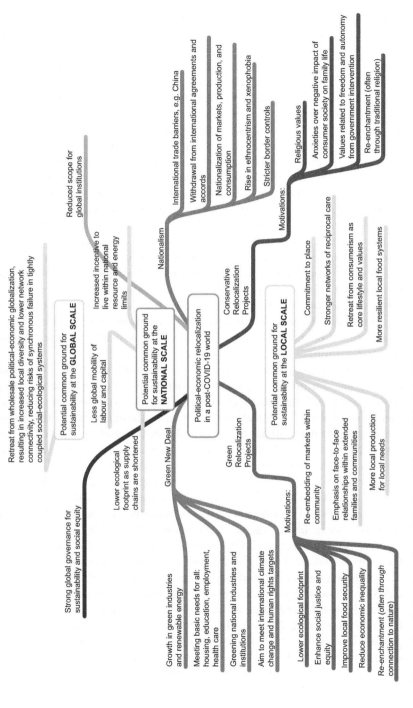

Source: Created by the author, originally published in Kish et al. 2021.

The regenerative farming or soil health movement (see chapter 4) provides a clear illustration of this dynamic in the realm of planetary health. In the United States, many of the movement's leaders are Christian farmers motivated by "the profound spiritual belief that their job is to restore God's creation" (Didi Pershouse, personal communication). Gabe Brown and his son Paul, for instance, who own and operate Brown's Ranch in North Dakota and are sought-after educators and consultants on regenerative agriculture, say on their website: "We believe that faith, family and working with the natural resources that God has provided allows us a meaningful life. We enjoy using these resources to regenerate landscapes for a sustainable future" (www.brownsranch.us). Didi Pershouse has noticed that these kinds of motivations are prevalent among regenerative farmers, but that they tend to be ignored by the progressive left because they are correlated with conservativism and in some cases may coexist with beliefs that the left does not support, like the right to life or objections to gender fluidity. Having seen them in action, Didi describes the Christian values of regenerative farmers as significant "motivational factors that could move a lot of people" to adopt practices that have positive outcomes for sustainability and health. However, she notes that on the whole, these values "haven't been tapped into yet" on a societal scale (personal communication).

Conservative regenerative farmers are often reticent to be identified as "organic" farmers because of the sociopolitical connotations of the word "organic," the economic costs of certification, and the governmental control that certification entails, even though many of them use approaches that go above and beyond what would be needed to be certified organic (Pershouse, personal communication). And, for some conservative farmers, narratives around restoring God's creation gain more traction than narratives about drawing down carbon, but ultimately have the same effect for planetary health. Didi describes how many midwestern and conservative regenerative farmers "feel at odds with the typical 'liberal agenda'" (Pershouse 2020b, 279). Instead, many midwestern famers are initially drawn to regenerative methods because they can no longer make a living using industrial farming techniques. The costs of genetically modified seeds, chemical fertilizers and pesticides, and machinery are increasingly too much for farmers to shoulder, and at the same time these industrial methods are rapidly degrading the land, rendering it less productive and less profitable (Pershouse, personal communication; Pershouse 2016). As the land loses its productive capacity, socially conservative farmers find themselves in a situation where they are relying on government subsidies, which makes them uncomfortable because it goes against their values. Switching to a regenerative farming approach is often a better way to make a living. It also aligns with their conservative values of pulling themselves up by their bootstraps, looking after their family, taking care of the land around them, and contributing positively to their community. Farmers may also take pride in and see a spiritual value in keeping the land the way it was (a mainstay of small-c conservatives) and not allowing it to degrade further under their tenure (Pershouse, personal communication). For instance, what Didi calls the "Soil Health Principles," Gabe Brown calls "Nature's Way" (Pershouse 2017a, 52), intimating a return to the way things are supposed to be. It is notable that despite these deep political divides, liberal and conservative farmers are often able to develop meaningful working relationships when they are focused on landscape-level health (see Pershouse 2017b).

Didi explains that while mainstream climate movements often focus on needing to buy something or stop doing something to live more sustainably (see chapter 4), engaging in the regenerative farming movement is an opportunity to do simple things that create tangible and immediate benefits that people can feel good about in their daily lives (Pershouse, personal communication; Pershouse 2020b). They may notice that the land on their farm absorbs water in new ways or that birds return to their property. In regenerative agriculture, "you're involved in actually creating the infrastructure of life." Didi recounts how Gabe Brown told her that on his farm he's not "'growing crops,'" he's 'growing microbes.' He says, 'I used to wake up every morning and think what can I kill, and now I wake up and I think what can I support, or what can I help live?'" (Pershouse, personal communication). This is a powerful shift in perspective, and as the regenerative farming movement demonstrates, such important realignments of the ways in which people interact with the planet, with other species, and with one another not only emerge on the left, but can arise at different places along the political spectrum, or confound binary political divides altogether.

8.3 Facing the Wicked Tensions of Relocalization

As a "plausible response" (Raymond De Young, personal communication) to intersecting economic and ecological problems, relocalization could support planetary health by enabling human societies to live within ecological limits. It is also possible that human health could improve in a relocalized future, with a simpler life reducing anxiety and stress and creating more opportunities to make tangible contributions to community (Schumacher 1973; Hopkins 2008; De Young and Princen

2012). And adopting some degree of relocalization before it is forced upon us could help high-income countries to better manage the inherent risks of a highly interconnected world that is becoming increasingly vulnerable to cascading global crises (Homer-Dixon 2020; De Young 2014; also see chapter 13). But becoming more place-bound and losing layers of economic complexity has implications for the technological and social complexity of human societies, which in turn shapes the kinds of ideas, practices, and approaches that are able to take root. This raises wicked questions that can never be definitively solved, but only negotiated and worked through on an ongoing basis by diverse actors across social-ecological systems.

As we consider more place-bound futures, it makes sense to look to past modes of political-economic and social organization for hints as to the kinds of structures, practices, and worldviews that might find themselves suited to a life lived within ecological limits. However, it is also important to recognize that *re*-localization will not be a straightforward process of modernization in reverse. First, there is no historical precedent for experiencing economic contraction on a global scale. Second, in the language of complexity science, we are starting from dramatically different "initial conditions" that will influence the course and character of future system configurations. While it is impossible to know what, exactly, these systems might look like, it is worth thinking through the wicked dilemmas that are coming to light as various drivers of relocalization converge. In particular, it is worth turning our attention towards the ways in which political alignments are shifting. As we do so, it is important not to discount the very real potential that positive outcomes for planetary and human health could arise as a result of the activities, choices, and commitments of actors whose politics and values may not align with mainstream sustainability discourses. The following four chapters will consider a range of approaches, practices, and ideas that could enable health systems within relocalized, post-growth political economies to advance both human and planetary health.

9 Community Organizing for Health and Well-Being in a Global Pandemic

Pandemics have long been a force for societal disruption and transformation (Geobey and McGowan 2019). As a shock to the system, the COVID-19 pandemic and the measures taken by governments and communities to slow the spread of the virus could contribute to pushing the political economy – and society more broadly – into an alternative state, one that could be more – or less – conducive to planetary health than capitalist modernity (Homer-Dixon 2020; Hancock 2020b; Kish et al. 2021). Shocks to the system offer glimpses of alternative political economies that exist within what complexity scientists call the "adjacent possible," a space of promise and potential at the margins of the current regime (Kauffman 1999). In the same way that community organizing and government responses during the Second World War laid the groundwork for the Keynesian welfare state to be established post-war, the community-organizing and government approaches to recovery that gain momentum during the COVID-19 pandemic could prepare the ground for a care-based, ecologically regenerative future (Hancock 2020b; Kish et al. 2021). Yet it is also very possible that the system could tip in the other direction, and that policy choices aimed at patching up the cracked foundation of the status quo and temporarily restarting the engines of growth economies could further entrench inequities, deepen political divides, and stymie any hope to step back from ecological overshoot.

As ecological public health expert Trevor Hancock (2020b) reflected in the early weeks of the pandemic, "we stand yet again at a crossroads of history. Too often in my lifetime we have stood at this same crossroads, and each time we have taken the wrong path. Will we get it right this time?" From the outset, Hancock saw the pandemic as opening a window of opportunity for a new political economy of care and well-being to gain ground: "It may be that with this combination of reduced consumption and reduced environmental harm, coupled with societal commitment to ensuring the meeting of basic needs for all, we will find ourselves unintentionally creating the wellbeing economy we need in the 21st century" (n.p.). António Guterres (2020), UN secretary general, similarly urged people to think of the pandemic as a chance to make long-overdue changes to the ways in which the political economy operates: "Now is the time to redouble our efforts to build more inclusive and sustainable economies and societies that are more resilient in the face of pandemics, climate change and other global challenges. The recovery must lead to a different economy" (n.p.).

Drawing on complexity theories and systems science, Thomas Homer-Dixon (2020) also argued that one of the upsides of the pandemic is the extent to which it is "revealing critical vulnerabilities in humanity's planet-spanning economic, social and technological systems." The pandemic, he insisted, is a global "'tipping event,' in which multiple social systems flip simultaneously to a distinctly new state." Exacerbating the likelihood of such state changes are the interconnectivity of our current globalized world as well as its uniformity (see chapter 13). Homer Dixon concluded:

> Today's emerging pandemic could help catalyze an urgently needed tipping event in humanity's collective moral values, priorities and sense of self and community. It could remind us of our common fate on a small, crowded planet with dwindling resources and fraying natural systems ... I place my own hope in the possibility of virtuous cascades of such positive, "normative" change. The coronavirus emergency is already causing terrible human suffering. But it's also just possible that it could put us, together, on a far better path into the future. (n.p.)

This chapter will not take a strong stance on whether the transformative possibilities alluded to by Hancock, Guterres, and Homer-Dixon at the onset of the pandemic can be realized or not. It will not be easy to use the systemic window afforded by the COVID-19 pandemic effectively, and as transformations set in motion by past pandemics have taught us, much is likely to be out of our control as individuals and organizations, with patterns only becoming apparent after the fact (Geobey and McGowan 2019). The goal of this chapter is rather to explore aspects of the adjacent possible political economy revealed by the pandemic and to consider how it might be able to secure long-term human and planetary health. To do so, I will focus on the work of a community organizer in Toronto, Canada, who supported the development of the Canadian "Principles for a Just Recovery" (www.justrecoveryforall.ca)

as well as a national network of mutual aid groups in the early months of the pandemic.

9.1 Principles for a Just Recovery

Julia Steinberger argues that lessons in "pandenomics: the economics we need in a time of pandemic" can aid in navigating the broader transition towards a more equitable and ecologically resilient political economy (2020, n.p.). She insists that amid a global pandemic compounded by a climate crisis, "the struggle for a new economics is without hyperbole the fight of our lives, for our lives" (n.p.). This insight is embodied in a range of plans that seek to leverage COVID-19 economic recovery policies to support the transition towards a more healthful, equitable, and ecologically sustainable political economy (see Stratford and O'Neill 2020; Edger et al. 2020; Corkal, Gass, and Cosbey 2020; Büchs et al. 2020; "Open Letter," n.d.; Open Letter Working Group, n.d.). Amara Possian, a campaigner and convenor who has spent a decade running national and international campaigns to build a more just and caring society, helped to bring together one such movement in Canada. In April 2020 as part of her role at 350.org, Amara began organizing with groups including the Climate Action Network and the Canadian Association of Physicians for the Environment to articulate a set of shared principles for a just recovery from COVID-19.[1] The Canadian principles were inspired by 350.org's US principles for a just recovery, which aimed to create a framework and call to action for a "united global response" to COVID-19 to secure a healthier, more equitable, ecologically resilient future ("Open Letter," n.d.; "US Just Recovery Principles," n.d.). The goal of the principles in Canada was to demonstrate that a critical mass of civil society organizations is united in pushing for "intersectional policy solutions to steer us out of crisis" (Possian, personal communication). Amara explained:

> Fundamentally we were trying to build relationships and trust across organizations that understood that we're already facing intersecting economic and social and ecological crises so the response to COVID was an opportunity to build back better. To build those relationships and to demonstrate to governments that a broad range of groups are pushing for us to come out of this crisis better and stronger through investments that prioritize the health of people and the planet. (personal communication)

The work progressed quickly, as the organizers knew that the window of influence to affect government relief efforts was limited.

They had heard that there was a group of Liberal ministers in cabinet who wanted to proceed with corporate bailouts, while another group wanted to put money in people's pockets, to invest in green infrastructure, and to use this moment to accelerate the transition away from fossil fuels. There were also a lot of people in the middle who were undecided about which course of action to support. In this political context, the principles were intended to "show the people in the middle that this was a path that they could take and a path on which they would be supported" (Possian, personal communication). Close to two hundred organizations signed in support of the principles before their launch on 25 May 2020; by the time I spoke with Amara in July 2020, nearly five hundred organizations had formally endorsed the principles.

In addition to influencing cabinet ministers to support more equitable, green approaches to COVID-19 recovery, the process of developing the "Principles for a Just Recovery" also had organic effects across a network of civil society organizations in Canada. Amara described how "from a relationship-building perspective, I think it has had a very big impact. There are definitely organizations that are supporting each other's efforts and amplifying each other's work that previously didn't talk to each other" (personal communication). Because meaningful political-economic change is not only about government policy but also about the ideas and approaches that take root at the community level, stronger relationships and connections among civil society organizations could continue to generate positive outcomes into the future (also see section 14.3). When people know and trust one another, it is easier to work towards shared goals (brown 2017), and it is clear that not only government but also national non-profits, community-based organizations, grass-roots networks, and social-purpose businesses would all need to be central players in a political economy organized around health, care, and ecological regeneration (see Hough-Stewart et al. 2019). Amara reflected:

> There's polling showing that three quarters of the population doesn't think that we'll be going back to normal. This is a moment where everyone is expecting transformation. So the question is, what kind of transformation? The choices that we are making now are going to shape our society for decades. In this moment, we need a high-level declaration from as many groups as possible so we can present a united front to government, and then we need to work together to actually make things happen in many, many different ways. (personal communication)

Other coalitions and countries also developed principles intended to guide COVID-19 recovery efforts and in the process support a benevolent transition towards a more just and ecologically sustainable political economy. For instance, the degrowth movement put forward five recommendations for political-economic change:

1. put life at the centre of our economic systems;
2. radically re-evaluate how much and what work is necessary for a good life for all;
3. organize society around the provision of essential goods and services;
4. democratize society; and
5. base political and economic systems on the principle of solidarity. (Open Letter Working Group, n.d., n.p.)

The Wellbeing Economy Alliance's principles include:

1. New goals: ecologically safe and environmentally just
2. Protecting environmental standards
3. Green infrastructure and provisioning
4. Universal basic services
5. Guaranteed livelihoods
6. Fair distribution
7. Better democracy
8. Wellbeing economics organisations
9. Cooperation
10. Public control of money (Büchs et al. 2020, 5)

In the United Kingdom, there was even a COVID-19 recovery plan developed to align with Kate Raworth's doughnut economics framework, proposing a range of approaches that could enable the United Kingdom to reduce its dependence on economic growth while creating an economy that can meet basic needs without surpassing planetary boundaries. These recommendations include:

1. Safeguard basic needs
    - Introduce a Minimum Income Guarantee and better Statutory Sick Pay
    - Provide comprehensive adult social care
    - Reform energy tariffs to create a free minimum energy entitlement
    - Invest in free and affordable alternatives to private car travel

2. Empower and protect workers
   - Provide support to firms to cut hours, not jobs
   - Create well-paid secure jobs through a Green New Deal
   - Use equity-based bailouts to increase worker rights over the long term
   - Raise the minimum wage and end insecure work
   - Strengthen sectoral bargaining and democratise workplaces
3. Reduce exposure to debt crises
   - Make more extensive use of central bank financing of government deficits, to reduce the burden of public and private debt
   - Facilitate interest holidays and debt write-downs for households
   - Reduce the cost of borrowing for small and medium sized enterprises
   - Shift from debt to equity financing, and prevent the use of debt for tax avoidance
   - Use macro-prudential tools to discourage inflationary lending and reduce asset price booms and busts
4. Tackle rent extraction
   - Prevent public bailout money being captured by rentiers
   - Tax capital gains and property wealth more fairly
   - Protect tenants and reduce rent extraction in the housing market
   - Protect small and medium sized enterprises, while taxing monopolies (Stratford and O'Neill 2020, 5–6)

Each set of principles listed above articulates a political economy that is more conducive to human and planetary health than the status quo. While distinct, these principles directly acknowledge that the integrity of natural systems is a prerequisite for human well-being. They also:

- Prioritize health equity, with a goal of reducing or eliminating inequitable health outcomes rooted in the social and ecological determinants of health
- Question the value of economic activity that does not contribute to well-being or that actively undermines health
- Emphasize the need for more democratic and inclusive governance systems
- Advocate for the provision of basic human needs regardless of individual circumstances like income or immigration status

These approaches will have to contend with many of the wicked dilemmas discussed in chapters 7 and 8, especially related to the capacity of the welfare state to maintain strong social safety nets without economic growth, as well as the more long-term risk to cosmopolitan value systems posed by economic contraction. However, they articulate a compelling vision for a well-being-centric political economy and are rapidly gaining momentum. The proliferation of such principles across countries and sectors demonstrates that a growing coalition of organizations is committed to working towards these goals, not only by influencing government responses but by taking action within their own professional networks and communities. Diverse sets of principles for a just recovery from the COVID-19 pandemic shine a light on some of the characteristics of an adjacent possible political economy that could secure human and planetary health at a lower ecological cost.

9.2 Mutual Aid

The rise of mutual aid networks illuminates another facet of the adjacent possible political economy taking shape in response to the COVID-19 pandemic. Mutual aid groups are informal, often neighbourhood-level networks that offer reciprocal forms of support to community members. Operating outside of formal markets, they perform essential "economic work in producing and distributing goods and services," and often support people who experience marginalization (Mair 2020, e593). Mutual aid is in many ways a traditional, perhaps even ancient form of human social security (Chamberlin 2018). While it has continued to be part of community life even within capitalist economies, especially among Indigenous people, racialized communities, and people with disabilities, the first few weeks of the pandemic saw a rapid resurgence and mainstreaming of the approach across North America and the United Kingdom (Moscrop 2020; COVID-19 Mutual Aid UK 2020). In its many diverse forms, mutual aid could become a crucial component of post-growth economies designed to enable human well-being (Steinberger 2020). It also has positive implications for planetary health in that mutual aid networks have a minimal ecological footprint, making space for livelihood-based health and care activities to flourish in place of high-overhead, profit-driven approaches (see Quilley and Zywert 2019a). Amara Possian initiated one such hyper-local network in her neighbourhood in Toronto, and soon became involved in supporting others to establish their own "neighbourhood pods" across Canada (Possian 2020; Moscrop 2020).

On 13 March 2020 Amara dropped off a note at her neighbours' homes offering to help in "whatever way was needed" (Possian, personal communication). At the time, she felt like she wasn't particularly vulnerable to the virus, and recognized that although she didn't know her neighbours very well, many of them might need support accessing essential goods while self-isolating. She then posted the note online, which led many other people who were doing the same kind of thing to reach out to her. Together, the group decided to develop a toolkit to help others wishing to organize what they called a "neighbourhood pod," a group of five to thirty people living in close proximity who would assist each other by providing "support, connection, and solidarity" (How to Start a Neighbourhood Pod, n.d., 3). They also set up a Slack workspace where mutual aid groups across the country could coordinate their activities and share what they were learning. Over the next few months, the national network created a map to track and help people connect with local pods. The Slack workspace also became a place to share resources, troubleshoot challenges, and organize for related causes.

I asked Amara what the purpose of a neighbourhood pod was in the early stages of the COVID-19 pandemic; she explained, "I think fundamentally it's about connecting people to each other to help meet each other's needs" (personal communication). On Amara's block, neighbours tended to support each other with things like grocery runs and picking up medications, "anything that would require someone who is vulnerable to leave the house and be at greater risk." Other pods had a stronger focus on community building and established more complex infrastructures that many expect will have a life beyond the COVID crisis. I was curious to know whether Amara had intended to start a mutual aid movement when she sent the letter to her neighbours and posted it online, but she said that, sparked by the trigger events of the pandemic, she suddenly found herself in the middle of a growing movement that was rapidly gathering momentum. I asked her why she thought the pandemic provided such a strong impetus for mutual aid to re-emerge and go to scale so quickly. She suggested:

> I think it has something to do with how alienated we are from each other at a hyper-local level ... All of a sudden, everyone was told to stay in place. At least this is what happened for me. I'm a very relational person, I have lots of strong relationships of trust, and they're kind of all over the world. And the moment I was told I had to stay in place, I realized that I didn't really know the people who were geographically closest to me. I'm sure if I had tried harder as an individual, it would have made a bit of a difference,

but in big cities and under capitalism, the entire world is structured to make it difficult to connect with one another. So I think a lot of people had that experience, where they realized that they would have to depend on each other, but they didn't even know the names of the people they might need to help or who might need to help them.

The mutual aid movement had an impact beyond ensuring that neighbours were able to call on one another for help running errands and accessing basic needs. Although many leaders of local mutual aid groups were already community organizers, many others had never participated in or led any community initiatives before. They simply found that when faced with a crisis, they "wanted to help their neighbours." For these individuals, the onset of the COVID-19 pandemic was the moment when they became active and engaged in their communities and connected to others who were also active and engaged. They learned how to manage volunteers and gained community-organizing experience. Amara said that "for many of them, it was a huge capacity and leadership development opportunity." She also noted that for many people, participating in mutual aid inspired new, more inclusive ways of thinking about their community, such as "shifting from [the idea that there are] people who need help and helpers to mutual aid where everybody needs something and everyone can offer something."

In an article about Canada's "caremongering" movement published in the *Washington Post* at the end of March 2020, David Moscrop argues that we should be careful not to romanticize mutual aid, as such networks often arise where economic inequities have cut people off from access to basic needs. As a society, we should instead focus on permanently eliminating these inequities. He says that we

> can and should strive to render many functions of the caremongering movement obsolete in the future. Movements of care and solidarity ought to be built into policy and institutions to create a supporting framework for navigating life during and after crises ... The caremongering movement is an inspiring bright spot in dark times. Even brighter still would be not having to rely on mutual aid so extensively in the first place. (n.p.)

Although I share Moscrop's conviction that as a society we need to commit to ensuring that everyone has their basic needs met, I argue that it would be unwise to try to institutionalize all community-based, reciprocal support structures that are rooted in relationships of mutual obligation. In a world of declining material and energetic resources and reduced welfare state capacity (see chapters 7 and 8), the simplicity and informality of such approaches is one of their greatest strengths; mutual aid networks could easily become a vital part of ecologically and socially regenerative health systems (see Mair 2020). They could even offer livelihood opportunities to organizers, and more roles could emerge for community members to act as liaisons between informal grass-roots supports and formalized health and community services (see, e.g., Government of Ireland 2020). In this way, diverse forms of mutual aid could complement public health initiatives, support community-based approaches aimed at addressing the social and ecological determinants of health, and nurture relationships that build community resilience at the hyper-local scale.

9.3 Piecing Together a Resilient Post-Growth Political Economy

This chapter presented two stories from the early days of the COVID-19 pandemic, the development of principles to guide COVID-19 recovery in Canada, and the rise of hyper-local mutual aid groups. The "Principles for a Just Recovery" sought to articulate and institutionalize alternative forms of value – health, well-being, equity, planetary health, dignity, democracy, and community resilience – over the pursuit of profit. Mutual aid networks expanded the diversity of livelihood activities taking place to support those most vulnerable to transmission. Both efforts strengthened existing relationships and nurtured new connections at different scales; the principles at the scale of civil society organizations and mutual aid at the scale of neighbourhoods and networks of grass-roots community organizers across the country. Although we can't yet predict the long-term outcomes of the connections and capacities built through these two initiatives, both reveal facets of an emergent post-growth political economy that could be more resilient to economic, social, and ecological disruptions, as well as more conducive to human and planetary health over long time horizons.

NOTE

1 The six Principles for a Just Recovery are (https://justrecoveryforall.ca):
   1. Put people's health and well-being first. No exceptions.
   2. Strengthen the social safety net and provide relief directly to people.
   3. Prioritize the needs of workers and communities.
   4. Build resilience to prevent future crises.
   5. Build solidarity and equity across communities, generations, and borders.
   6. Uphold Indigenous rights and work in partnership with Indigenous peoples.

10 Health and Care in Two Ecovillages

Ecovillages are intentional communities organized around principles of social and ecological sustainability (Lockyer and Veteto 2013; Litfin 2014). They are often grounded in theories of bioregionalism and permaculture and aim to enable residents to lead ecologically integrated, place-based lives, meeting their subsistence needs locally with a minimal ecological impact. Ecovillages also often seek to advance social and ecological justice. They embody these ideals by organizing collective decision-making processes, cooperative or common property arrangements, labour exchange and trading systems, and (in some communities) income sharing (Lockyer and Veteto 2013). For these reasons, ecovillages are seen as important sites of prefigurative experimentation for the kinds of structures and practices that could make it easier for people in high-income, Westernized countries to adopt less individualistic, lower-consumption, ecologically regenerative lifestyles (Dawson 2013; Le Vasseur 2013). I was curious to understand more about how ecovillages approach health and care, and how these activities are integrated into their governance systems. To do so, I spoke with two members of the care team at Earthaven Ecovillage in North Carolina, as well as a long-time resident of an income-sharing ecovillage in the United States. Our conversations explored the extent to which ecovillages create conditions for healthy living, the structures they use to support those who require care in their communities, and how ecovillage residents interact with health care institutions.

10.1 Creating Conditions for Health

Although health in and of itself is not always an explicit goal of ecovillage life, ecovillage residents acknowledge that living sustainably and prioritizing "care for the earth, care for people," has direct benefits for individual and community health (da Silva 2009, 16). Arjuna da Silva, a founding member of Earthaven Ecovillage, explains:

> The whole lifestyle is self-health care. Living as close as possible to unpolluted Earth and creating a relationship with a place that is as reciprocal as possible. We're not quite capable of giving back as much as we're given in terms of opportunity to live resiliently on the Earth. Living at Earthaven influences almost everybody who lives here to follow a kind of health-oriented lifestyle. Local food, food you can trust … and learning about the long-lost advantages of plants and herbs and other resources that people have used for thousands of years to maintain well-being in their communities. (personal communication)

Monique Mazza, a naturopathic doctor and member of Earthaven's care team, adds that even experiences like not having wi-fi outside of common areas can promote health, for instance by encouraging a lifestyle of

> being in harmony with the nature of light and dark. We're using solar powered homes, so there's not a lot of usage of electricity in the evening, so it's kind of getting to bed earlier, rising earlier. We have a lot of ritual around the solstice times, so there's a lot of connection to the natural cycle. Rotating our diet according to what's growing in season and being awake and sleeping and [varying] our activities according to the season. And then there is lots of emotional support too, which is a big piece of the health of what happens here, the connection between the friends and neighbours. (personal communication)

A resident from an income-sharing ecovillage in the United States further describes how the ways in which work and life are structured within ecovillages are inherently health promoting. She reflects:

> Our bodies and our minds are most healthy when we're doing a mix, I believe, of physical and mental work, and I get to do that here … As an ecovillage we're providing a lot for ourselves. Fifty percent of our own food we're growing, we have our own dairy, we harvest and split our own wood. All of that is physical work. And we're a pretty big place, we're 450 acres, and so we're always walking around. Even if you do sedentary work, you're walking in the morning, at noon, at dinner, so there's inherently more physical activity. And definitely our bodies evolved to be physical creatures. Our underlying bodily systems work better when we have some physical activity in our lives. Our blood flow, our lymph flow, and all that side of stuff. But also, because we're providing so much of

our own food, we're eating a lot of whole food, and we're not 100 per cent organic, but we're significantly organic, so of course a healthier choice ... Even if people living here didn't do anything else to try to enhance their health, just the daily lifestyle already makes us healthier than the average Westerner, for sure. (personal communication)

Further, collectivization allows people to prioritize their well-being and reduces many of the stressors that characterize life in conventional modern society, such as the need to make rent every month and the stress that comes from being solely responsible for the economic stability of oneself and one's family:

> The sharing that we do enables us to live in a really different way. You know, sharing houses, sharing vehicles, sharing money. If we just did nothing else, if we didn't even try to be a certain way, we didn't try to be more eco, we didn't use any solar energy, or whatever, it wouldn't matter. Our ecological footprint is still so much lower than the average North American's. But even on other levels, because we share our labour, every single person doesn't have to be out there pounding the pavement to pay their personal rent. So we're able to have a more, in a way, flexible and relaxed labour system. You can do this variety of work because we are collectivized. If it's just you, it's all on your shoulders and you've just got to do it. When it's shared, there's more wiggle room, there's more flexibility, so people can make choices that are more suited to our well-being rather than the bottom dollar. (ecovillage resident, personal communication)

However, ecovillage residents recognize that their way of life can also involve trade-offs when it comes to health and well-being. In the income-sharing community, for instance, living together in homes of ten to twenty residents who share work and money can create tension and conflict: "When you have less autonomy and you're tied up with more people, there's more opportunity for people to have different opinions and for stress to happen ... It's not that we have more stress than the mainstream, it's just a different kind of stress (ecovillage resident, personal communication).

At Earthaven, Arjuna and Monique also speculate that there could be trade-offs for physical health. For instance, the limited availability of electricity in the community could mean that if older people wanted to access high-tech treatments or supports to keep them comfortable at the end of their lives, it might not be possible for them to do so while remaining in their homes. However, Arjuna notes that the values many people in the community hold may mean that they do not want such treatments at the end of their lives, though how that would play out remains to be seen. Monique also mentioned that living in community can create susceptibility to infectious diseases, with colds and flus and stomach viruses sweeping through the community at a rapid pace. Ecovillage residents may also experience more environmental stressors such as dealing with inadequate heating during the winter months or overheating due to lack of air conditioning in the summer. Despite these possibilities, Monique considers that such environmental stressors could represent positive rather than negative stress:

> We're building our immunity, and we go through it, and we support each other to share when someone's sick, so we give an alert that something might be happening. But that is one thing that maybe in an urban setting you can kind of separate and maybe take a little bit more, not precaution, but I think you're just not together so much. We have potlucks, we have coffee, we have playdates, we have a lot of time when we're together. And there's a lot of sharing of good things, and sometimes germs. That's just the way we live. I thought to myself, well, maybe living here is a little bit harder on the general body because we're dealing with weather more. All of our houses are not comfy-cozy warm. We have to deal with some stressors like cold and heat because we're not in air conditioning, and we're not in heat all the time. But I think about [environmental stressors] and then I wonder, I think it makes us more resilient in the end ... This is what we call good stress. If we're always comfortable, our system never gets a chance to work. So I flip-flop on that one, wondering if we're ageing more because we're dealing with these stressors, but then I think no, it's helping us build our stress capacity, and that's like exercising that muscle.

There may also be trade-offs in terms of the extent to which ecovillages can support people with serious ongoing mental health issues or addictions. The income-sharing community, for instance, recognizes that when people live communally in an egalitarian context, one individual can have a significant influence on the group, either positively or in more complex and challenging ways (ecovillage resident, personal communication). As a result, though the community understands that everyone at some point in their lives will experience a mental health challenge, they have a public statement on their website saying that the community is not a good fit for people with serious mental illnesses. In taking on new members, they are careful to make sure that the living situation will work for the new member as well as for the community as a whole. When potential new members are vetted, the individual or family will be invited to the farm for a three-week visit. During that time, if they do have ongoing issues they have a referral with the health team or the mental health team to check in on the status of their condition, whether it is under control and if they have a plan in place to live with their challenges. If the team feels like things are under control and it could work, they will give it a try. However, the community will generally not accept new members with active mental illnesses (ecovillage resident, personal communication).

10.2 Heath/Care Teams

Both Earthaven and the income-sharing ecovillage have organized systems to oversee health and care in their communities. At Earthaven there is a care team made up of residents that ecovillage members can engage if they need assistance solving a conflict through mediation, or if they require physical care or any other form of community support due to illness or other difficulties. Monique Mazza says that the role of the care team is:

> Always holding space for people to come to us, alert us as to what's going on, what issue has come up, and then we often form specialized teams that are individual caregivers. Some may be care team members, some not, because in some cases folks are elderly and stricken with illness and they need round-the-clock care. So the care team is like the starting place for, ok, what is this going to develop into, and how much time, how much attention does this need? We're kind of a place to vet out what the rest of the needs are, and then put a spark to the formation of whatever that individual needs. (personal communication)

The care team at Earthaven meets monthly to discuss the care that is being provided throughout the community. They then conduct a "community sweep" in which they consider each neighbourhood in turn to identify any areas where people may need support (Arjuna da Silva, personal communication). Participating in the care team fulfils residents' requirements for service to the community and is tracked as part of their labour exchange and trading system. Arjuna says that "all those kinds of caring things make the difference. It's exactly what people don't have so often, or have to work so hard to have when your friends are strewn over an urban or even sub-urban area" (personal communication).

The care team at Earthaven forms part of the broader governance structure of the ecovillage, which includes a board of directors, safety committee, currency committee, and other special committees that look after community needs. When the care team organizes the community to support one of its members, it will engage an individual's friends and neighbours to provide support where they can, occasionally enlisting the guidance of health professionals. For example, when two elderly community members became chronically ill and required twenty-four-hour care, a team was formed to make it possible for the couple to live their final days in comfort and die at home at Earthaven. To support this process, lay community members attended trainings by nurse practitioners who taught them how to provide more specialized care to the couple, one of whom eventually became paralyzed as her condition progressed. Monique describes how supporting their older neighbour at the end of her life "required folks to learn all-new things about body dynamics, and it was a really incredible learning experience, and folks who may have been a little bit shy had to be present with this woman – there was nothing to hide at that point. It was really nice to see how resilient this community is. When we need to get things done, we can (personal communication).

The income-sharing ecovillage also integrates health and care work into the organization of community life. The community has been around for fifty years and was founded on egalitarian values by social scientists focused on process, methodology, and structure. Its health team is made up of around three individuals and serves an administrative function within the broader governance of the community. It is the health team's "job to help members access and get their health care needs met through the community or through the support of other people or through themselves" (ecovillage resident, personal communication). Residents who are experiencing health-related challenges can contact the health team, which will help to coordinate care, support, or access to services. If needed, the health team then convenes a care team, a group of five or six people who will come together for a few months to support an individual through physical or mental illness or other challenges. Often the care team is made up of people who have a strong connection to the individual and who make themselves available for daily check-ins and other support as needed.

At the income-sharing ecovillage, health care is one of their top community expenses, alongside food. The community's income-sharing structure means that the close-to-ninety adults who live in the community all qualify for subsidized health care at the local hospital. They also pay into a mutual aid health care fund organized by a federation of other ecovillages that share similar egalitarian values to cover unforeseen expenses not available through Medicaid. The resident explains:

> How [the fund] operates is that every year the communities pay a certain amount of money per person per year into this fund that exists. And

that fund just grows and grows and grows and sits there until someone in one of the communities has some catastrophic health care issue, and at that point, their home community is responsible for the first $5,000 of treatment, but after that the health care fund kicks in and will cover, you know, hip replacement, cancer, heart attack, those sorts of things. So it's not insurance, technically it's a mutual aid fund based on a Mennonite model. And that's great, we are providing for our own health care into the future through this money collection. (personal communication)

When a new individual or family joins the community, the community commits to looking after their health care needs. Yet although they are assured that they will not have to pay for their health care individually, there are costs that are perceived to be reasonable and costs that would not be deemed reasonable; moreover, what is defined as a "need" is determined collectively, with the health team taking on a large role in the communal decision-making process (ecovillage resident, personal communication).

10.3 Integration with Mainstream Health Systems

As illustrated above, although ecovillages convene health or care teams that are responsible for coordinating health needs and providing community support to residents, they do not generally create self-contained, fully sustainable health systems. Instead, they remain integrated into mainstream health systems, while also providing opportunities to access holistic health practitioners who live on site as well as natural herbal medicines and other remedies produced by community members. Both ecovillages discussed here have thriving herbal medicine practices that were initiated by community residents. At Earthaven, Arjuna describes how, through trainings offered on site, people are learning to cultivate medicinal mushrooms and process them into tinctures. Three local herbalists also make other herbal medicines that they sell at rates that are much more affordable than commercial herbal products. One resident is a respected herbalist who offers courses in the community to members and guests. Through her work, many residents have completed internships in herbalism or have become her apprentices or students, raising the level of understanding of herbal medicines throughout the community. As a result, Arjuna says that "a lot of people just finally make their own medicine and they make enough to last for years, so medicine isn't something you go to the store for every month" (personal communication).

At the income-sharing ecovillage, an herbalist joined the community around thirty years ago. Over time her initiatives were recognized and valued and as a result gained community support and resources. Each year, the community looks at how much money they will have and how much labour, and divides it according to the areas of the community that will require money and work. The herbalist began in a modest fashion by growing a personal herb garden: "Over time, we gave her herb work area more and more money and more and more hours so she could do more. So it was building slowly to the point that now, she's a part of our life here, and that aspect is a part of our life" (ecovillage resident, personal communication). Today, there is a half-acre herb garden wherein the herbalist produces St. John's wort, elderberry, and echinacea tinctures, salves, and herbs for cooking. These herbal medicines grown on site have become an important part of many community members' preventative health regimens and are sometimes used in combination with allopathic medical care. The resident says she thinks about health care at her ecovillage in terms of four quadrants:

> There's on the farm and off the farm and then there's typical Western medicine and alternative therapies. So there's four different categories, and you can sort of mix and match ... If you've twisted your ankle or you need a pelvic exam or an eye exam or whatever, we go to the hospital and get subsidized mainstream health care. Whether it's maintenance or an emergency like appendicitis. We mostly don't provide Western medical care [on the farm] ... And then for more alternative health care, we do have a certain number of practitioners who live here. We have an herbalist who lives here, she makes herbs, she makes tinctures, she makes salves, she can give those to people. We have reiki practitioners who live here, we have homoeopaths who live here, we have a massage therapist, so we can provide a certain amount of that on the farm. And those people get labour credits. Again, briefly, everyone in the community works forty-two hours a week in the community. So that health care work, like giving somebody a massage, that counts for your work that week. (personal communication)

At Earthaven, Arjuna and Monique speculate that people who live in ecovillages might be more likely to try a holistic health intervention before seeking out conventional allopathic treatments, though they did not have data to support this intuition. Nonetheless, Earthaven is home to a range of health practitioners, including an acupuncturist and other body workers who regularly trade their services as part of the community's labour exchange and trading system and through informal trades between community members. They may also be paid for their services by those who can afford market rates (da Silva, personal communication). Many people at Earthaven see health care as a significant sustainability issue (da Silva 2009). Monique Mazza, for instance, notes:

> My whole motivation in coming to Earthaven is to really change the way health care is depended upon as a last resort when someone is so sick they're broken, then they need major intervention. Like the case of a diabetic who ends up on dialysis because their kidneys are so diseased. Diabetes is absolutely a lifestyle type of disorder that can be prevented and reversed, and so what I'm hoping to do, when I really dig in and get my passion flowing here, is to teach people that food is medicine, and lifestyle is medicine, movement and connection, heart connection with friends and family is medicine. And so we prevent some of these major illnesses that result in trillions of dollars in health care spending that we don't have. We look at the United States, we spend more dollars [on health care] and we're not the healthiest nation. So money doesn't equal health. What we're trying to do is be empowered to know how to take care of ourselves and be responsible for ourselves so we don't just live recklessly and then show up expecting something to fix us. That is a broken model itself. So, especially young people, adolescents, to get the message early so that they walk through life having this understanding. (personal communication)

10.4 Grounding Health and Care Work in Community

My conversations with ecovillage residents confirm key themes in the literature on health and ecovillage life, including:

- The psychological and physical benefits of living in close-knit communities that foster meaningful relationships to people and place
- The advantages of eating locally grown, nutritious, seasonal, organic foods
- The ways in which collectivized labour can reduce stress and promote well-being
- The existence of trade-offs such as the potential for interpersonal conflict (for instance, see Lockyer and Veteto 2013; Mychajluk 2020; Baker 2013)

Ecovillage structures such as health/care teams could have broader application for health and care beyond intentional communities, especially in a post-growth political economy (see Dawson 2013). The ways in which ecovillages integrate holistic health practices like herbalism into place-based community life also suggest avenues for prioritizing preventative health and incorporating herbal medicine-making into community livelihood activity. Yet as the resident at the income-sharing ecovillage correctly points out, although people in close-knit neighbourhoods, for instance, could pool resources and organize themselves in ways that mirror ecovillage approaches,

> I think the tricky part is the lastingness of it, the stickiness of it. Because of course, life is change and people move or the priority shifts or something comes up. What's different here than, say, in the mainstream, a neighbourhood or some similar thing, the bonds that are otherwise holding those people together are weaker than the bonds that are holding us together. It's like electrons or something. There's less energetic hold when things do get a little shaky, which happens in life. There's less of that holding on. The bonds are weaker, so the electrons just fly off. (personal communication)

Substantive relocalization of the political economy could facilitate the kind of "stickiness" needed to make such forms of labour and resource sharing more enduring outside of intentional communities. Or mutual aid groups such as those that gained traction during the pandemic (see chapter 9) could potentially develop into more long-lasting structures of reciprocal support over time, given favourable conditions. Although these prospects remain uncertain, my conversations with ecovillage residents suggest that intentional sustainable communities have developed effective strategies for grounding health and care work within community-based systems of shared labour and reciprocal support, while remaining integrated into mainstream health care systems to access more specialized, technical services. As such, strategies that have arisen within ecovillages could become models for post-growth community organizing around health and care.

11 Community Nursing

Community Nurse Connection (formerly the Upper Valley Community Nursing Project) aims to integrate professional nurses into existing networks of volunteer caregivers so that older community members can stay in their homes and maintain their independence as they age. Grounded in a holistic approach to nursing, the project draws its inspiration from mid-nineteenth-century parish nursing, a model in which a nurse would care for the individuals and families within a religious congregation according to their need, regardless of their ability to pay for services (Laurie Harding, personal communication; also see www.communitynurseconnection.org). Community Nurse Connection was founded by Dr. Dennis McCullough, a key figure in the slow medicine movement and author of *My Mother, Your Mother: Embracing "Slow Medicine," the Compassionate Approach to Caring for Your Aging Loved Ones*, and Laurie Harding, a registered nurse and state legislator in New Hampshire. I spoke with Laurie Harding (RN, MSN), former co-director and board member of Community Nurse Connection, as well as Sarah Jo Brown (RN retired, PhD), board member, to understand how community nursing works and what lessons it might teach us about designing sustainable health systems that can enable elders to age in place.

Laurie Harding says that before founding Community Nurse Connection, she and Dennis McCullough had noticed that

> more communities were making an effort to establish small volunteer groups that would support community residents as they aged in community. Volunteers were getting frustrated because they could only do so much without having some clinical input as to how to get someone with a new hip replacement into a car, or how to have a conversation with someone about the difference between hospice and palliative care, or respond to problems that people were having with medication reconciliation. As

a result, communities that we spoke to early on started saying, "we'd really like a nurse." Dennis and I got together with the three existing parish nurses and started to understand their role a bit better, and were able to appreciate that their role is more clinical care management, working with primary care physicians and working with some aspects of people's clinical diagnoses, but there was also a lot of work involved with supporting the caregivers. We started to work with communities that said, "well how can we get a nurse?" We recognized that communities were willing to actually hire the nurse themselves, to do some fundraising, and have the nurse be *their* community nurse.

Community Nurse Connection does not administer the work of community nurses directly. Instead, it fosters the community nursing movement in the small New England towns bordering the Connecticut River, which separates New Hampshire and Vermont. The organization helps communities to establish the structure that is needed to hire and fund a community nurse. It offers support to nurses in this new role, which can be quite different from what they were used to in a conventional nursing job. The community nurse supports people who may be frail or ageing but are not in acute distress, filling an important gap in care for older community members:

> In all states, Medicare will provide skilled home care services, but at some point the client stabilizes, they no longer need skilled care from the nurse or a physical therapist, and they get discharged from the home care service (often Visiting Nurse Association service). However, the individual is still ninety years old and still living at the end of the road by themselves. (Harding, personal communication)

The community nurse's role is not to provide hands-on clinical care, but to act as a "care manager" (Harding, personal communication). The nurse helps families to connect to the resources they need, to coordinate with visiting nurses and the hospital and senior services such as Meals on Wheels. Ongoing communication with the primary care provider is critical. The purpose of this work is to support elders to "have a decent quality of life and not be anxious all the time" (Sarah Jo Brown, personal communication). The nurse will help people find ways to avoid falls, ensure that medications are organized correctly, and determine whether symptoms are being managed to their satisfaction. Community nurses can also help older people to overcome resistance to small changes like putting up a handrail or getting a hearing aid and will make sure that systems are in place to meet the person's basic daily needs. For many older residents, just being able to call the nurse to ask a question or to check in helps to reduce their anxiety (Brown, personal communication). Sarah Jo Brown explains:

> There's a tremendous amount of angst among older people because they're losing ground on a number of fronts. They're losing control of their ability to manage their home. They're managing whatever illness or frailty problems they're dealing with. They may have had pets over the years and now they're having trouble with that. They had barn animals and now they can't get to the barn. So it's loss after loss and that sense of vulnerability, I think, particularly in the over-eighty group ... [In this context] you get these kinds of resistance to almost any kind of change that happens. But at the same time there's this angst about dealing with daily life. That's what the nurse can calm down. If she can get some of those things under control, get some regular way of getting food into the household, or someone they can call if they're not feeling well, or they can call the nurse. Just being able to call the nurse is a huge thing for some of them. The fact that the nurse will call them once a week. Once she's seen them initially and stabilized, maximized everything that she can, she might go in and she might not see them but once every three [or] four months, but she might talk to them once every week or once every two weeks, and that's a huge sense of anxiety relief for many of them.

Rather than assessing physical health, the community nurse works to maximize a person's functional well-being within their social context (Harding, personal communication). To do so, community nurses will also support the networks of informal caregivers and family members that surround seniors who are aging at home.

> Because the caregiver is often very much alone, with nobody to ask questions of, the reality that the nurse will come every couple of weeks or will make a phone call, or is there when the caregiver has a question or a concern, has been very reassuring. In a couple of instances when we've looked at some of the data, the decrease in anxiety on the part of the caregiver and the client is one of the consistent positive outcomes of this program. (Harding, personal communication)

In addition to reducing the psychological pressure and isolation experienced by people caring for elders, the nurse will mobilize family and community networks as needed. "The nurse uses people in the community to the extent that she/he can. They will tap into neighbors or family members. They know the social services in the area, the Councils on Aging, and are able to patch together a team to better support caregivers" (Harding, personal communication). When I spoke with Sarah Jo Brown, Community Nurse Connection was also in the process of designing a caregiver support group to provide further assistance to those caring for seniors at home.

By 2021, eleven community nurses had been hired with the support of Community Nurse Connection. Hiring a nurse for ten to twelve hours each week usually costs the community between twenty and twenty-three thousand dollars per year. The towns that choose to take on a nurse have so far all been small towns or cities with populations between 1,800 and 13,000. The average is a population of 2,000 to 3,000 in the smaller towns. In each town, oversight for the community nursing project is provided by a steering committee of three to four volunteers, which will often include a retired nurse. The steering committee drives the program forward by securing funding for the nurse and by hiring the community or parish nurse. In some communities, the nursing project has been remarkably successful, securing multiyear funding from municipal governments. The town of Thetford, Vermont, for instance, now contributes $8,500 USD to the local community nursing project on an annual basis. Part of the success of the project has to do with the fact that it is community based, sitting outside of traditional health care services: "This whole project exists at the community level, unfunded, in a sense we're outside of the health care system, and that provides a great deal of freedom. We aren't burdened by all their rules and regulations and so on in terms of hours or in terms of documentation or who you can see or not see (Brown, personal communication).

All the community nurses hired when I spoke with Laurie and Sarah Jo were currently licensed and several were recently retired from "very challenging jobs." Laurie says that many of them

> transitioned into this role because they are women for the most part who tend to be in their late fifties/early sixties, they're smart, highly motivated, not ready to no longer be a nurse. They've been highly motivated to take this job, because they love their community, they want to give back. They want to continue nursing and utilizing the skillset they've gained over the years. All are paid.

As experienced nurses, they are well positioned to be highly effective in the care management role because they know their communities and their local health care system well, have strong relationships with individuals across health care and community organizations, and can easily access tools that are necessary to improve an older person's quality of life.

In the community nursing role, nurses are freed – often for the first time in their careers – from the need to adhere to productivity metrics. "If they need to spend two hours sorting out a problem," Laurie says, "they can do it without having somebody holding a time clock." Sarah Jo notes that community nurses find the role to be meaningful and rewarding, and that it fits well with their career and personal goals; although it represents a significant decrease in pay compared to working in acute care, that is acceptable to the nurses because they see the role as a partly voluntary commitment to serve their communities. Laurie adds that for the nurses themselves, "it's been a gift, they've loved the role. They tell us that it's 'the best job they have ever had.'"

Community nursing is steeped in the principles of slow medicine, which aims to help people live well at the end of life without subjecting them to "inappropriate," "harmful," and dehumanizing medical procedures (McCullough 2008, n.p.). Dennis McCullough wanted to create a sea change in geriatric care that would reverse the growing trend of highly medicalized, invasive, and ultimately "fruitless" medical interventions being administered in the final stages of life, resulting in "Death by Intensive Care." Although he valued the life-saving, heroic capacities of modern medicine in certain contexts, he argued that when applied to, for instance, a "vulnerable and failing great-grandmother," the approach "may not save her life so much as torturously and inhumanely complicate her dying" (McCullough 2008, n.p.). One of Dennis and Laurie's goals in developing Community Nurse Connection was to ensure that people's wishes were respected at the end of their lives (Harding, personal communication). Sarah Jo Brown says that the community nurse supports health at the end of life by

> doing all the things to make life better after age eighty that don't involve interventions in the sense that the medical world uses the term "interventions." No medications, no intensive treatments. It's more focusing on the person and what they want from life ... For some people, they still want to travel a bit. "Well, I want to get back to Ireland at least once," that kind of thing. I think what Dennis really appreciated is that, as life is nearing its last phase, there are certain things that are still important to people and that they want to continue, so that's what the nurse zeros in on.

Unlike other health care practitioners, the nurse "has time to" find out what people want and focus on their quality of life (Brown, personal communication). Laurie explains:

> We work very hard to make sure that people have advance directives completed and that there's a conversation that goes on between the

nurse and the family and the individual about what they really want. The nurses are all over early referrals to hospice, for example, to make sure that people, when they have an event that is scary for them, they don't necessarily need to go to the emergency room. The nurses strive to get their clients to plan ahead and realize that they need someone to call, and consequently the nurse is pretty assertive about getting people who are frail and declining onto hospice programs. The last thing we want is for a ninety-year-old to end up in the emergency room for ten hours only to be admitted to an ICU where they're getting expensive tests and yet some of their basic needs are not being met.

For many older people, going to the emergency room is inherently problematic because once you are in hospital

> there's a cascade of events that occurs that very often ends up in expensive interventions that people, when you really talk to them about what their desires are, don't really want. But it's hard to stop the train once it starts down the track ... We really try to listen to people and pay attention to what their desires are, and work with families to help people accept that people have made decisions about what they want at the end of their lives. Very often, once the health care system starts intervening, it's very hard to ensure that people are going to get what they want. (Harding, personal communication)

This approach has implications for the quality of life of elders, as well as for the utilization of highly energy- and resource-intensive approaches within the health care system. Laurie notes: "While it's very hard to prove in terms of data, I would say that on a number of different occasions the nurse's intervention has dissuaded families from calling 911. Also, it's saved probably thousands of dollars because people don't end up going to the emergency room."

When I spoke with Laurie and Sarah Jo, they were in the process of establishing an electronic documentation system for the nurses that would enable them to track the progress of their client as well as give them a better understanding of the impact of the community nursing project in each community. However, nurses themselves had already identified the prevention of emergency department visits, hospitalizations, and fast squad calls as one of the important outcomes of their work, along with preventing adverse medication-related events and reduced anxiety for elders and their caregivers (Brown, personal communication).

11.1 Strengthening Community Care Networks

Community nursing exemplifies how professional medical care can be effectively integrated into informal care work undertaken primarily by family, friends, and neighbours. When community nurses bring their expertise as care managers to voluntary networks of caregivers, it reduces the stress and isolation associated not only with ageing in place but with caring for elders who choose to age in place. In so doing, they support and strengthen community care networks, making them less onerous for those involved. By working with older people and their families to discuss their wishes for the final stage of life, community nurses also promote hospice and palliative care approaches that enable quality of life while diverting people away from highly invasive, expensive, and ecologically intensive medical interventions that do not offer substantive benefits to elders or their families (see McCullough 2008; Gawande 2014). In a context of economic contraction and relocalization, community is likely to become the "epicentre of health care," with hospital-based care reserved for addressing medical issues that cannot be solved at the community level (Eduardo Missoni, personal communication). The community nursing model could gain traction in such conditions, as it offers an affordable and scalable approach that could be rapidly adopted to increase the quality of care to vulnerable members of the community. While Community Nurse Connection aims to support elders, the model could easily be retooled to support other populations such as people living with chronic illnesses, people with disabilities, or new mothers and infants. It could also become one of the foundational elements of a hyper-local approach to primary care provision in a post-growth political economy.

12 Community Care for Severe Mental Illnesses in Geel, Belgium

In Belgium, a non-medical model of community-based mental health care has persisted for centuries. The town of Geel, with a modest population of around thirty-five thousand, is widely recognized to be the oldest therapeutic community in Europe (van Bilsen 2016). In Geel, families make lifelong commitments to foster people with serious mental illnesses. The foster care program places people with chronic mental illnesses or learning disabilities into the homes of local families (Openbaar Psychiatrisch Zorgcentrum [OPZ] staff, personal communication). Once a strong match has been made between a family and a boarder, the boarder will often live with their host family for decades; the average tenure in the program is thirty years (van Bilsen 2016). Care has also been known to span generations, with children who grew up with a boarder taking him or her in as their parents age or pass on (OPZ staff, personal communication; Jay 2014). Geel's foster care model is context specific, rooted deeply in religious and cultural traditions, and buttressed by strategic supports provided by Belgium's state health care system (Goldstein and Godemont 2003; van Bilsen 2016; Arnold 2015; Jay 2014). The circumstances that led to the emergence of Geel's family care system are culturally unique, making scaling to other communities difficult, if not impossible. However, Geel embodies principles that could be indispensable for place-bound health systems operating within the constraints of a local resource base. By considering the history and structure of Geel's family foster care model, as well as the motivations that keep families engaged in the practice, this chapter will reveal some of these principles.

12.1 History and Structure of Geel's Family Foster Care Model

Geel's family foster care model for people with severe mental illnesses is steeped in Catholic tradition. The story is said to have begun with Dymphna, an Irish princess born of a marriage between a pagan king and a Christian queen. When Dymphna's mother died, her father went insane with grief and rage and commanded that she marry him. Dymphna left her home to escape, but her father found her in Geel, where he had her beheaded. A shrine was built in her honour, and Dymphna became known as a saint with the ability to cure or intervene on behalf of people experiencing mental illness (Jay 2014; Goldstein and Godemont 2003; Van Bilsen 2016). Religious pilgrimages to Geel to cure mental illness are thought to have begun as early as the year 600. By the thirteenth century, the town was renowned as a "haven for those with mental illness" (Aging 1974 as cited in van Bilsen 2016, 208). A church hospital was built to house Geel's many pilgrims, but it soon became too small to accommodate the number of visitors arriving in town. Geel's mental health care model emerged when farmers and community residents began to offer pilgrims to St. Dymphna's shrine accommodation in their homes. Pilgrims who remained in the community became the first boarders in the nascent family foster care system. Geel's history is unique in that the model was created by the community itself – by lay farmers and tradespeople – rather than by health professionals or the church, as was the case for most other early therapeutic communities. Nevertheless, the Catholic Church administered the project for at least five centuries, remaining in charge until 1852, after which time the state took control. The family foster care system expanded significantly during the 1930s, with Geel housing close to four thousand boarders in 1938 (van Bilsen 2016).

In the family foster care model, host families do not try to change the behaviour of their boarder or to fix or cure his or her illness (Godemont 1992, Roosens and Van de Walle 2007, both as cited in Arnold 2015). Families are not expected to deliver any kind of "therapeutic intervention," nor are boarders required to engage in a therapeutic or medical regimen of any kind (Roosens and Van de Walle 2007 as cited in Arnold 2015, 61). Families are not professionally trained to provide care, but instead implement a "common-sense approach" (van Bilsen 2016, 210). In contrast to many mental health programs, family foster care is characterized by the absence of rules, regulations, and reporting requirements. Foster families do not need to demonstrate to anyone that they are adhering to any formal plan in their care, but instead keep in contact with nurses through regular, in-person check-ins (van Bilsen 2016).

The foster care system employs teams of health professionals that offer shared services to boarders on an as-needed basis. Nurses are assigned to support the well-being of around forty boarders each. They are there to: advocate for the interests of boarders and their foster families, ensure that interactions in the household are positive and healthy, mediate conflicts, provide assistance with medications, and visit as often as necessary during challenging times (Roosens and Van de Walle 2007 as cited by van Bilsen 2016). Nurses take the pressure off families, who know they can access support around the clock. Families also receive assistance from a "team group" that includes a coordinator, social worker, psychiatrist, and general practitioner (Arnold 2015, 56). Team groups are assigned to support foster families within a particular district of the community (there are twelve districts), and the foster family itself is an equal partner on the team (Roosens and Van de Walle 2007 as cited by Arnold 2015). In acute crises, boarders can also access care at the local hospital, Openbaar Psychiatrisch Zorgcentrum Geel (OPZ Geel), and can be admitted temporarily if necessary (Roosens and Van de Walle 2007 as cited by Arnold 2015). When I spoke with a staff person from OPZ Geel, he noted that in most cases the hospital plays a very minimal role in day-to-day life, but that its presence makes it possible for the program to exist. He reflected that the foster care system would not work nearly as well if families were left to deal with crises on their own. One of the reasons the model has such strong outcomes, he explained, is that families always know that help is there if they need it.

Historically, prospective foster families had to be "certified" to take on a boarder (van Bilsen 2016, 209). Certification depended upon everyone in one's family being perceived to act in legal and moral ways. Being certified was considered to be "a matter of pride and social standing; not to be certified meant that something was not right with the family" (209). Today, families that want to participate in the program need to demonstrate that they are capable of coping with stress, have a steady income, have a space in the home where the boarder can live comfortably, and can provide an environment of care and stability (Roosens and van de Walle 2007 as cited in van Bilsen 2016). Boarders accepted into the program have a range of mental illnesses and/or intellectual disabilities. People who can be violent, who have a history of sexual assault or other serious criminal behaviours, or who are in an acute crisis are not considered eligible for the program (van Bilsen 2016). Other criteria include being able to communicate, form emotional attachments, and complete daily tasks independently (Goosens and van de Walle 2007 as cited in van Bilsen 2016).

One of the most crucial components of the family foster care model is the matching process between the family and the individual experiencing psychiatric challenges (OPZ Geel staff, personal communication). Families are first screened, a process that includes asking them what they think will fit into their existing family life. Prospective boarders are screened in a similar way, by being asked about the kinds of support they think they will need. Hospital staff create initial matches, after which the foster family and the boarder meet several times, first over a short period and then for a longer time, for instance a weekend visit to the foster family's home. During these visits, families do not ask people what is wrong with them. Instead, they ask them what they like to do and what their hobbies are. Families recognize that even if boarders may have difficult behaviours, they also have abilities, skills, and talents and can make an important contribution to family life (OPZ Geel staff, personal communication). When boarders join a foster family, they soon develop a fulsome identity and a role within that family. They are also integrated into a broader social network and are given responsibilities within their household and community (van Bilsen 2016, 209; OPZ Geel staff, personal communication). They may contribute by walking the family dog, picking up the newspaper in the morning, doing the dishes, or going to the bakery. Often, boarders take on simple tasks that make them feel needed and responsible while easing the burden of domestic work for their host family. Once families and boarders have had one or more longer visits, they decide together whether they think the match will work. Both parties are encouraged not to make the match if it would mean drastically changing anything about their lives. Over time, it has been found that if families change the way they are living to make family life with a psychiatric patient possible, it works against the match. Instead, the emphasis is on finding a good fit between the needs, behaviours, and personalities of boarders and those of their foster families. Nonetheless, there is often an initial adjustment period in which boarders and their host family must get used to living together (OPZ Geel staff, personal communication).

On the whole, foster families accept that boarders have serious problems and that these problems will not go away. There is a saying in Geel that if someone is a boarder, "it's not because of their smelly feet." This saying implies that everyone involved recognizes that there are real problems, but that it isn't worth complaining about them because for the most part they can't be changed. Instead, unusual behaviours simply exist, and it is part of the foster family's role to help people have as normal a life as possible (OPZ Geel staff, personal communication). Instead of looking for medical solutions, foster families employ social approaches to cope with unusual behaviours. Toni Smit and her husband, for instance, who have taken in many boarders throughout their marriage, had to chase away the lions that one of their boarders saw coming out of his bedroom wall every night. They also had to find ways to deflect one of their boarder's overwhelming physical attachment and affection for Smit (Chen 2016). Another foster family had a boarder who would twist off all the buttons on his clothes every day. Rather than trying to stop him from doing so, they patiently sewed his buttons back on every evening. Such behaviours are not seen as a burden in Geel. Host families generally do not seek out pharmaceutical solutions or other medical interventions, but instead find workable strategies to live with behavioural idiosyncrasies (Chen 2016; Godemont 2006 as cited in van Bilsen 2016).

12.2 Motivations, Outcomes, and Future Prospects

A range of motivations lead families to want to participate in Geel's family foster care program. Most of the host families that choose to take in boarders today have some connection to the foster care system, often generationally. New foster families tend to be either relatives or neighbours of other foster families. As such, most of them are already familiar with the system. Those who grew up with a boarder in their home when they were children, for instance, will often know even better than the hospital staff what it means to live with someone with serious psychiatric issues. Some families may decide to take in a boarder because they want to continue to look after someone whom their parents were previously fostering and whom they lived with as a child. In other cases, young widows or widowers will take in a boarder because they want to have company and a reason to get up in the morning (OPZ Geel staff, personal communication). In the past, there was always a clear "win-win" for families and boarders. Boarders would often help on the family farm in the days when Geel was largely agricultural, or help the family run a small business (OPZ Geel staff, personal communication; Jay 2014). However, this dynamic was easier to maintain when one member of the family was the income earner and the other was responsible for caring for children, performing certain jobs on the farm, and looking after the boarders, who would in turn provide some help and bring in a bit of income for the family (OPZ Geel staff, personal communication). People's motivations for taking on a boarder are often layered. For some, the financial aspect is important, for others the help or company is the main driver, and still others are motivated to carry on a family tradition (OPZ Geel staff, personal communication). Although many of the motivations that anchor ongoing participation are rooted in the community's unique, place-bound religious and cultural tradition of family care, the financial component of family foster care is a key motivator for participation, without which the program could not persist (Roosens and van de Waal 1979, 2007 as cited in Arnold 2015; OPZ Geel staff, personal communication).

Today, families receive around five hundred euros per month to care for boarders (van Bilsen 2016), which equates to around a sixth of the cost of a bed in a hospital in Belgium and half the cost of other supported living programs (Roosens and van de Walle 2007 as cited in Arnold 2015; Verbiest, Genes, and Joosens 2014 as cited in van Bilsen 2016). The model is therefore highly cost-effective when compared to other forms of care for people experiencing severe mental illnesses, and has significant relevance for the transition towards a post-growth economy. Geel's approach is also exceptionally effective at utilizing resources that are already present in the community, such as the extra space in people's homes and their capacity to devote time and energy to caring for people with psychiatric illnesses or disabilities (OPZ Geel staff, personal communication). But aside from being inexpensive and leveraging existing community assets, Geel's model of mental health care also generates strong health outcomes for boarders. In Geel, relationships between boarders and their host families are reciprocal and grounded in dignity, respect, and care. In some cases, the care provided to boarders is even returned in the form of care for foster parents as they age or support provided to families experiencing crises like illness or death (OPZ Geel 2014 as cited in van Bilsen 2016). Researchers also note that due to their full integration into family and community life, many boarders do not require pharmaceutical medications, or require less medication than they took before entering the program (van Bilsen 2016). When I asked a staff member at OPZ Geel whether families were able to provide something that could not be offered in other settings, he answered that the real relationships and real context created through the foster care model were critical benefits. Psychologist Marc Godemont, who worked in Geel for twenty-eight years, similarly identified the following factors as being crucial to the success of the family foster care approach:

1. People recognize and accept the idiosyncrasies of boarders.
2. Boarders' needs are met through social engagement and meaningful work.
3. Boarders become members of not only a foster family, but also a broader foster community. (Godemont 2006 as cited in van Bilsen 2016)

In 2018, there were two hundred people being fostered as part of Geel's family care program. The demographics of participants and host families have changed over the course of modernization, with new families now joining when they are older, often waiting until after their children have left home to take in a boarder. Younger couples who are just married are in general no longer joining the program because it is not economically feasible for them to do so. Being a foster family requires dedicated time and attention and is not compatible with having two members of a household working outside the home. As a result, some argue that engaging more people in the foster program in the future will depend on its capacity to compensate people more so that their care work can cover a more significant proportion of their household's expenses, making it possible to meet basic needs without both members of the household requiring full-time employment (OPZ Geel staff, personal communication). The program may also be able to attract more people in their fifties who are suffering from burnout in challenging careers. If these individuals could be decently compensated for fostering, it could generate mutual benefits for boarders while reducing the health care and social costs associated with people burning out and leaving the workforce (OPZ Geel staff, personal communication). While the economic circumstances of modern life seem to be causing a decline in the number of foster families willing to take in boarders at present, the decline may also reflect a trend within the field of mental health care. Community care is now seen as the gold standard and institutionalization is a last resort; as a result, there are many more supported living options available to people experiencing mental illness now than there were in the past (Jay 2014). In general, Geel's model of mental health care has displayed remarkable resilience to the forces of modernization that eroded the majority of reciprocal place-based systems of care that once existed in traditional communities. It is easy to see how a model like Geel's could inform care arrangements in post-growth contexts in which welfare states are looking for ways to lower costs at the same time as families are looking for ways to earn an income and individuals are looking for new sources of meaning, status, and identity.

12.3 Identifying Principles of Design

In an *Aeon* article about Geel's approach to mental health care, Mike Jay draws attention to a paradox inherent to the model in a modern context. He suggests that expanding family foster care amid rising rates of mental illness

> would demand a reform not simply of medicine but of society itself. It's ironic but probably not coincidental that the need for a community response to mental illness is becoming obvious just as the structures that might provide it are failing ... Who would not wish to live in a community where such extraordinary resources of time, attention and love were available to those who needed them – but who these days can imagine being in a position to offer them? (2014, n.p.)

Jay's insight reveals a core challenge facing health systems within a growth-centric political economy: even when we know what works, it is often difficult to act on this knowledge because nearly everyone is locked into an economy that requires all members of a household to be employed outside the home, leaving little time or energy to participate in reciprocal networks of community support (see Granados and Roux 2009). The obligation for all adult family members to have full-time employment has also been identified as a driver of the decline of the family foster care model in Geel (OPZ staff, personal communication). Growth economies can erect barriers to implementing simpler solutions such as community care or preventative approaches to health grounded in exercise, diet, and time spent in nature. Instead, growth economies create path dependencies towards professionalized approaches to health and care that remove burdens from individuals and families, displacing care activities from the home and into the realm of professionalized state- and profit-driven, market-based services. In a post-growth economy, however, this trend could be reversed. If formal markets and states contract, the domain of livelihood could expand, renewing the relevance of models such as Geel's family foster care system (Quilley and Zywert 2019a; also see chapter 8). Although Geel's approach cannot be transplanted, the success of nineteenth-century family care systems in the United States that were inspired by Geel demonstrates that similar outcomes can be achieved even in the absence of Geel's singular religious and cultural history (Tuntiya 2006). As such, Geel's family foster care model for mental illness suggests a list of principles that might guide the design of other community-based approaches to health and care in a post-growth political economy. These principles include:

- Using resources that are already in the community to provide high-quality care
- Integrating people who are often excluded from community life into reciprocal family and community networks
- Prioritizing radical acceptance of idiosyncratic behaviours and social rather than medical/therapeutic solutions
- Providing round-the-clock access to a team of professional care providers while also reducing reliance on professionalized care
- Compensating families adequately for their time and effort while also lowering costs for the state
- Leveraging non-rational motivations such as religious/cultural traditions, moral obligation, and intergenerational continuity.

PART 3

Social-Ecological Systems Change for Health

Part 3 considers how social-ecological systems change happens, bringing together strategies for health system adaptation as broader ecological, economic, and social transformations unfold. It focuses on the role of human agency within complex and emergent systems change processes, suggesting that even though systems change is inherently unpredictable, promising practices can be used to steward systems transitions towards desirable outcomes. Part 3 then tells three stories that demonstrate how practitioners, including medical doctors and herbalists, put these insights into practice.

To begin, chapter 13, "How Social-Ecological Systems Change Happens," presents theories from the fields of sustainability transitions, social innovation, and complexity studies to explore the dynamics of complex systems change processes. The chapter outlines common characteristics of social-ecological systems transformations, such as multidimensionality, diverse actors, and uncertainty. Next, it presents evidence that the current configuration of our global social-ecological regime in the Anthropocene makes it particularly vulnerable to rapid, cascading failures. It then argues that as change is a constant within complex systems, human actors can play a meaningful role in stewarding social-ecological systems towards greater health and sustainability. Promising strategies include guiding the natural process of self-organization and building and strengthening prefigurative alternatives to make it more likely that the system will tip in a benevolent direction when transitions occur.

These ideas are further developed in chapter 14, "Promising Systems Change Strategies for Cultivating Human and Planetary Health," which presents key themes from my conversations with change makers working to shift complex systems towards greater well-being, equity, and sustainability. First, it shares reflections on whether a managed, benevolent transition to a post-growth world is possible. Next, it presents three promising approaches for stewarding systems change: adopting multiple, diverse worldviews and paradigms to enable long-term health; creating conditions in which communities have the capacity to positively contribute to resilience and adaptation; and supporting self-organization within complex systems. Within each of these overarching strategies, more specific approaches are discussed, such as reframing ecological problems as health problems, building trusting relationships within networks engaged in systems change work, and accelerating momentum around key leverage points for human and planetary health.

Three ethnographic examples then illustrate how change makers enact these strategies in their respective communities. Chapter 15, "The Midnight Kitchen," follows the emergence of community initiatives, including a virtual kitchen table that supported change makers as they mobilized in response to the first wave of the COVID-19 pandemic. Drawing on Dr. Jane Myat's voice diaries from the early days of the pandemic in the United Kingdom, it illustrates how doctors can steward systems change by working with the forces of emergence, self-organization, and relationship building to shift how primary care practices approach health and well-being.

Chapter 16, "Complexity Medicine Group," tells the story of Dr. William Sutherland's weekly psychotherapy group co-designed by participants and grounded in the principles of complexity medicine. Participant experiences are shared to illustrate the potential of enabling communities to self-organize to improve mental health. Within the group, what emerges is a co-created, non-theoretical, and body-centric medicine that demonstrates what a complexity-informed, contextually whole approach to mental health care can look like in practice.

Chapter 17, "Herbalism in a Post-Growth Transition," concludes part 3. The chapter draws on insights from three herbal practitioners to consider how herbalism enables individuals and communities to access inexpensive medicines and build relationships to plants and place. The chapter also explores tensions related to regulation and informality, commodification, and access to land to cultivate medicines, tensions that arise as the approach gains popularity in the United States and Canada. In doing so, it demonstrates how herbalists can contribute to stewarding the transition towards a more sustainable and healthful social-ecological regime.

13 How Social-Ecological Systems Change Happens

> Contributing to the transition to a sustainable, just, and healthy future has become an integral part of the health sector's role – and responsibility. (Parkes et al. 2019, n.p.)

Social-ecological systems change is an inherently unpredictable process. The scale and scope of systemic transformation required to enable human societies to step back from planetary ecological disruption and find more sustainable paths forward is unprecedented – almost unthinkable. The metaphor of stepping back, of choosing a new path, implies agency. It implies, as the quotation above suggests, first that it is possible for human actors to intentionally influence the dynamics of social-ecological systems at the planetary scale. It also implies that individuals, communities, and organizations feel a sense of responsibility and have the capacity to act in ways that can enhance sustainability and health. To a certain degree, our ability to even understand the dynamics of change within complex systems as transformations unfold around us is limited. We are part of the systems we seek to change; all our interventions, and our attempts to comprehend the outcomes of our actions, feed back in an iterative way to affect the behaviour and characteristics of complex systems (see Geobey and McGowan 2019). Nevertheless, many people do try to understand the complexity within which we find ourselves and to make collective sense of emerging transformations (Geobey and McGowan 2019). This chapter represents such an effort. It brings together theories from the fields of complexity science, social innovation, and sustainability transitions to (1) present a working understanding of why and how the transition towards a social-ecological regime with the potential to uphold human and planetary health over the long term might occur; and (2) consider the extent to which humans can steward social-ecological systems change processes towards such a future. In doing so, this chapter highlights the value of prefigurative movements for developing promising ideas, practices, and approaches that could become the cornerstones of post-growth health systems.

13.1 Complex Social-Ecological Systems in Transition

The complex social-ecological problems before us – the climate crisis, biodiversity loss, and the breaching of other planetary boundaries – have been described as "grand societal challenges" (Köhler et al. 2019, 2). Technological innovation, managerial approaches, and incremental shifts in individual behaviours have proven to be insufficient responses to the scale and complexity of such challenges. Instead, these challenges demand more sweeping "sustainability transitions" towards novel social-ecological regimes that can provision social goods in more sustainable ways (Köhler et al. 2019, 2; also see O'Neill et al. 2018). Transformations of this magnitude have been conceptualized as "major shifts in pathways of development" that set a system on an entirely new course (Carpenter et al. 2019, n.p.). Past examples of transitions from one social-ecological regime to another include the agricultural and industrial revolutions (Holling, Gunderson, and Ludwig 2002; Homer-Dixon 2006). Many have argued that only a transition of comparable depth and scope will enable humanity to escape its dependence on economic growth, individualism, and mass consumption, among other systemic dynamics that create and perpetuate ecological destruction within the current regime (D'Alisa, Demaria, and Kallis 2015; Homer-Dixon 2006; Westley et al. 2011). Research into sustainability transitions suggests that social-ecological systems transformations are characterized by dynamics including:

- Co-evolution and multidimensionality – diverse elements of complex systems (e.g., markets, cultural values, policies, technologies) constantly interact and influence one another.
- Multiple, diverse actors – individuals, families, disciplines and professions, social movements, and industries all exert different kinds of agency within a system according to their interests, capacities, and resources.
- Tension between change and stability – forces of transformation and novelty constantly interact with vested interests and entrenched ways of thinking and structuring society.
- Long time horizons – innovations seeded within protective niches often take decades or longer to begin influencing the regime and frequently run up against resistance.

- Uncertainty – multiple potential pathways for transition exist and the complexity of a system's interacting variables makes it impossible to know which path a system will follow.
- Contestation and disagreement – diverse actors within the system hold divergent, sometimes opposing values and often disagree about the kinds of systemic change that would be desirable.
- Normative directionality – the ways in which transitions unfold are influenced by the environments created by regulators, governments, and policy makers, which in turn are shaped by prevailing societal norms. (Köhler et al. 2019; also see Westley et al. 2011; Wiseman, Edwards, and Luckins 2013)

As a result of these properties, change in complex systems is a nonlinear process that can never be fully understood nor predicted with anything close to certainty (Scheffer et al. 2012; Helbing 2013; Köhler et al. 2019). This dynamic holds true in all complex systems, even mathematical systems created only for the purpose of modelling complex behaviours. When we move into the realm of complex social-ecological systems, the number of variables and their interactions become nearly inconceivable. The nature and sheer quantity of feedback loops in social-ecological systems is so vast that any statements about the future of such systems must be made humbly, with recognition that what emerges may be very different than what one might expect (Helbing 2013). Within a context of co-evolutionary processes, diverse and sometimes competing interests, and dependence on initial starting conditions and the current state of the system, management and control of complex change processes are exceedingly difficult and top-down control is usually impossible (Helbing 2013; Homer-Dixon et al. 2015). Instead, the behaviours of complex systems in transition are shaped by processes of self-organization and emergence, processes in which unanticipated or even "counterintuitive" outcomes often arise (Helbing 2013, 52). Due to non-linearity, network effects, randomness, and time lags, complex systems can also be highly sensitive to what may initially appear to be minor perturbations. This dynamic makes it even more difficult to predict, prepare, or intervene in complex systems change processes (Helbing 2013).

Nevertheless, change is inevitable within complex systems. And the configuration of our existing social-ecological system leaves it particularly vulnerable to crises that could precipitate a rapid transition to an alternative social-ecological regime (Homer-Dixon 2006; Homer-Dixon et al. 2015). While crises have always visited human communities and ecosystems, past crises were better at staying put. Not only were they more local geographically, but they did not generally cross systemic boundaries to affect multiple aspects of society and the planetary processes on which civilization depends (Biggs et al. 2011 as cited in Homer-Dixon et al. 2015). Homer-Dixon and colleagues argue that three interconnected elements of the current regime's systemic architecture make it increasingly prone to "synchronous failure," serious disruptions that unfold rapidly and cascade across interconnected social-ecological domains (Homer-Dixon et al. 2015, n.p.). These elements are:

1. the degree to which human economic activities are putting untenable pressure on our planet's resources and biophysical processes;
2. the increasing speed at which global systems are connected through flows of information, energy, and materials; and
3. the homogenization and declining diversity of technologies, institutions, cultures, practices, and policies. (Homer-Dixon et al. 2015)

Globalization is a key driver of systemic vulnerability, as it increases the connectedness of nodes within the social-ecological system, facilitates the rapid spread of resources, people, and crises from one network node to another, and reduces the diversity of nodes (Young et al. 2006; Homer-Dixon et al. 2015). Loss of diversity in technologies, practices, values, institutions, languages, and cultures "entails a loss of local knowledge" (Young et al. 2006, 311). At the scale of social-ecological systems, this loss amounts to a reduction in the number of components available to support processes of innovation, adaptation, renewal, and repair (Young et al. 2006; Homer-Dixon et al. 2015). However, globalization also makes it possible for learning and resources to spread quickly through an interconnected network and therefore potentially increases available options for repairing the damage caused by cascading crises (Scheffer et al. 2012; Young et al. 2006; Homer-Dixon et al. 2015). As a result, globalization is an ambiguous driver, creating both risks and opportunities for coupled human and ecological systems (Helbing 2013).

When we consider the nature of social-ecological systems change in the Anthropocene, it is important to remember that "the emergence for the first time in human history of a single, tightly coupled human social-ecological system of planetary scope" only occurred over the past half-century (Homer-Dixon et al. 2015, n.p.). The dynamics of this single planetary system are novel, and the degree of interconnectedness, coupling, and complexity within it are only increasing over time (Young et al. 2006). As linked crises deepen and spread, few areas of human and non-human life are left untouched (Homer-Dixon et al. 2015; Gallopín 2002). The rising impact of human activities on planetary-scale processes also unhinges the assumption that change will occur quickly on the local scale and more slowly on the global scale (Young et al. 2006). This shift represents a "fundamental reversal" of traditional hierarchies within complex systems and further compounds risks because changes that occur on similar timescales are more likely to interact and influence one another (Allen and Starr 1982; Mesarovic et al. 1970; O'Neill et al. 1986; Simon 1973 as cited in Young et al. 2006, 310). Within more tightly coupled systems, changes tend to unfold more quickly and more often, and are also more likely to build upon one another (Helbing 2013).

External shocks can contribute to pushing social-ecological systems across thresholds, creating a critical transition beyond which the system reorganizes in novel ways (Scheffer et al. 2012). When a system is already approaching a threshold, even a small change can instigate a self-propagating transition to an alternative state. Systems that display threshold effects include dominant positive feedback patterns that, pushed beyond a certain range, cause the system to flip into an alternative dynamic equilibrium. Networks characterized by more homogeneous, more tightly connected nodes tend to resist change until a threshold is reached, at which point they shift rapidly to a new regime. This pattern gives highly connected networks like our globalized world the appearance of resilience and stability; because they contain so many close connections, they are able to repair themselves easily and quickly within certain parameters. However, this apparent resilience is deceptive, often masking an accumulation of stressors across the entire network. In contrast, modular networks that have more diverse components and looser connectivity are more able to adapt to change over time without being thrown into a critical transition (Scheffer et al. 2012). As discussed above, the current social-ecological regime displays the high connectivity and low diversity that characterizes a system prone to experiencing critical transitions (Scheffer et al. 2012; Homer-Dixon et al. 2015). If we hope to avoid or at least mitigate some of the damage that could be caused by a rapid state-change at the scale of the global social-ecological system, there are two broad options to consider: buttress the current state of the system, or attempt to make the system more modular in nature so that it is better able to adapt as the current state becomes increasingly untenable (Scheffer et al. 2012). Pursuing the second course of action would involve finding ways to increase diversity and reduce connectively within the global social-ecological system to make it less vulnerable to synchronous failure (Helbing 2013). This option would entail some degree of relocalization and local self-determination, raising many of the wicked questions discussed in chapter 8.

Yet within all complex systems, change is a key component of long-term stability (Lovelock 2014; Meadows 2008; Walker and Salt 2006). The dynamic equilibrium that characterizes complex systems is dependent upon a balance of resilience (the capacity to absorb disturbance without losing the system's identifying structure and function) and transformability (the capacity to create new systemic possibilities when existing structures and functions are no longer adaptive) (Walker and Salt 2006). A system's ability to cope with stress is thus reflected not only in the degree to which it can maintain its current state, but also in its capacity to "noncatastrophically" transition to a new stable configuration (Homer-Dixon et al. 2015, n.p.). In the Anthropocene, achieving a noncatastrophic transformation of the global social-ecological system will depend upon how resilience and transformability play out at diverse scales. For complex human societies to be sustained within planetary boundaries, for example, maintaining the resilience of the Earth's biophysical systems will require both significant transformations of the political economy as well as changes to the provisioning systems through which we meet human needs for health and care, food, energy, and education (Hahn and Nykvist 2017). At the same time, efforts to build resilience across scales must recognize that the meaning of resilience shifts when considered from the perspective of an individual, a community, a population, a nation, or the planet as a whole (National Research Council 2010 as cited in Frumkin and Myers 2020). Further, when it comes to the pursuit of health in the context of social-ecological transformation, unintended consequences, including surprising and unanticipated results of ecological changes on human health (results that may be either positive or negative), are "inevitable" (Cole 2019a, xii). Nonetheless, diverse human actors, communities, and movements are engaged in attempts to steward the process of global social-ecological change with a goal of transitioning towards a regime that can support human and planetary health over long time horizons. Section 13.2 will identify some potential paths through which the self-organization of complex systems may be stewarded, while recognizing the extent to which uncertainty remains ever-present in conditions of complexity.

13.2 Stewarding Social-Ecological Transformation

> To reach the desired states of symbiosis and homeostasis, whether individual humans with their microbial diseases, or planets infested with people, it is the sentient partners, the people, who need the will to live with their partners in symbiotic harmony. Whether humans are the host or the parasite seems to matter less. (Lovelock 1991, 171)

The human capacity to design an ideal social-ecological system or to intentionally manage the transition from the current regime to one that is more sustainable and healthful is inherently limited (Köhler et al. 2019; Scheffer et al. 2012; Homer-Dixon et al. 2015). Yet despite these constraints on our agency, countless individuals, communities, and organizations across all sectors continue to devote their time, resources and energy to the work of shifting complex systems (Westley et al. 2013). James Lovelock articulates the paradoxical nature of the situation in which we find ourselves. He warns that humankind does not yet (and may never) have a comprehensive enough understanding of climate systems or other planetary biophysical processes to confidently manipulate the environment using technological approaches like geo-engineering (Lovelock 2014). At the same time, human beings remain the only species that can understand the scale of the global problems we face in the Anthropocene and that can choose to act in ways that could increase "Gaia's chances of survival" (148). To do so effectively, Lovelock argues that "we need both intuition and reason, both part of our evolutionary past and equally necessary for survival" (57). In this section and in chapter 14, I aim to highlight some of the promising ways in which people are using their intuition and reason to steward processes of social-ecological transformation.

The literature on social-ecological systems is polarized when it comes to identifying the most influential mechanisms of change within complex systems (Hahn and Nykvist 2017; Westley et al. 2013). Ecologists and other natural scientists tend to attribute change to adaptations that occur naturally among unconsciously self-organizing actors (e.g., shifting relationships between species within an ecosystem or changes to planetary biophysical processes due to altered concentrations of molecules in the atmosphere or soil). Social scientists, on the other hand, generally attribute change to the activities of agentic, intentionally self-organizing actors (e.g., network-building and social-learning processes undertaken by communities and interest groups, industries, disciplines, social movements, or governments) (Hahn and Nykvist 2017; Westley et al. 2013). Both fields of practice present robust conclusions (Hahn and Nykvist 2017; Westley et al. 2013), suggesting that both human agency and autonomous self-organization could together have an important role to play in social-ecological systems change. As such, learning to think in systems and to recognize the diverse influences on processes of change across scales could enable human actors to leverage the agency they do have more effectively (Meadows 2008; Westley, Zimmerman, and Patton 2007). Equipped with greater knowledge of systems dynamics, we may indeed find ways to "proactively navigate away from this new kind of crisis – globally extensive and intersystemic – that could otherwise irreversibly degrade the biophysical and economic basis for human prosperity" (Homer-Dixon et al. 2015, n.p.).

An alternative to top-down control, strategies that enable "guided self-organization" provide promising opportunities to nudge systems towards desirable states from the bottom up (Helbing 2013, 54). Such strategies entail working with rather than against a complex system's innate tendency to self-organize into a stable state. They involve cultivating feedback patterns that create desirable outcomes, encouraging specific beneficial interactions between components of the system, and developing institutional settings in which it is easier for valued forms of self-organization to emerge. Bottom-up approaches that support self-organization to achieve goals like health and sustainability are inherently more participatory and grounded in local needs, capacities, and resources (Helbing 2013). They may also create opportunities to make use of cascade effects to generate positive outcomes, for instance by using cascades to rapidly spread new ideas, approaches, and solutions or to mobilize to address collective challenges (Helbing 2013). Supporting self-organization is a process of taking strategic actions that align with specific opportunities that arise within the shifting context of a complex system (Westley et al. 2013), for example, activating positive tipping points by creating enabling conditions (adjusting social network structure, increasing desirability and accessibility) and designing interventions (social, technological, or ecological innovations) to enable systemic transformations towards sustainability (Lenton et al. 2022).

Perhaps one of the most promising ways to steward processes of social-ecological systems change is to contribute to building a "backup system" that operates in tandem with the dominant system and that can serve as a "fallback" in the case of cascading failures (Helbing 2013, 55; Westley et al. 2011). To effectively support the transition towards a more desirable regime and to avoid becoming entangled in the collapse of the primary system, this backup system must rely on a fundamentally different underlying logic (Helbing 2013). Prefigurative political movements are instrumental to the development of such backup systems, as they represent collective attempts to live out alternative values, worldviews, and social arrangements in the present, despite pressures from the dominant regime (Leach 2013; Boggs 1977). Prefigurative movements are radically committed to embodying new ways of relating to one another and the world that do not reproduce existing values, ideologies, and power structures (Leach 2013). Their rejection of mainstream ideas and practices can make it difficult for most prefigurative movements to gain traction so long as existing systemic conditions prevail

(Cornish et al. 2016). However, prefigurative experiments act like seeds in the cultural and political landscape, germinating possible but as yet unattempted approaches that, as external conditions begin to shift, can root down and flourish surprisingly quickly (Westley et al. 2011). These seeds are particularly essential in the Anthropocene, when the changes required are so substantial and fundamental that "if the innovation proposed does not actively alter the path that underlies the Anthropocene, the innovation may end up reinforcing them" (Olsson et al. 2017, 3).

Prefigurative approaches are well positioned to demonstrate the advantages of alternative ways of being, thinking, and addressing problems when existing systems break down and people begin searching for different kinds of solutions. Social movements and civil society organizations, for instance, often contain prefigurative elements and have been shown to offer nurturing spaces in which niche values, practices, and policies can grow, eventually gathering enough momentum to influence the mainstream (Köhler et al. 2019). Developing prefigurative alternatives in advance of systems transformations can also help achieve a more benevolent transition from one regime to another by enabling catagenesis, the creative flourishing that can follow phases of creative destruction or localized collapse (Homer-Dixon 2006; Walker and Salt 2006). The diversity of prefigurative movements can also help to highlight multiple potential trajectories of transformation, increasing options for action (Walker and Salt 2012). The fields of resilience studies, social innovation, and sustainability transitions have all recognized the key role that prefigurative political movements can play in social-ecological systems transformation (Beddoe et al. 2009; Westley, Zimmerman, and Patton 2007; Köhler et al. 2019).

Figure 13.1 uses a heuristic drawn from complexity science to illustrate the potential of prefigurative alternatives to contribute to the transition towards an alternative modernity that is more conducive to human and planetary health than the current regime. Complex systems seek equilibrium, but every social-ecological system has different potential attractors or steady states, represented in figure 13.1 as valleys on a three-dimensional plane, or "basins of attraction" (see Zywert and Quilley 2020a; Carpenter et al. 2019; Walker and Salt 2012). The existing dominant basin of attraction is modern consumer capitalism. As discussed in chapters 2 and 3, consumer capitalism has generated unprecedented improvements to health and quality of life around the world, but has also been responsible for planetary ecological disruptions such as the climate crisis and biodiversity loss (Myers and Frumkin 2020; Whitmee et al. 2015; Zywert and Quilley 2017). At the same time, modern consumer capitalism has eroded the capacity of

Figure 13.1. The three basins of attraction of the global social-ecological system

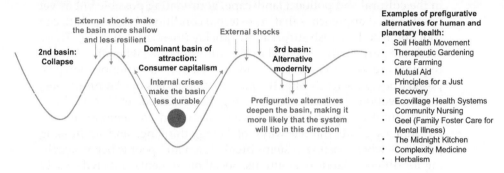

Source: Adapted from Zywert and Quilley 2020a.

communities to meet their members' needs for care, connection, and meaning. Modernity has, for instance, enabled widespread individualization (Weber 1968; Beck and Beck-Gernsheim 2002), the disintegration of community bonds of mutual obligation (Tönnies and Loomis 1999), alienation (Marx 1992), anomie (Durkheim 1897), the encroachment of the formal economy into every aspect of life (Polanyi 1944), and the colonization of Indigenous cultures (Kimmerer 2013). Despite these challenges, the basin of consumer capitalism has proven to be extremely resilient. Resilient basins of attraction (represented as a deep valley on a two-dimensional plane) are held in place by the complex interplay of cultural frameworks, institutional structures, and power dynamics, as well as by a general societal agreement that the status quo is, for the most part, acceptable (Carpenter et al. 2019). When they experience disturbances, the system returns to the stable attractor; when systems are within a resilient basin, it would take a substantial amount of energy to push them into an alternative stable state (Carpenter et al. 2019).

Yet evidence is accumulating that the resilience of consumer capitalism as a dominant basin of attraction is quickly eroding (Homer-Dixon 2006; Homer-Dixon et al. 2015). Planetary ecological changes are now severe enough to substantially lower the threshold between the existing regime and alternative basins of attraction (Zywert and Quilley 2020a). As the basin of modern consumer capitalism becomes increasingly untenable, the social-ecological system is likely to shift into one of two other possible steady states: collapse (second basin in figure 13.1) or an alternative modernity (third basin in figure 13.1). Collapse has often been described as a sudden, precipitous loss of complexity within social, political, or economic systems, though it can also refer to a rapid transition from an established to a novel regime (Cumming and Peterson 2017; Tainter 1988, 2014). Cumming and Peterson (2017) argue that a system has collapsed when:

1. It has lost its identity – characteristic system components and interactions disappear.
2. Loss of identity proceeds quickly – in less than one generation of the relevant actors in the system.
3. There are significant losses of social-ecological capital – for instance, a loss of population, resources, productivity, or relationships.
4. There are long-term consequences – it takes longer than a generation for the system to recover, or recovery may be impossible.

Collapse of consumer capitalism would likely represent a catastrophic, rapid, and enduring contraction of global trade and economic activities alongside rising sociopolitical conflict and upheaval, as well as (at least initially) a worsening of planetary ecological changes already set in motion since the Great Acceleration (Zywert and Quilley 2020c). Alternative modernity, in contrast, is a much more desirable steady state in which humanity finds ways to preserve many of the benefits of modern societies while using resources and energy in an ecologically sustainable fashion and regenerating ecosystems and communities that have been disrupted over the course of industrial modernization (Zywert and Quilley 2020c; Kish et al. 2021). Yet even if the transition towards such an "alternative modernity" is mostly benevolent, it will inevitably involve relinquishing many aspects of the current regime, some of which are highly valued (Kish and Quilley 2017; Kish 2018; Quilley 2020b). As discussed in chapters 7 and 8, an alternative modernity would be characterized by a profound decomplexification of the economy, with implications for the capacity of the welfare state, the availability of cheap material goods, and the scope of the health care sector (Zywert and Quilley 2020a; Kish et al. 2021; Zywert 2017). Many of the approaches discussed throughout this book prefigure the kinds of relationships, worldviews, and practices that could enable health systems to flourish despite such economic contraction (see examples listed in figure 13.1). They do so not only by offering solutions to some of the most troubling aspects of modern societies, like disconnection from nature and community life, but by creating contexts to improve preventative health, thus taking pressures off biomedical health care. They also address aspects of health for which modern health systems have struggled to make inroads, such as mental health, nutrition, physical activity, social connectedness, and the social and ecological determinants of health. Although each prefigurative approach discussed in this book is unique and grounded in the full context in which it arose, there is substantial evidence that fostering numerous, diverse approaches with the potential to strengthen the resilience of possible alternative regimes can help ensure that the transition between basins of attraction unfolds in a way that upholds rather than undermines human well-being (Westley 2013).

13.3 Understanding Change in Complex Systems

This chapter has outlined some of the ways in which researchers studying social-ecological systems transformations understand the dynamics of change in complex systems. By all accounts, social-ecological transitions are unpredictable processes that cannot be controlled or managed, at least not from the top down (Helbing 2013; Scheffer et al. 2012; Homer-Dixon et al. 2015). What's more, the extreme interconnectivity, rising uniformity, and degree of ecological disruption that exist within the current system are increasingly likely to precipitate a systemic transformation that could be as profound and long lasting as the agricultural or industrial revolutions (Homer-Dixon 2006; Homer-Dixon et al. 2015). Yet even within a context of deep uncertainty, human agency can play a role in nudging complex systems in a desirable direction or in building a backup system that can help hollow out an alternative basin of attraction to anchor the system in a new state of dynamic equilibrium (Westley et al. 2011; Westley, Zimmerman, and Patton 2007; Köhler et al. 2019). Prefigurative political movements hold particular promise for leveraging what agency does exist within conditions of complexity (Zywert and Quilley 2020a; Kish et al. 2021). It is worth repeating that the emergence of a single, tightly coupled social-ecological system only occurred within the past fifty to seventy years (Homer-Dixon et al. 2015). Indeed, it is only relatively recently that humanity has even been able to think about "the planet" as a complex system that we can seek to both understand and affect (Steffen et al. 2015b). There is much that we don't know about how to steward planetary processes of social-ecological change and much that we may never know. Regardless, we continue to act, guided by both "intuition and reason" (Lovelock 2014, 57) to create conditions in which human and planetary health can thrive. Chapter 14 assembles strategies that medical doctors, researchers, and social change practitioners across diverse fields are using to steward social-ecological systems transformations amid the profound complexity, uncertainty, and novelty that characterize the Anthropocene.

14 Promising Systems Change Strategies for Cultivating Human and Planetary Health

> There are very large health costs to our current way of life, and thus very large potential health benefits from a shift to a more sustainable society. (CPHA, 2015, 16)

In this chapter I gather insights from the many conversations I had about *how* to achieve social-ecological systems change to enable health in the Anthropocene. Some of what is proposed below applies specifically to transforming health systems, but most is relevant to social change work more broadly. Making it possible for human and planetary health to flourish in a period when the Earth has already been fundamentally altered by human activities is not a task for only those parts of the system that are formally responsible for health and care. This idea was frequently emphasized by those interviewed for this book and has been discussed at length in the literature on health in the Anthropocene (see Whitmee et al. 2015; Butler 2016; McMichael 2014; Zywert and Quilley 2020b). Health systems are an important but insufficient leverage point for improving health outcomes and pulling back from ecological overshoot. Lasting social-ecological systems change for health must shift the overall *trajectory* of human activities and their impact on the biosphere and on the diverse human and non-human communities that inhabit our planet (see Olsson et al. 2017).

To contribute to this effort, this chapter considers how those working towards long-term human and planetary health might approach stewarding social-ecological systems change processes. The strategies and approaches presented below are shared as a place to start. They were assembled by triangulating (1) the many literatures I have drawn on in the course of this research, (2) common experiences and tactics used by the researchers and practitioners I interviewed for this project, and (3) my own hunches[1] about which paths have the most potential to lead towards a better future at this particular juncture in time. The last component is inevitably influenced by the professional and personal spaces that I inhabit, by my individual interests and biases, and by my own interactions within the complex social-ecological systems of which I am a part. As such, the themes presented here should be taken as a situated contribution to the landscape of social-ecological systems change strategy, rather than as best practice guidance. These approaches are shared as useful principles for diverse health and social change practitioners to consider as they work to effect the transformative changes that will be needed to secure human and planetary health into the long-term future.

I begin by reiterating a concept that was introduced in chapter 8 and developed further in chapter 13; given the complexity of existing social-ecological systems and the unprecedented nature of our current circumstances, it is highly unlikely that we can bring human activities back into alignment with planetary boundaries by pursuing only managerial solutions, technological innovations, or governance strategies. I then argue that those interested in contributing to social-ecological systems change may get more traction by directing their efforts towards strengthening humanity's collective ability to

1. adopt multiple, diverse worldviews and paradigms that are conducive to long-term human and planetary health;
2. create conditions in which people and communities have the capacity to contribute to social-ecological resilience and/or adaptation; and
3. support the self-organization of social-ecological systems.

In what follows, I consider each of these promising strategies in turn, highlighting many useful ideas, tactics, and ways of working discussed by subject-matter experts and practitioners across diverse fields related to human and planetary health.

14.1 Prospects for a Managed, Benevolent Post-Growth Transition

When speaking with academic researchers and health practitioners who had shared interests in limits to growth and health systems, I often turned the conversation towards whether it would be possible to achieve a benevolent transition from the world we live in today to a healthful and sustainable future. Most of the people I spoke to who had devoted considerable attention to this question in their careers thought that an intentionally designed, benevolent transition would be difficult or perhaps even impossible to achieve. Don Spady, for instance, reflects that the transition towards a new social-ecological regime would be more likely to unfold "largely [as] a series of responses to circumstance." He suggests that "there may be isolated pockets where people can plan, but even the planning can't be that far ahead" (personal communication). Peter Gray similarly argues that a benevolent transition "is a bit of a tall order." Given the scale of the problems, from oil dependence to rising populations, he says he is unable to see "an easy way down from that." The best we can do, he says, is to work locally, building the will and capacity to practice medicine in ways that are suited to the changing circumstances around us (personal communication).

Colin Butler, who has written over one hundred articles and academic book chapters that consider the relationship between limits to growth and health, thinks we had a much better chance of purposefully navigating towards a more sustainable future in the 1970s. Today, wealthy nations seem to be focused increasingly on "fortifying ourselves" (Butler, personal communication). With less money and less goodwill for other nations to go around, as well as evidence for the emergence of regional limits to growth (Butler 2020), Butler warns that "all I can see is an intensification of mini-collapse in growing regions over a decadal period" (personal communication). Dan Bednarz, former editor of the "Health after Oil" blog on resilience.org, also thinks it is unlikely that we will be able to manage a planned transition from the current regime to an alternative, more sustainable state. He explains: "A new system must be a decentralized, low-tech, less complex one that's in line with thermodynamic and ecological realities while simultaneously overcoming the corrupting class-based, neoliberal social policies now dominant in society. At this time it's hard to imagine how we get to this system in anything approaching a consciously designed and orderly fashion" (2014, n.p.)

Bednarz suggests that a more sudden collapse of the kind described by Tainter (1988, 2014) is probably the most likely scenario, though the collapse could also proceed more slowly, perhaps over fifty or one hundred years as a series of plateaus or "incremental steps" downward (personal communication). While we won't be able to avoid descent in some fashion, Bednarz notes that collapses do provide windows of opportunity: "You have to have some kind of partial collapse for the system to open up enough for people to realize what's going on, and then for some kind of movement to build" (personal communication).

Epidemiologist Hank Weiss also thinks it is unlikely that we will be able to design our way through a sustainability transition simply by making good decisions, primarily, he says, because human beings find it exceptionally difficult to conceptualize a slow threat. "If people saw an invading army over the horizon, they'd do exactly what was necessary. But this is not that kind of problem" (personal communication).

Unfortunately, widespread "climate inertia" means that by the time things have become dire, it will probably be too late to do anything about it. However, as changes unfold, some areas will likely be able to adapt more effectively than others: "Things aren't going to change overnight, there will be a series of escalating crises over a long period of time. It's how we adapt to each one of those in the long-term that defines where we go. I think that some people will do it right, both from an internal and an external basis, and other places will have problems" (personal communication).

Localization researcher Raymond De Young also argues that a "stepwise descent" in which we find opportunities to adapt at intervals over the course of years or decades is more likely than a planned retreat from ecological overshoot:

> My hunch is we're going to have what I think of as a step-wise descent, where we'll have events that occur that shake us out of our complacency, or social or technical or organizational behavioural complacency. But then there will be periods of stability. So we'll have a failure of replacement of fossil fuel reserves, and then slowly there'll be a lack of long-distance transportation. Suddenly getting goods from a long distance will be impossible. Everything else will be functioning quite normally, but there'll be a change in the consumption landscape and we'll have to get used to that ... Then there will be another step down, and another and another, but it will be like a staircase, not unlike the way we came up during the Industrial Revolution ... Which means it's not just a constant slide, there's these punctuated moments of stability in which we can look around. (personal communication)

After experiencing several of these descents and plateaus, communities may develop greater capacity to respond in ways that are more creative and forward-looking (personal communication).

The researchers and practitioners I spoke to often noted that as ecological constraints begin to make themselves felt, people will have no choice but to change. Indeed, small and large collapses may turn out to be strong drivers of sustainability transitions, creating conditions in which change becomes psychologically possible and materially necessary. Bednarz explains, for instance, that it is "very hard to get people to consciously give up something they're benefiting from, or to go to something they're uncertain of. But Mother Nature's really great about this, because when you run out of stuff, it just happens" (personal communication). He says that to instantiate a regime change, it would take "an economic breakdown, a cultural crisis. The analogy would be, our culture is an alcoholic that has to hit bottom." James Truong, a GP with a practice in northern Ontario, also spoke about how crisis and collapse can open opportunities for healing at different scales:

> It simply may be too much to ask people to change without change being thrust upon them. In a weird way then, I mean, not that I wish hardship upon anybody, but I do love it when systems collapse in upon themselves in sort of an observable way, to prove that we can't do that anymore … The same way as, not that I want any of my patients to have a heart attack, but the time when I've been most able to leverage change with people in a health care situation is ironically in a health care crisis. (personal communication)

Truong emphasizes that in medicine, periods of crisis are often "when we do our best work … when we do our most effective, long-lasting work. You wouldn't think that somebody landing in my emergency department with a heart attack can be in any way a good thing, but it is a teachable moment, and it seems to do something to galvanize people to the idea of change. (personal communication)

Those concerned about limits to growth and health often emphasized that even if a planned sustainability transition is out of reach, strategic actions grounded in hope are still important:

> We don't want to lose a sense of purpose, we don't want to lose a sense of hope. We don't want to have a sense that we are on a downward slope that has no bottom. And I think that if we have a sense of who we are and how we like to deal with things, then we may still end up in deep trouble, but we might be able to deal with it a bit more effectively. We have to be able to understand what we can do and what we can't do. (Don Spady, personal communication)

Colin Butler similarly reflects that as we face profound social-ecological systems changes that will disproportionately affect vulnerable communities and individuals, it is essential to continue working towards positive outcomes for health across scales:

> You and I may live out our lives and sort of see this happen around us and have reasonably fulfilling lives, so we can't be totally pessimistic. But I think we have an ethical duty to consider these things, and I don't think you can be truly happy in the world where these things are going on, and you've got to try and fight. And you have to light a candle, because a candle can be seen in the darkness, even if it's just a tiny candle. (personal communication)

In the sections that follow, I will discuss some of the hopeful actions and approaches leaders are using to steward social-ecological systems change in the direction of long-term sustainability and health.

14.2 Adopt Multiple, Diverse Worldviews and Paradigms That Are Conducive to Long-Term Human and Planetary Health

> I think seeing the world differently is one of the most powerful tools we can use to help people get ready to respond. Pre-familiarize themselves with what might be happening. And if we're wrong, and it's not as bad as people say, or it works out even better than we can hope, we're not worse off. (Raymond De Young, personal communication)

In her book *Thinking in Systems*, Donella Meadows (2008) identifies the paradigms and mindsets that underpin a system as being among the most influential leverage points for transformation. Alternative paradigms make it possible for new goals, behaviours, and structures to emerge within a system (Meadows 2008). As such, enabling widespread adoption of ways of seeing the world that are conducive to human and planetary health must be a key focus of systems change efforts in the Anthropocene (Zywert and Quilley 2020a). I argue here that some of the most important ways that worldviews can lay the groundwork for health across social-ecological scales are by:

- Helping people to perceive and make decisions based on interconnectedness and long time horizons
- Increasing people's comfort with death and other limitations
- Framing ecological problems as health problems.

I present a brief rationale for focusing on these three domains below. However, I first want to emphasize that each of these domains could be usefully approached through the lens of diverse and even opposing ways of seeing the world, including radical green politics, traditional conservativism, Indigenous worldviews, Judeo-Christian traditions, alternative and traditional medicines, and biomedicine (see Quilley 2020a; Kish et al. 2021; Kimmerer 2013; Sutherland 2015). I encourage those aiming to work with paradigms as a leverage point for systems change to avoid seeing one worldview as "bad" and another as "good." Instead, be willing to consider tapping into existing values, traditions, and ways of seeing the world, even when this approach raises wicked questions or requires uncomfortable conversations across ideological divides (see chapter 8).

Perceive and Make Decisions Based on Interconnectedness and Long Time Horizons

The challenges of the Anthropocene – planetary ecological disruptions, mass extinction of biodiversity, resource limits, social inequities, health disparities – can only be navigated effectively by attending to the interconnections between human and ecological systems. Moreover, time lags between past and current economic activities and their future implications for human health and ecological change suggest the need to think and act based on longer time horizons (Olsson et al. 2017; Quinn Patton 2021; Cole 2019c; Myers and Frumkin 2020). As anthropologist Stephanie Schnorr argues: "We can't just think one hundred or even fifty years ahead of us at a time, we need to really extend this out. What are the trajectories of our society, of our species, of our existence on this planet in thousands of years, in the kind of millennial terms that we evolved in?" (personal communication).

There are multiple pathways for expanding capacities to perceive interconnectedness and long-term cause and effect. In practice, for instance, supporting solutions that can generate both near-term and long-term benefits could enable a paradigmatic shift towards more widespread recognition of the interconnectedness between components within complex systems.

> I think sometimes one has to get some quick wins, which may not be fully attuned to a systems-based approach, but nevertheless do represent a step forward. But at the same time, one does need to promote and support systems-based thinking, because otherwise you get adverse unintended consequences ... I think sometimes there can be a tension between a systems approach and near-term benefits, and I suppose in the future, our research is going to really be focusing on how we can maximize the near-term benefits while at the same time thinking in a longer-term systems-based way. One way we've been trying to do this, of course, is through the health co-benefits of low carbon technologies and strategies, for example. As well as reducing climate and other long-term changes, it also produces near-term benefits to health through, for example, reductions in air pollution. That's an attempt to square the circle in a sense, or achieve both near-term benefits while at the same time thinking in a long-term, profound, systemic way. (Andy Haines, personal communication)

A shift in mainstream experiences of time could also be accomplished by leveraging ritual as a technique for stepping out of the regimented, linear, and productivity-focused experience of time that is a signature of modern capitalist societies (see Quilley 2020b; Zywert and Quilley 2017; Davy 2020). Ritual brings collectives of people into a liminal space in which the present can evoke shared experiences of the timeless, or of a more cyclical flow of time across generations, linking the current moment to both the past and the future (Quilley 2020b; Seligman et al. 2008; Turner 1977; Turner 2012). Historically, rituals tended to be enacted during times of resource scarcity, or to redress social conflict, to build community solidarity, and to give meaning to milestones experienced in the life course (Turner 1977; Katz 1982; Turner 2012; Solomon, Greenberg, and Pysczynzki 2015). As such, the resource constraints and crises of the Anthropocene may inspire a resurgence of ritual as a source of meaning-making activity (see Lorea 2020 on ritual during the COVID-19 pandemic) that could make it easier for people to experience and attend to the longer timescales on which patterns of human and planetary health play out.

While many of these rituals may be religious or spiritual in nature, others may be more grounded in the tasks of ordinary life that support the provision of basic needs for families and communities. As Dr. Jane Myat describes, for instance, her intention in establishing a community garden at her medical practice was about more than "just gardening" (personal communication). As a "complex activity," gardening is linked to the fundamental activities of human survival and creates a living connection to "where we come from as human beings and what we used to do together." The act of gardening therefore holds potential to mend the broken connections between the human and the ecological components of complex social-ecological systems while helping to re-establish "that link with where we've come from." In this way, diverse kinds of rituals can help to establish greater awareness of both the interconnectedness of components within a system and a greater sense of connection to the future and the past.

Increase Acceptance of Death and Ecological Limits

Modern consumer societies deny both death and ecological limits. Within formal health systems, death denial results in the proliferation of treatments and interventions aimed at extending the individual lifespan regardless of the ecological and economic costs and often despite the toll such procedures can take on quality of life (Quilley 2020b; Gawande 2014; McCullough 2008). In the political economy more broadly, denial of limits has fuelled the Great Acceleration and the breaching of planetary boundaries, undermining human and planetary health in the process (Steffen et al. 2015a; Evison and Bickersteth 2020; Zywert and

Quilley 2020a). From an ontological standpoint, these two dynamics are interconnected, embedded within our bodies and in the priorities of our health systems. Death, as Dan Bednarz notes, is "the ultimate limit," and yet we seem just as determined to reject its existence as we are to ignore the limits to growth (personal communication).

Bednarz sees our collective inability to face death and "the extraordinary lengths doctors are willing to go to now in terms of resource consumption, habitat destruction, et cetera, to keep people alive" as "severe impediments" to sustainable health systems (personal communication). Dr. William Sutherland similarly reflects that as a culture

> we're not good with dying. We're not good with limits. Death is a limit on our humanness. And look at all the other bounded limits that we're just crashing past, never mind carbon limits, our petrol limits and our extraction limits of all the other limited resources in the world. The ignoring of limits is probably because we ignore the fundamental limit on ourselves. And that fundamental limit is also what creates notions of intergenerational relationship, the idea that we do things not for us but for people down the road. We plant the acorn not for the tree that we'll see the shade of, but for our great-great grandkids, this kind of thing. So the system is not dealing well with those sorts of notions either. (personal communication)

As Sutherland suggests, accepting death and limits could help to bring humanity back into alignment not only in terms of our ecological impact but also in our relationship to our communities and to future generations (also see Quilley 2020b). Other researchers and practitioners also emphasize the importance of shifting towards ways of thinking that can help people to accept limits across scales. Peter Gray, for instance, says that "our best hope for moving forward in a coordinated way" is to help people understand that you "can't have infinite growth from a finite planet" (personal communication). Yet while "people have to believe that things really are scarce, and that their best method of survival is by cooperating, not competing" (Dan Bednarz, personal communication) to establish structures that can enable human and planetary health, there are multiple systemic barriers to widespread acceptance of death and limits. Bednarz explains that many people "are unable emotionally to accept the idea that there are limits to growth, that modernity is not the best thing that ever happened" (personal communication). He adds, "as dire as the situation is, we're not ready to face what the situation is. To really come to grips with what it is. And if you don't know what it is, you keep doing the wrong things."

Another barrier may lie in the extent to which fear of death leads people to seek comfort in ingrained cultural worldviews that offer symbolic immortality through, for instance, beliefs about the afterlife or the enduring importance of one's actions in the world (Becker 1973; Solomon, Greenberg, and Pysczynzki 2015). A substantial body of evidence from the field of terror management theory demonstrates that in modern societies, material consumption is the primary source of status and prestige. As such, fear of death translates directly into increased consumption, driving unsustainable behaviours and contributing to ecological disruptions in the Anthropocene (Solomon, Greenberg, and Pysczynzki 2015; Solomon 2020). In this context, significant potential may lie in approaches that aim to re-embed individuals within networks of reciprocal gift-giving and intergenerational continuity through, for instance, practices of ancestor veneration (Davy 2020). Green "hero projects," or activities that turn sustainable behaviours into sources of cultural heroism (for instance, contributing to ecological conservation projects), could also offer alternatives to mass consumption as a way of finding enduring meaning in life and death (Dickinson 2009). Within health systems more specifically, hospice and palliative care approaches can help to reduce the ecological and economic costs of end-of life interventions by creating opportunities to speak with elderly people about "what they value" as they near the end of life (Jessica Pierce, personal communication). While so much of the focus on caring for ageing people is about prevention of injuries and death, bioethicist Jessica Pierce explains: "I think what a lot of people nearing the end of life want is exactly the opposite of that. They want to live rather than be protected from dying. So letting them do that would be, I think, really life-affirming and would use fewer resources. They don't need as much care or want as much care as we're forcing on them" (personal communication). These and other practices could begin to lay the groundwork for mindsets that are more accepting of death and ecological limits, both key components of a paradigm that can enable human and planetary health.

Reframe Ecological Problems as Health Problems

Although scientists and sustainability advocates have been speaking out about impending climate catastrophes since the 1970s, human impacts on the biosphere have continued to expand at an accelerating pace (see Steffen et al. 2015a). Increasingly, researchers in the social sciences warn that we may be telling the wrong stories about the climate crisis, stories that have the unintended effects of reinforcing consumeristic worldviews and unsustainable patterns of behaviour by invoking fear, denial, and hopelessness (Davy 2021; Solomon 2020; Kaplan 2000). Within the field of planetary health, researchers are proposing a new story that emphasizes interdependence by reframing ecological problems as health problems. Andy Haines explains: "I think the health community does have a real potential to reframe the environmental challenges as health challenges. Particularly climate change needs to be rethought of as a health issue, not solely an environmental issue – and that's why we need to act" (personal communication).

Unlike environmental problems that can feel distant and impersonal, health problems are easier to perceive as personal and urgent. As Sarah Whitmee describes, "If you start to show people that it impacts their own life and they can do things about the environment to make themselves maybe feel good, but also have an impact on their health, then it's quite a different way to talk to people, and it's also a very powerful argument, because people are naturally very self-interested (personal communication).

This approach does not shy away from anthropocentrism, but rather aims to tap into existing individualistic values and harness these for ecological good. Andy Haines says that planetary health can be seen as

> quite anthropocentric in the sense that it could be conceived of as self-interest on the part of *Homo sapiens* as a collective species recognizing that its own future is inextricably bound up with the future of natural systems ... In fact I see quite serious limitations in some of those who propose a sort of deep ecology approach. Because I don't think that politically it's going to have a lot of traction. I think what might have traction is the recognition that our health and our future ultimately depend on the integrity of the natural systems which have allowed our species to flourish, and if we undermine those, we undermine the prospects of health for our descendants, for future generations, and indeed for some current populations as well. So I do see it as a form of enlightened self-interest and not necessarily putting aside notions of anthropocentrism, which I think are almost inevitable really in the way in which we envision our place in the world. (personal communication)

Leveraging anthropocentrism to inspire ecologically sustainable behaviours may seem contrary to the development of the kind of more embedded, place-bound and community-centric worldview that could enable human and planetary health into the long-term future. However, it is a practical place to start. Telling new stories that make connections between human health and ecological disruption in contextually appropriate ways could dramatically shift support for environmental action.

In particular, such stories could potentially appeal to the sensibilities of people across the political spectrum who may not care about or even believe in climate change, but who strongly value the health of their families and communities (see Hochschild 2017; also see chapter 8).

14.3 Create Conditions in Which People and Communities Have the Capacity to Contribute to Social-Ecological Resilience and/or Adaptation

In my conversations with researchers and health practitioners, many shared the conviction that social-ecological systems change for human and planetary health would be possible if the human components of the system – individuals and communities – had greater capacity to support change across scales. In practice, the transition towards more sustainable regimes involves building local resilience and enabling adaptation where needed, as well as coordinating action across problem domains to steward broader transformative processes (Walker and Salt 2006; Quinn Patton 2021). The capacities needed to do so are diverse, contextual, and interdependent, yet participants identified several enabling conditions that could make it easier for people to engage in effective systems change work. Research participants often spoke, for instance, about the need to make it easier for individuals to think clearly and act strategically to ensure that people in all walks of life can make good decisions and stay the course in challenging times. Many also noted the central importance of cultivating relationships across networks involved in transformative efforts, with strong relationships seen as the primary determinant of impact in social change movements. Participants also repeatedly highlighted two external conditions: equity and unnecessary complexity. Equity was seen as not only an important outcome of systems transformation but also an enabling condition of healthful and sustainable social-ecological change. Without greater equity both within and between communities and nations, human and planetary health can only ever be realized by a small percentage of the population, creating risks to sustainability further down the line and upholding many of the social dynamics that originally led to global ecological overshoot (see Karliner 2020; Edger et al. 2020). The second condition, itself a wicked problem to negotiate, was the need to rethink the balance of complexity within health systems. To a certain degree, layers of social and institutional complexity can facilitate positive health outcomes, but too many layers can stifle innovation, erode informal support systems, and overshadow preventative approaches. Many medical doctors, for instance, reported that excessive regulations and bureaucracy erect multiple barriers to patient care and innovation, especially social innovations involving closer patient-doctor relationships and more common-sense approaches to care. Each of these enabling conditions for building the capacity to contribute to social-ecological resilience and adaptation is discussed below.

Support the Capacity to Think and Act Well

Systems change work is inherently complex, messy, and uncertain. As such, it is important to support the capacity of individuals and communities to engage in this work by ensuring that people have the space and resources they need to think clearly and to act effectively within highly complex situations. Didi Pershouse explains, for instance, that

> society doesn't provide information, framing, or access to the tools and strategies necessary for people to create the relational support systems they need to process the challenging circumstances we face as capitalism collapses and the environmental conditions shift. Without those simple tools and strategies, our instinctual fear-based reactions of freeze, appease, fight, flight, and play dead take over, we turn to addictions and patterned reactive behaviours, and we don't have access to our full intelligence, resilience, and responsiveness. (personal communication)

Raymond De Young similarly argues that people need meaningful and frequent opportunities to engage in behaviours that restore their attention to avoid the burnout that is often associated with living through difficult social change processes:

> Coping with resource descent, energy descent, climate disruption, requires being clever and controlling your emotions and managing your behaviour, all of which require directed attention. A good response to those current challenges and future challenges requires that we have a lot of directed attention restoration. So I consider restorative behaviours, spending time in nature, spending time in meditation or mindfulness-based stress reduction as preconditions to being able to creatively manage and coordinate our behaviour and coordinate our emotional response to all the challenges we have. I have this saying, burned-out people can't save the planet. They're mentally burned out, they're no use to us, we're not any use to ourselves in that state. That means that restoration in nature or mindfulness-based practices, having some reflection, time for inner thought, time to clear our mental landscape of distractions, is an essential part of learning to respond to energy descent, resource descent, and the social challenges of those things. (personal communication)

Colin Butler also emphasizes the need to engage in psychological practices that enhance individual resilience while cultivating the hope needed to keep going when working on intractable challenges:

> Especially if you tackle a problem that's very hard to solve, it's actually very hard to make progress, in anything ... You've got to walk some sort of balance and have some practice to keep yourself level-headed. Otherwise you're going to become grandiose and think you are solving it, or you're going to become hopelessly depressed and give up. Many times in my life I felt like giving up and a few times I've felt like I'm grandiose, but overall you just struggle on. And you've also got to have the long view of history. It can seem hopeless, but eventually, you know, slavery in America was abolished even though it might be making a little bit of a comeback. But you're part of a big movement. So you've got to keep your hope up. Professor Ron Labonté, I don't know if he coined the phrase, but he said you can be optimistic as a political action. Because as soon as you give up having some hope, well, you just lose all possible influence you might have. (personal communication)

Several others identified specific approaches, mindsets, and tools that can support people's internal capacity to engage in complex systems change work. GP Jane Myat, for instance, talks about working in a way that focuses on process over destination. She describes using the guiding principles of the transition town movement to create positive experiences rooted in connection, hope, and a willingness to act without needing everything to be perfect (see Transition Network 2020). In developing The Listening Space garden, for instance (see chapter 5), she says: "Right from the first day we decided to start, I cooked soup for eighty volunteers in our waiting room and we had a party ... If it becomes fun and enjoyable, then it doesn't really matter if you've got that community kitchen that's shiny and lovely looking" (personal communication).

Tanya Darisi, co-founder of Openly, an impact strategy, research, and evaluation company that specializes in working with organizations pursuing social change, says:

> I often lead off conversations about working in complexity with an emphasis on the kinds of mindsets we bring to working in complex systems. The tensions between a fixed mindset, where we approach the world as if it is ordered and knowable, as if there's a right answer and a wrong answer, as opposed to a growth mindset which is open ended, recognizing that the state we are in right now is not the end state, but there's always the

potential for learning and doing more and an unfolding, organic growth. If we're going to work in complexity, we need to bring into it a strong growth mindset.

I think we also need comfort with ambiguity. Trying to get people to reflect on how comfortable they are with not knowing something, and being ok with just moving forward and not having all of the answers. I think that is a really big one. Because complex systems have so many different components and dynamics, relationships and actions. It's impossible for anyone to hold all of that in our head. We can only ever hold a slice of that. People get overwhelmed thinking they need to know everything or they need to grasp everything ... I think having an approach orientation is also important, where we recognize that there are challenges, but that whatever resources we have, we can leverage those resources and learn. (personal communication)

In addition to practices that can help people avoid psychological burnout and mindsets that can support engagement in systems change, it is also important to consider how these individual capacities are connected to the external conditions in which we live and work. Didi Pershouse, for example, is genuinely concerned that our capacity to think well about complex, systemic issues could be compromised in the future due to damage and contamination to the microbiome, which can affect both physical and mental health (see chapter 2). Our relationship to the ecological systems around us through practices such as glyphosate and antibiotic use within agricultural systems, for instance, can have implications for our ongoing capacity to respond effectively as social-ecological transformations unfold (Pershouse, personal communication). Individual capacities must therefore always be considered within the context of broader patterns of feedback within social-ecological relationships.

Build Trusting Relationships across Networks Engaged in Systems Change

The literature on social innovation, resilience, and systems thinking highlights the essential role of relationships in enabling or erecting barriers to social change (brown 2017; Bird and Westley 2011; Westley, Zimmerman, and Patton 2007; Gunderson and Holling 2001; Meadows 2008). Research demonstrates that strong coalitions of actors with shared values and interests are often responsible for making positive tipping points for sustainability possible (Lenton et al. 2022). Participants equally reflected on the need to cultivate strong relationships across problem domains and scales to prepare the ground for social-ecological transformation. Lisa Villeneuve, co-founder of Openly and an experienced coach who has worked with leaders across the social services, health, and public sectors, notes:

> We know that what makes networks and collaborations work is the effectiveness of the relationships more than anything. I've seen the most dysfunctional networks you can imagine trying to work on collective change together, and there was so much distrust and power issues, it eventually fell apart. In one case there was initially a space for healing and a really interesting thing that happened where we were able to move into a new space of regeneration with this network and then the leadership changed and a new leader came in with the iron fist, and everything completely went back, all that old stuff got resurfaced and it broke. I see that happen over and over again. Then I see how little conversations that happen between people, just trusting little moments, supporting one another, makes it happen. It deepens that connection. I always think when I teach on network theory or system leadership or system change, the heart of it is the power of people to connect with one another, to learn from one another and to understand and build perspective empathy. I think it changes everything. (personal communication)

Amara Possian, a community organizer who supported the mutual aid movement and the development of the "Principles for a Just Recovery" during the COVID-19 pandemic (see chapter 9), also describes trusting relationships as an important enabling factor that can allow movements to take advantage of windows of opportunity when they emerge. During the pandemic, she noticed that some collaborations were able to move forward quickly, while others were more strained and difficult to get off the ground. Reflecting on the differences between these efforts, Possian says, "It really got me thinking about the level of preparation you need before a crisis in order to quickly and meaningfully build the infrastructure needed to scale a response in the moment of crisis. And I've come out of this experience feeling like yes, we're in a crisis right now, and everything is possible, and I want to slow down and focus on building something that could actually seize a similar moment" (personal communication).

Within social-ecological systems it is important to think not only about human-to-human relationships but about the relationships between people, non-human species, and ecological wholes. Shifting our attention towards ecological relationships can ensure that we have a more inclusive understanding of what planetary health means and who it can benefit. Didi Pershouse explains:

We care about the things we're connected to, that's our wiring as mammals. That sense of caring and nurturing and stewardship – as pack animals or tribe animals, if we feel this is part of us and part of our community, then we have some sort of an instinct to protect it and care for it and we can tell that by caring for it, things are going to go better. I think that's built right into our system. (personal communication)

Relationships were also seen as a key motivating factor for people working in social innovations for health and care. Although working in new ways is often time consuming and challenging, relationships are what kept people engaged in the work over the long term. Care farmer Floor de Canter, for instance, says:

We always look at the person and we think, ok for this person, we'll give him a chance, and it would be very good for this person to have a place where he feels at home and he feels useful. So that keeps us going. And sometimes with all the new regulations, because that's a problem here, the regulation grows and grows. That makes it sometimes that you think, I'm going to quit. All these reports, nobody reads them, it's just for the quality stuff, etc. So then you sometimes think, I'm going to stop this, why am I doing it? But just for the people, and I was just called today by a mother, a young person, and he's getting very depressed and I hear the story and I think, give him a chance. Maybe it works, let's try it. So we would never say no. That's what keeps us going. (personal communication)

Enable More Equitable Health Outcomes and Dismantle Systemic Barriers to Health and Well-Being

Inequity and inequality were highlighted by multiple researchers and practitioners as primary barriers to long-term human and planetary health. At the same time, moving towards more equitable health outcomes was seen to be one of the most important potential outcomes of social-ecological systems transformation and a necessary precondition for achieving health across scales. Colin Butler, for instance, says that ultimately, "inequality is threatening the survival of civilization." He reflects that elites seem to think they can live in a fortress world in which the wealthy have pockets of green space around them and it doesn't matter that ecological functions are degraded and pollinators are dying out. Elites, Butler argues, are behaving as though they can "manage the inequality" in its many forms without any blowback, but that this is dangerously unrealistic. He suggests that mounting global and local inequalities are likely to continue generating massive social conflicts unless wealthy nations and the wealthy within nations take tangible actions to "make the world a little bit fairer" (personal communication). Hank Weiss similarly says that the most profound challenge facing human health is "inequity," both in his home country of the United States and at a global level (personal communication). Addressing inequitable health outcomes was also seen to be a moral imperative and a key ethical question for the field of planetary health. As Sir Andy Haines reflects, "There is a profound ethical dilemma at the root of all this, which is that those who are most vulnerable have the least responsibility for driving the changes" (personal communication).

There is a growing sense within the climate movement that expanding equity is a precondition for enabling long-term human and planetary health by changing the mindsets and paradigms that contributed to planetary ecological change in the first place (see Karliner 2020; Edger et al. 2020). Amara Possian, for instance, explains:

> I think the same mindset that leads people to colonize, to pursue limitless growth and expansion, to conquer other peoples, also exacerbates climate change, both in how we do things and how much carbon is produced and also in whether or not we do anything about it or are willing to change. Whether or not you talk about climate change in that way really depends on what it is you're trying to do. I think it's helpful for people to understand that things are connected. (personal communication)

Creating the conditions that can enable equity is about learning to listen to people in new ways and embedding attention to diverse perspectives into processes of institutional decision making:

> Even in the best utopia we can imagine, there will still be harm and there will still be mistakes. Once in a while we will still collectively probably go down a path that is not good for us. It's not about never making mistakes. It's just about how we respond to that and how quickly. Who are we listening to when they say "there's a problem here," or "I'm being hurt here," or "my needs aren't being met"? And then, what do we do about it? (Possian, personal communication)

While the connections between climate justice and equity are rapidly gaining attention, it will be an undeniably massive challenge to find ways to effectively redistribute resources and ensure equitable access to health care and preventative health opportunities in a context of "decline and contraction" (Dan Bednarz, personal communication). Creating the conditions for equity will not only involve securing more resources for people and communities that have little within the current system, but also encouraging people and communities with abundant resources to live with less (Bednarz, personal communication; Steffen et al. 2013). For this reason, Bednarz says that we would "need an ethic of egalitarianism" to achieve the potential benefits of relocalization strategies to ease the transition away from fossil fuels towards a post-carbon regime, an ethic that is currently absent from both political parties in the United States. Further, an ethic of egalitarianism cannot be created through rational argumentation: "You have to have some really profound, existential crisis that threatens your being for you to give up these kinds of beliefs" (personal communication).

Rethink the Balance of Complexity within Health Systems

Researchers and practitioners working within health systems often discussed a tension between establishing enough complexity to facilitate positive health outcomes without putting in place so many layers of complexity that they unintentionally undermine health. Research participants spoke, for instance, about the barriers created by excessively complex regulatory environments in the health sector, which make it difficult to practice in innovative ways. As Floor de Kanter notes above, the regulatory burden that has come to be associated with care farming, particularly the overwhelming number of reports to write, can at times make her think "I'm going to quit. All these reports, nobody reads them, it's just for the quality stuff, etc. So then you sometimes think, I'm going to stop this, why am I doing it?" (personal communication). Jane Myat discussed this same dynamic in chapter 5, adding that bureaucratic reporting requirements within primary care can stifle health practitioners' capacity to meet the needs of their patients, especially those experiencing multiple vulnerabilities.

Peter Gray identified legal liability issues as one of the key constraints preventing doctors from moving towards the kinds of practices the profession may need to adopt in a future of economic contraction and resource limitations:

> A lot of the things that we may have to do once the oil supplies diminish, we can't really do at the moment because they wouldn't be according to accepted standards. So it really wouldn't be acceptable for me to go out to a remote farmhouse and deliver a baby in the kitchen, because if something went wrong, I'd be out on the streets without a medical licence. So [at the moment I don't practice in these ways; instead I am focused on]

thinking and prepping, and really thinking through what I might have to do, or what other people coming after me might have to do. I think it really is a good idea to try and think about some of these things before you actually have to do them. (personal communication)

Given that the current legal system is structured entirely around the rights of individuals, it is not particularly surprising that the culture of perfection is so entrenched within the medical system. Peter Gray suggests, however, that modern liability concerns probably won't be relevant in the future, or at least not to the same extent: "I think once you get into the twenty-second century, then the concept of medical liability is going to probably go back to something like it was a hundred years ago, where physicians did their best, and if things went wrong, well that was just unfortunate, but no one was going to come after the doctor with lawyers and malpractice suits" (personal communication).

James Truong also discussed this culture of perfectionism within medicine and the challenges it can pose for doctors concerned about the ecological footprint of health care. He said that when he teaches students, he tries to instil alternative values grounded in working with patients to achieve the best outcomes possible within uncertain circumstances, an important competence for doctors working in the Anthropocene. He says that his approach is rooted in

> a version of my parents' sort of immigrant pragmatism, where they're like "ok, let's just give this an honest, best go." It won't work out all of the time, but so long as we're both trying hard, the healer and the patient, it will probably go ok. That concept unfortunately is lost somewhat on people who demand perfection. So part and parcel with everything that I teach my medical students is, OCD aside, we need to be ok even in the medical world with the idea that things start out imperfect and they're going to end up imperfect, and that's alright. (personal communication)

While legal liability and the culture of perfectionism in medicine may be good places to start when it comes to reducing barriers to ecologically minded innovation in health systems, these considerations must be part of a broader conversation about how health systems approach complexity more generally. For instance, are more complex, energy-intensive approaches always the go-to solution, or can other, less ecologically and economically expensive options be considered first? James Truong says he is highly uneasy with the extent to which the current system presents high-tech or pharmaceutical interventions as the first, default course of action without addressing the more immediate drivers of ill health:

> Most of the medical world lives by the philosophy of, we'll just find things and we'll treat them and pretend our lives won't need to change. Well, that's not really the way of things. And part of what I do in my practice is I make a pact to my patients that when possible, we're going to try to get rid of their diseases without using meds if I can. I mean I'll use them over the short term, I'm not scared of them, but most of the type 2 diabetes I get rid of without meds ... Do we have to constantly be adding on more meds which people can't afford, and do more surgeries which the health care system can't afford, and complain about wait times for procedures that technically are optional? Or can we just say ok, what's what here? Do we really need to be doing all these knee replacers, when people can just lose weight? (personal communication)

If the goal is to support lower-overhead approaches to health and care that are both preventative and draw on the support of informal community networks, it will be necessary to ask new questions about taken-for-granted levels of social and institutional complexity in health-related fields. We may need to ask, for example: How do the various layers of social complexity within health systems (e.g., professional bodies, administration, measurement and evaluation systems, legal departments) support innovation, strategic learning, and evidence-based decision making, and how do they create barriers? Which specific regulatory requirements are most stifling to practitioners trying to work in more ecologically and economically sustainable ways, and why? How can we put in place measurement and evaluation systems to enable evidence-based practices and decision making while at the same time creating conditions for low-overhead, preventative, and common-sense approaches to thrive?

The case of Geel, Belgium (see chapter 12), is a positive deviant in this space. The family foster care system is supported by the state, which added layers of social complexity to the practice such as financial compensation and twenty-four-hour supports from teams of health professionals. However, families were not bogged down by administrative reporting or regulatory requirements, or even medical intervention into the process of care. In Geel, a common-sense approach prevailed. This case is an outlier, and one that could serve as a strong model for how to put in place enough social complexity to enable positive health outcomes without establishing so much complexity that it undermines effective care or makes the commitment untenable for those involved. There is some evidence that the COVID-19 pandemic has created glimmers of change in this direction, but it is unclear whether the experience of temporarily working in more collaborative, less bureaucratic ways will create space for a more permanent rethinking of regulatory practices (Giulio et al. 2020; McCartney 2020; Jane Myat, personal communication; and see chapter 15). In stewarding processes of social-ecological change for human and planetary health, it will be important to pay closer attention to levels of social complexity within health-related fields, and especially to instances in which social complexity may need to be scaled back to increase the potential for more sustainable practices and structures to emerge.

14.4 Support the Self-Organization of Social-Ecological Systems

Social innovators, recognizing the inherent complexity of the conditions in which they work, often refrain from trying to control systems change processes and instead "see their work as managing or designing the contest for self-organization" (McCarthy 2017 as cited in McGowan and Westley 2017, 103). This strategy may be particularly important when working within living systems that have both ecological and social components (see Olsson et al. 2017). As Didi Pershouse notes, "biological systems know how to function and how to heal and how to evolve and adapt" (personal communication). For this reason, she lists "creating conditions for self-organizing systems" as one of the key principles that characterize ecological models of health care (Pershouse 2016, 48–9). Pershouse expands:

> The essence of life is that organisms naturally tend to work together in *self-organizing* systems, where they solve problems and evolve in creative ways, without external control or constant intervention. This is true on many scales. Yet in our ways of managing society, bodies, and land, we constantly try to control and regulate the creative processes around us, to *make* those self-organizing groups do things, instead of *letting them*. (286)

In this section, I present three approaches that can enable self-organization for human and planetary health: accelerating momentum around key leverage points, expanding community networks of care, and co-designing solutions with all who have a stake in the change. Each of these approaches is illustrated by sharing the story of an initiative that embodies what it means to work in this way.

Accelerate Momentum around Key Leverage Points for Human and Planetary Health

Nourish is an initiative that sees food as "a powerful way to build health for both people and the planet" (Nourishhealthcare.ca, "About"). The project works to create the conditions in which health care institutions can become leaders in climate action and health equity by cultivating healthier food systems within hospitals. At the core of the approach is the idea that healthier food systems within health care institutions can have a systemic impact by encouraging prevention, acting on the social and ecological determinants of health, and increasing the well-being of patients, hospital staff, and the broader community (Hayley Lapalme, personal communication). With a mission of increasing the health of people and the planet, Nourish sees food as an opportunity for broader social-ecological change. As executive director Hayley Lapalme explains:

> Right from the get-go, we had made a systems map about how our current food culture increased the burden on the health system. These are things like rates of malnutrition, high rates of diet-related disease, inequitable access to food, lots of poor coordination and distribution in the system, lots of processed foods. Through these, we see a contribution to the already overburdened health system. So we see the opportunity with food as an intervention to break down that burden. (personal communication)

In the early days of the project, food lived metaphorically and literally in the basement of hospitals (Lapalme, personal communication). Nourish's aim was to shift the paradigm on food from being a cost centre for organizations to being a leverage point to create health. Through the work of their Innovator cohort, they began to see the emergence of more windows of opportunity for transformation (see Westley, Zimmerman, and Patton 2007) within the health care sector:

> We started to see a lot of space opening up in terms of hospitals internally directing resources toward food efforts, whether it was local sustainable food procurement efforts for contracting agreements with local farmers, reorganization of the food services structure, say, to a room service model, investment by the hospital foundation in a hospital garden, willingness from the board to start to build relationships with local First Nation or Métis community members to have them guide the development of Indigenous foodways or traditional recipes or selection of plants in design for gardens. (Lapalme, personal communication)

Nourish accelerated this momentum by supporting food system leaders within hospitals to shift their food procurement and preparation practices, activating a series of "food for health levers" collectively identified by subject matter experts and staff (https://www.nourish healthcare.ca/nourish-levers). Lapalme describes how "the goal with the program was really to be finding innovative ways of demonstrating how a more closed-loop holistic approach to these connections between the land, food systems, and personal and planetary health actually builds health (personal communication).

After two and a half years, the project shifted towards engaging the whole system of the hospital, including senior leaders, to enhance hospital food systems in collaboration with local community partners and policy partners who would help take the learnings to scale. In this new approach, Nourish decided to focus on supporting

> collaboratives that would be organized around principles of place-based leadership, collaboration with community, understanding and embracing complexity and wanting hospitals to work beyond their walls with communities, recognizing the wisdom that communities hold in terms of caring for themselves and looking for opportunities to address the more upstream social and ecological determinants of health, and not just treating sick people when they come through the door. (Lapalme, personal communication)

The anchor collaborative model works across three scales: health care institutional stakeholders, from senior leadership through to hospital patients; community organizations that bring a grass-roots perspective; and policy sponsors that can take the learnings into the broader policy environment: "We see Nourish's role as being able to create the conditions for that kind of collaboration to come about where it might not otherwise. So there was a pivot because I don't think we thought we were getting far enough fast enough (Lapalme, personal communication).

Within the new approach, food remains a useful entry point into deeper conversations about health care and planetary health. Lapalme reflects that "at Nourish, we talk about the power of food to bring people together to have a complex conversation that maybe otherwise wouldn't be happening" (personal communication). Reimagining the relationship that health care institutions have with food creates unexpected space to reimagine the purpose and potential of hospitals to create well-being in their communities. Lapalme comments on "the number of times I've seen a conversation go somewhere that the people in the conversation did not expect. Especially, shifts toward a more preventative health care system, or working to advance reconciliation, it happens more times than I can count, but food opens up the space for that conversation to happen (personal communication).

In this way, Nourish accelerates momentum for change within health care institutions and communities. Although the long-term effects of the project continue to emerge, the developmental evaluation has already tracked systems changes in the areas of resource flows (e.g., allocation of budgets to support the work), power and authority flows (e.g., increased commitment to food-for-health work among health care decision makers), and relationships (e.g., relationships between Indigenous and non-Indigenous colleagues and increased credibility within professional networks) (Hsu et al., n.d.).

Expand Community Networks of Care

The time-banking movement clearly illustrates the value of expanding community networks of care to support health across scales. Time banks connect community members to give and receive diverse kinds of support such as help picking up groceries, painting a fence, changing a lightbulb, or learning a new language. Community members who provide services earn time credits that they can then use when they need support in turn. The effect is a stronger network of caring relationships, reduced social isolation, and meaningful participation in community life. In the United Kingdom, many time banks were originally established in connection with local GP practices. The Rushey Green Time Bank, for instance, was founded over twenty years ago when Dr. Richard Byng at the Rushey Green Group Practice noticed that a significant number of his patients were presenting with issues related not to physical health but to mental health and well-being; many people, especially those who were older, were feeling "socially isolated and lonely" (Simone Riddle, community engagement lead, Rushey Green Time Bank, personal communication; Rushey Green Time Bank, n.d.). When the time bank was first established, referrals to it came directly through the local doctor's office in an early form of social prescribing, which is a prescription from a doctor "to an exercise club, or a gym, or a walking club, or a book club, or a time bank. It is giving some practical guidance or direction to a patient to integrate them into a new community that may help to solve their problems in a non-medical way" (Sebastian Yuen, trustee, Timebanking UK, personal communication).

In addition to facilitating connections between community members to provide one-on-one support, time banks run initiatives specifically designed to increase health and well-being. Rushey Green's

Wildcat Wilderness project, for example, offers access to a community green space where people can play, garden, learn about nature, learn outdoor skills, and participate in other community programs. The time bank also runs exercise classes for seniors and a walking group (Simone Riddle, personal communication). Simone Riddle, community engagement lead at the Rushey Green Time Bank, says that these activities take an asset-based approach that views everyone as having something to contribute and that begins with people's skills and interests rather than aiming to solve people's problems (personal communication). Sebastian Yuen, trustee of Timebanking UK, an agency that supports the development and success of the time-banking movement across the United Kingdom, confirms that this approach is characteristic of the time-banking movement as a whole. Time banking, he says, recognizes that

> health isn't simply the absence of illness. Health is a product of our education, interactions, it can be affected by isolation, domestic violence, unemployment, divorce, all these things have an impact. Time banks can help by reducing isolation, bringing people together, having a purpose. It can make the people feel valued. Following the principles of asset-based community development, it sees people as assets and values them and their contributions, as opposed to the traditional view, probably from the state sector or NHS that someone might be elderly, or they might be diabetic, or they might have cancer. That is a deficit model. (personal communication)

Time banking strengthens community networks of reciprocal care by creating a simple structure to bring people together. Often, isolated and vulnerable older adults don't have anyone to call on when they are in need. Time banks foster these connections between individuals and facilitate greater engagement in group activities that deepen relationships and expand networks (Riddle, personal communication). In doing so, time banks can also take the pressure off of formal health care infrastructures: "The fact that members have that network means that they're probably not calling the social worker, the doctor, or emergency services. Some of our more vulnerable members find having that network means you're preventing crises or problems from escalating" (Riddle, personal communication). Yuen also discussed this potential impact of time banking, describing a program in Stockport that sought to address the problem of delayed transfer of care, in which people who are discharged from hospitals are unable to return home due to barriers like not having anyone to drive them home or check on them after they have been discharged. In Stockport, the time bank stepped in to fill this gap by coordinating members to pick people up at the hospital, look in on them regularly, and run errands for them like shopping for groceries and medications. This arrangement benefits participants who are able to return home sooner while freeing up beds in NHS hospitals for people who require more acute care (Yuen, personal communication).

Most of the Rushey Green Time Bank's members are older people, and the membership reflects the full diversity of the local Lewisham community. The time bank also has many members with additional needs, including people with learning difficulties (Riddle, personal communication). This membership is typical for time banks across the United Kingdom, which tend to engage members who are older, who have long-term disabilities, and who do not work full time (Yuen, personal communication). Members of the Rushey Green Time Bank say that engaging with the organization improves "their quality of life emotionally and physically" (Riddle, personal communication). By participating in the activities of the time bank, they report "feeling valued through those relationships and by helping one another." Participants also say that they enjoy the fact that the time bank's programs engage community members across diverse age cohorts and backgrounds. People with learning disabilities, for instance, appreciate participating in groups that are not only for others with learning disabilities, but that include other members of the community as well, creating a more fulsome sense of integration into local networks of care (Riddle, personal communication).

Co-design Solutions with All Who Have a Stake in Change

Designing public services in ways that include meaningful input from the communities that will be affected by the service has been shown to "foste[r] social norms that favour the long term over the short, the future over the present, and others over the self" (Helliwell and Hall 2020, 277). Co-design can also help social change makers to accomplish Meadows's recommendations for living in a world of systems (see Meadows 2008, 194). Engaging those who have a stake in systems change is an effective strategy for taking what Meadows describes as "the beat of the system" (194). It can also challenge one's assumptions about how a system operates and why it reinforces certain patterns of behaviour, certain flows of resources and power, and certain social and ecological outcomes over others (Meadows 2008). To illustrate how this approach can work in practice, I will share my conversation with Lamis Bayar, chair of the board of trustees for Mental Fight Club, a London-based charity founded, led, and delivered by people with mental health experience.

Mental Fight Club runs three key projects, the Dragon Café, the Dragon Café in the City, and Re:Create Psychiatry. The Dragon Café is "an open mental health space, open hearted, and open to everyone absolutely ... It exists to offer a space of safety or mutual support, of commonality, of empathy, and I hope of joy" (Bayar, personal communication). Its medium is art, which is used as a tool to articulate and share experiences of vulnerability. It sees art as a social practice, a tool to think with, and a way of "enabling intelligent conversations, personal, social, and collective, about health and being in the world." At the Dragon Café, "it's not a prescription of the space that you must recover." The space serves people in diverse positions across the health system, from people suffering from extreme mental health distress to those experiencing milder challenges, people experiencing physical health conditions that affect their mental health, individuals who refuse formal medical assistance, as well as carers, clinicians, NHS managers, social workers, researchers, artists, and the local community. Lamis Bayar describes the space as having "a kind of dynamic, almost-slightly-befuddling diversity to it."

The other program run by Mental Fight Club is Re:Create Psychiatry, "an exploratory dialogical platform" that enables more equal forms of dialogue between those who use mental health services and those who provide them. Bayar explains:

> Re:Create Psychiatry conversations tend to elicit these rather magical moments where ... hierarchies inherent in the medical model as it currently exists in our context are stripped away and, dare I say, for a moment reversed. What Re:Create Psychiatry as a project then does is it tries to piece together these collective, multiperspectival yet genuinely shared understandings of the mental health care system and suggests approaches to remedy some of the urgent issues within it.

In this way, the project creates opportunities for "patient-doctor learning ... The professionals tend to get really detailed insights into the unfathomed aspects of service user experience." By establishing more equal dialogue and understanding between users of the mental health system and mental health practitioners, the project "helps professionals provide better care." At the same time, for people who use the mental health care system, it is

> an empowering route to understanding where they fit in within that system and to somewhat mitigate the weight of the system on their everyday lives. Because once you're using the health care system it's just

absolutely ever-present in your daily life ... The hope is that by understanding the way the system is set up, by understanding the systemic pressures under which those who wield the system exist, there's an opportunity for people who use the system to take the lead in establishing better onward relationships with the people who provide their health care.

Co-design is inherent in the structure and operation of Mental Fight Club and all its initiatives. Those who do the labour of running the organization have mental health experience, as do those who participate in Mental Fight Club's projects. This embedded co-design approach allows the organization and its projects to harness the

> real intelligent knowledge which comes from navigating systems ... the expertise which comes from navigating the complex health care system which we have is very valuable, and it ought to be understood as such, and compounded into a communal voice which speaks to the system about what systems do.

This approach is not about consulting people or engaging them tokenistically on the odd committee, but about trying to centre the voice of experience as an integral feedback process that informs the transformation of the health system so that it can serve people more effectively. This approach is key to creating what Bayar describes as "non-fragmented" mental health services that are less expensive for the state, are more efficient, and work for service users and health practitioners. While Mental Fight Club works within the mental health system, I would argue that the insights gleaned about the value of genuine co-design processes apply equally to initiatives aiming to improve planetary health.

14.5 Bringing about a Healthier, More Sustainable World

A benevolent transition from the current social-ecological regime to one that can secure human and planetary health into the long-term future may be, as Peter Gray suggests, "a bit of a tall order" (personal communication). Nonetheless, people from all walks of life choose to turn their attention, time, and skills towards trying to bring about a more sustainable, healthier world. Based on my conversations with health practitioners and with leaders and participants in social innovations for health and care, several strategies stand out as promising places to start in the effort to steward social-ecological change processes towards new patterns of organization that are more conducive to human and planetary health. As described above, these approaches fall into three categories:

1. Adopting paradigms and worldviews that could create a foundation for ways of life that can uphold planetary health
2. Creating enabling conditions in which people across diverse local contexts can effectively support the resilience and/or adaptation of the systems in which they have some agency
3. Supporting the self-organizing capacities of complex systems in the direction of health and sustainability

Each of these three domains are interconnected and overlapping. The specific practices and approaches discussed in this chapter have been offered up as suggestions – as strategies to think with – for those who participate in the uncertain work of systems change. Not only is it beyond the scope of this book to offer more concrete guidance, but such an approach would be counter to effectively working in complex systems, which requires above all attention to context and to the emergent nature of social-ecological change (Westley, Zimmerman, and Patton 2007; Quinn Patton 2021; brown 2017).

NOTE

1 Westley, Zimmerman, and Patton (2007) argue that, given the complexity of social change work, attending to embodied "hunches" about how to proceed can play a crucial role in the success of social innovations.

15 The Midnight Kitchen

In the spring of 2020, as the first wave of the COVID-19 pandemic rose across Europe and the United Kingdom, I began working with GP Jane Myat at the Caversham Group Practice to track emerging processes of community self-organization for health and well-being. Thrown headlong into new ways of working when London went into lockdown, Jane and her collaborators drew on their experiences co-creating The Listening Space garden (see chapter 5) to mobilize in imaginative ways. While navigating novel restrictions, they developed a community kitchen, distributed food parcels to patients, connected as a virtual community around food and storytelling, and came together for distanced story walks between green spaces in South London. Throughout this time, Jane sent me regular voice memos reflecting on the effects of the unfolding COVID-19 pandemic on her practice and her patients. I also joined a transdisciplinary team of doctors, cooks, artists, makers, and students engaged in creating the Midnight Kitchen, a space we described as a "virtual kitchen table where we gather to cook, eat, craft, laugh, and connect" (www.midnightkitchen.co.uk). This chapter draws on Jane's voice diaries, my participation in the development of the Midnight Kitchen, and a group interview with Jane Myat and collaborator Jim Jones on why and how the Midnight Kitchen came into being. In sharing this story, I aim to highlight how Jane leverages processes of emergence and self-organization to steward transformative change. As a doctor committed to using the power of gardening and crafting to enable health through social connection, Jane's work during the COVID-19 pandemic reveals multiple lessons about how primary care doctors can act as change makers in times of social-ecological transition.

15.1 The Birth of the Midnight Kitchen

The first weeks of the COVID-19 pandemic were shocking and disorienting, perhaps especially for those working in health care. The pandemic unsettled long-standing practices in health care institutions, accelerating changes that had been difficult to implement in normal times due to resistance and institutional inertia (see McCartney 2020). With the crisis creating new urgent priorities, bureaucratic demands were loosened, colleagues felt a renewed sense of purpose, and some of the boundaries between organizational silos became more permeable (McCartney 2020). Jane described many of these trends in her voice diary, sharing in real time the tensions and the highs and lows of practising medicine in a crisis. These early experiences formed the backdrop for the emergence of the Midnight Kitchen and the other social supports that Jane initiated in collaboration with health practitioners and volunteers at the Caversham Group Practice. On 18 March 2020, less than a week after the WHO declared COVID-19 to be a global pandemic, Jane said:

> I think the reality hit me today. I think I've been a bit like a machine until now, trying to get things organized, which I think had been a bit of denial about what's actually unfolding here. I think that this is going to be really difficult, actually. We had a lot of staff in tears today at different points in the day for all sorts of different reasons. I think it's an unfolding of grief and trying to get on under pressure and wondering how everybody's going to cope and at the same time worrying about things outside and family … I think we were also shocked because a young man who had come to the practice yesterday is now in intensive care on a ventilator at University College Hospital. I think we thought that the first patients we would hear about would be some of our vulnerable elderly and we didn't think that we would already be seeing people in the practice who were young with no co-morbidities. So I hope that was not a taste of what's to come, but I fear that it might be.

As Jane described, the onset of the pandemic created fear and uncertainty for health care workers, who were often the first to witness people's ill health, their distress, and the suffering of their families. Doctors and other health practitioners were also required to suddenly pivot the ways in which they worked, an experience that was both challenging and, in some instances, energizing. Each day brought new personal and professional difficulties, but there were also moments in which the potential for renewal became palpable. On 20 March, Jane heard this potential clearly in the form of a fetal heartbeat sounding through her office wall:

> Got to the end of the week – amazing. I've just been desperate to get to this point because we've had a plan to totally transform the practice into a new way of working to keep everyone safe and try to manage all the demand that we're facing with less and less people around and we've actually managed to do it on very little sleep. We were laughing because we had a strategy meeting early on in the year and almost every year the same things come up because we never get anything done, and we've now transformed in about two and a half weeks things we've been trying to change for twenty years or so. What an achievement that has been, and I'm sure it's going to be a completely different world for everybody after all this. I was just thinking that I often look forward to Fridays because it's the end of the week, but also in the day on Fridays we have an antenatal clinic and the midwife runs it from next door to my room. For some reason the fetal heartbeats always transfer through the wall. It's always really lovely when you suddenly hear a baby's heartbeat through the wall. Today, things were difficult, and then there was this lovely little chuk-a-chuk-a-chuk-a as the heartbeat came through the wall and it just felt like one of those amazing moments where it reminded you just to be in the now. It made me think about this baby being birthed into a new world that's being birthed at the moment. The mood in the team was quite buoyant today. We're feeding people every day and there is lots of laughter, I think because people have been feeling really scared. The mood dipped a bit later in the afternoon because all the news came out about everything shutting down and some people thought that meant lockdown. Some of our staff who travel in from just outside London were really worried they wouldn't be able to get home, but that's not the case. But it's all change all the time.

Although London didn't lock down that day, three days later on 23 March a full lockdown went into effect. The NHS began preparing for a surge of hospitalizations that was expected to overwhelm the health care system's existing capacity. At the same time, the first wave of the pandemic brought with it a sense that paradigmatic change was possible. Reflecting on the first weekend of the London lockdown, Jane said she experienced

> all sorts of whiplash between different emotional states and situations. It was really nice to have a bit of downtime away from the practice and some sleep finally. Really strange, quite upbeat atmosphere in London.

It was really sunny, and everybody was out on the street and chatting to neighbours, albeit at a slight distance. Kids were out playing in the street, lots of people going on the heath for walks, which is going to stop now. It felt like going back in time to the sixties or seventies. No planes in the sky or very little. I think people were feeling a sort of wave of possibility and a little bit of excitement, I think, that things are changing, which very much contrasted with other things that happened today being back in the practice. It's a new world for everybody and strange, we're having to make all sorts of different kinds of decisions. So, throwing up all sorts of moral mazes and difficult scenarios, and I think it's going to get a lot worse. We had a really sobering briefing from NHS London about what's going to pan out and the preparations that are being made. Clearing out leisure centres and halls to get people out of hospital as soon as possible, a bit like army field hospitals, which I think we were sort of expecting, but it feels a bit scary because it's going to be quite soon I think. They're anticipating that we're going to be running out of intensive care beds in the next two weeks or so and I think that's the scenario that we're really worried about, because essentially it may mean that we're having to manage people who are very distressed and dying and can't get into hospital, without much resources ourselves. So we're trying to gear ourselves up as much as possible for that while trying to manage everyone's anxiety and all sorts of things besides. And knowing that we've got to not burn out before we get there.

In the weeks that followed, Jane worked incredibly long hours at the practice in addition to stewarding an evolving range of community efforts. She began by coordinating daily cooking for all the staff at her practice, then helped create a system to collect and distribute food parcels to vulnerable patients. Soon the idea for the Midnight Kitchen, a virtual space of connection centred on food and storytelling, began to materialize. As these initiatives took hold, the realities of the pandemic continued to set in. In late March, Jane shared:

Our young man who was really unwell and who ended up in ICU sadly died yesterday, so that came as a real shock and was quite unnerving for all of us because I think we thought that once he received treatment he would be ok. He's part of a big extended family in our area, so already the impact of that is being felt. That's just one person. We had a second person die in his fifties yesterday, and this is just the beginning of the upswing … I was meant to be having a day off today, but I'm not sure if that's going to happen, although I'm absolutely exhausted at the moment. One thing that's been lovely has been the communications with patients.

> I did a full clinic by phone yesterday. I managed to catch up with lots of people that I have looked after for many years, and it really felt basked in warmth and – love, I guess. I think it's really bringing out, as these things do, the best and worst in different people and the sort of multiplicity of our selves. I'm going to try to do a bit of concentration on the community effort today, but interestingly it seems like lots of things are happening on their own, including harnessing some of the skill sets [of the collaborators involved]. We've set up a rudimentary community kitchen along the lines we'd wanted to, partly because it's hard to get food and things on a day-by-day basis. Even though there are delivery services, to make sure we've got enough for our staff we've started cooking at the practice, so I'm gathering ingredients in the mornings.

For Jane, connections with her patients continued to be a source of meaning, joy, and grief as the pandemic progressed. As a primary care provider with sometimes decades-long relationships with patients, she found institutional preparations for an upswing of illness and death from COVID-19 not abstract and practical, but deeply personal. She explained:

> I think everything's escalating here. I've just been sent some sobering guidance from North Central London about how to manage all the patients that don't get into hospital, knowing that we've got a shortage of palliative care drugs and just trying to speed through decisions, contact all our vulnerable patients, do some speedy advanced care planning for those who we haven't done, which makes me feel upset because they're all people who we know! I think that's one of the beauties and also painful things about primary care, is that we know all our patients, we've often known them for years, so it always feels painful when we lose people. I think we're going to have a lot of that and not a lot of time to sort things out and digest and process things. So that feels difficult, and having to have difficult conversations without being able to be with people, without face to face contact a lot of the time, without being able to hold people's hands, which feels really hard as well.

In the midst of Jane's navigating intensely sensitive conversations with vulnerable patients and preparing the practice to respond to the pressures of COVID-19, plans for the Midnight Kitchen began to take shape. Jane drew together a group of collaborators, including a socially engaged artist, a social prescriber, an adolescent psychiatrist, and the founder of an international charity focused on nature-based education. The Midnight Kitchen was envisioned as an online space to host virtual cooking and eating experiences, feasts that could be shared across distance. The initiative drew on work that had been done as part of an earlier collaboration between The Listening Space and the SEED project, an art and gardening collective at another London GP practice. The collaboration had produced The Lonely Aubergine Cookbook, an assemblage of the community's recipes and art that aimed to build health by reducing loneliness and creating social connections through food. About the emergence of the Midnight Kitchen, Jane said:

> I do feel rather buoyed up by the idea of having a virtual kitchen table, if we can all find a way to make that happen. I'd rented the domain name The Midnight Kitchen quite a number of years ago imagining that it was going to morph into something in the future. It had come from having a laugh about always cooking late at night, but I like that idea of transitions and doing things under the cloak of darkness. Something quite exciting and secretive and maybe a bit subversive about it. And crafting something in darkness that will be new and hopeful when the light returns. Anyway, let's see what happens. I always think with these things if they're meant to be then they will be born and if they're not, they're not quite right, so let's see.

While the Midnight Kitchen gestated within a growing network of volunteers, the themes of food, social connection, and well-being continued to arise in Jane's work with her patients. During the pandemic, lack of access to healthy food became an urgent need for many vulnerable people experiencing mental illnesses and lacking strong social ties in the community. With the closure of day centres and other in-person supports for people with complex needs, difficult situations were quickly exacerbated. In this context, the Caversham Group Practice built its capacity to gather and distribute food to people who found themselves without, an intervention that Jane described as "better than any medicine":

> I had an encounter with a patient of mine that I've been worrying about. She's somebody that has schizoaffective disorder, is very disturbed, is very isolated because she can be very difficult. So she's isolated not just because she has no family in the UK, but because she tends to push people away. She had been coming to our crafting group, which had been the first time when she's gone through a period of being relatively settled, a place where she felt that she was accepted and could come and could show off her very considerable sewing talents. I had been worrying about her because I hadn't managed to get hold of her in order to check that she

was doing ok. And I did see her today and sadly she was in a terrible state. I was thinking how hard it is for us all, with all our privilege and all the people we have around us, and I couldn't imagine how difficult it must be if you're lost in a world with only the voices that are punishing you, and with no comfort. Also she then told me that she'd been without food for a few days, which just made my heart break. And so it was really good with all the food gathering that we've been doing that I was able to send her off with a food parcel, which was better than any medicine, or any other comfort or solace we could have offered her.

As the weeks went on, Jane began to see increasing numbers of patients suffering from worsening mental illnesses. Living through a global pandemic was anxiety provoking in and of itself, coupled with lockdown measures cutting people off from the social supports that play such a crucial role in maintaining their mental health and well-being. With socially distant interactions becoming the new norm, The Listening Space garden at the practice was more widely recognized and valued than ever:

Things are really picking up here in a different way than before. Lots of people having all sorts of different types of suffering from the lockdown and neglected health issues, lots of mental health problems. So we're all busy busy busy. What's difficult is that the bureaucrats and the administrators have come back out to play, casting obstacles in our way again, which feels rather depressing after a lovely period of time without that. I do feel really enriched having the project [the Midnight Kitchen] around us and having the garden, it's been a complete godsend. So as well as using it for ourselves and our staff, we've increasingly used it to meet patients, particularly ones who have no place of respite or solace. There's a bit of a queue developing now for who can use the garden, and lots of other services are asking if they can have it for a period as well. It's interesting how that happens, when nobody was interested for a while, and certainly it was often difficult to get support and help in developing it. But I think people sometimes can't conceptualize something until it's properly in fruition. There are quite exciting developments in our plans for our link between the Story Garden and our Listening Space garden and the idea of mapping it with trees. I feel very fortunate in who we have in our congregation here, because it suddenly feels like there's a lot of magic going on, a lot of threads coming together.

In early June, the Midnight Kitchen ran its first "Zoom Eating" event, a virtual "picnic by the hedge" hosted by Jim Jones, a rural skills practitioner, storyteller, and PhD student based at Mount Wolfe Farm in Ontario. At the picnic participants shared stories, discussed the foods they had brought to the picnic and their meanings and origins, and ate together at a virtual kitchen table that built community at a distance. Although this was the only formal event of the virtual Midnight Kitchen to date, the process of collaborating around the development of the initiative became a support network for those involved, a place of human connection centred on experiences of growing, preparing, and enjoying food. As Jane suggested above, the Midnight Kitchen, Story Walks, and the community kitchen that developed at her practice during the pandemic all represent connected, emergent strands of a broader approach to health and well-being. In offering her time and attention to these initiatives, Jane did not proceed with a firm plan, but instead took an approach rooted in the power of relationships and the self-organizing capacities of community networks. About the Midnight Kitchen in particular, Jane said:

> It feels like it's one of those long-rooted things that has been brewing under the surface for some time. It felt like one of those hazy pictures where you feel something but you can't quite see it. Gradually over time, lots of things have come together. It feels like a sudden recognition, "oh that's why that happened," or "that's why." I think it's more a felt-sense of something that's been going on underneath. Then feeling like when things come together at a certain point, certain aspects land and others don't. So I guess it's been more a way-finding experience rather than having a firm plan.

The network engaged in the Midnight Kitchen was inspired by personal experiences of food as a social connector. Jane said that growing up, her life was "always rooted around a table. So lots of people, refugees for different reasons coming through our household, and people sitting around a table and finding their place of comfort and a place to be and then being able to move off into the world." Other collaborators shared similar experiences of food and tables acting as a centre of gravity in their childhood homes. Jim Jones, for instance, reflected:

> This idea of a community coming together and having a kind of creative space, and particularly around the idea of a kitchen. I grew up with this really really strong image of the kitchen being the place where not only meals were cooked, but I have this strong image of my father standing in the kitchen door and looking out over the garden and talking. Just talking about Beethoven and Jung and all these fantastic things, and my mind was swelling with this idea of intellectual endeavour and discovery ... So the

kitchen has always been therefore the place of doing and also the place of thinking and endeavour.

During the pandemic, the process of developing some structure around the virtual Midnight Kitchen took on a dual role. Although the vision behind "Zoom Eating" events was to reduce loneliness and increase health for people who found themselves isolated and cut off from other community supports, the collaboration itself became a support network for Jane and her collaborators. In her voice diary, Jane referred to the Midnight Kitchen as an "imaginary community" and a "virtual home" offering connections through a challenging time. In a subsequent interview, she elaborated:

> I think that the sort of virtual Midnight Kitchen for me offers a space which provides confidence and solace and respite, even when we're not always doing the things together, almost like a family, and knowing the people are there. I think that sometimes if you're quite active and a doer, you can be quite isolated because people don't always understand what's going on in your head or whether it's connected, or whether you're just off doing another madcap thing. And I know from establishing the garden at work, there's a lot of people who enjoy it now that didn't get it at all at the beginning, or thought it was just about gardening. Which of course it's a bit about that, but it's not just about that. And it's really nice to have a bunch of people to whom you don't have to explain that. It's certainly helped me to feel more grounded and rooted.

When developing community initiatives during the pandemic, Jane took an emergent approach, building on the momentum that surrounded certain activities as they unfolded and not being afraid to let others go if they weren't gaining traction (see brown 2017). Working in this way was an intuitive and embodied process, a skill learned over time:

> I know I feel it in my body when I'm on the right track and I feel it equally when I'm not. I think I'm getting a better balance, not feeling like it's all got to be successful or it's all got to happen a certain way, because it sort of feels like things happen in their own time. I don't always feel like it's me doing it, I genuinely feel like it's something being channelled and I just happen to be there. I know there are times when I try to make things happen and it doesn't work, so I've kind of let go of that. It just felt at the beginning like there was a need for people to be fed, and I had the energy for it, even though I was working really long hours clinically.

Jane's approach stands in contrast to the way in which health care institutions generally function. Health care settings, Jane argues, tend to impose too many specific requirements around activities, outcomes, and measurement, creating formalized structures and processes that can impede the "alchemy" of social change work:

> I think the sort of modern way of doing things – mechanistic, we've got to plan, and we know exactly what outcomes we want – it doesn't allow for that kind of third way. Where you've got the tension between two things, and something new emerges. Which is why I like the kitchen metaphors as well, you have the alchemy between ingredients. If you mix flour and water together, you can get amazing bread, but you can get all kinds of things besides, including a stinky mess if you just mix it and leave it in the wrong place.

The initiatives that Jane supported during the pandemic illustrate the value of contributing to the self-organization of community systems without being overly prescriptive about structure or results. Jane described this work as a form of play, an imaginative improvisation that makes it possible to act, learn, and act again in rapid cycles as community needs shift:

> At the beginning we were really busy because we were cooking every day. It was really gratifying because then when I was on the phone to people who couldn't get food, to be able to say, "don't worry, we'll just bike it round," and we had loads of volunteers. But then that need was lessened because as things have eased up, people were able to get hold of things, and also I think people wanted to get a bit more back to normal. It provided an easy pause in the whole thing so that we didn't get exhausted and people didn't get fed up. And I think it felt a bit like playing. I always think the things we've done are a bit like how kids do it. You play it first. It might be a bit rough and ready and not the bright, shiny, whatever you imagine it could be, and you make your mistakes that way. But you also do something straight away, without it having to be perfect. And then you have different iterations and it feels like it somehow brings it into being. We did it with the garden, so we kind of imagined, each time we imagined the kitchen, and eventually we've built on extra bits, so it's actually been quite easy and it's been quite light touch. It's not that you have to raise all kinds of money and build a proper kitchen. It's very makeshift, and I quite like that. It's fairly fluid, what's happening. But I think that as a result, it's always been relational, we've built lots of relationships with other people and things have happened.

The relationships formed and deepened through the activities of the Midnight Kitchen have already begun to give rise to new initiatives, including the Arete International Craft Consortium, a collaboration of artists, makers, farmers, researchers, and doctors working on questions of sustainability, health, and well-being through engagement in craft and storytelling. Jim Jones, a member of the Midnight Kitchen and the Craft Consortium, noted that

> the crafting thing may not have happened if the feast hadn't happened. It was at least for me a way of deepening relationships with people like Bess and Jane, and you, to get us ready to shift into that next phase of doing deeper work … All of a sudden, these people within the Midnight Kitchen, their context is much deeper. All of a sudden I can say a word or a series of words and you will understand, without me elaborating, because we've had that deepening of context. So the feasts and the ongoing, just sitting around the kitchen table, is incredibly important.

15.2 Working with Emergence and Self-Organization

As the first wave of the COVID-19 pandemic gave way to the second, the work of the virtual Midnight Kitchen was paused as other urgent needs arose and collaborators began to come together on new initiatives like the Craft Consortium and Story Walks. These shifting priorities mirrored broader changes in the landscape created by government responses to the COVID-19 pandemic, as well as new trends in the organic self-organization of the community. In a final voice diary entry sent mid-October 2020, Jane reflected:

> I think there have been different phases at the practice. I think we had the first bit at the beginning of the pandemic, where it felt like all the patients scattered, management scattered, there was a lot of bewilderment and we flexed and changed lots of things at the practice. It was quite a lot of energy, that's when we started our social kitchen, all sorts of other activities alongside managing the patient contacts and visiting, and linking in with social care. Then I think there was a middle bit where it became more business as usual, where I think as the lockdown eased and people started to come back, there was also a sense of dissatisfaction, people having plenty of time on their hands, having examined all sorts of bits of their body, and with all the new ways into primary care, we've had lots and lots of people who are worried but well consulting. It's meant that there's quite a lot of white noise I guess, because there's a lot of people who are sick and a lot of people at a lot of disadvantage who aren't able to access services. I think

once again we're seeing the inverse care law play out. So those people who are younger, more tech savvy, are able to access services much more easily than our patients whose first language isn't English, or people who are disadvantaged in other ways, either through poverty, education, all sorts of other reasons. So we've been trying to do a bit of reaching out, but I think we're all rather exhausted as well because of everything that's been going on. I guess now we're moving into a third phase, which I think looks like more lockdown restrictions going into winter. Certainly more illness, rising levels of COVID again, but with the exhaustion of this not being new and more confusion in the world. But again, I see it also as a time of real opportunity to make changes.

Jane's voice diaries demonstrate that the COVID-19 pandemic unearthed the potential for significant transitions within health care institutions. During the first wave, changes that had been in the works for years were implemented in a matter of weeks (see also McCartney 2020). Yet new practices like telemedicine and videoconferencing, which helped to keep people safe from the virus, simultaneously erected novel barriers to care for vulnerable patients. Social isolation and the weight of living through a global crisis exacerbated existing mental illnesses and loneliness among Jane's patients. In this context, places and approaches like The Listening Space garden and the community kitchen at the Caversham Group Practice offered solace, respite, and connection. In a time of crisis, the value of these initiatives was recognized more broadly than ever before, even by those who had formerly resisted the changes that such projects entailed. During this period the Midnight Kitchen also came into being, a virtual kitchen table that cultivated relationships and helped to sustain Jane and her collaborators through the challenging, exhausting, and at times paradoxically energizing first phase of the pandemic. The stories of the Midnight Kitchen and the other community initiatives led by Jane and her colleagues illustrate how working with the forces of emergence, self-organization, and relationship building can support change makers to effectively use windows of opportunity such as those afforded by the COVID-19 pandemic to fundamentally shift the ways in which primary care practices approach health and well-being in the communities they serve.

16 Complexity Medicine Group

> This is a group about life on life's terms. We are all life, living life.
>
> (Dr. William Sutherland, personal communication)

In 2018 Dr. William (Bill) Sutherland, a general practice physician and innovator of the complexity medicine paradigm, invited me to attend his Wednesday night psychotherapy group. At the time Bill was a member of my dissertation committee, and I had read his book *Grand Rounds: Healing Medicine for a Complex World*. We had even begun to co-author a paper together on the medicines that are needed to support complex adaptive systems in precarious times (see Zywert and Sutherland 2020). However, I had yet to understand what complexity medicine could look and feel like in practice. Over ten weeks in the fall and winter of 2018, I attended Bill's complexity medicine psychotherapy group to experience the approach first hand. During that time, I participated in the group's discussions and processes, interviewed participants, and held a focus group about the purpose and impact of the group. The discussion that follows draws from all these experiences, as well as from additional conversations with Bill about the purpose of his Wednesday night group and about the characteristics and potential of complexity medicine.

16.1 Enacting Complexity Medicine Together

Bill would be the first to say that the practice of "complexity medicine" could be as diverse as the practitioners and participants involved, and as the contexts (cultural, ecological, historical) in which they live. Complexity medicine, as described in *Grand Rounds: Healing Medicine for a Complex World*, is at its heart health-centric and holistic, with both terms understood in the widest sense. A health-centric medicine does not take disease as its starting point. It sees symptoms not as unpleasant experiences to be suppressed, but as a primary "gateway" to healing that reveals important aspects about the systems and relationships in which an individual is embedded (Sutherland, personal communication; Keeney 1983). When one adopts a health-centric ontology (understood here as a way of seeing the world), healing becomes a process of learning to access the "systemic wisdom" that exists within wholes – whole people, whole families, whole cultures, whole social-ecological systems (Sutherland 2015, 90). It also requires one to act in ethical ways that "nurture" the complexity of nested wholes as they continue to evolve (90). While biomedical paradigms are often criticized for being inherently reductionistic, they are not necessarily so. As an emergency room doctor, Bill notes that emergency medicine is often holistic in that doctors do "what is required to maintain the integrity of the whole person in light of immediate trauma" (18). Complexity medicine is therefore not an alternative to biomedical health care, but can be integrated by health practitioners across diverse biomedical or traditional fields if they attend to the dynamics of complex systems when providing care.

Complexity medicine approaches like Bill's weekly group enact an "epistemology of wholeness" rooted in embodied understandings of the nature of complex systems (Sutherland 2015, 57). Notions of self-organization, emergence, and the inability to separate the observer and the observed figure prominently, if not always explicitly, in the approach. Bill reflects that although the group may on the surface appear to be little more than group psychotherapy, a practice that was developed in the 1960s and is nothing new, it is more accurately an attempt

> to correct an inversion, the idea of what a group is, and we're trying to reinvert that inversion ... Already just the form of it, we're already breaking all these rules as to what it is ... it doesn't have a theoretical stance, it's not specific diagnostically. We're not coming in with an agreed-upon thing, other than we have a mental health journey, or there's some concern for our health in that way. (personal communication)

Each week, Bill would open the group with a theme. Some would be psychological, such as "cognitive distortions," while others were abstract, like "persona." Still others were simply provocative phrases like "in reach, out of reach." At the first group I attended, he began the session by showing a video of a professional surfer riding an incredibly enormous wave. These ideas, phrases, and images acted as the starting point for the group's engagement in their own and each other's health. The wave, for instance, evoked feelings of mastery, being overwhelmed, and awe at humanity's bravery and competence; several people likened the experience of the surfer riding the wave to coping with the rise and fall of emotions in the body. Bill said, "When I would put those up, I had no idea where I really wanted to go with them, they were just story starters." Participants reflected that this aspect of the structure of the group was useful and unique compared to other groups they had attended in the past. One focus group participant explained:

> I'm really grateful to be in a situation where the person in authority doesn't already have an idea of how you're going to heal and what you need to do to heal, and that arrogance. Allowing for interplay and interactiveness and dynamicness of moments and not just this, "well, I know how you're going to heal and I'm going to tell you."

Another focus group participant noted that the group felt "human" and that the lack of an agenda and pre-determined focus helped to create a context in which change and healing could arise:

> I was just thinking there's a humanness to this group that's not contrived. In a lot of therapies it's contrived, it's a theory, they have a goal to get to and theories. Here, I don't know what's going to happen! At first it was scary, but it's ok for me now. And kind of just looking back at my life in the last year, I can't believe how many changes I've made in the face of some tragedy and I'm thinking, "How did that happen?" I was at a point when I was just so stuck and I was terrified at the condition of my mental health and my physical health, and now I see them as all just health, right? I don't know what the nugget in this group is that's different, but I think it's partly that nobody's pushing us toward their own agenda.

Bill has found that this open approach that invites but does not direct engagement helps the group to circle around and tap into the lived experience of health, something that is difficult or perhaps impossible to access directly:

> Every week it seems that we do something different, and yet every week I think we're just reaffirming, validating that we're doing the same. There's something magic in the different and the same. We're speaking to something that can't be spoken to directly, and we do that in a different way each week. We point towards it, we move towards it, we get pulled towards it. We don't know what it is, but every week we circle around in a new and different way, and I think there's something really generative about that. I think it's confirming too, because we come back really knowing that we're

being pulled back to that same something that none of us can name but we're looking for, and then we rediscover it every Wednesday. And we recreate it anew and we restate it anew, and we make up all new things around it. I think there's something in that new but completely expected. (Sutherland, personal communication)

In my discussions with group members, many commented that the Wednesday group was different from any other psychotherapeutic process in which they had previously engaged (many participants emphasized that they had worked with multiple counsellors and therapists and had participated in numerous groups over the course of their mental health journey). Above all, they said that Bill's approach was distinctive because of its focus on the whole person and on embodied feelings experienced in the present. Both of these characteristics align with what Bill believes is required to hold and nurture complexity for health: rejecting epistemologies that separate the mind and body, and becoming more attuned to emotion and sensation to get back in touch with one's embeddedness within complex living systems (see Sutherland 2015). Both of these core components of the approach were highly valued by participants. One focus group participant said, "I have so much appreciation for dealing with not just the psychotherapy aspect of it, but dealing with the person as a whole. Where my experience in other groups has really been focused on just the mental health aspect." Another reflected that the group creates the space to begin to think of oneself through the lens of holism: "the power of putting ourselves back together in some sort of whole way, or of tapping into some sort of wholeness that's already in us and that we only lost in some way, or we couldn't find another way."

Others described how the group takes a "body-centred approach" that aims to help people work with feelings as they arise. Bill's approach was seen to depart significantly from typical talk therapy sessions that often involve "rehashing the past and trying to come to terms with it." Instead, "it's more present here-and-now focused around your feelings and bodily sensations and the emotions within your body." One participant said that this body-centred approach works well for him because he tends to be overly analytical in many aspects of his life: "I try to figure out everything. What's going on with me, what's wrong with me, what's wrong with you. And I think that's been a diversion from actually dealing with my core feelings, learning to regulate my feelings properly." He further reflected that what he does in the group and in individual sessions with Dr. Sutherland is

> not psychotherapy, where you're digging up what mum did. It's what's arising. So whatever's evoked in the moment, that's what we're working

with. I never know what to expect here anymore. I used to try to figure out what he does, so I would be like the student in the group like you, trying to figure out what techniques or modalities he's using, but I can see it's more, it's not Western-focused.

Similarly, a woman who came to see Dr. Bill because she was suffering from chronic pain, fibromyalgia, and PSTD resulting from domestic abuse and a near-death experience, said that the body-centric approach "made a tremendous difference":

First session I just did a kind of a run-on sentence like I am with you right now about my medical history, and then he said, in typical Dr. Bill fashion, "well that's not going to help us much. I'm bored with listening to people talk about the past, let's do some work." So I started to learn about dropping into the body and feeling the emotions that I was feeling and where I was feeling them, and how to process them. And that in itself has been a godsend. So I know when I'm feeling anxious or I'm feeling sad or whatever, I know how to drop in and deal with the emotions.

In contrast to previous groups she had attended where people could become fixated on telling the stories of their past traumas, often repeating the same stories week after week, with facilitators merely asking people how they feel or what they think about various parts of the story, the Wednesday night group was more like a "class." The participant said it provided "a good support structure" by reinforcing concepts in creative ways, reiterating ideas from individual sessions, and focusing on teaching skills for processing emotions in the body. Another participant reinforced this insight:

This group is unlike any other group I've been in, and I've been in a lot of group therapy settings that have only focused on past events in my life and processing those past events. It's been very mind-story oriented. This is the first time I've been introduced to feelings as a body sensation, and treating the whole body. This group isn't so focused on story and past life content and processing that. So there is content, but we learn from each other. But it is whole-body focused and that is very unique to me and unlike anything I've experienced before, and I've done a lot of counselling.

When speaking with participants in semi-structured interviews and in the focus group, I asked them whether they thought being part of the group had affected their health, and if so in what ways. People said that their mental health had improved, that they were better able to cope with chronic pain, and that they had a greater capacity to process feelings in the moment by using the approaches they practised together every Wednesday night. A man who experiences chronic pain and who has struggled with depression and addiction said that, in combination with approaches like yoga, osteopathy, and nutrition, his work in group and individual sessions with Dr. Sutherland has made his pain more tolerable:

> I'm more accepting of the pain ... now instead of focusing on the pain, I'm focusing on the feelings associated with the pain, like fear or anger or frustration or whatever, and I sit with those. As a consequence, the pain becomes more acceptable, if that makes sense. I'm not struggling with the pain ... The pain hasn't reduced, the pain is still there, but ... you learn to live with the pain rather than struggle and fight it all the time.

Some participants reflected that taking part in the group evoked a paradigm shift in the way they think about and pursue health. One person said that the group's effect on her health has been "invaluable":

> I've been coming here for a while, and I was just thinking, lately I've actually caught myself being excited about life and different things. I don't even know the last time that was there. Like I said before, I was just stuck in such an inflexible way of thinking. Another word that is used is "spacious." Just having the space in your body and mentally to exist in a way that I guess isn't painful.

Another participant explained:

> I just feel like this is pulling together a lot of things in a new paradigm where I'm starting to catch myself and say, "oh, I put value judgements on things. Dysregulation is bad, regulation is good." This is part of a new framework of thinking about not just mental health, but all of life. Observing things as they are and not just putting value judgements on them instantaneously. It's moving me into a place where if I allow myself, I'll be able to expand and grow. I feel like every week we're building a framework, a holistic framework, that's bigger and more powerful than we think, than I've ever encountered until now.

A woman who came to Bill's group facing anxiety and depression, PTSD, and a sense of hopelessness about the state of the world also described how the group helped to illuminate the frameworks through which we understand health, creating space for group members to engage with these frameworks directly and consider whether or not they ring true. She said that by drawing attention to the ways in which we understand health, Dr. Sutherland "invites you into the story of health and you and health, and everyone in health and him in health, and how that evolves." At the Wednesday night group, Bill would often share insights from complexity theories, his experiences living and working with Indigenous people, and his training in psychology to spark new ways of thinking about what health is and how one can move towards health. Participants said that they particularly appreciated and enjoyed the opportunity to learn from the group: one said, "I really love the educational part, the teaching. The teaching really challenges my preconceived notions of therapy and what I want to get out of therapy."

From his own perspective, Bill also felt that his health was affected by his participation in the group. Even though the focus of the group was on others, his participation in the experience circled back to create positive changes in his own health:

> I'm the facilitator, but I actually am a participant in all this too. Especially when you ask the question "what does this do for one's health?" How does this affect my health? It's interesting because of course as far as intent, I don't come in and say, "well, what am I going to do for my health today?" I'm thinking about the group, but inevitably each time when I leave, my health has been affected, directed, redirected, given momentum in a positive way. And in a way that I can't take self-credit for. I can't take credit and say it was my doings that allowed me to feel that in myself. There's something in this that deeply feeds me and I'm surprised and grateful and full of wonderment every time it happens, every week. It's an interesting place to be the so-called facilitator of the group and enjoy the perpetual surprise that that brings. Because I never get to see it coming until it does, and it affects me profoundly every time as well. So I think there must be something unique in the structure that I can't claim credit for and I don't think anyone can claim credit for, but something in the alchemy of when we get together that somehow finds a place to hold us all in our roles. It's interesting, because in many ways I think my role could hold me as separate, but somehow the group doesn't allow that to happen. I feel like I'm part of this as well in a way that helps me to slip more into my wholeness and my health each time.

Similar to Bill's reflection, participants also often had a hard time identifying exactly what it was about the group that facilitated a change in their health, yet they nonetheless recognized the change when it occurred.

There was a sense that being together in the room every Wednesday night to work with the ideas and practices being shared offered an opportunity to think and act in new ways that allowed health to emerge:

> Let's call it a practice. The thing we come here and do every week. I think it has something to do with consistency of being here and doing it, every week. And the practice, yes, you're supposed to take it into the world and do the practice in the world. But because we're consistently coming here on Wednesday night and sitting amongst each other, and sitting with uncomfortable feelings, and really doing the practice of going in and seeing how it feels, doing it in this room, then this becomes a regular thing. They say to be able to make something a habit, you need to consistently do it for a number of times. That's what this brings. And then we can take it into the world. More often then, I find myself being in the car, or being in an uncomfortable situation out there, and because I've been here on Wednesday having to put these things in practice in the group, that's what I think happens. There's something to be said about that.

Doing the work in a group also held tremendous value for participants. Several people said that it was helpful to be with others who shared similar struggles and experiences:

> The purpose of me being in this group is that you can talk amongst people who are kind of like yourself. As opposed to people and friends and family that you may hang out with, they never seem to acknowledge that you may have something else going on, i.e., mental health problems. I'm sure everyone knows about me, but I can also assure you that no one has ever talked to me about it, voluntarily. So it's nice to be acknowledged by people who are going through the same things.

Interacting with others to nurture health as opposed to working through one's mental health challenges alone provided useful opportunities to practise new ways of reacting to and "digesting" experiences that could later be applied outside the group:

> The value of doing it in a group is that I can't do it in a vacuum. I can't have a relationship in a vacuum. For me it's like, I can relate to a lot of what people in this group are saying and that helps me get in touch with some of my feelings around what you guys are sharing, and I can actually practice in the group the self-regulation that Bill talks about. Sitting in the group and digesting. So it gives me that opportunity to do that, because what you share evokes stuff in me. I get to sit with that.

Over time, the group has become a place for peer support, learning, and connection. One participant described how in the group "people are not intrusive, but they're friendly. And they're also people who have found that other groups or other modes of therapy haven't worked for them. And they're respectful and intelligent people." Another explained that the group was a place where she felt trusted and valued:

> I come here, it's like sitting down in my living room with friends and actually having a conversation. I feel relaxed, I feel that I'm trusted in this room. I know that a lot of therapy places where I was at, I didn't feel like I was trusted. What I was saying, I didn't feel like my trust was confidential or secure or whatever, but here I do. I feel validated, I leave here excited, and I go home and I bring what I've learned in the group back home and I try to instil it for the week. It doesn't work all the time, but I like going from the body to the mind to the feelings. I also put myself back where I should be. There's not a place that I was before that I could do that, and I've never done it before, before this group.

In the focus group, participants expressed gratitude and appreciation for the learning and support they had received from other members of the group:

> Everybody who's here, all your insights and all that you talk about and have done, I have implemented that in my life since I've been here. And everyone has their stories and everything, but I take a little bit from every one of you guys home with me. And right now I think I'm a better person for it, and I know there's still work to be done, but I want to thank everyone here. I greatly appreciate your insights and you guys have helped me, more than you know.

From Bill's perspective, doing the work in community was one of the primary reasons that health emerged every Wednesday night. He explained, "the community of the group is what allows for intimacy and vulnerability, it is a private public space. More than anything we do, that is actually the therapy." Within the community that is the group, the content and structure are co-created among all who are present. Bill said that over time, the way he interacted as the facilitator changed as trusting relationships deepened between participants:

> My role at the beginning was often just to say "not that" – to stop people from going into the same old story, instead shift into the feelings, where that's moving in the body. Over time how much I would even interject

became less. Somehow along the line we developed truly a culture. Something switched and they would start asking each other, they would speak to their experience of the other's sharing.

Once the culture of the group was established, new people who joined were able to learn it easily. Although many participants said that the group provided them with useful tools and practices that helped to improve their mental health, Bill noted that these tools were "holistically held. The group action, culture, movement, interaction held all of those tools and actions simultaneously – acting, listening, receiving, doing, but you couldn't say 'this is my cognitive behavioural therapy tool' or 'this is my breathing.' There was no skillset or modality base." And while participants experienced meaningful improvements to their mental health and shifts in their perspective as a result of participating in the group, the culture of the group was not always heavy, serious, or even aimed at any particular outcome. Instead, Bill said, it was about process, interaction, and aesthetics:

> There's a lot of play, a lot of laughter. There's no goal orientation, it's all process. None of us are trying to get somewhere. We end up somewhere at the end of the two hours, we end up somewhere collectively over time, but we're never trying to get there. It's about play, process, and aesthetics. Every time we're trying to make something beautiful in its interaction. Every night, even though it's the same format, feels unique, and we all go, "we just made something beautiful again." That's what drives it. The fact that we continue to call it a psychotherapy group is really a guerrilla tactic ... We keep utilizing that word as an invite, and then people will tell you very quickly, this is like no other group I've been to.

16.2 Adopting Systems-Based Approaches to Health

Bill's weekly group began, he said, as a way "to get people in quickly to become part of a therapeutic process." As a sought-after, OHIP-billing psychotherapist, Bill had a waitlist frequently between a year and two years long. While participants waited to begin individual sessions, they could join the Wednesday night group. Bill reflected:

> By the time they would see me a year, year and a half later, we would have a relationship, or sometimes they would say the reason I came to you has been taken care of, or most of the work had been done. Then the individual sessions became like finishing school. We went into their specific experience, but we knew how to go into it. There was this priming that

had happened. But I couldn't tell you what it was. Probably I couldn't do a dissection about exactly how the change happened.

Participants in their turn came to the group to address mental health issues, many of which were acute and long-standing. One man described how after "crushing defeat and heartache and all kinds of tough, tough severe lessons in my life, I have come to a point where the only thing I can do is something about my mental health." Another said:

> the purpose of me being in this group is if I don't get my mental state into a normal state, I'm at a point where I'm going to have a heart attack and die. So it's my health. I have a fifteen-year-old son. I have a life that I want to still have, and if I can't get my mental issues under control, then I have a very good chance of not being here. And I'm not willing to do that, and that's why I'm here.

Still others sought to unlearn unhealthy patterns of thought and action and to adopt new ways of being to support their own and their family's health:

> [The purpose of the group for me is] to be able to guide my children the best way that I can and learn what I can for myself so that I can have the tools to raise my children differently from what I learned. Because I guess I sort of learned along the way some not so great things. So to learn from that and revamp it, fix it up, and be able to be a good person in the world.

Through the engagement of these and many other participants seeking to improve their mental health, Bill's Wednesday night group became a co-created, non-theoretical, body-centric, holistic space in which participants could engage with one another to learn, offer support, and "digest" their emotions and experiences (group participant, personal communication). The group can therefore be seen as one unique manifestation of a complex medicine suited to and arising within its own specific context. By making use of familiar ideas like group psychotherapy – a framing Bill refers to as a "guerrilla tactic" – the group offers opportunities to practise new ways of perceiving health and of relating to others to build health while continuing to operate within the confines of existing biomedical institutions and resource flows. In this way, the group illustrates what complexity medicine can look like in practice and how health systems could begin to shift towards adopting more systems-based approaches without the need to establish new structures or to overcome resistance to paradigmatic change.

17 Herbalism in a Post-Growth Transition

In the early spring of 2021, I spent many evenings after my son had gone to sleep standing at the kitchen sink, filling little pots with wet soil. I scattered seeds onto the dark surface of the soil, and after pressing them down set them in their trays to germinate under grow lights. This year I seeded many plants that were new to me: tulsi, motherwort, elecampane, arnica, ashwagandha, calendula, camomile, skullcap, and marshmallow. Over the winter I had worked with Nikola Barsoum, a community herbalist and founder of Half Moon Herbals, an herb farm and apothecary, in what she calls a "medicine garden mentorship." The mentorship consisted of eight sessions in which Nikola conducted a health assessment to determine which plants could offer the most useful medicines for my family and me, made recommendations on which plants to grow, created a preliminary medicine garden design grounded in permaculture principles, and taught me the basics of medicinal plant propagation, harvesting, and medicine making. Nikola's weekly mentoring sessions were enlivening during the paradoxical pandemic winter, which for so many families was both isolating and frantically busy. Although I had known that I wanted to grow a medicine garden for several years and had basic knowledge of gardening passed down from my grandmother and mother, I had little confidence about where to start when it came to growing and preparing medicinal plants. The medicine garden mentorship gave me a way to enter into relationship with nutritive herbs that could enhance my family's well-being while also transforming our unused lawns into more biodiverse landscapes that contribute to ecological resilience (also see chapter 5). Working with Nikola felt like an important step in my effort to put some of what I was learning in this research into practice in my life. Increasingly, I was coming to see herbalism as an important component of a post-growth health system that can generate benefits across social-ecological scales at a low ecological and economic cost. In this chapter, I convey some of the potential of herbal medicine to both uphold thriving post-growth health systems and support the transition towards such a system. I will also discuss some of the tensions that are inherent in the approach.

Susan Leopold, executive director of United Plant Savers, an organization with a mission to conserve native medicinal plants and their habitats in the United States and Canada while securing an abundant supply of herbs into the future, describes herbal medicine as the "root" of all medicine. Herbalism is, as Leopold sees it, humanity's "primary medicine," an approach that has been with us throughout our evolutionary history (personal communication). Today, around half the population in industrialized countries reports using traditional medicines (e.g., 42 per cent in the United States, 70 per cent in Canada), many of which include culturally grounded herbal traditions (WHO 2018a). In low- and middle-income countries, the WHO estimates that a third of the population lacks access to biomedical health care and relies on traditional medicines for primary care (WHO 2015). The WHO formally recognizes that herbalism and other forms of traditional and complementary medicines can support long-term health system sustainability by lowering costs, making health care more accessible to communities, and helping to "balanc[e] curative services with preventative care" (WHO 2019b, 5; see also WHO 2018a). As such, modern health systems around the world are working to increase integration between allopathic and traditional and complementary medicines (WHO 2018a, 2019b). To date, thirty-four WHO member states also include herbal medicines in their nation's list of "essential medicines," medicines that are seen to contribute most to population health and that should therefore be made affordable and readily accessible to all (WHO 2018a).

Herbal medicine is best understood as "an overall tonic and preventative. It's not the 'save your life' kind of thing. A lot of people turn to herbal medicine because everything else has failed" (Leopold, personal communication). 7Song, founder of the Northeast School of Botanical Medicine, explains that one of herbalism's key strengths is its ability to offer tonics that blur the line between food and medicine. In combination with good nutrition, herbal medicines can also at times be better than allopathic medicines at addressing the underlying causes of illness. For instance, conditions like fibromyalgia that present as a collection of different symptoms can be exceedingly difficult to treat with pharmaceuticals, but can be effectively managed using a variety of herbs that can help reduce symptoms like pain and insomnia (7Song, personal communication).

7Song works as an herbalist at the Ithaca Free Clinic, where he has the opportunity to collaborate with allopathic doctors in an integrated practice. Through this work, he has found that herbs and modern pharmaceuticals can be complementary in the sense that plants can often do things that drugs don't do and, in some instances, can increase the effectiveness of pharmaceuticals (personal communication). Patients taking antibiotics for Lyme disease, for example, can be prescribed herbs to help them with the pain and cognitive difficulties associated with their illness. He notes that the Ithaca Free Clinic offers a meaningful opportunity for integration of herbalism and biomedicine within a formal health care context, likely because patient needs are so urgent, leading doctors and patients alike to be more open to non-conventional approaches (personal communication). In a future of more constrained resources, herbalists could play an increasingly important role in primary care, both within formal health care settings like the Ithaca Free Clinic and in informal community and family settings.

From a planetary health perspective, a resurgence of interest in herbalism also has the potential to begin shifting the way people interact with the plants and landscapes around them. Susan Leopold says that ideally, herbal medicine is "something that you're connected with," something that is embedded in one's culture and daily life (personal communication). In many high-income nations, we have moved away from "that idea of your grandmother making a cup of tea, and having mint growing in your garden or incorporating bitters into your diet." However, Leopold would "really like to think that as we learn about herbal medicine, we learn about how to take care of the planet. Because if we can't heal the planet, we can't heal ourselves." Engaging in the practice of herbalism can draw attention to the connections between the integrity of local ecosystems, global consumer forces, individual and family health, and planetary ecological change:

> If you start to learn about the plants around you and you start to understand the role these plants play in the ecosystem, I think you're going to shift this idea that a plant is just there to be harvested or manoeuvred or it doesn't matter, what we do to our ecology has no impact. Many of these native medicinal plants, especially in the Appalachia region, are only going to be found and are only going to grow in ecosystems that are functional, that are intact, that have the soil structure, they're not eroded, they're not taken over by invasives, they haven't been depleted of their nutrients in the soil. These really functional hardwood, often mesic, forests are often those areas that are sequestering carbon ... If we manage those forests differently, we could totally shift the climate change in that

region. We could be sequestering carbon and at the same time protecting biodiversity and safeguarding our medicinal plants. So it's a win-win. (Leopold, personal communication)

Nikola Barsoum described herbal medicine as "the people's medicine," as a tradition of self-sufficient home healing that is low cost, widely accessible, and grounded in local cultural and ecological knowledge (personal communication). Learning to grow and prepare herbal medicines can support people to develop more reciprocal relationships with plants and with the landscapes in which we live while potentially reducing reliance on global supply chains to furnish households with an expanding array of pharmaceutical treatments. One of the benefits of herbalism, in the context of relocalization and a post-growth transition, is the extent to which the plants that thrive within a particular ecosystem are particularly well suited to supporting the health of the people living in that bioregion. Leopold argues:

> We don't need to be importing herbal medicine from the Amazon. Herbs that are in our environment are there to treat things that we're environmentally struggling with. We live in a temperate climate, the plants go through seasonal changes just like we go through seasonal changes. So there's a deep connection with plants serving our bodies as they adapt to the environment that we're both experiencing together. I think there's a total shift in how we see ourselves and how we see our role in the environment as stewards and caretakers. (personal communication)

She also says that there can be a spiritual component to growing and preparing plant medicines that can increase general well-being and healing, and create opportunities for meaning making:

> There's that whole other spiritual aspect of making your own medicine, that in itself is healing. We're in this instant gratification mentality. I think it's a process, but if you really want to connect with herbalism, the best thing you can do is start by learning about the plants that grow around you. And then, what plants can you make medicine from? And going through that process. The harvesting of the plant. And the crux of everything, of course, is total communication. So if you're going to communicate with that plant and you're going to harvest that plant you're going to build a relationship, and then there's this whole reciprocity that starts to take place. Now you have a deeper appreciation of yourself, you have a deeper appreciation of the plant that just spoke to you that you harvested. Then when you make that medicine, there's a sense of ownership, there's

a sense of connectivity and it takes on a meaning. It's a much different process than "I'm going to go to CVS [Pharmacy] and buy that thing off the shelf." But maybe that's the first step. (personal communication)

For 7Song, making his own medicines, mostly from wild-crafted herbs, is part of what it means to be an herbalist. 7Song is a botanist and a naturalist, and he sees harvesting and medicine making as part of his broader study of the natural world. He also makes his own medicine as a way to "disconnect" from a profit-driven medical system, though he recognizes that even his work at the free clinic is tied into that system in that it alleviates the worst of the suffering it causes, which may ultimately contribute to allowing it to persist rather than collapse. Nevertheless, 7Song says that some of the people who come to him for herbal medicines also do so to separate themselves from what they perceive to be a destructive pharmaceutical industry. He explains, "I've always had my ear to the ground, and I do feel like herbal medicine, even though it's not always applicable, many people appreciate the idea that we can not be beholden to companies" (personal communication).

Although herbalism offers tangible ways to build connections between human and planetary health and to potentially reground preventative health practices within family- and community-level production, renewed interest in herbalism within a capitalist political economy has also created its own ecological and social challenges. Susan Leopold says that the herbal medicine industry has consistently grown by 10 to 15 per cent every year for the past fifteen years and is now a six billion US dollar/year industry in the United States alone (personal communication; data from American Botanical Council 2017). As a result of this growth, herbalism is an ambiguous driver of ecological change. Growth in the herbal medicine industry has, for instance, contributed to the decline of wild-harvested medicinal plants at the same time as it has opened up space to reduce dependence on resource-intensive biomedical treatments. Yet over-harvesting of herbal products is not the only driver of decline in medicinal species:

> It's very easy to see this decline in wild-harvested plants, because they cannot reproduce at the rate they're being harvested. Even up to probably the 1920s, maybe leading up until World War I, you could go into the pharmacy and the majority of what you saw were all herbal products. Actually, many of the wild plants were being cultivated, even in a woodland environment, to support that. But then you had this total drop-off in demand, people stopped growing these plants, and now that this industry has picked up at such a rapid pace, people are just going back out and

they're harvesting from wild populations. So what we're seeing is a dramatic decline in these plants. Then you add fragmentation of the land, so these plants aren't able to have wildlife corridors to reproduce and to court genetic diversity. We're seeing increased logging on public lands, we're seeing rapid development and then on top of that we're seeing mountaintop removal, we're seeing fracking, we're seeing this incredible loss of habitat. And then you throw into that whole mix this unsustainable, unregulated harvesting, and that we do not prioritize conservation of native plants at all. (Leopold, personal communication)

Leopold suggests that declines in medicinal plant populations may be "even more desperate in other places" outside the United States and could lead to health crises in regions where people do not have access to allopathic health care and rely on herbal medicines for primary care. She notes that "as people are losing their access to medicinal plants, they're losing their only access to health care" (personal communication).

A key problem for organizations trying to address these issues is that there isn't enough data to quantify the loss of medicinal plants. Tracking plant populations would require significant knowledge and resources dedicated to multiyear monitoring, and these activities are difficult to fund. Leopold explains that United Plant Savers "was founded in 1994 specifically out of concern about the native medicinal plants that were being harvested out of the wild for an herbal trade that was growing exponentially." The organization was established by prominent herbalist Rosemary Gladstar, who recognized that

> we need to know where these plants are coming from if we're going to consume them, and more importantly if we're going to use these plants for healing ourselves, we need to ask ourselves what these plants need from us in return. So this idea of reciprocity, and being more conscientious of choices when it comes to herbal products and the whole development of herbalism as a practice. (Leopold, personal communication)

Growth in the for-profit herbal medicine industry also creates problematic dynamics for people who wish to practise herbal medicine as a livelihood activity. With so much mass marketing of herbal products, many people get their information about herbs from the media and from popular culture sources like Dr. Oz (7Song, personal communication). As such, they tend to self-diagnose rather than consult qualified herbal practitioners. This trend makes it difficult for practitioners to make a living from their trade, further perpetuating lack of access to herbal expertise at the community level. Commodification of herbalism also tends to favour more simplified ways of thinking about herbs as "good for" specific illnesses, rather than as complex actors with multiple physiological effects in the body (7Song, personal communication). For these reasons, the commodification of herbal medicine is a barrier to realizing some of the transformative potential of the approach within the current regime. However, if commodification in general is curtailed during a post-growth transition, the herbal medicine industry could become more local, more regenerative, and more reliant on skilled and experienced practitioners.

Lack of formal regulation of education and accreditation in the herbal medicine sector is another point of tension, creating both challenges for scaling up the approach as well as opportunities for alternative ideas and practices to take root at the community level. Without any formality in herbal medicine, 7Song says that standards of practice are highly uneven (personal communication). Anyone can call themselves an herbalist regardless of the extensiveness of their training or experience. Lack of formality in herbalism also limits the capacity of the sector to collect data and conduct formal research that might lend more mainstream credibility to the health benefits of herbs. As an herbalist with a sceptical streak, 7Song often questions whether herbal medicines actually do what people think they do, but says that it is challenging to research herbs on par with pharmaceuticals due to the degree to which medical research funding is driven by profit-based incentives to develop and market new drugs. Yet the absence of formal studies does not mean that herbalists can't learn more about what works and what doesn't over time. 7Song notes that working in an integrated health care setting has allowed him to track the effects of different herbs, primarily because it expands the reach of his practice, making it possible to collect more data. The informality of herbalism also facilitates greater accessibility, for instance by enabling different kinds of learners from all walks of life to build their knowledge and begin practising even if they wouldn't necessarily be interested in or have the time or capacity to pursue a more conventional medical education (7Song, personal communication). And, as Peter Gray suggests, herbalists may have more leeway to work in ways that could become increasingly practical in a context of limited resources:

> If you're an herbalist or an acupuncturist or a traditional midwife, you're probably practising some skills that are going to be needed fifty or one hundred years down the line. If you're a physician then you're really in a straitjacket. You have to conform to the guidelines, to what the Royal College wants, to what the medical malpractice laws want. It's very difficult to do anything outside of those boundaries. (personal communication)

In a post-growth world, herbalism could become more integrated into a pluralistic system of primary care providers, working at a hyperlocal level to prevent illnesses, increase well-being, and at the same time regenerate ecosystems and cultivate reciprocal relationships with the land around us. As Leopold says, "the best type of medicine is the medicine you can grow in your backyard that's bioregional, that you can source locally." But realizing this potential will require reckoning with the reality that "many people don't have access to land where that's possible." Around the world, people continue to be denied access to land to harvest or cultivate medicines, particularly Indigenous peoples whose land has been or is being taken from them, or who are otherwise prevented from using traditional lands to support their health. Many urban landscapes are also barren of medicinal value, and can be seen not only as "food deserts" but as "herbal deserts" (Leopold, personal communication).

However, if these inequities can be addressed, herbalism as a diverse set of contextual practices and relationships has the potential to enable human and planetary health even as ecological disruptions become more severe. When I asked 7Song whether he was worried that the climate crisis would result in the loss of key medicinal plants that are essential for human health, he said:

> I'm worried about ecological devastation because I'm worried about the effects on people who lack resources. It's a social justice issue. A lot of the plants I use, they're survival plants. I mean, if we kill ourselves, these plants – golden rod is not going anywhere, nor are oak trees. Probably about eighty to ninety species that I use are really very weedy, common plants, and sure they can be destroyed, but not easily.

And, while Susan Leopold's doctoral study of cultural traditions in the Bull Run Mountains was about the loss of ethnobotanical knowledge, it ended with an unexpectedly hopeful conclusion:

> I realized that the people I was studying actually gained that knowledge in a very short amount of time. I mean, it wasn't like it took them thousands of years to acquire a relationship with the land that had all the characteristics of something that you would find in an Indigenous culture … We have the potential to shift things very rapidly, and the plants respond really quickly to a shift in consciousness. So that's the hopeful side, is that plants are extremely forgiving and if we actually just shift our perspective, there's an incredible opportunity to change what's happening very quickly. (personal communication)

17.1 Building Reciprocal Relationships between People and Plants

Herbalism, as humanity's "primary medicine" (Leopold, personal communication) and the "medicine of the people" (Barsoum, personal communication), could become – as it once was and still is in places that lack access to biomedical health care (WHO 2015) – a cornerstone of post-growth health systems. The approach is low cost and creates space to enter into reciprocal relationships with plants, shifting the way people steward and care for the land as they learn to perceive medicinal herbs as key partners in health. To realize the transformative potential of herbalism, tensions related to regulation and informality, commodification, and access to land to cultivate medicines will need to be addressed in generative ways by communities, herbal practitioners, and health systems. Offerings like the medicine gardening mentorship that I participated in during the pandemic could provide a starting place for people like myself who have been disconnected from lineages of herbal knowledge through processes of modernization, migration, and generational discontinuity. Practising herbalism in the Anthropocene could forge stronger relationships between people and plants, draw connections between human and planetary health, and regenerate local ecosystems while providing an abundant source of low-cost preventative medicine for communities as they step back from ecological overshoot. It is an approach that has been with us throughout our evolutionary history and that can continue to be instrumental to health as we transition into a post-growth political economy in a novel social-ecological regime.

Conclusion: Cultivating Human and Planetary Health for a Sustainable Future

To cultivate a healthy future for people and the planet, there is an urgent need to radically reimagine health systems. This reimaging must begin with greater recognition of the inseparability of human and planetary health outcomes, of the extent to which human beings can only thrive when the Earth is also thriving. As we reimagine health systems, it is also important to do so as part of broader transformations in our economic systems to uphold sustainability and equity as prerequisites for human survival. We must replace our quest for economic growth with a quest for sufficiency and well-being. We cannot achieve human and planetary health without rethinking the purpose of the economy. Up to this point, human economic activity has been responsible both for improvements to quality of life around the world and for civilization-threatening ecological destabilizations. We can no longer afford to trade short-term gains for long-term destruction. We must find a workable path through these paradoxical outcomes, knowing that no option will be easy or perfect, only better or worse. To do so, we must reimagine health systems in ways that are informed by complexity and systems thinking. In a complex system composed of so many different ecological and social components, relying only on top-down management is not going to work. Systems change will need to be stewarded by people equipped with the skills to live with uncertainty, to continually learn and adapt to emergence, and to work with the inherent power of self-organization.

This book has shown how we might approach such a reimagining by sharing stories of the promising practices communities are enacting to seed systemic change. These diverse initiatives hold potential to ground health systems in ways of thinking, relating, and approaching health that are well positioned to flourish in a future sustainable society. Some, such as ecovillage health teams and the "Principles for a Just Recovery," were developed with the specific aim of structuring community life in more socially and ecologically sustainable ways. Others like community nursing and mutual aid respond directly to deepening resource limitations within the health care sector. Still others like care farming, therapeutic gardening, and Geel's family foster care model address the need for greater community inclusion and for alternative approaches to care for mental illness. Practitioners and participants who engage in such initiatives may not identify their work as capable of addressing pressing challenges to human and planetary health in a time of social-ecological transformation. However, these practices nonetheless begin to show us what an outcomes-focused, post-growth health system that relies increasingly on community-based, preventative, and low-cost approaches to health and care might look like. They also all represent movements that, while deeply context specific or even somewhat marginal within the current system, could become attractors that build energy and momentum as social-ecological conditions shift. Material resource and energy limitations, for instance, could bring low-throughput approaches like the soil health movement or Geel's family foster care model for serious mental illness further into the mainstream. We might also see a proliferation of initiatives like The Listening Space garden or the complexity medicine group, which operate within the health care sector while bringing in alternative ways of thinking, acting, and relating to one another in the pursuit of health.

It is increasingly urgent that we find workable alternatives for health and care as social-ecological transformations unfold. These alternatives must not only be effective, but also be able to move through the innovation cycle from conceptualization to implementation and institutionalization much more rapidly than ever before to address social-ecological challenges *in time* (Olsson et al. 2017). This book demonstrates that there is an abundance of promising alternatives that together can make meaningful contributions to human and planetary health. In this conclusion, I will return to the original questions that inspired the book. I will also consider the limitations of this work, identify areas where further research would be useful, and offer some concluding remarks.

What Could a Health System That Meets Population-Level Health and Care Needs without Consuming Unsustainable Levels of Resources and Energy Look Like?

In a post-growth political economy with fewer material and energetic resources available across all sectors of society, health systems will need to use the resources they do have much more strategically to maintain positive population-level health outcomes. At the same time, sectors beyond formal health care may be expected to take on a larger role in preventing physical and mental illnesses and enabling social connectedness, healthy behaviours, good nutrition, and meaningful engagement in community life. The research assembled in this book suggests that in practice, such a health system could be characterized by:

1. *A health care sector with greater capacities in prevention and primary care.* In a context of sustained economic contraction, welfare states are likely to be significantly constrained in their ability to fund high-overhead, resource-intensive health care services (Bailey 2015; Zywert 2017; Quilley 2020b; also see section 7.2). Health care is a large and rising expense for high-income nations, and this level of investment may not be able to be maintained in a post-growth future (Bailey 2015; Hensher and Zywert 2020). However, research shows that health care is only responsible for a relatively small percentage of population health outcomes, between 5 and 20 per cent (Woolf 2019; Hancock 2017). Prioritizing prevention and primary care could enable high-income countries to continue delivering high-quality, accessible, and universal health care services such as emergency medical care and treatments for some rare and common illnesses while reducing the burden on health systems created by preventable infectious and non-communicable diseases. Such an approach proved effective for Cuba during a period of extreme resource and energy deprivation, and the lessons learned from this experience could be useful as high-income nations transition away from growth economies (Borowy 2013). Evidence that health indicators like life expectancy have become decoupled from income and carbon consumption in cross-country comparisons over the past two decades also indicates that it may be possible to maintain population-level health outcomes achieved with the transition to global modernity even if GDPs and ecological footprints begin to fall around the world (Fanning and O'Neill 2019).
2. *Increased investment in social change initiatives that address the social and ecological determinants of health.* The social determinants of health have been shown to be responsible for 30 to 55 per cent of human health outcomes; sectors outside of health systems exert a stronger influence on population health than health-related fields (WHO n.d.-a). While medical research and technological development receive substantial funding and resources within the current regime, studies indicate that investing in social change would generate better health outcomes than continuing to invest in medical advancement (Woolf et al. 2007, 2019). In a smaller economy, it may become imperative to shift resources away from activities that generate only incremental gains for human health while contributing significantly to the

pollution and waste generated by health care (see Thiel et al. 2015 and Venkatesh et al. 2016 for comparisons of the ecological footprints associated with low- and high-tech surgical techniques; also see Missoni and Morales Galindo 2020). The potential cost savings and well-being gains associated with addressing the social determinants of health have been apparent for decades. Prolonged economic contraction combined with increasing calls for health equity could at last create the necessary conditions to generate the political will to implement such an approach (see section 9.1). In this context, we may see initiatives like affordable housing, universal basic income, ecological restoration, waste and pollution reduction, and poverty alleviation contributing substantially to population health.

3. *Thriving networks of contextually whole health and care initiatives that attend to social, physical, and mental health while also regenerating local ecosystems.* As a complement to more robust primary care and prevention capacities within the health care sector, the success of sustainable health systems will depend upon developing strong networks of local health and care initiatives that meet community needs. Initiatives could include, for instance, care farms, enabling gardens, mutual aid networks, community nursing, herbal farms and practices, and family foster care for people with mental illnesses. These initiatives are more likely to be successful to the extent that they are "contextually whole," or grounded in the cultural, ecological, and historical contexts in which they arise while at the same time acting across social-ecological scales to cultivate health (Zywert and Sutherland 2020, 291). Practices like co-designing an approach with all who have a stake in its outcomes make it more likely that initiatives will be able to meet local needs in meaningful ways (see section 14.4 and chapter 16). Community-based approaches to health and care generally have a low ecological and economic cost while requiring substantial social commitments from those involved. As such, they are well suited to the circumstances of a more place-bound existence (see section 8.2). Approaches that simultaneously build resilience at the human and ecological scales hold the greatest potential to contribute to meeting local needs within ecological limits (see chapters 5, 6, and 17).

4. *Expanded livelihood opportunities related to health and care.* Degrowth scholars often argue that in a post-growth health system that prioritizes prevention and the social and ecological determinants of health, we can expect to see a proliferation of formal and informal roles that support health and care (Missoni 2015; D'Alisa, Demaria, and Kallis 2015; Aillon and D'Alisa 2020). Formal roles

may arise in the non-profit sector and within small and medium-sized social enterprises, while informal caregiving roles will be more necessary than ever and may garner increased value and prestige. As the formal economy contracts and people are no longer obliged (or able) to devote the majority of their time to paid work, community-based networks for health and care could expand, benefitting from the time and energy of a large corps of volunteers. Activities such as caring for children and elders, supporting people experiencing physical and mental illnesses, growing preventative medicines, exercising, and provisioning for one's own and one's community's basic needs for food, shelter, and clothing could increasingly fall into the livelihood domain (Quilley 2020b; Quilley and Zywert 2019a). These activities could generate a greater sense of meaningful contribution and satisfaction than the market-based work that occupies such a substantial portion of people's time in growth economies (see chapters 7 and 8). Participating in these livelihood activities could therefore create a positive feedback loop through which the more people engage in supporting the health of their families, communities, and local ecosystems, the more their individual health and well-being increase.

What Existing Ideas, Behaviours, Structures, and Relationships Prefigure Such a Health System and How Might They Enable Its Emergence in High-Income Nations?

As discussed above, an abundance of promising alternatives for health and care in the Anthropocene already exist. These alternatives embody ways of thinking, acting, and relating as well as practices and structures that can contribute to upholding human and planetary health into the long-term future. Within the current regime, many of the alternatives I investigated remain marginal or highly place-bound (e.g., Geel), while others thrive across nations (e.g., mutual aid, care farming). Multiple, diverse prefigurative alternatives can collectively contribute to deepening a novel "basin of attraction" that could eventually represent a new state of dynamic equilibrium for complex social-ecological systems as conditions within the dominant regime become untenable (Zywert and Quilley 2020a; Carpenter et al. 2019; Walker and Salt 2012; also see section 13.2). In the transition to a social-ecological system defined by rising ecological constraints, economic decomplexification, and relocalization of community life, such prefigurative alternatives could move rapidly from the margins into the mainstream. The examples I included in this work all have the potential to enable the emergence of more healthful and sustainable health systems by:

1. Generating synergistic benefits for human and planetary health across social-ecological scales
2. Embodying ways of thinking and acting with the potential to disrupt the current trajectories of the Anthropocene by foregrounding alternative sources of meaning, social commitments, and connections to place
3. Achieving positive health outcomes at a low ecological and economic cost
4. Re-embedding aspects of health and care work in networks of family and community reciprocity

In table C.3, I summarize the ways in which each of the initiatives profiled in this book prefigure a health system that could secure human and planetary health into the long-term future while also responding to the unprecedented challenges of the Anthropocene. The table also draws attention to some of the wicked tensions inherent in each approach, many of which may be exceedingly difficult to reconcile (see chapters 3 and 8). The insights presented in table C.3 are preliminary and have not been measured or proven. They instead indicate the potential of each initiative in theory; further research would be needed to determine whether this potential is being or can be realized in practice.

How Can We Nudge Health Systems towards Greater Long-Term Sustainability and Resilience as Broader Social-Ecological Systems Transformations Unfold in the Coming Decades?

In part 3, I draw on literatures from social innovation and social-ecological systems studies to argue that change in complex systems cannot be managed or controlled, but that it *can* be stewarded by attending to emerging trends, feedback patterns, tensions, and opportunities (see chapters 13 and 14). Chapter 14 presents promising strategies for building more sustainable and resilient health systems that can contribute to shifting the trajectories of health in the Anthropocene, including:

1. Adopting multiple, diverse worldviews and paradigms that are conducive to long-term human and planetary health
2. Creating conditions in which people and communities have the capacity to contribute to social-ecological resilience and/or adaptation
3. Supporting the self-organization of social-ecological systems

Table C.3. How prefigurative alternatives align with inclusion criteria

Prefigurative natural experiment	Criteria 1: Synergistic benefits across scales	Criteria 2: Disrupt Anthropocene trajectory	Criteria 3: Low ecological and economic cost	Criteria 4: Re-embed health and care work	Wicked tensions
Soil health	Improves water cycle; cools the land; reduces flooding, drought, and wildfire; increases nutrient content of food Improves health of the microbiome (land and gut) Reduces exposure to toxic agricultural chemicals in land, water, and food	Prevents and reduces impact of extreme weather events caused by climate change Increases economic viability of small-scale farms Could affect planetary boundaries related to climate change, freshwater use, land use change, and biochemical flows	Reduces reliance on expensive chemical inputs in agriculture Lowers costs to states, communities, and families by preventing damage caused by natural disasters Labour-intensive methods can leverage appropriate technologies	Increases livelihood opportunities on small-scale, regenerative farms Growth in community networks that apply soil health principles in urban agriculture, community gardens, parks, public land, home gardens	Taking regenerative farming to scale in a world with significant corporate interests in industrial agriculture and dependence upon cheap, highly processed foods Supporting both socially conservative and liberal farmers to adopt regenerative farming methods
Gardening for health	Increases mental health, physical activity, and community inclusion Contributes to local ecological restoration and cooling	Gardening becomes a source of meaning and connection to place Contributes to displacing consumption as a source of status and prestige Shift towards preventative vs. curative health systems	Can lower cost and raise effectiveness of mental health care Engagement in gardening can be inexpensive and accessible Gardens generate a high return on investment in health care and long-term care settings	Community gardens build social inclusion and well-being Increases livelihood opportunities related to provisioning basic needs such as food and medicine Horticultural therapies in health care, long-term care, and community settings promote inclusion of populations that experience marginalization	Ensuring equitable access to land to grow food and medicines

(Continued)

Table C.3. (Continued)

Prefigurative natural experiment	Criteria 1: Synergistic benefits across scales	Criteria 2: Disrupt Anthropocene trajectory	Criteria 3: Low ecological and economic cost	Criteria 4: Re-embed health and care work	Wicked tensions
Care farms	Increases physical, mental, and social health of participants Facilitates adoption of organic farming practices Ecological benefits of returning hand work to the rural landscape	Increases community inclusion for people experiencing significant mental health issues, long-term disabilities, behavioural issues, and dementia Socially engaged farms use organic farming methods and rely heavily on hand work	Lowers costs of mental health support for the state Organic farming methods reduce reliance on expensive and destructive chemical inputs Farmers are paid to incorporate the labour of people with diverse health needs	New societal role for farmers who adopt multifunctional approaches to agriculture that include health and social care Populations that experience marginalization, including people with mental illnesses and long-term disabilities have opportunities to do meaningful work that contributes to their communities	Requires long-term commitment from farmers and (often) participants Need to keep reporting requirements manageable to reduce administrative burden for farmers
Principles for a Just Recovery	Increases societal resilience to social-ecological crises that damage human and planetary health Addresses social and ecological determinants of health and builds health equity across communities and nations	Redistributes wealth from the ultra-rich to workers Advocates for divestment of government support to fossil fuel and other ecologically destructive industries	Reduces upstream health care costs by addressing social and ecological determinants of health	Aims to build community solidarity	Relies on economic growth to fund fiscal transfers to workers and communities Unclear whether welfare states will have sufficient resources to support a strong social safety net as economic growth declines

Mutual aid	Supports individual and community health Engaging networks of volunteers to support aspects of health and care at a hyper-local scale could lower the ecological footprint of health systems	Fosters a collective sense of responsibility for community health and well-being Operates in the domain of livelihood, reducing reliance on both state and market	Negligible economic and ecological cost	Mobilizes hyper-local networks of volunteers to support health and care Builds connections between neighbours	Unclear whether existing community networks are viscous enough to sustain long-term engagement in mutual aid
Ecovillage health systems	Individuals and families benefit from living close to nature and eating healthy, local food Ecovillages aim to reduce their ecological footprint by using renewable energy, farming organically, and living communally	Shift towards sustainable, communal social arrangements and collective organization to meet basic needs Community members take responsibility for the health and care of their neighbours in a close-knit, intentional community	Health/care teams have a negligible economic and ecological cost	Volunteers support community members by coordinating care, checking in when needed, and taking on care roles that would otherwise be professionalized	Communal living can increase interpersonal challenges with negative effects on well-being Challenges integrating people with serious mental health issues

(*Continued*)

Table C.3. (Continued)

Prefigurative natural experiment	Criteria 1: Synergistic benefits across scales	Criteria 2: Disrupt Anthropocene trajectory	Criteria 3: Low ecological and economic cost	Criteria 4: Re-embed health and care work	Wicked tensions
Community nursing	Allows elders to remain in their communities as they age, reducing social isolation Low ecological cost reduces environmental footprint of health systems, benefitting planetary health	Promotes "slow medicine," an approach to caring for elders that prioritizes quality of life and reduces invasive medical procedures in the last phase of life	Reduces the number of calls made to emergency services Reduces the number of invasive medical procedures performed near the end of life Promotes palliative and hospice care approaches that are associated with a lower ecological and economic cost than hospital-based end-of-life care	Nurses support networks of caregivers, making it easier for them to care for elders who choose to remain in community	Unknown
Geel	Social inclusion of people with serious mental illnesses and long-term cognitive disabilities Low ecological cost reduces environmental footprint of health systems, benefitting planetary health	Promotes social vs. medical/therapeutic approach to mental health care that challenges biomedical assumptions about what is needed to generate health and well-being for people with serious mental illnesses and cognitive disabilities Leverages non-rational drivers of behaviour rooted in religion, history, and culture	Family foster care is lower cost for the state than institutionalization or other forms of community care Boarders reduce reliance on pharmaceuticals and professionalized care Makes use of existing community resources (time, space in homes)	Families care for boarders by integrating them fully into family and community life Boarders contribute to their families and communities in meaningful ways	Rooted in historical tradition and difficult to scale out Requires individual and family sacrifices and commitments that are unthinkable to most people in modern societies

The Midnight Kitchen	Coming together around food can reduce social isolation and improve mental health and community well-being Implication for planetary health unknown	Food and social connection seen as key leverage points for mental, social, and physical health Peer support for doctors working in innovative ways enables more effective social change work	Dispersed global network brought together virtually has a relatively low ecological cost	Builds networks of health practitioners and other social change professionals to seed new ideas, approaches, and connections	Unclear whether the approach has traction or whether the network will be sustainable over time
Complexity medicine group	Attention to health across nested complex systems and long time horizons Potential to generate contextually diverse medicines that increase the health and well-being of individuals, families, and other living systems	Integrates insights from complexity science within a biomedical health care setting, increasing the capacity to attend to the health of living systems across scales Can leverage existing health care infrastructure and resource flows to enable new ways of thinking and doing related to health	Weekly group has a low ecological cost (generated by the footprint of the facility and transportation to and from the site)	Engages people in their health while building a community within which to explore the nature of health and how it emerges	Paradigmatic differences between biomedical approach and complexity medicine approaches may be difficult to negotiate in some contexts

(*Continued*)

Table C.3. (Continued)

Prefigurative natural experiment	Criteria 1: Synergistic benefits across scales	Criteria 2: Disrupt Anthropocene trajectory	Criteria 3: Low ecological and economic cost	Criteria 4: Re-embed health and care work	Wicked tensions
Herbalism	Use of preventative and nutritive herbs can increase individual, family, and community health Can increase time spent in nature, sense of connection to local ecosystems, and mental health Supports ecological restoration by planting native species and rewilding communities	Paradigm shift towards the value of herbs to support preventative health Cultivating plant medicines as a source of well-being and meaning making Growing and using medicinal plants promotes reciprocity between human communities and non-human species in local ecosystems	Herbal medicines used for prevention, nutrition, and symptom management could reduce reliance on high-cost pharmaceuticals and other resource- and energy-intensive treatments Herbs are readily available and can support health when biomedical treatments are unavailable	Can enable intergenerational and intercultural knowledge sharing about medicinal plants Promotes reciprocal relationships between humans and plant species	Ensuring equitable access to land to grow herbal medicines Tension between informality (supports flexibility and inclusion) and formalization (enables standards of practice and Western scientific research) Expansion of the approach can lead to unsustainable harvesting

Enacting these strategies depends upon our ability to listen to the systems around us and to negotiate the paradoxes that inevitably arise as social change unfolds (see Meadows 2008; Westley, Zimmerman and Patton 2007; Quilley 2013; Kish and Quilley 2017; Kish et al. 2021). In particular, we need to meaningfully attend to the wicked tensions that arise when attempting to build health across nested social-ecological scales and pull back from ecological overshoot, such as the implications of moving away from individualism and economic growth as organizing principles for modern society (see chapters 3, 7, and 8).

The stories assembled in this book also support a growing body of literature arguing that prefigurative movements can enable more humane social-ecological systems transformations (see Homer-Dixon 2006; Walker and Salt 2006; Beddoe et al. 2009; Westley, Zimmerman and Patton 2007; Köhler et al. 2019; Kish et al. 2021). Prefigurative movements provide a glimpse of what an alternative social-ecological regime might look and feel like. By embodying healthy and sustainable societal arrangements in the present, they contribute to lowering the threshold between this regime and the next and could become attractors for systems seeking a new dynamic equilibrium (see chapter 13). Having diverse prefigurative alternatives ready to take the place of approaches that become untenable under new conditions is one of the best ways to ensure that systems tip in a benevolent direction rather than falling into a deep collapse (Köhler et al. 2019; Homer-Dixon 2006; Walker and Salt 2006). The more alternatives there are, the more options for action arise as systems transform (Walker and Salt 2012). For this reason, one of the most important things we can do to steward social-ecological systems change may be to support prefigurative alternatives to grow, flourish, and spread their seeds across the landscape.

This book has highlighted the potential value of a diverse range of prefigurative alternatives for human and planetary health, but there are countless others. The level of complexity that characterizes human societies and Earth systems in the Anthropocene means that we cannot be assured that our actions will have their intended effects. However, humankind is an influential part of the self-organization of the Earth's nested living systems. As communities, families, and individuals, we can contribute to this self-organization by creating, learning about, and lending our time and attention to alternatives like those discussed in this book.

Limitations and Directions for Future Planetary Health Research

The purpose of this research was to bring together a set of ideas, practices, approaches, and structures that could cultivate human and planetary health in a sustainable future. To identify promising initiatives and research participants to interview, I used a snowball approach combined with an extensive literature search. These methodologies allowed me to compile a diverse range of promising alternatives, components of which could become cornerstones of sustainable health systems in the Anthropocene. However, as noted above, the prefigurative alternatives I investigated are by no means comprehensive. I have no doubt that a myriad of other equally promising approaches exist that I did not even encounter in the course of this work. My situatedness as a white, middle-class, liberal, anglophone, Canadian researcher shaped the networks I was able to access and therefore affected the initiatives that made their way into this book. It would be useful in future to collaborate with researchers, health practitioners, and social innovators across multiple diverse backgrounds to identify additional prefigurative alternatives for cultivating human and planetary health in the Anthropocene. Assembling prefigurative alternatives identified by people from varied national, professional, disciplinary, racial, ideological, political, class, linguistic, and gender backgrounds and identities would draw together a more holistic picture of the spectrum of alternatives that could gather momentum in the coming decades.

Such an undertaking would also make it possible to test the criteria for inclusion that I developed for this project (see above, introduction, and appendix) to determine whether they hold true in other regions and populations. In particular, it would be useful to investigate initiatives emerging in low-resource settings in the global south, which could provide specific insights into the kinds of appropriate technologies that might enable health in a post-growth political economy, as well as the ways in which biomedical health care can be effectively structured in low-resource settings. Incorporating examples from low- and middle-income countries was for the most part beyond the scope of my current research, which purposefully focused on initiatives arising within high-income nations. I made the decision to focus on high-income contexts because it is imperative to consider the kinds of prefigurative alternatives that already have some traction in the places that most urgently need to step back from ecological overshoot. Understanding more about these initiatives and drawing attention to their potential in academic and practitioner networks could help to position them as attractors for health systems as social-ecological conditions shift. Scoping the work in this way, however, also limited the findings as it omitted a wide range of potential alternatives from investigation.

In addition, this research did not specifically identify which aspects of the existing biomedical health care sector could be expected to survive the transition to a post-growth political economy in high-income countries. In this book I have suggested that the continued expansion of high-technology approaches such as robotic surgeries may not be feasible as the economic and ecological resources available to the health care sector are increasingly curtailed (see section 8.1). This argument was not difficult to make given the high ecological cost of such approaches and the availability of less resource-intensive options (see Thiel et al. 2015; Venkatesh et al. 2016). But what of pain medications, antibiotics, the rapid development of vaccines, cancer treatments, and genetic medicine? It was beyond the scope of this research to compare various biomedical treatments and practices in order to produce definitive recommendations about which aspects of health care make the most meaningful contributions to planetary health and which may be difficult to maintain in a global-scale sustainability transition. In this work I only began the conversation by making the case that we can expect to be faced with significant trade-offs (also see Zywert and Quilley 2017, 2020b). Instead of pursuing these questions further, I chose to investigate practices, approaches, and structures that might be able to take some of the burden off professionalized health care services so that the resources that are earmarked for this economically and ecologically intensive sector can be used more strategically to enhance quality of life at a population level. As I have argued strongly here and elsewhere (Zywert 2017; Zywert and Quilley 2020b), it is preferable to avoid a scenario in which societies lose the biomedical knowledge and capacities we have developed over the past two centuries of modernization. Negotiating the details of which components of health care in high-income nations are most likely to remain relevant and feasible in a post-growth political economy must be the subject of future work.

A Medicine Garden of Social Approaches to Human and Planetary Health

I like to imagine that those reading this book are walking through a medicine garden of social approaches to human and planetary health. Many of the initiatives lining the path are old plants, well established and flourishing. Others are seedlings only recently transplanted, plants that may not bloom until next season. Still others are only seeds, their potential for life not yet certain. In the Anthropocene, unpredictable global social-ecological systems transformations are unfolding around us. The prospects for human health and well-being are uncertain and are tied to the health of our communities, our local ecosystems, and the planet's biophysical processes. Before us is an incredibly immense task – enabling health in the broadest sense of the word to emerge and thrive across the diverse, nested, living systems that make up our world. To do so, I have argued that we must move away from pursuing ecologically destructive economic growth to achieve social goods like health. Instead, we must find ways to provision human health systems that do not erode the foundations of health at higher or lower scales. The prefigurative alternatives that hold the greatest potential to secure health in the transition to a novel social-ecological regime are those that generate benefits across multiple scales, disrupt trajectories of ecological destruction, operate at a low ecological and economic cost, and are sustained by reciprocal community networks. By supporting these alternatives to take root, we can cultivate human and planetary health for a sustainable future.

Appendix: Justification for Inclusion Criteria

Criteria	Justification for Inclusion	Key References
1. Generate synergistic benefits for human and planetary health across social-ecological scales	• Planetary health is the foundation for human health and thriving human civilizations; planetary ecological disruptions undermine the health of current and future generations. • Prioritizing the health of humans over the integrity of social-ecological systems as a whole has created emergent problems at higher and lower scales. • There is significant potential for health, well-being, and care-focused initiatives to simultaneously build social-ecological resilience and human health.	Whitmee et al. 2015; Cole 2019c; Myers and Frumkin 2020; CPHA 2015; Steffen and Stafford-Smith 2013; Rockström et al. 2009; McMichael 2014; Pershouse 2016
2. Embody ways of thinking and acting with the potential to disrupt the current trajectories of the Anthropocene by foregrounding alternative sources of meaning, social commitments, and connections to place	• The Anthropocene creates a context that is unprecedented and highly uncertain; managerial and technological approaches are insufficient to address the scale of current social-ecological challenges.	Olsson et al. 2017; O'Neill et al. 2018; Field et al. 2020; Steffen et al. 2015a; Watts et al. 2019; Köhler et al. 2019; Quilley 2017, 2020b; Zywert and Quilley 2020b

(*Continued*)

Criteria	Justification for Inclusion	Key References
	• Addressing the complex problems of the Anthropocene demands a comprehensive reimagining of the political economy and the systems through which we provision social goods like health, food, housing, education, and cultural meaning. • The ways in which we currently provide for social goods use resources at unsustainable levels and contribute substantially to breaching planetary boundaries.	
3. Achieve positive health outcomes at a low ecological and economic cost	• Economic growth cannot be decoupled from ecological destruction; as such, it undermines health across social-ecological scales. • A post-growth transition is necessary to secure human and planetary health into the future, but also creates multiple wicked problems related to how we structure, fund, and operate modern health systems. • Health, well-being, and care initiatives with a low ecological and economic cost could take pressure off of formal health care systems, enabling them to use a contracting resource base more strategically to maintain the capacity for modern medical care through a period of dramatic economic contraction.	Engelman, Bongaarts, and Patterson 2020; Ward et al. 2016; Meadows et al. 1972, 2004; Büchs and Koch 2019; Fanning and O'Neill 2019; Missoni and Morales Galindo 2020; Hensher and Zywert 2020
4. Re-embed aspects of health and care work in networks of family and community reciprocity	• Relocalization and economic contraction are likely to create greater reliance on informal networks of support rooted in place-based relationships of mutual obligation (e.g., within extended families, neighbourhoods, or grass-roots community associations).	De Young and Princen 2012; Borowy 2013; Polanyi 1944; Schumacher 1973; Hopkins 2008; Quilley, Hawreliak, and Kish 2016; Kish and Quilley 2017; Zywert and Quilley 2020a; Quilley 2020b

Criteria	Justification for Inclusion	Key References
	• Informal family and community supports for health and care have a low ecological and economic cost and could enable a sustainable retreat from current levels of complexity within health systems while achieving comparable outcomes. • Re-embedded relationships to place, family, and community challenge the underlying logic of the existing social-ecological regime by offering alternative sources of value, status, and well-being.	

References

Aerts, Raf, Olivia Honnay, and An Van Nieuwenhuyse. 2018. "Biodiversity and Human Health: Mechanisms and Evidence of the Positive Health Effects of Diversity in Nature and Green Spaces." *British Medical Bulletin* 127: 5–22. http://doi.org/10.1093/bmb/ldy021. Medline:30007287.

Aillon, Jean-Louis. and Giacomo D'Alisa. 2020. "Our Affluence Is Killing Us: What Degrowth Offers Health and Wellbeing. In *Health in the Anthropocene: Living Well on a Finite Planet*, edited by Katharine Zywert and Stephen Quilley, 306–32. Toronto: University of Toronto Press.

Alley, C., and J. Sommerfeld. 2014. "Infectious Disease in Times of Social and Ecological Change." *Medical Anthropology* 33, no. 2: 85–91. http://doi.org/10.1080/01459740.2013.850590. Medline:24512379.

Armelagos, G.J., P.J. Brown, and B. Turner. 2005. "Evolutionary, Historical and Political Economic Perspectives on Health and Disease." *Social Science and Medicine* 6, no. 4: 755–65. http://doi.org/10.1016/j.socscimed.2004.08.066. Medline:15950089.

Arnold, Luke. 2015. "Moving beyond Geel: Developing an Adult Foster-Care System for Those with Schizophrenia and Other Psychoses." PhD diss. Chicago School of Professional Psychology.

Asafu-Adjaye, John, Linus Blomqvist, Steward Brand, Barry Brook, Ruth Defries, Erle Ellis, Christopher Foreman, et al. 2015. *An Ecomodernist Manifesto.* https://static1.squarespace.com/static/5515d9f9e4b04d5c3198b7bb/t/552d37bbe4b07a7dd69fcdbb/1429026747046/An+Ecomodernist+Manifesto.pdf.

Asayama, Shinichiro, Seita Emori, Masahiro Sugiyama, Fumiko Kasuga, and Chiho Watanabe. 2020. "Are We Ignoring a Black Elephant in the Anthropocene? Climate Change and Global Pandemic as the Crisis in Health and Equality." *Sustainability Science* 16, no. 2: 695–701. https://doi.org/10.1007/s11625-020-00879-7. Medline:33193903.

Baer, H.A., M. Singer, and I. Susser. 2013. *Medical Anthropology and the World System*. 2nd ed. Westport, CT: Praeger.

Bailey, Daniel. 2015. "The Environmental Paradox of the Welfare State: The Dynamics of Sustainability." *New Political Economy* 20, no. 6: 793–811. https://doi.org/10.1080/13563467.2015.1079169.

Baker, Ted. 2013. "Ecovillages and Capitalism: Creating Sustainable Communities within an Unsustainable Context." In *Environmental Anthropology Engaging Ecotopia: Bioregionalism, Permaculture, and Ecovillages*, edited by J. Lockyer and J.R. Veteto, 285–300. New York: Berghahn.

Barnett, Steve, and Tom Foot. 2018. "Happy Birthday NHS! GP Surgery in Kentish Town Joins the Party." *Camden New Journal*, 30 June 2018. http://www.camdennewjournal.co.uk/article/happy-birthday-nhs-gp-surgery-in-kentish-town-joins-the-party.

Barrett R., C.W. Kuzawa, T. McDade, and G.J. Armelagos. 1998. "Emerging and Re-emerging Infectious Diseases: The Third Epidemiological Transition." *Annual Review of Anthropology* 27: 247–71. https://doi.org/10.1146/annurev.anthro.27.1.247.

Basu, Gaurab. 2020. "Want to Prevent the Next Pandemic? This Doctor Is Prescribing Climate action." *Grist*, 12 May 2020. https://grist.org/fix/want-to-prevent-the-next-pandemic-this-doctor-is-prescribing-climate-action/.

Bauman Z. 2012. *Liquid Modernity*. Cambridge: Polity.

Beck, U., and E. Beck-Gernsheim. 2002. *Individualization: Institutionalized Individualism and Its Social and Political Consequences*. London: Sage.

Becker, E. 1973. *The Denial of Death*. New York: Free Press.

Beddoe, R., R. Costanza, J. Farley, E. Garza, J. Kent, I. Kubiszewski, L. Martinez, et al. 2009. "Overcoming Systemic Roadblocks to Sustainability: The Evolutionary Redesign of Worldviews, Institutions, and Technologies." *PNAS USA* 106: 2483–9. https://doi.org/10.1073/pnas.0812570106.

Bednarz, Dan. 2014. "Public Health's Response to Decline: Loyalty to the 1%." *Health after Oil*. https://healthafteroil.wordpress.com/2014/12/15/public-healths-response-to-decline-loyalty-to-the-1/#more-999.

Belesova, Kristine, David L. Heymann, and Andy Haines. 2020. "Integrating Climate Action for Health into Covid-19 Recovery Plans." *BMJ* 370: m3169. http://doi.org/10.1136/bmj.m3169. Medline:32878746.

Beresford-Kroeger, Diana. 2013. *The Sweetness of a Simple Life: Tips for Healthier, Happier and Kinder Living Gleaned from the Wisdom and Science of Nature*. Toronto: Random House Canada.

Bernard, H.R. 2006. *Research Methods in Anthropology: Qualitative and Quantitative Approaches*. Lanham, MD: Alta Mira.

Bird, Frederick, and Frances Westley. 2011. *Voices from the Voluntary Sector: Perspectives on Leadership Challenges*. Toronto: University of Toronto Press.

Boggs, C. 1977. "Marxism, Prefigurative Communism, and the Problem of Workers' Control." *Radical America* 11: 99–122.

Borowy, Iris. 2013. "Degrowth and Public Health in Cuba: Lessons from the Past?" *Journal of Cleaner Production* 38: 17–26. https://doi.org/10.1016/j.jclepro.2011.11.057.

Borowy, Iris, and Jean-Louis Aillon. 2017. "Sustainable Health and Degrowth: Health, Health Care and Society beyond the Growth Paradigm." *Social Theory and Health* 15, no. 3: 346–68. http://doi.org/10.1057/s41285-017-0032-7.

Brown, Adrienne Maree. 2017. *Emergent Strategy: Shaping Change, Changing Worlds*. Chico, CA: AK Press.

Brown, Italo M., Ayesha Khan, Jamar Slocum, Linelle F. Campbell, Jahmil R. Lacey, and Alden M. Landry. 2020. "COVID-19 Disparities and the Black Community: A Health Equity–Informed Rapid Response Is Needed." *American Journal of Public Health* 110, no. 9: 1350–1. http://doi.org/10.2105/AJPH.2020.305804. Medline:32783709.

Bryan, Sterling, Craig Mitton, and Cam Donaldson. 2014. "Breaking the Addiction to Technology Adoption." *Health Economics* 23: 379–83. http://doi.org/10.1002/hec.3034. Medline:24590701.

Buch-Hansen, Hubert. 2018. "The Prerequisites for a Degrowth Paradigm Shift: Insights from Critical Political Economy." *Ecological Economics* 146: 157–63. https://doi.org/10.1016/j.ecolecon.2017.10.021.

Büchs, Milena, Marta Baltruszewicz, Katharina Bohnenberger, Jonathan Busch, James Dyke, Patrick Elf, Andrew Fanning, et al. 2020. "Wellbeing Economics for the COVID-19 Recovery: Ten Principles to Build Back Better." 11 May 2020. Wellbeing Economy Alliance (website). https://wellbeingeconomy.org/ten-principles-for-building-back-better-to-create-wellbeing-economies-post-covid.

Büchs, Milena, and Max Koch. 2019. "Challenges for the Degrowth Transition: The Debate about Wellbeing." *Futures* 105: 155–65. https://doi.org/10.1016/j.futures.2018.09.002.

Buck, David. 2016. *Gardens and Health: Implications for Policy and Practice*. The King's Fund. https://www.researchgate.net/publication/303436076_Gardens_and_health_Implications_for_policy_and_practice.

Buist, Yvette. 2016. *Connect, Prioritize and Promote: A Comparative Research into the Development of Care Farming in Different Countries from the Transition Perspective*. Wageningen: Wageningen University and Research Center.

Butler, Colin. 2014. *Climate Change and Global Health*. Wallingford, UK: CABI.

– 2016. "Sounding the Alarm: Health in the Anthropocene." *International Journal of Environmental Research and Public Health* 13: 665. https://doi.org/10.3390/ijerph13070665. Medline:27376314.

– 2020. ""Regional Overload" as an Indicator of Profound Risk: A Plea for the Public Health Community to Awaken." In *Health in the Anthropocene: Living Well on a Finite Planet*, edited by Katharine Zywert and Stephen Quilley, 60–85. Toronto: University of Toronto Press.

Canadian Hunger Foundation and Brace Research Institute. 1983. *A Handbook on Appropriate Technology*. 3rd ed. Ottawa: Canadian Hunger Foundation.

Canadian Public Health Association (CPHA). 2015. *Global Change and Public Health: Addressing the Ecological Determinants of Health*. Ottawa: CPHA.

– 2019. *Position Statement: Climate Change and Public Health*. Ottawa: CPHA. https://www.cpha.ca/climate-change-and-human-health.

Canadian Women's Foundation. 2022. "The Facts: Women and Pandemics." Last updated October 2022. https://canadianwomen.org/the-facts/women-and-pandemics/.

Carpenter, Stephen R., Carl Folke, Martin Scheffer, and Frances R. Westley. 2019. "Dancing on the Volcano: Social Exploration in Times of Discontent." *Ecology and Society* 24, no. 1: 23. https://doi.org/10.5751/ES-10839-240123.

Carson, K.A., 2010. *The Homebrew Industrial Revolution: A Low Overhead Manifesto*. Booksurge. https://theanarchistlibrary.org/library/kevin-carson-the-homebrew-industrial-revolution.

Ceballos, Gerardo, Paul R. Ehrlich, and Peter H. Raven. 2020. "Vertebrates on the Brink as Indicators of Biological Annihilation and the Sixth Mass Extinction." *PNAS* 117, no. 24: 13596–602. https://doi.org/10.1073/pnas.1922686117. Medline:32482862.

Chamberlin, Shaun. 2018. "The Sequel: Life after Economic Growth." Resilience.org, 13 December 2018. https://www.resilience.org/stories/2018-12-13/the-sequel-life-after-economic-growth/.

Chen, A. 2016. "For Centuries, a Small Town Has Embraced Strangers with Mental Illness." NPR. http://www.npr.org/sections/health-shots/2016/07/01/484083305/for-centuries-a-small-town-has-embraced-strangers-with-mental-illness.

Cole, Jennifer. 2019a. "Foreword." In *Planetary Health: Human Health in an Era of Global Environmental Chang*, edited by Jennifer Cole, x–xiii. Wallingford, UK: CABI.

– 2019b. "Introduction to Planetary Health." In *Planetary Health: Human Health in an Era of Global Environmental Change*, edited by Jennifer Cole, 1–8. Wallingford, UK: CABI.

– 2019c. "Key Concepts in Planetary Health." In *Planetary Health: Human Health in an Era of Global Environmental Change*, edited by Jennifer Cole, 9–22. Wallingford, UK: CABI.

Cole, Steven W. 2014. "Human Social Genomics." *PLOS Genetics* 10, no. 8: 1–7. https://doi.org/10.1371/journal.pgen.1004601. Medline:25166010.

Complexity Medicine. n.d.-a. "Align and Design – Community Explorations in Health Design – Week 1." YouTube. Accessed 23 March 2021. https://www.youtube.com/watch?v=D7jyc5Od-Rw.

– n.d.-b. "Align and Design – Community Explorations in Health Design – Week 2." YouTube. Accessed 23 March 2021. https://www.youtube.com/watch?v=D7jyc5Od-Rw.

Cooper Marcus, Clare, and Naomi Sachs. 2014. *Therapeutic Landscapes: An Evidence-Based Approach to Designing Healing Gardens and Restorative Outdoor Spaces*. Hoboken, NJ: John Wiley and Sons.

Corkal, Vanessa, Philip Gass, and Aaron Cosbey. 2020. "Green Strings: Principles and Conditions for a Green Recovery from COVID-19 in Canada." International Institute for Sustainable Development. https://www.iisd.org/publications/green-strings-recovery-covid-19-canada.

Cornish, F., J. Haaken, L. Moskovitz, and S. Jackson. 2016. "Rethinking Prefigurative Politics: Introduction to the Special Thematic Section." *Journal of Social and Political Psychology* 4: 114–27. https://doi.org/10.5964/jspp.v4i1.640.

COVID-19 Mutual Aid UK. 2020. "Local Organizing to Support the Most Vulnerable in Our Communities." Accessed 26 February 2021. https://covidmutualaid.org.

Crate, S. 2011. "Climate and Culture: Anthropology in the Era of Contemporary Climate Change." *Annual Review of Anthropology* 40: 175–94. https://doi.org/10.1146/annurev.anthro.012809.104925.

Cumming, Graeme S., and Garry D. Peterson. 2017. "Unifying Research on Social-Ecological Resilience and Collapse." *Trends in Ecology and Evolution* 32, no. 9: 695–713. https://doi.org/10.1016/j.tree.2017.06.014. Medline:28734593.

Dale, G. 2010. *Karl Polanyi: The Limits of the Market*. Cambridge: Polity.

D'Alisa, G., F. Demaria, and G. Kallis. 2015. *Degrowth: A Vocabulary for a New Era*. New York: Routledge.

Daly, Herman. 2019. "Some Overlaps between the First and Second Thirty Years of Ecological Economics." *Ecological Economics* 164: 1–3. https://doi.org/10.1016/j.ecolecon.2019.106372.

Dartnell, Lewis. 2014. *The Knowledge: How to Rebuild Our World from Scratch*. New York: Penguin.

da Silva, Arjuna. 2009, Winter. "Growing a Culture of Community Health and Wellbeing at Earthaven Ecovillage." *Communities*, no. 145, 16–17.

Davy, Barbara Jane. 2020. "To Become Ancestors of a Living Future." In *Health in the Anthropocene: Living Well on a Finite Planet*, edited by Katharine Zywert and Stephen Quilley, 419–31. Toronto: University of Toronto Press.

– 2021. "How Gratitude for Nature Can Reign In Your Existential Angst about Climate Change." *The Conversation*, 7 April 2021. https://theconversation.com/how-gratitude-for-nature-can-rein-in-your-existential-angst-about-climate-change-156840.

Dawson, Jonathan. 2013. "From Islands to Networks: The History and Future of the Ecovillage Movement." In *Environmental Anthropology Engaging Ecotopia: Bioregionalism, Permaculture, and Ecovillages*, edited by J. Lockyer and J.R. Veteto, 217–34. New York: Berghahn.

"Deep Time Walk." n.d. Empathy Media. Accessed 21 October 2020. https://vimeo.com/236050600.

Del Bianco, Ann, David Mallery, Kamal Paudel, and Martin J. Bunch. 2020. "The Exploration of Socioecological Approaches and Indicators in the Anthropocene." In *Health in the Anthropocene: Living Well on a Finite Planet*, edited by Katharine Zywert and Stephen Quilley, 357–82. Toronto: University of Toronto Press.

Demaria, F., G. Kallis, and K. Bakker. 2019. "Geographies of degrowth: Nowtopias, resurgences and the decolonization of imaginaries and places." *Nature and Space* 2, no. 3: 431–50. https://doi.org/10.1177/2514848619869689.

De Young, Raymond. 2014. "Some Behavioral Aspects of Energy Descent: How a Biophysical Psychology Might Help People Transition through the Lean Times Ahead." *Frontiers in Psychology* 5, no. 1255: 1–16. https://doi.org/10.3389/fpsyg.2014.01255. Medline:25404926.

De Young, Raymond, and Thomas Princen. 2012. *The Localization Reader: Adapting to the Coming Downshift*. Cambridge, MA: MIT Press.

Dickinson, J. 2009. "The People Paradox: Self-Esteem Striving, Immortality Ideologies, and Human Response to Climate Change." *Ecology and Society* 14, no. 1: 34. https://doi.org/10.5751/ES-02849-140134.

Dryzek, J. 2013. *The Politics of the Earth: Environmental Discourses*. Oxford: Oxford University Press.

Duff, H., C. Faerron Guzmán, A. Almada, C. Golden, and S. Myers. 2020. "Planetary Health Case Studies: An Anthology of Solutions." https://doi.org/10.5822/phanth9678.

Durkheim, E. 1897. *Suicide: A Study in Sociology*. Glencoe, IL: Free Press.

Eckelman, Matthew J., Jodi D. Sherman, and Andrea J. MacNeill. 2018. "Life Cycle Environmental Emissions and Health Damages from the Canadian Health Care System: An Economic-Environmental- Epidemiological Analysis." *PloS Medicine* 15, no. 7: e1002623. https://doi.org/10.1371/journal.pmed.1002623. Medline:30063712.

Edger, Robin, Courtney Howard, Melissa Lem, Jean Zigby, C. Pétrin-Desrosiers, H.M. Doyle, G.T. Kitching, et al. 2020. *Healthy Recovery Plan for a Safe and Sustainable Future*. Canadian Association of Physicians for the Environment. Toronto: CAPE. https://cape.ca/wp-content/uploads/2020/07/CAPE_Report2020_EN_HealthyRecoveryPlan.pdf.

Eisenstein, Michael. 2020. "The Hunt for a Healthy Microbiome." *Nature* 577: S6–S8. https://doi.org/10.1038/d41586-020-00193-3. Medline:31996823.

Elias, Norbert. 2011 [1939]. *The Civilizing Process*. Rev. ed. In *On the Process of Civilisation*, vol. 3 in *The Collected Works of Norbert Elias*. Oxford: Blackwell.

Elings, Marjolein. 2012. *Effects of Care Farms: Scientific Research on the Benefits of Care Farms for Clients*. Wageningen: Plant Research International.

- 2020. "Care Farming: Making a Meaningful Connection between Agriculture, Health Care, and Society." In *Health in the Anthropocene: Living Well on a Finite Planet*, edited by Katharine Zywert and Stephen Quilley, 226–40. Toronto: University of Toronto Press.
Engelman, Robert, John Bongaarts, and Kristen P. Patterson. 2020. "Population, Consumption, Equity, and Rights." In *Planetary Health: Protecting Nature to Protect Ourselves*, edited by Samuel Myers and Howard Frumkin, 37–70. Washington, DC: Island Press.
Evison, Will, and Sam Bickersteth. 2020. "A New Economics for Planetary Health." In *Planetary Health: Protecting Nature to Protect Ourselves*, edited by Samuel Myers and Howard Frumkin, 387–424. Washington, DC: Island Press.
Fanning, Adrew L., and Daniel W. O'Neill. 2019. "The Wellbeing-Consumption Paradox: Happiness, Health, Income, and Carbon Emissions in Growing versus Non-growing Economies." *Journal of Cleaner Production* 212: 810–21. https://doi.org/10.1016/j.jclepro.2018.11.223.
Field, Chris, David Tilman, Ruth DeFries, David R. Montgomery, Peter Gleick, Howard Frumkin, and Philip Landrigan. 2020. "A Changing Planet." In *Planetary Health: Protecting Nature to Protect Ourselves*, edited by Samuel Myers and Howard Frumkin, 71–110. Washington, DC: Island Press.
Fitzgibbon, Marian L., Joanna Buscemi, Molly Cory, Anjana Jagpal, Bridget Brush, Angela Kong, and Lisa Tussing-Humphreys. 2018. "Understanding Population Health from Multi-level and Community-Based Models." In *The Handbook of Health Behaviour Change*, 5th ed., edited by Marissa E. Hilliard, Kristin A. Riekert, Judith K. Ockene, and Lori Pbert, xvii–xx. New York: Springer.
Fleming, David. n.d. "Appropriate Technology." In *Lean Logic: A Dictionary for the Future and How to Survive It*. Accessed 29 January 2021. https://leanlogic.online/glossary/appropriate-technology/.
Foucault, M. 1994. *The Birth of the Clinic*. New York: Vintage.
Frey, B.S., and S. Meier. 2004. "Pro-social Behavior in a Natural Setting." *Journal of Economic Behavior and Organization* 54, no. 1: 65–88. https://doi.org/10.1016/j.jebo.2003.10.001.
Frumkin, Howard. 2020. "Climate Change and Human Health." In *Planetary Health: Protecting Nature to Protect Ourselves*, edited by Samuel Myers and Howard Frumkin, 245–59. Washington, DC: Island Press.
Frumkin, Howard, Gregory N. Bratman, Sara Jo Breslow, Bobby Cochran, Peter H. Kahn Jr., Joshua J. Lawler, Phillip S. Levin, et al. 2017. "Nature Contact and Human Health: A Research Agenda" *Environmental Health Perspectives* 125, no. 7: 1–18. https://doi.org/10.1289/EHP1663. Medline:28796634.

Frumkin, Howard, and Andy Haines. 2020. "Global Environmental Change and Noncommunicable Disease Risks." In *Planetary Health: Protecting Nature to Protect Ourselves*, edited by Samuel Myers and Howard Frumkin, 165–88. Washington, DC: Island Press.

Frumkin, Howard, and Samuel Myers. 2020. "Afterword: Coronavirus and Planetary Health." In *Planetary Health: Protecting Nature to Protect Ourselves*, edited by Samuel Myers and Howard Frumkin, 487–96. Washington, DC: Island Press.

Gallopín, G.C. 2002. "Planning for Resilience: Scenarios, Surprises, and Branch Points." In *Panarchy: Understanding Transformations in Human and Natural Systems*, edited by L.H. Gunderson and C.S. Holling, 361–94. Washington, DC: Island Press.

Gawande, A. 2014. *Being Mortal: Medicine and What Matters in the End*. New York: Metropolitan Books.

Gellner, E. 1998. *Language and Solitude: Wittgenstein, Malinowski and the Habsburg Dilemma*. Cambridge: Cambridge University Press.

Geobey, Sean, and Katharine McGowan. 2019. "Panarchy, Ontological and Epistemological Phenomena, and the Plague." *Ecology and Society* 24, no. 4: 23. https://doi.org/10.5751/ES-11089-240423.

Giddens, A. 1990. *The Consequences of Modernity*. Stanford, CT: Stanford University Press.

Giulio, Mary, Dario Maggioni, Isacco Montroni, Giampaolo Ugolini, Patrizio Capelli, Lorenzo Ceppi, Paolo Bonfanti, Andrea Mariani, and Felice Achilli. 2020. "Being a Doctor Will Never Be the Same after the COVID-19 Pandemic." *American Journal of Medicine* 133, no. 6. https://doi.org/10.1016/j.amjmed.2020.03.003. Medline:32240630.

Goldstein, J., and M. Godemont. 2003. "The Legend and Lessons of Geel, Belgium: A 1500-Year-Old Legend, a 21st-Century Model." *Community Mental Health Journal* 39: 441–58. https://doi.org/10.1023/a:1025813003347. Medline:14635986.

Government of Ireland. 2020. *Government Action Plan to Support the Community Response*. Department of Rural and Community Development. https://www.gov.ie/en/publication/70be56-government-action-plan-for-community-response-to-covid-19/.

Granados, Jose, A. Tapia, and Ana V. Diez Roux. 2009. "Life and Death during the Great Depression." *PNAS* 106, no. 41: 17290–5. https://doi.org/10.1073/pnas.0904491106. Medline:19805076.

Gravlee, Clarence C. 2020. "Systemic Racism, Chronic Health Inequities, and COVID-19: A Syndemic in the Making?" *American Journal of Human Biology* 32, no. 5: e23482. https://doi.org/10.1002/ajhb.23482. Medline:32754945.

Greer, John Michael. 2009. *The Ecotechnic Future: Envisioning a Post-Peak World*. Gabriola Island, BC: New Society.

Gunderson, L.H., and C.S. Holling, eds. 2001. *Panarchy: Understanding Transformations in Human and Natural Systems*. Washington, DC: Island Press.

Guterres, António. 2020. "UN Secretary General: Recovery from the Coronavirus Crisis Must Lead to a Better World" *The Guardian*, 2 April 2020. https://www.theguardian.com/commentisfree/2020/apr/02/un-secretary-general-coronavirus-crisis-world-pandemic-response.

Hager, Thomas. 2019. *Ten Drugs : How Plants, Powders, and Pills Have Shaped the History of Medicine*. New York: Abrams.

Hahn, Thomas, and Björn Nykvist. 2017. "Are Adaptations Self-Organized, Autonomous, and Harmonious? Assessing the Social-Ecological Resilience Literature." *Ecology and Society* 22, no. 1: 12. https://doi.org/10.5751/ES-09026-220112.

Halikiopoulou, Daphne. 2015. "Austerity Brings Extremism: Why the Welfare State Is the Key to Understanding the Rise of Europe's Far Right." *Huffington Post*, 23 September 2015. https://www.huffingtonpost.co.uk/daphne-halikiopoulou/austerity-brings-extremis_b_8182866.html.

Hancock, Trevor. 2015. "Population Health Promotion 2.0: An Eco-social Approach to Public Health in the Anthropocene" *Canadian Journal of Public Health* 106, no. 4: e252–e255. https://doi.org/10.17269/cjph.106.5161. Medline:26285199.

– 2017. "Beyond Health Care: The Other Determinants of Health." *Canadian Medical Association Journal* 189, no. 50: e1571. https://doi.org/10.1503/cmaj.171419. Medline:29255107.

– 2020a. "A Different Perspective on COVID-19." *Healthy People, Healthy Communities, a Healthy Plant* (blog). 20 March 2020. https://trevorhancock.org/2020/03/23/a-different-perspective-on-covid-19/.

– 2020b. "A Tale of Two Futures: This Time, Let's Choose the Right One." *Healthy People, Healthy Communities, a Healthy Plant* (blog). https://trevorhancock.org/2020/04/14/a-tale-of-two-futures-lets-choose-the-right-one-this-time/. 14 April 2020.

Hanlon, P., S. Carlisle, M. Hannah, D. Reilly, and A. Lyon. 2011. "Making the Case for a 'Fifth Wave' in Public Health." *Public Health* 125: 30–6. https://doi.org/10.1016/j.puhe.2010.09.004. Medline:21256366.

Harmer, Andrew, Ben Eder, Sophie Gepp, Anja Leetz, and Remco Van de Pas. 2020. "WHO Should Declare Climate Change a Public Health Emergency." *British Medical Journal* 368: 1–3. https://doi.org/10.1136/bmj.m797. Medline:32229481.

Harrison, M. 2004. *Disease and the Modern World: 1500 to the Present Day*. Cambridge: Polity.

Hassink, Jan. 2017. "Understanding Care Farming as a Swiftly Developing Sector in the Netherlands." Ph.D. diss., University of Amsterdam.

Hassink, Jan, Herman Agricola, Esther J. Veen, Roald Pijpker, Simone R. de Bruin, Harold A. B. van der Meulen, and Lana B. Plug. 2020. "The Care Farming Sector in the Netherlands: A Reflection on Its Developments and Promising Innovations." *Sustainability* 12: 1–17. https://doi.org/10.3390/su12093811.

Hassink, Jan, and Marjolein Elings, eds. 2006. *Farming for Health: Green-Care Farming across Europe and the United States of America*. Dordrecht: Springer.

Hassink, Jan, Willem Hulsink, and John Grin. 2014. "Farming with Care: The Evolution of Care Farming in the Netherlands." *NJAS – Wageningen Journal of Life Sciences* 68: 1–11. https://doi.org/10.1016/j.njas.2013.11.001.

Hazeltine, B., and C. Bull. 2003. *Field Guide to Appropriate Technology*. Boston: Amsterdam Academic.

Hedges, S. Blair. 2009. "Life." In *Timetree of Life*, edited by S.B. Hedges and S. Kumar, 89–98. Oxford: Oxford University Press.

Hedges, S. Blair, Julie Marin, Michael Suleski, Madeline Paymer, and Sudhir Kumar. 2015. "Tree of Life Reveals Clock-Like Speciation and Diversification." *Molecular Biology and Evolution* 32, no. 4: 835–45. https://doi.org/10.1093/molbev/msv037. Medline:25739733

Helbing, Dirk. 2013. "Globally Networked Risks and How to Respond." *Nature* 497: 51–9. https://doi.org/10.1038/nature12047. Medline:23636396.

Helliwell, John F., and John Hall. 2020. "Happiness on a Healthier Planet." In *Planetary Health: Protecting Nature to Protect Ourselves*, edited by Samuel Myers and Howard Frumkin, 261–82. Washington, DC: Island Press.

Hensher, Martin, Katie Kish, Joshua Farley, Stephen Quilley, and Katharine Zywert. 2020. "Open Knowledge Commons versus Privatized Gain in a Fractured Information Ecology: Lessons from COVID-19 for the Future of Sustainability." *Global Sustainability* 3, e26, 1–5. https://doi.org/10.1017/sus.2020.21.

Hensher, Martin, and Katharine Zywert. 2020. "Can Health Care Adapt to a World of Tightening Ecological Constraints? Challenges on the Road to a Post-Growth Future." *BMJ* 371: m4168. https://doi.org/10.1136/bmj.m4168.

Heyd, Thomas. 2020. "Covid-19 and Climate Change in the Times of the Anthropocene." *Anthropocene Review* 8, no. 1: 1–16. https://doi.org/10.1177/2053019620961799.

Hickel J., and G. Kallis. 2019 "Is Green Growth Possible?" *New Political Economy* 25: 469–86. https://doi.org/10.1080/13563467.2019.1598964

Hidaka, BC. 2012. "Depression as a Disease of Modernity: Explanations for Increasing Prevalence." *Journal of Affective Disorders* 140: 205–14. https://doi.org/10.1016/j.jad.2011.12.036. Medline:22244375.

Hilliard, Marissa E., Kristin A. Riekert, Judith K. Ockene, and Lori Pbert. 2018. "Preface." In *The Handbook of Health Behaviour Change*, 5th ed., edited by

Hilliard, Marissa E., Kristin A. Riekert, Judith K. Ockene, and Lori Pbert, xvii–xx. New York: Springer.

Hochschild, Arlie Russel. 2017. *Strangers in Their Own Land: Anger and Mourning on the American Right*. New York: New Press.

Holling, C.S., L.H. Gunderson, and D. Ludwig. 2002. "In Quest of a Theory of Adaptive Change." In *Panarchy: Understanding Transformations in Human and Natural Systems*, edited by L.H. Gunderson and C.S. Holling, 3–24. Washington, DC: Island Press.

Holling, C.S., L.H. Gunderson, and G.D. Peterson. 2002. "Sustainability and Panarchies." In *Panarchy: Understanding Transformations in Human and Natural Systems*, edited by L.H. Gunderson and C.S. Holling, 63–102. Washington, DC: Island Press.

Homer-Dixon, Thomas. 2006. *The Upside of Down: Catastrophe, Creativity and the Renewal of Civilization*. Toronto: Vintage Canada.

– 2020. "Coronavirus Will Change the World. It Might Also Lead to a Better Future." *Globe and Mail*, 5 March 2020. https://www.theglobeandmail.com/opinion/article-the-coronavirus-is-a-collective-problem-that-requires-global/.

Homer-Dixon, Thomas, Brian Walker, Reinette Biggs, Anne-Sophie Crepin, Carle Folke, Eric F. Lambin, Garry D. Peterson, et al. 2015. "Synchronous Failure: The Emerging Causal Architecture of Global Crisis." *Ecology and Society* 20, no. 3: 6. https://www.jstor.org/stable/26270255.

Hopkins, R. 2008. *Transition Handbook: From Oil Dependency to Local Resilience*. Totnes, UK: Green Books.

Horton, Richard. 2012. "Global Burden of Disease 2010: Understanding Disease, Injury, and Risk." *The Lancet* 380, no. 9859: 2053–4. https://doi.org/10.1016/S0140-6736(12)62133-3. Medline:23245595.

– 2020. "Offline: COVID-19 Is Not a Pandemic." *The Lancet*, 396, no. 10255, 874. https://doi.org/10.1016/S0140-6736(20)32000-6. Medline:32979964.

– 2021. "Offline: The Origin Story." *The Lancet* 398, no. 10317: 2136. https://doi.org/10.1016/S0140-6736(21)02786-0. Medline:34895520.

Horton, Richard, Robert Beaglehole, Ruth Bonita, John Raeburn, Martin McKee, and Stig Wall. 2014. "From Public to Planetary Health: A Manifesto." *The Lancet* 383, no. 9920: 847. https://doi.org/10.1016/S0140-6736(14)60409-8. Medline:24607088.

Hough-Stewart, Lisa, Katherine Trebeck, Claire Sommer, and Stewart Wallis. 2019. *What Is a Wellbeing Economy? Different Ways to Understand the Vision of an Economy that Serves People and Planet*. Wellbeing Economy Alliance. https://wellbeingeconomy.org/wp-content/uploads/2019/12/A-WE-Is-WEAll-Ideas-Little-Summaries-of-Big-Issues-4-Dec-2019.pdf.

Howard, Courtney. 2020. "Coronavirus and Climate Change: How to Save Lives during Crises." *The Narwhal*, 21 April 2020. https://thenarwhal.ca/coronavirus-and-climate-change-how-to-save-lives-during-crises/.

"How to Start a Neighbourhood Pod." n.d. https://docs.google.com
/document/d/17iMBTzaM4tPsUym-wyiEqOcOAiHVKiXN3XSjJ26TBKM
/edit#. Accessed 25 February 2021.

Hsu, Cheryl, Beth Hunter, Hayley Lapalm, and Jennifer Reynolds. n.d. *Nourish: The Future of Food in Health Care: Phase 1 Developmental Evaluation (2016–2019).* https://static1.squarespace.com/static/58829365c534a576e10e3a5c/t
/5d7bf27365fd1713e6526cee/1568404085673/Final+Nourish+Developmental
+Evaluation+Report_2019Sept13.pdf. Accessed 18 May 2019.

Hu, Ben, Hua Guo, Peng Zhou, and Zheng-Li Shi. 2021. "Characteristics of SARS-CoV-2 and COVID-19." *Nature Reviews Microbiology* 19: 141–54. https://doi.org/10.1038/s41579-020-00459-7.

Illich, I. 1973. *Tools for Conviviality.* New York: Harper and Row.

IPCC. 2022. "Summary for Policymakers." In *Climate Change 2022: Impacts, Adaptation and Vulnerability. Working Group II Contribution to the Sixth Assessment Report of the Intergovernmental Panel on Climate Change,* edited by H.-O. Pörtner, D.C. Roberts, M. Tignor, E.S. Poloczanska, K. Mintenbeck, A. Alegría, M. Craig, et al., 3–33. Cambridge: Cambridge University Press. https://doi.org/10.1017/9781009325844.001.

Jackson, T. 2009. *Prosperity without Growth: Economics for a Finite Planet.* London: Earthscan.

Janevic, M., and Connell, C. "Individual Theories." In *The Handbook of Health Behaviour Change,* 5th ed., edited by Marissa E. Hilliard, Kristin A. Riekert, Judith K. Ockene, and Lori Pbert, 3–24. New York: Springer.

Jay, M. 2014. "The Geel Question." *Aeon,* 9 January 2014. https://aeon.co
/essays/geel-where-the-mentally-ill-are-welcomed-home.

Johnson, S. 2010. *Where Good Ideas Come From: The Natural History of Innovation.* New York: Riverhead.

Kaplan, S. 2000. "New Ways to Promote Proenvironmental Behavior: Human Nature and Environmentally Responsible Behavior." *Journal of Social Issues* 56, no. 3: 491–508. https://doi.org/10.1111/0022-4537.00180.

Karliner, Josh. 2020. "Coronavirus and the Climate Crisis; Common Causes and Shared Solutions." Health Care Without Harm. *Medium,* 26 March 2020. https://medium.com/@HCWH/coronavirus-and-the-climate-crisis
-227c36bf07d0.

Katz, Richard. 1982. *Boiling Energy: Community Healing among the Kalahari Kung.* Cambridge, MA: Harvard University Press.

Kauffman, S. 1999. *At Home in the Universe.* New York: Oxford University Press.

Keeney, Bradford. 1983. *The Aesthetics of Change.* New York: Guilford.

Kimmerer, Robin Wall. 2013. *Braiding Sweetgrass: Indigenous Wisdom, Scientific Knowledge and the Teachings of Plants.* Minneapolis: Milkweed.

Kirksey, S.E., and S. Helmreich. 2010. "The Emergence of Multispecies Ethnography." *Cultural Anthropology* 25, no. 4: 545–76. https://doi.org/10.1111
/j.1548-1360.2010.01069.x.

Kish, Kaitlin. 2018. *Ecological Economic Development Goals: Reincorporating the Social Sphere in Ecological Economic Theory and Practice*. Waterloo: University of Waterloo, School of Environment, Resources and Sustainability.

Kish, K., and S. Quilley. 2017. "Wicked dilemmas of scale and complexity in the politics of degrowth." *Ecological Economics* 142: 306–17.

Kish, Kaitlin, Katharine Zywert, Martin Hensher, Barbara Jane Davy, and Stephen Quilley. 2021. "Socioecological System Transformation: Lessons from COVID-19" *World* 2, no. 1: 15–31. https://doi.org/10.3390/world2010002.

Köhler, Jonathan, Frank W. Geels, Florian Kern, Jochen Markard, Elsie Onsongo, Anna Wieczorek, Floortje Alkemade, et al. 2019. "An Agenda for Sustainability Transitions Research: State of the Art and Future Directions." *Environmental Innovation and Societal Transitions* 31: 1–32. https://doi.org/10.1016/j.eist.2019.01.004.

Kohn, Eduardo. 2013. *How Forests Think: Toward an Anthropology beyond the Human*. Berkeley: University of California Press.

Kovacic, Z., M. Spano, S. Lo Piano, and A.H. Sorman. 2018. "Finance, Energy and the Decoupling: An Empirical Study." *Journal of Evolutionary Economics* 28: 565–90. https://doi.org/10.1007/s00191-017-0514-8.

Kumar, Sudhir, Glen Stecher, Michael Suleski, and S. Blair Hedges. 2017. "TimeTree: A Resource for Timelines, Timetrees, and Divergence Times." *Molecular Biology and Evolution* 34, no. 7: 1812–19. https://doi.org/10.1093/molbev/msx116.

Lal, Rattan. 2020. "Home Gardening and Urban Agriculture for Advancing Food and Nutritional Security in Response to the COVID-19 Pandemic." *Food Security* 12: 871–6. https://doi.org/10.1007/s12571-020-01058-3. Medline:32837634.

Leach, D.K. 2013. "Prefigurative Politics." In *The Wiley-Blackwell Encyclopedia of Social and Political Movements*. Chichester, UK: Wiley-Blackwell.

Lenton, T.M., S. Benson, T. Smith, T. Ewer, V. Lanel, E. Petykowski, T.W.R. Powell, Jesse F. Abrams, Fenna Blomsma, and Simon Sharpe. 2022. "Operationalising Positive Tipping Points towards Global Sustainability. *Global Sustainability* 5, no. e1: 1–16. https://doi.org/10.1017/sus.2021.30.

Le Vasseur, Todd. 2013. "Globalizing the Ecovillage Ideal: Networks of Empowerment, Seeds of Hope." In *Environmental Anthropology Engaging Ecotopia: Bioregionalism, Permaculture, and Ecovillages*, edited by J. Lockyer and J.R. Veteto, 251–68. New York: Berghahn.

Litfin, K. 2014. *Ecovillages: Lessons for Sustainable Community*. Cambridge: Polity.

Lock, M., and V.-K. Nguyen. 2010. *An Anthropology of Biomedicine*. Chichester: Wiley-Blackwell.

Lockyer, J., and J.R. Veteto, eds. 2013. *Environmental Anthropology Engaging Ecotopia: Bioregionalism, Permaculture, and Ecovillages*. New York: Berghahn.

Lorea, Carola Erika. 2020. "Religious Returns, Ritual Changes and Divinations on COVID-19." *Social Anthropology* 28, no. 2: 307–8. https://doi.org/10.1111/1469-8676.12865. Medline:32836937.

Lovelock, James. 1991. *Healing Gaia: Practical Medicine for the Planet*. New York: Harmony.

– 2014. *A Rough Ride to the Future*. New York: Overlook.

Lurie, Nicole, Melanie Saville, Richard Hatchett, and Jane Halton. 2020. "Developing Covid-19 Vaccines at Pandemic Speed." *New England Journal of Medicine* 382: 1969–73. https://doi.org/10.1056/NEJMp2005630. Medline:32227757.

MacDonald, Valerie. 2020. "Community Gardens Sprout during Pandemic." *Ontario Farmer*, 7 July 2020, B18.

Mahmoudi Farahani, Leila, Cecily Maller, and Kath Phelan. 2018. "Private Gardens as Urban Greenspaces: Can They Compensate for Poor Greenspace Access in Lower Socioeconomic Neighbourhoods?" *Landscape Online* 59: 1–18. https://doi.org/10.3097/LO.201859.

Maier, Karl J., and Mustafa al'Absi. 2017. "Toward a Biopsychosocial Ecology of the Human Microbiome, Brain-Gut Axis, and Health." *Psychosomatic Medicine* 79: 947–57. https://doi.org/10.1097/PSY.0000000000000515. Medline:28719406.

Mair, Simon. 2020. "Neoliberal Economics, Planetary Health, and the COVID-19 Pandemic: A Marxist Ecofeminist Analysis." *The Lancet Planet Health* 4: e588–96. https://doi.org/10.1016/S2542-5196(20)30252-7. Medline:33278376.

Marcus, George E. 1995. "Ethnography in/of the World System: The Emergence of Multi-sited Ethnography." *Annual Review of Anthropology* 24: 95–117. https://doi.org/10.1146/annurev.an.24.100195.000523.

Maroko, Andrew R., Denis Nash, and Brian T. Pavilonis. 2020. "COVID-19 and Inequity: A Comparative Spatial Analysis of New York City and Chicago Hot Spots." *Journal of Urban Health* 97: 461–70. https://doi.org/10.1007/s11524-020-00468-0. Medline:32691212.

Marx, Karl. 1992. "Economic and Philosophical Manuscripts." In *Early Writings*, translated by Rodney Livingstone and Gregor Benton, 279–400. Penguin Classics. Harmondsworth, England: Penguin.

Maxmen, Amy, and Smriti Mallapaty. 2021. "The COVID Lab-Leak Hypothesis: What Scientists Do and Don't Know. *Nature* 594: 313–15. https://doi.org/10.1038/d41586-021-01529-3. Medline:34108722.

McCartney, Margaret. 2020. "Medicine: Before Covid-19, and After." *The Lancet*, 31 March 2020. https://doi.org/10.1016/S0140-6736(20)30756-X.

McCullough, Dennis. 2008. "Slow Medicine." *Dartmouth Medicine*, Spring 2008. https://dartmed.dartmouth.edu/spring08/html/grand_rounds.php.

McElroy, A., and P.K. Townsend. 2014. *Medical Anthropology in Ecological Perspective*. Boulder, CO: Westview.

McGowan, Katharine, and Frances Westley. 2017. "Constructing the Evolution of Social Innovation: Methodological Insights from a Multi-case Study." *European Public and Social Innovation Review (EPSIR)* 2, no. 1: 93–109. https://doi.org/10.31637/epsir.17-1.7.

McMichael, Anthony J. 2014. "Population Health in the Anthropocene: Gains, Losses, and Emerging Trends." *Anthropocene Review* 1, no. 1: 44–56. https://doi.org/10.1177/2053019613514035.

Meadows, Donella H. 2008. *Thinking in Systems: A Primer*. White River Junction, VT: Chelsea Green.

Meadows, Donella H., D.L. Meadows, J. Randers, and W.W. Behrens III. 1972. *The Limits to Growth: A Report for the Club of Rome's Project on the Predicament of Mankind*. New York: Universe Books.

Meadows, Donella H., J. Randers, and D.L. Meadows. 2004. *Limits to Growth: The 30-Year Update*. White River Junction, VT: Chelsea Green.

Mejia, Angie, Manami Bhattacharya, Amanda Nigon-Crowley, Kelley Kirkpatrick, and Chandi Katoch. 2020. "Community Gardening during Times of Crisis: Recommendations for Community-Engaged Dialogue, Research, and Praxis." *Journal of Agriculture, Food Systems, and Community Development* 10, no. 1: 1–7. https://doi.org/10.5304/jafscd.2020.101.006.

Melgar-Melgar, Rigo E., and Charles A.S. Hall. 2020. "Why Ecological Economics Needs to Return to Its Roots: The Biophysical Foundation of Socio-economic Systems." *Ecological Economics* 169: 1–14. https://doi.org/10.1016/j.ecolecon.2019.106567.

Mikkonen, Juha, and Dennis Raphael. 2010. *Social Determinants of Health: The Canadian Facts*. Toronto: York University School of Health Policy and Management.

Missoni, Eduardo. 2015. "Degrowth and Health: Local Action Should Be Linked to Global Policies and Governance for Health." *Sustainability Science* 10, no. 3: 439–50. https://doi.org/10.1007/s11625-015-0300-1.

Missoni, Eduardo, and Edmundo Morales Galindo. 2020. "Health Workers and Sustainable Systems for Health in a Post-growth Society." *Visions for Sustainability* 14: 83–98. https://doi.org/10.13135/2384-8677/4545.

Montefrio, Marvin Joseph F. 2020. "Interrogating the "Productive" Home Gardener in a Time of Pandemic Lockdown in the Philippines." *Food and Foodways* 28, no. 3: 216–25. https://doi.org/10.1080/07409710.2020.1790142.

Morgan, T. 2016. *Life after Growth: How the Global Economy Really Works – And Why 200 Years of Growth Are Over*. Petersfield: Harriman House.

– n.d. *Coronavirus: The Economics of De-growth*. Surplus Energy Economics. Accessed 19 January 2021. https://surplusenergyeconomics.files.wordpress.com/2020/04/coronavirus-the-economics-of-de-growth.pdf.

Morris, D.S., T. Wright, J.E.A. Somner, and A. Connor. 2013. "The Carbon Footprint of Cataract Surgery." *Eye* 27: 495–501. https://doi.org/10.1038/eye.2013.9. Medline:23429413.

Moscrop, D. 2020. "In Canada, an Inspiring Movement Emerges in Response to the Coronavirus." *Washington Post*, 24 March 2020. https://www.washingtonpost.com/opinions/2020/03/24/canada-an-inspiring-movement-emerges-response-coronavirus/.

Mullins, Lisa, Sylvain Charlebois, and Janet Music. 2020. "Home Food Gardening in Response to the COVID-19 Pandemic." Agri-Food Analytics Lab, Dalhousie University. https://www.dal.ca/sites/agri-food/research/home-food-gardening-during-covid-19.html.

Mychajluk, Lisa. 2020. "'Food as Thy Medicine': How Ecovillages Foster Population and Planetary Health through Regenerative Food Systems." In *Health in the Anthropocene: Living Well on a Finite Planet*, edited by Katharine Zywert and Stephen Quilley, 210–25. Toronto: University of Toronto Press.

Myers, Samuel, and Howard Frumkin. 2020. "An Introduction to Planetary Health." In *Planetary Health: Protecting Nature to Protect Ourselves*, edited by Samuel Myers and Howard Frumkin, 3–16. Washington, DC: Island Press.

Nourish. n.d. "Nourish Food for Health Levers." Accessed 18 May 2021. https://www.nourishhealthcare.ca/nourish-levers.

Odum, H.T. 2007. *Environment, Power, and Society for the Twenty-First Century: The Hierarchy of Energy*. New York: Columbia University Press.

Olsson, Per, Michele-Lee Moore, Frances R. Westley, and Daniel D.P. McCarthy. 2017. "The Concept of the Anthropocene as a Game-Changer: A New Context for Social Innovation and Transformations to Sustainability." *Ecology and Society* 22, no. 2: 31. https://doi.org/10.5751/ES-09310-220231.

O'Neill, Dan, Andrew Fanning, William Lamb, and Julia Steinberger. 2018. "A Good Life for All Within Planetary Boundaries." *Nature Sustainability* 1: 88–95. https://doi.org/10.1038/s41893-018-0021-4.

"Open Letter: Principles for a Just Recovery from COVID-19." N.d. Accessed 30 November 2020. https://350.org/just-recovery/.

Open Letter Working Group. n.d. "Re-imagining the Future after the Corona Crisis." Accessed 28 August 2023. https://degrowth.info/en/open-letter.

Ostfeld, Richard S., and Felicia Keesing. 2020. "Planetary Health and Infectious Disease." In *Planetary Health: Protecting Nature to Protect Ourselves*, edited by Samuel Myers and Howard Frumkin, 141–64. Washington, DC: Island Press.

Parkes, Margot W., Blake Poland, Sandra Allison, Donald C. Cole, Ian Culbert, Maya K. Gislason, Trevor Hancock, Courtney Howard, Andrew Papadopoulos, and Faiza Waheed. 2019. "Preparing for the Future of Public Health: Ecological Determinants of Health and the Call for an Eco-social

Approach to Public Health Education." *Canadian Journal of Public Health* 111, no. 1: 60–4. https://doi.org/10.17269/s41997-019-00263-8. Medline:31792844.

Pepper, John W., and Simon Rosenfeld. 2012. "The Emerging Medical Ecology of the Human Gut Microbiome." *Trends in Ecology and Evolution* 27, no. 7: 381–4. https://doi.org/10.1016/j.tree.2012.03.002. Medline:22537667.

Pershouse, Didi. 2011. "Didi Pershouse Speaks in Woodstock, VT after Flooding 10/9/11." Youtube. Accessed 8 December 2020. https://www.youtube.com/watch?v=Q26VKSTCSxk.

– 2016. *The Ecology of Care: Medicine, Agriculture, Money, and the Quiet Power of Human and Microbial Communities*. Thetford Center, VT: Mycelium Books. Kindle.

– 2017a. *Understanding Soil Health and Watershed Function: A Teacher's Manual*. Project of USDA Natural Resources Conservation Service, USDA Southern Plains Climate Hub, Soil Carbon Coalition, Redlands Community College, and Dixon Water Foundation. https://www.didipershouse.com/understanding-soil-health-and-watershed-function.html.

– 2017b. "Audacious August Goals" (blog). 1 September 2017. https://www.didipershouse.com/blog/audacious-august-goals.

– 2020a. "Parallels between Sustainable Agriculture and Sustainable Medicine." *Medium*, 24 September 2020. First published by Post Growth Institute, 2013. https://medium.com/post-growth-institute/parallels-between-sustainable-agriculture-and-sustainable-medicine-33abbbf0d2d2.

– 2020b. "The Soil Sponge: Collaborating with the Work of Other Species to Improve Public Health, Climate Change, and Resilience." In *Health in the Anthropocene: Living Well on a Finite Planet*, edited by Katharine Zywert and Stephen Quilley, 266–84. Toronto: University of Toronto Press.

Pershouse, Didi, and Regenerative Economy Collaborative. 2020. "Other Species Are Essential Workers, Whose Economies Enfold Our Own." *Medium*, 2 December 2020. https://medium.com/the-regenerative-economy-collaborative/other-species-are-essential-workers-whose-economies-enfold-our-own-50deaa2f649f.

Persson, Linn, Bethanie M. Carney Almroth, Christopher D. Collins, Sarah Cornell, Cynthia A. de Wit, Miriam L. Diamond, Peter Fantke, et al. 2022. "Outside the Safe Operating Space of the Planetary Boundary for Novel Entities." *Environmental Science & Technology* 56: 1510–21. https://doi.org/10.1021/acs.est.1c04158. Medline:35038861.

Polanyi, Karl. 1944. *The Great Transformation: The Political and Economic Origins of Our Time*. Boston: Beacon.

Pörtner, H.-O., D.C. Roberts, H. Adams, I. Adelekan, C. Adler, R. Adrian, P. Aldunce, et al. 2022. "Technical Summary." In *Climate Change 2022: Impacts, Adaptation and Vulnerability. Contribution of Working Group II to the Sixth Assessment Report of the Intergovernmental Panel on Climate Change*, edited by

H.-O. Pörtner, D.C. Roberts, M. Tignor, E.S. Poloczanska, K. Mintenbeck, A. Alegría, M. Craig, et al., 37–118. Cambridge: Cambridge University Press. https://doi.org/10.1017/9781009325844.002.

Possian, Amara. 2020. "How to Start a Neighbourhood Pod." Google Slide Deck. Accessed 25 February 2021. https://docs.google.com/presentation/d/1eX-vPI5PqA2nkNp3X6sIss4Vq8I78R4A1LrpLKqKsKI/edit#slide=id.p.

Pray, Leslie. 2008. "Antibiotic Resistance, Mutation Rates and MRSA." *Nature Education* 1, no. 1: 30. https://www.nature.com/scitable/topicpage/antibiotic-resistance-mutation-rates-and-mrsa-28360/.

Prescott, Susan L., Rachel A. Millstein, Martin A. Katzman, and Alan C. Logan. 2016. "Biodiversity, the Human Microbiome and Mental Health: Moving toward a New Clinical Ecology for the 21st Century?" *International Journal of Biodiversity* 2016: 1–18. https://doi.org/10.1155/2016/2718275.

Prüss-Üstün, A.J. Wolf, C. Corvalán, R. Bos, and M. Neira. 2016. *Preventing Disease through Healthy Environments: A Global Assessment of the Burden of Disease from Environmental Risks*. Geneva: World Health Organization.

Puterman, Eli, Jordan Weiss, Benjamin A. Hives, Alison Gemmill, Deborah Karasek, Wendy Berry Mendes, and David H. Rehkopf. 2020. "Predicting Mortality from 57 Economic, Behavioral, Social, and Psychological Factors." *PNAS* 117, no. 28: 16273–82. https://www.pnas.org/doi/10.1073/pnas.1918455117.

Quercia, S., M. Candela, C. Giuliani, S. Turroni, D. Luiselli, S. Rampelli, P. Brigidi, et al. 2014. "From lifetime to evolution: Timescales of human gut microbiota adaptation." *Frontiers in Microbiology* 5: 1–9. https://doi.org/10.3389/fmicb.2014.00587.

Quilley, S. 2012. "System Innovation and a New 'Great Transformation': Re-embedding Economic Life in the Context of 'De-growth.'" *Journal of Social Entrepreneurship* 3, no. 2: 206–29. https://doi.org/10.1080/19420676.2012.725823.

– 2013. "De-growth Is Not a Liberal Agenda: Relocalisation and the Limits to Low Energy Cosmopolitanism." *Environmental Values* 22, no. 2: 261–85. https://doi.org/10.1080/19420676.2012.725823.

– 2017. "Navigating the Anthropocene: Environmental Politics and Complexity in an Era of Limits." In *Handbook on Growth and Sustainability*, edited by B. Dolter and P. Victor, 439–470. Cheltanham: Edward Elgar.

– 2019. "Green Politics and the Right: Possible Alliance?" Paper presented at 12th Biennial Conference of the Canadian Society for Ecological Economics, Waterloo, ON, 22–25 May 2019.

– 2020a. "Between MAGA and E.F. Schumacher: A Post-Pandemic Political Economy." *British Intelligence*, 1 May 2020. https://www.british-intelligence.co.uk/british-intelligence-articles/LONG-READ--BETWEEN-MAGA-AND-E.F.-SCHUMACHER-%3A-A-POST-PANDEMIC-POLITICAL-ECONOMY.

- 2020b. "Individual or Community as a Frame of Reference for Health in Modernity and in the Anthropocene." In *Health in the Anthropocene: Living Well on a Finite Planet*, edited by Katharine Zywert and Stephen Quilley, 25–59. Toronto: University of Toronto Press.
- Quilley, S., J. Hawreliak, and K. Kish. 2016. "Finding an Alternate Route: Towards Open, Eco-cyclical, and Distributed Production," in "Alternative Internets," edited by Félix Tréguer, Panayotis Antoniadis, and Johan Söderberg, special issue, *Journal of Peer Prod Special Issue* 9 (September). http://peerproduction.net/issues/issue-9-alternative-internets/peer-reviewed-papers/finding-an-alternate-route-towards-open-eco-cyclical-and-distributed-production/.
- Quilley, Stephen, and Katharine Zywert. 2019a. "Livelihood, Market, and State: What Does a Political Economy Predicated on the 'Individual-in-Group-in-PLACE Actually Look Like?" *Sustainability* 11, no. 15: 4082. https://doi.org/10.3390/su11154082.
- – 2019b. "The One Earth Approach: Planetary Health in an Era of Limits." In *Planetary Health: Human Health in an Era of Global Environmental Change*, edited by J. Cole, 35–41. Wallingford, UK: CABI.
- Quinn Patton, Michael. 2021. "Evaluation Criteria for Evaluating Transformation: Implications for the Coronavirus Pandemic and the Global Climate Emergency." *American Journal of Evaluation* 42, no. 1: 53–89. https://doi.org/10.1177/1098214020933689.
- Rampelli, Simone, Stephanie Schnorr, Clarissa Consolandi, Alyssa N. Crittenden, Amanda G. Henry, and Marco Candela. 2015. "Metagenome Sequencing of the Hadza Hunter-Gatherer Gut Microbiota." *Current Biology* 25: 1682–93. https://doi.org/10.1016/j.cub.2015.04.055. Medline:25981789.
- Raworth, Kate. 2012. "A Safe and Just Space for Humanity." Oxfam Discussion Paper, 13 February 2012. https://www.oxfam.org/en/research/safe-and-just-space-humanity.
- – 2017. "A Doughnut for the Anthropocene: Humanity's Compass in the 21st Century. *The Lancet Planetary Health* 1: e48–e49. https://doi.org/10.1016/S2542-5196(17)30028-1. Medline:29851576.
- Reep. 2021. "Rain Garden Coach." Accessed 27 July 2021. https://reepgreen.ca/gardencoach/.
- Regeneration International. 2017. "What Is Regenerative Agriculture?" https://regenerationinternational.org/why-regenerative-agriculture/.
- Rittel, H., and M. Webber. 1973. "Dilemmas in a General Theory of Planning." *Policy Sciences* 4, no. 2: 155–69.
- Roa, Lina. Lotta Velin, Jemesa Tudravu, Craig D. McClain, Aaron Bernstein, and John G Meara. 2020. "Climate Change: Challenges and Opportunities to Scale Up Surgical, Obstetric, and Anaesthesia Care Globally." *The Lancet*

Planet Health 4: e538–43. https://doi.org/10.1016/S2542-5196(20)30247-3. Medline:33159881.

Rockström, J., W. Steffen, K. Noone, Åsa Persson, F. Stuart Chapin III, Eric F. Lambin, Timothy M. Lenton, et al. 2009. "A Safe Operating Space for Humanity." *Nature* 461: 472–5. https://doi.org/10.1038/461472a. Medline:19779433.

Rogers, E.M. 1983. *Diffusion of Innovations*. New York: Free Press.

Ross, Jennifer A., Gediminas Gliebus, and Elisabeth J. Van Bockstaele. 2018. "Stress Induced Neural Reorganization: A Conceptual Framework Linking Depression and Alzheimer's Disease." *Progress in Neuro-Psychopharmacology and Biological Psychiatry* 85, no. 13: 136–51. https://doi.org/10.1016/j.pnpbp.2017.08.004. Medline:28803923.

Rushey Green Time Bank. n.d. *Rushey Green Time Bank Celebrating 20 Years*. Accessed 18 May 2021. https://12f72b88-9300-43fa-8236-554631e28054.filesusr.com/ugd/7db68e_7973982eea664295acfc668f4e242a1b.pdf.

Sachs, Naomi A. 2017. "The Case for Nature or Nature-ish." *Health Environments Research and Design Journal* 10, no. 5: 157–61. https://doi.org/10.1177/1937586717732653. Medline:29056091.

– 2019. "Research on Nature in Health Care: What Do We Still Need?" *Health Environments Research and Design Journal* 12, no. 2: 162–7. https://doi.org/10.1177/1937586719848861. Medline:31088174.

– 2020. "Our Health Care System Is Broken: A Personal Account." *Health Environments Research and Design Journal* 13, no. 2: 256–63. https://doi.org/10.1177/1937586720917946. Medline:32364842.

Sandifer, Paul A., Arianna E. Sutton-Grier, and Bethney P. Ward. 2015. "Exploring Connections among Nature, Biodiversity, Ecosystem Services, and Human Health and Wellbeing: Opportunities to Enhance Health and Biodiversity Conservation." *Ecosystem Services* 12: 1–15. https://doi.org/10.1016/j.ecoser.2014.12.007.

Savage, Neil. 2020. "Gut Reaction." *Nature* 577: S10–S11. https://media.nature.com/original/magazine-assets/d41586-020-00196-0/d41586-020-00196-0.pdf.

Scheffer, Martin, Stephen R. Carpenter, Timothy M. Lenton, Jordi Bascompte, William Brock, Vasilis Dakos, Johan Van de Koppel, et al. 2012. "Anticipating Critical Transitions." *Science* 338: 334–48. https://doi.org/10.1126/science.1225244. Medline:23087241.

Schepper-Hughes, N., and M. Lock. 1987. "The Mindful Body: A Prolegomenon to Future Work in Medical Anthropology." *Medical Anthropology Quarterly* 1, no. 1: 6–41. https://doi.org/10.1525/maq.1987.1.1.02a00020.

Schnorr, Stephanie. 2015. "The Diverse Microbiome of the Hunter-Gatherer." *Nature* 518: S14–S15. https://doi.org/10.1038/518S14a. Medline:25715276.

Schnorr, Stephanie, and Harriet A. Bachner. 2016. "Integrative Therapies in Anxiety Treatment with Special Emphasis on the Gut Microbiome." *Yale Journal of Biology and Medicine* 89: 397–422. Medline:27698624.

Schumacher, E.F. 1973. *Small Is Beautiful.* London: Blond and Briggs.
Schwab, Klaus. 2017. *The Fourth Industrial Revolution.* New York: Crown.
Seligman, A.B., R.P. Weller, M.J. Puett, and B. Simon. 2008. *Ritual and Its Consequences: An Essay on the Limits of Sincerity.* Oxford: Oxford University Press.
Silvast, Antti, and Mikko J. Virtanen. 2019. "An Assemblage of Framings and Tamings: Multi-sited Analysis of Infrastructures as a Methodology." *Journal of Cultural Economy* 12, no. 6: 461–77. https://doi.org/10.1080/17530350.2019.1646156.
Sithey, Gyambo, Mu Li, and Anne Marie Thow. 2018. "Strengthening Noncommunicable Disease Policy with Lessons from Bhutan: Linking Gross National Happiness and Health Policy Action." *Journal of Public Health Policy* 39, no. 3: 327–42. https://doi.org/10.1057/s41271-018-0135-y. Medline:29950574.
Søgaard Jørgensen, Peter, Didier Wernli, Carl Folke, and Scott P Carroll. 2017. "Changing Antibiotic Resistance: Sustainability Transformation to a Promicrobial Planet." *Current Opinion in Environmental Sustainability* 25: 66–76. https://doi.org/10.1016/j.cosust.2017.07.008.
Solomon, Sheldon. 2020. "Death Denial in the Anthropocene." In *Health in the Anthropocene: Living Well on a Finite Planet*, edited by Katharine Zywert and Stephen Quilley, 404–18. Toronto: University of Toronto Press.
Solomon, S., J. Greenberg, and T. Pysczcynski. 2015. *The Worm at the Core: On the Role of Death in Life.* New York: Random House.
Steffen, W., W. Broadgate, L. Deutsch, Owen Gaffney, and Cornelia Ludwig. 2015a. "The Trajectory of the Anthropocene: The Great Acceleration." *Anthropocene Review* 2, no. 1: 81–98. https://doi.org/10.1177/2053019614564785.
Steffen, Will, Katherine Richardson, Johan Rockström, Sarah E. Cornell, Ngo Fetzer, Elena M. Bennett, Reinette Biggs, et al. 2015b. "Planetary Boundaries: Guiding Human Development on a Changing Planet." *Science* 347, no. 6223: 1259855-1–1259855-10. https://doi.org/10.1126/science.1259855. Medline:25592418.
Steffen, Will, and Mark Stafford Smith. 2013. "Planetary Boundaries, Equity and Global Sustainability: Why Wealthy Countries Could Benefit from More Equity." *Current Opinion in Environmental Sustainability* 5: 403–8. https://doi.org/10.1016/j.cosust.2013.04.007.
Steinberger, Julia. 2020. "Pandenomics: A Story of Life versus Growth." Open Democracy. 8 April 2020. https://www.opendemocracy.net/en/oureconomy/pandenomics-story-life-versus-growth/.
Stratford, Beth, and Dan W. O'Neill. 2020. *The UK's Path to a Doughnut-Shaped Recovery.* University of Leeds, UK. https://goodlife.leeds.ac.uk/doughnut-shaped-recovery.
Sultana, A., and C. Ravanera. 2020. *A Feminist Economic Recovery Plan for Canada: Making the Economy Work for Everyone.* 28 July 2020. The Institute

for Gender and the Economy (GATE) and YWCA Canada. https://static1.squarespace.com/static/5f0cd2090f50a31a91b37ff7/t/5f205a15b1b7191d12282bf5/1595955746613/Feminist+Economy+Recovery+Plan+for+Canada.pdf.

Sutherland, William. 2015. *Grand Rounds: Healing Medicine for a Complex World* [e-book]. Waterloo: Institute for Complexity and Connection Medicine.

Swinburn, Boyd A., Vivica I. Kraak, Steven Allender, Vincent J. Atkins, and Phillip I. Baker. 2019. "The Global Syndemic of Obesity, Undernutrition, and Climate Change: The Lancet Commission Report." *The Lancet* 393: 791–846. https://doi.org/10.1016/S0140-6736(18)32822-8. Medline:30700377.

Tainter, J.A. 1988. *The Collapse of Complex Societies*. Cambridge: Cambridge University Press.

– 2014. "Collapse and Sustainability: Rome, the Maya, and the Modern World." *Archeological Papers of the American Anthropological Association* 24, no. 1: 201–14. https://doi.org/10.1111/apaa.12038.

Therapeutic Landscapes Network. n.d. "Gardens in Health Care and Related Facilities." Accessed 15 December 2020. http://www.healinglandscapes.org/healthcare-gardens/index.html#z.

Thiel, C.L., M. Eckelman, R. Guido, M. Huddleston, A.E. Landis, J. Sherman, S.O. Shrake, et al. 2015. "Environmental Impacts of Surgical Procedures: Life Cycle Assessment of Hysterectomy in the United States." *Environmental Science and Technology* 49, no. 3: 1779–86. https://doi.org/10.1021/es504719g.

Thomson, C., and M. Jakubowski. 2012. "Toward an Open Source Civilization: Innovations Case Narrative: Open Source Ecology." *Innovations* 7, no. 3: 53–70. https://doi.org/10.1162/INOV_a_00139.

Tönnies, F., and C.P. Loomis. 1999 [1887]. *Community and Society (Gemeinschaft und Gesellschaft)*. New York: Routledge.

Tran, Viet-Thi, and Philippe Ravaud. 2016. "Frugal Innovation in Medicine for Low Resource Settings." *BMC Medicine* 14: 102. https://doi.org/10.1186/s12916-016-0651-1. Medline:27383644.

Transition Network. 2020. "Principles: The Values and Principles that Guide Us." Accessed 14 December 2020. https://transitionnetwork.org/about-the-movement/what-is-transition/principles-2/.

Tsing, Anna Lowenthaupt. 2005. *Friction: An Ethnography of Global Connection*. Princeton: Princeton University Press.

– 2015. *The Mushroom at the End of the World: On the Possibility of Life in Capitalist Ruins*. Princeton: Princeton University Press.

Tuntiya, Nana. 2006. "Making a Case for the Geel Model: The American Experience with Family Care for Mental Patients." *Community Mental Health Journal* 42, no. 3: 319–30.

Turner, E. 2012. *Communitas: The Anthropology of Collective Joy*. New York: Palgrave Macmillan.

Turner, Victor. 1977. *The Ritual Process: Structure and Anti-structure*. New York: Cornell University Press.

"US Just Recovery Principles." N.d. Accessed 24 February 2021. https://350.org/us-just-recovery-principles/.

van Bilsen, Henck P.J.G. 2016. "Lessons to Be Learned from the Oldest Community Psychiatric Service in the World: Geel in Belgium." *BJPsych Bulletin* 40: 207–11. https://doi.org/10.1192/pb.bp.115.051631. Medline:27512591.

van Elsen, Thomas, Amelie Günther, and Bas Pedroli. 2006. "The Contribution of Care Farms to Landscapes of the Future: A Challenge of Multifunctional Agriculture." In *Farming for Health: Green-Care Farming across Europe and the United States of America*, edited by Jan Hassink and Marjolein Elings, 91–100. Dordrecht: Springer.

Venkatesh, R., S. van Landingham, A. Khodifad, A. Haripriya, C. Thiel, P. Ramulu, and A. Robin. 2016. "Carbon Footprint and Cost-Effectiveness of Cataract Surgery." *Current Opinion in Ophthamology* 27, no. 1: 82–8. https://doi.org/10.1097/icu.0000000000000228.

Vidal, John. 2020. "Tip of the Iceberg: Is Our Destruction of Nature Responsible for COVID-19?" *The Guardian*, 18 March 2020. https://www.theguardian.com/environment/2020/mar/18/tip-of-the-iceberg-is-our-destruction-of-nature-responsible-for-covid-19-aoe.

Walker, B., and D. Salt. 2006. *Resilience Thinking: Sustaining Ecosystems and People in a Changing World*. Washington, DC: Island Press.

– 2012. *Resilience Practice: Building Capacity to Absorb Disturbance and Maintain Function*. Washington, DC: Island Press.

Wall, Diana H., Uffe N. Neilson, and Johan Six. 2015. "Soil Biodiversity and Human Health." *Nature* 528: 69–76. https://doi.org/10.1038/nature15744. Medline:26595276.

Ward, James D., Paul C. Sutton, Adrian D. Werner, Robert Costanza, Steve H. Mohr, and Craig T. Simmons. 2016. "Is Decoupling GDP Growth from Environmental Impact Possible?" *PLoS ONE* 11, no. 10: e0164733. https://doi.org/10.1371/journal.pone.0164733. Medline:27741300.

Watts, Nick, Markus Amann, Nigel Arnell, Sonja Ayeb-Karlsson, Kristine Belesova, Maxwell Boykoff, Peter Byass, et al., "The 2019 Report of *The Lancet* Countdown on Health and Climate Change: Ensuring that the Health of a Child Born Today Is Not Defined by a Changing Climate." *The Lancet* 394: 1836–78. https://doi.org/10.1016/S0140-6736(19)32596-6. Medline:31733928.

Weber, M. 1968. *Economy and Society: An Outline of Interpretive Sociology*. Edited by G. Roth and C. Wittich. Translated by E. Fischo. New York: Bedminster Press.

Weinstein, N., A.K. Przybylski, and R.M. Ryan. 2009. "Can Nature Make Us More Caring? Effects of Immersion in Nature on Intrinsic Aspirations and Generosity." *Personality and Social Psychology Bulletin*, 35, no. 10: 1315–29. https://doi.org/10.1177/0146167209341649. Medline:19657048.

Westley, Frances. 2013. "Social Innovation and Resilience: How One Enhances the Other." *Stanford Social Innovation Review* 11, no. 3: 6–8. https://ssir.org/articles/entry/social_innovation_and_resilience_how_one_enhances_the_other.

Westley, F., P. Olsson, C. Folke, T. Homer-Dixon, H. Vredenburg, D. Loorbach, J. Tompson, et al. 2011. "Tipping toward Sustainability: Emerging Pathways of Transformation." *Ambio* 40: 762–80. https://doi.org/10.1007/s13280-011-0186-9. Medline:22338714.

Westley, F., O. Tjornbo, P. Olsson, C. Folke, B. Crona, L. Schultz, and O. Orijan Bodin. 2013. "A Theory of Transformative Agency in Linked Social-Ecological Systems." *Ecology and Society* 18, no. 3: 27. https://doi.org/10.5751/ES-05072-180327.

Westley, F., B. Zimmerman, and M. Patton. 2007. *Getting to Maybe: How the World Is Changed*. Reprint. Toronto: Vintage Canada.

Whitmee S., A. Haines, C. Beyrer, Frederick Boltz, Anthony G. Capon, Braulio Ferreira de Souza Dias, Alex Ezeh, et al. 2015. "Safeguarding Human Health in the Anthropocene Epoch: Report of the Rockefeller Foundation–*Lancet* Commission on Planetary Health." *The Lancet* 386: 1973–2028. https://doi.org/10.1016/S0140-6736(15)60901-1. Medline:26188744.

WHO. 2015. "Connecting Global Priorities: Biodiversity and Human Health: A State of Knowledge Review." Geneva: World Health Organization.

– 2018a. "Traditional and Complementary Medicine in Primary Health Care." Geneva: World Health Organization.

– 2018b. "WHO Compendium of Innovative Health Technologies for Low-Resource Settings, 2016–2017." Geneva: World Health Organization.

– 2019a. "Healthy Environments for Healthier Populations: Why Do They Matter, and What Can We Do?" Geneva: World Health Organization.

– 2019b. "WHO Global Report on Traditional and Complementary Medicine." Geneva: World Health Organization.

– 2020. "Antibiotic Resistance." 31 July 2020. https://www.who.int/news-room/fact-sheets/detail/antibiotic-resistance.

– 2021. "Antimicrobial Resistance." https://www.who.int/news-room/fact-sheets/detail/antimicrobial-resistance.

– n.d.-a. "Social Determinants of Health: Overview." Accessed 2 November 2020. https://www.who.int/health-topics/social-determinants-of-health#tab=tab_1.

– n.d.-b. "WHO Coronavirus Dashboard." Accessed 21 November 2022. https://covid19.who.int.

Wiseman, J., T. Edwards, and K. Luckins. 2013. "Post Carbon Pathways: A Meta-analysis of 18 Large-Scale Post Carbon Economy Transition Strategies." *Environmental Innovation and Societal Transitions* 8: 76–93. https://doi.org/10.1016/j.eist.2013.04.001.

Woolf, Stephen H. 2019. "Necessary but Not Sufficient: Why Health Care Alone Cannot Improve Population Health and Reduce Health Inequities." *Annals of Family Medicine* 17, no. 3: 196–9. https://doi.org/10.1370/afm.2395. Medline:31085522.

Woolf, Steven H., Derek A. Chapman, Roy T. Sabo, Daniel M. Weinberger, and Latoya Hill. 2020. "Excess Deaths from COVID-19 and Other Causes." *Journal of the American Medical Association*. 324, no. 5: 510–13. https://doi.org/10.1001/jama.2020.11787. Medline:32609307.

Woolf, Steven H., Robert E. Johnson, Robert L. Phillips, Jr., and Maike Philipsen. 2007. "Giving Everyone the Health of the Educated: An Examination of Whether Social Change Would Save More Lives than Medical Advances." *American Journal of Public Health* 97, no. 4: 679–83. https://doi.org/10.2105/AJPH.2005.084848. Medline:17329654.

Woolf, Stephen H., and Jason Q. Purnell. 2016. "The Good Life: Working Together to Promote Opportunity and Improve Population Health and Wellbeing. *Journal of the American Medical Association* 315, no. 16: 1706–8. https://doi.org/10.1001/jama.2016.4263. Medline:27063639.

Yilmaz, H., S. Toy, M.A. Irmak, and S. Yilmaz, and Y. Bulut. 2008. "Determination of Temperature Differences between Asphalt Concrete, Soil and Grass Surfaces of the City of Erzurum, Turkey." *Atmósfera* 21, no. 2: 135–46. https://www.revistascca.unam.mx/atm/index.php/atm/article/view/8599.

Young, Oran R., Frans Berkhout, Gilbert C. Gallopin, Marco A. Janssen, Elinor Ostrom, and Sander van der Leeuw. 2006. "The Globalization of Socio-ecological Systems: An Agenda for Scientific Research." *Global Environmental Change* 16: 304–16. https://doi.org/10.1016/j.gloenvcha.2006.03.004.

Zalasiewicz, Jan, Colin P. Summerhayes, Martin J. Head, Scott Wing, Phil Gibbard, and Colin N. Waters. 2019. "Stratigraphy and the Geological Time Scale." In *The Anthropocene as a Geological Time Unit: A Guide to the Scientific Evidence and Current Debate*, edited by Jan Zalasiewicz, Colin N. Walters, Mark Williams, and Colin P. Summerhayes, 11–31. Cambridge: Cambridge University Press.

Zalasiewicz, J., M. Williams, W. Steffen, and P. Crutzen. 2010. "The New World of the Anthropocene." *Environmental Science and Technology* 44, no. 7: 2228–31. https://doi.org/10.1021/es903118j. Medline:20184359.

Zhang, E., A. Kleinman, and W. Tu. 2011. *Governance of Life in Chinese Moral Experience: The Quest for an Adequate Life*. Abingdon, UK: Routledge.

Zowalaty, Mohamed E. El, Sean G. Young, and Josef D. Järhult. 2020. "Environmental Impact of the COVID-19 Pandemic – A Lesson for the Future." *Infection Ecology and Epidemiology*, 10, no. 1: 1768023. https://doi.org/10.1080/20008686.2020.1768023. Medline:32922688.

Zuckerman, M. 2014. "Introduction: Interdisciplinary Approaches to the Second Epidemiologic Transition." In *Modern Environments and Human Health: Revisiting the Second Epidemiological Transition*, edited by M. Zuckerman, 1–16. Hoboken, NJ: John Wiley and Sons.

Zywert, Katharine. 2017. "Human Health and Social-Ecological Systems Change: Rethinking Health in the Anthropocene." *Anthropocene Review* 4, no. 3: 216–38. https://doi.org/10.1177/2053019617739640.

Zywert, Katharine, and Stephen Quilley. 2017. "Health Systems in an Era of Biophysical Limits: The Wicked Dilemmas of Modernity." *Social Theory and Health*. Online First Article, 1–20. https://doi.org/10.1057/s41285-017-0051-4.

– 2020a. "Emerging Social Innovations for Health and Wellbeing: Prefiguring Viable Health Systems for the Anthropocene." In *Health in the Anthropocene: Living Well on a Finite Planet*, edited by Katharine Zywert and Stephen Quilley, 189–95. Toronto: University of Toronto Press.

–, eds. 2020b. *Health in the Anthropocene: Living Well on a Finite Planet*. Toronto: University of Toronto Press.

– 2020c. "Introduction." In *Health in the Anthropocene: Living Well on a Finite Planet*, edited by Katharine Zywert and Stephen Quilley, 285–305. Toronto: University of Toronto Press.

Zywert, Katharine, and William Sutherland. 2020. "Making Medicine Work in the Anthropocene: Tenets of a Meta-medicine for Complex Adaptive Systems in Precarious Times" *Health in the Anthropocene: Living Well on a Finite Planet*, edited by Katharine Zywert and Stephen Quilley, 285–305. Toronto: University of Toronto Press.

Index

adjacent possible, 8, 118, 167–8, 173
agriculture: regenerative, 72–80, 164–5, 285; urban, 82, 103–6, 125–6, 285
allopathic medicine, 184, 271–2, 275. *See also* biomedicine
alternative medicine, 118. *See also* complementary medicine; traditional medicine
Anthropocene, 6, 8–9, 15, 21, 27–9, 31–4, 51, 64–5, 76, 100, 119, 203, 208, 210–11, 213, 216–17, 222–4, 226, 236, 278, 283–93, 295–6
antibiotic resistance, 61–4, 70
antibiotics, 26, 44, 59, 61–4, 70, 75, 160–1, 272, 293
antimicrobial resistance, 11, 22, 27, 44, 52, 61–4, 70

bacteria, 22, 24, 29, 31, 45–9, 52, 62–4, 74–5, 80
biodiversity, 22, 24, 42, 57–61, 73, 76–7, 82, 95, 97, 113–14, 273
biodiversity loss, 10, 22, 28, 35, 49, 52, 57–61, 65–6, 69–70, 206, 213, 223
biomedicine, 10, 26, 33–4, 38–9, 44–5, 61–2, 73, 81, 118, 137, 215, 222, 260, 269, 271–2, 274, 278, 288–90, 292–3. *See also* allopathic medicine

biophilia, 60
bioregionalism, 177, 277

capitalism, 5, 8, 75, 79, 123, 128, 133–5, 138–9, 157–8, 161, 167, 173, 175, 213–15, 224, 229, 274
care, whole-systems, 31, 72, 75
care farming, 5, 7, 11, 22, 44, 50, 61, 99–116, 214, 233, 235, 280, 282–3, 286
caregivers, 70, 88, 118, 154, 181, 187–90, 192–3, 288
Catholicism, 12, 119, 194–5
change makers, 3, 13, 203–4, 243, 247, 258. *See also* social innovators
circular economy, 131
climate change, 10, 28, 37, 52–9, 64–7, 73, 76, 80, 137–8, 152, 162–3, 168, 227–8, 234, 272, 285
climate crisis, 4, 6, 11, 22, 29–30, 35–6, 43, 52–8, 60, 66, 68–70, 76–7, 155, 169, 206, 213, 226, 277
climate justice, 66–7, 234. *See also* environmental justice; social justice
co-design, 204, 238, 243–7, 267, 269, 282
collaboration, multisectoral, 57, 98, 154, 156, 170, 232, 240
collapse, social, 8, 42, 66, 76, 212–15, 219–21, 229, 291
colonization, 214

community building, 13, 14, 22, 41, 67, 85–7, 91, 174
community care for mental illness, 118–19, 160, 194–201, 282, 288
community-driven initiatives, 12, 143–4, 175–6, 204, 255–8, 282
community networks, 17, 118, 129, 147, 187–93, 201, 237–8, 241–2, 254, 282–3, 285, 287, 294; networks of family and community reciprocity, 9, 134, 155, 284, 296. *See also* informal networks of care
Community Nurse Connection, 12, 118, 187–93
community nursing, 5, 118, 160, 187–93, 214, 280, 282, 288
community organizers, 69, 168, 175–6, 232
complementary medicine, 129, 271–2. *See also* alternative medicine; traditional medicine
complexity: in health systems, 228, 235–8, 297; complexity medicine, 5, 7, 14, 15, 81, 204, 214, 259–69, 280, 289; complexity science, 14, 166–7, 205–6, 213, 289; societal, 26, 38, 42, 117, 137–8, 142, 156–8, 161, 165–6, 219, 291
complex systems, 13, 49–51, 203–16, 223–4, 230–1, 246, 259–60, 262, 279, 289
complex systems change processes, 203–46
consumerism, 79, 83, 144, 163, 226–7
consumption, 4, 10–11, 27, 34, 37–8, 42, 53, 57–8, 79, 126–32, 134, 138–40, 142, 144–8, 151, 57, 161, 163, 167–8, 177, 206, 220, 225–6, 281, 285
cosmopolitanism, 156–8, 173
COVID-19 pandemic, 11–13, 22, 41, 52, 59, 64–70, 82–3, 118, 122, 159, 161, 163, 167–76, 204, 224, 232, 238, 247–58, 270, 278
Cuba, special period, 82, 117, 124–6, 281

death, 5, 12, 25–7, 40–2, 54, 62, 64, 66, 70, 89, 125, 191, 199, 222, 224–6, 251, 263
decoupling, 11, 122, 127, 142, 296
deep time, 21, 23–30, 32, 222–8
degrowth, 81, 117, 123, 127–30, 133, 135–41, 150–1, 161, 171, 282. *See also* economic contraction; economic downscaling
disability, 11, 15–16, 22, 40, 91–4, 99–116, 119, 155, 173, 193, 195–201, 243, 286, 288
distributed production, 148–9, 155, 161–2
diversity, 5, 45, 47, 59–61, 64, 78, 81, 86, 159–60, 163, 176, 208–9, 213, 234, 243–4
doughnut economics, 36–7, 132–3, 171–2

Earth systems, 23, 27–8, 33, 35, 51, 74, 291
ecological constraints on human activities, 44, 115, 130, 140–2, 145–6, 150–1, 153, 165, 194, 220, 224, 272, 282–3
ecological determinants of health. *See* health: ecological determinants of
ecological disruption, 27, 29, 33, 35–6, 38, 60, 176, 205, 213, 216, 223, 226–7, 277, 295
ecological economics, 129
ecological footprint, 4, 28, 35, 70–1, 81, 114, 131, 149, 162–3, 173, 179, 236, 281–2, 287–8
ecological overshoot, 3, 11, 34, 36–7, 66, 81, 143, 167, 217, 220, 228, 278, 291–2

ecological regeneration, 11, 80, 84, 98, 100, 113–16, 164, 170, 177, 215, 277–8, 282
ecological restoration, 56, 116, 229, 282, 285, 290
economic contraction, 11, 94, 115, 117, 123–6, 133–4, 137–44, 147, 154, 157–9, 166, 173, 193, 215, 234–5, 281–3, 296. *See also* degrowth; economic downscaling
economic downscaling, 11–12, 36, 117, 137–42, 147, 166. *See also* degrowth; economic contraction
economic growth, 4–5, 11–12, 33, 53, 94, 117, 121–43, 148, 151, 167, 171, 173, 206, 279, 286, 291, 294, 296; effects on health, 53, 117, 122–33; limits to, 4, 11–12, 32, 81, 122, 130, 135, 140, 143–5, 148, 153, 155, 218–19, 221, 225. *See also* growth economy
economics, doughnut, 36–7, 132–3, 171–2
ecosystem services, 59, 95
ecovillages, 5, 12, 118, 177–86, 214, 279, 287. *See also* intentional communities
elder care, 12, 16, 33, 67, 90, 99, 101, 118, 125, 135, 155, 159, 181–2, 187–93, 283, 288
emergence (in complex systems), 13, 22, 70, 204, 207, 247, 257–8, 260, 279
energy, 3–4, 8, 10–11, 26–7, 36–8, 42, 53, 57, 122, 124, 128–31, 138, 148–9, 152–3, 156–7, 160–1, 163, 171, 179, 192, 208, 210, 214–15, 236, 280–1, 287, 290; energy descent, 143, 145, 229
environmental justice, 162. *See also* climate justice; social justice
environmental politics, 66, 118, 144, 154–66, 222, 228. *See also* left-right political divides

equity, 12–13, 32–3, 35–7, 52, 67, 127, 132, 134–5, 137–8, 148, 156, 159–60, 162–3, 169–70, 172, 203, 228, 233–5, 239, 279, 282, 285–6, 290. *See also* inequality; inequity
ethnography: multisited, 6; multispecies, 6–7
extinction, 57–8, 61, 223. *See also* biodiversity loss

Fiddlehead Care Farm, 99, 108–13, 115. *See also* care farming
food security, 55, 57, 59, 62, 73, 82–3, 96–7, 163
fossil fuels, 27, 53, 65–6, 68, 73, 82, 157, 170, 220, 235, 286
fungi, 22, 24, 45, 74–5, 77–80
future generations, 29, 32–3, 38, 51, 57, 95, 227, 295

Gaia, 23–4, 32, 211
gardens, 5, 7, 11, 22, 44, 50, 61, 74, 80–98, 214, 224, 239, 242, 247, 252, 255–6, 270–8, 280, 285; community gardens, 83–7, 94, 97, 224, 285; enabling gardens, 22, 91–4, 97–8, 282; Listening Space garden, 22, 84–7, 230, 247, 252–3, 258, 280; and mental health, 82–3, 90, 93, 99–116; and planetary health, 94, 97–8, 100, 115; therapeutic gardens, 44, 97, 214, 280; and well-being, 83, 94, 170
Geel, Belgium, 7, 12, 119, 194–201, 214, 237, 280, 283, 288
genetics, 21, 25, 32, 38–9, 43–4, 293
globalization, 13, 63, 65, 70, 143, 145, 156–7, 162–3, 168, 208–9
global north, 67
global south, 67, 130, 292
governance, 3, 12, 81, 129, 135, 139, 155, 160, 163, 172, 177, 181–2, 218

Great Acceleration, 21, 27, 32–3, 35–6, 215, 224
Great Depression, 123–4
greenhouse gasses, 4, 24, 53, 56–7, 68, 149
growth economy, 121–3, 128–9, 137, 140, 167, 201, 281, 283; limits to growth, 4, 11–12, 32, 81, 122, 130, 135, 140, 143–5, 148, 153, 155, 218–19, 221, 225. *See also* economic growth

Half Moon Herbals, 270
happiness, 127, 131–2, 142, 159
health: benefits of nature, 22, 49, 59–60, 88–9, 94–5, 97, 110–13; community, 11, 18, 26, 38, 84, 133, 178, 287; community-based approaches to, 82, 119, 134, 143–4, 167–201, 270–8; definition, 15–19, 144; ecological, 64; ecological determinants of, 10, 21, 32, 38, 42–4, 50, 69, 142, 172, 176, 239–40, 281–2, 286; global, 23, 34, 57, 62, 138; health promotion, 131, 151, 155; human, 10, 21–2, 25–6, 28–9, 31–5, 38–46, 51–61, 66, 68, 70–1, 73, 77, 79, 96, 123, 127, 131, 133, 141, 154, 165–6, 210, 223, 227, 234, 277, 281, 293–6; mental (*see* mental health); physical, 16–17, 22, 59, 79, 95, 99–100, 102, 111, 113, 115, 131, 136, 146, 179, 185, 189, 231, 241, 244, 261, 282, 286, 289; planetary (*see* planetary health); population, 10, 34, 40–3, 56, 63, 67, 97, 123, 128, 134, 138, 144, 271, 280–2; preventative, 14, 40, 56, 59, 63, 70, 97, 115, 121, 128, 131–2, 136–7, 151, 184–6, 192, 201, 215, 228, 234, 237, 239–41, 271, 274, 277–8, 280–3, 285, 290; public, 11–12, 26, 42, 56, 62, 65, 67, 72–3, 97–8, 125, 155, 167, 176; social determinants of, 10, 21, 27, 32, 38–44, 50, 68–9, 137, 142, 155, 172, 176, 215–16, 239–40, 281–2, 286; of social-ecological systems, 52, 69–71, 80; social-ecological approaches to, 40, 69, 72; systems-based approaches to, 21, 49–50, 72, 98, 268–9
health care, 10–11, 22, 31, 81–2, 84–5, 100–1, 117–19, 121, 124–5, 131, 133–6, 138, 190–5, 204, 221, 237–45, 248, 256, 260, 271–2, 276, 280–2, 286, 289, 292–3, 296; access to, 39, 41, 52, 68, 234, 271, 275, 278; capacity of, 63, 149, 153–4, 215, 249, 281–2; cost of, 35, 63, 97, 140–1, 147–51, 200, 271; in ecovillages, 177–8, 182–6; effect on health outcomes, 21, 26, 32, 38–40, 44, 52, 150; effects of climate change on, 54; environmental impact of, 4, 57, 236, 282; facilities, 87–91, 97–8, 125, 151, 153, 239–41, 285; gardens in, 87–91, 97–8, 100–1; institutions, 22, 87–91, 101, 107, 128, 131, 177, 239–41, 248, 256, 258, 269; mental, 101, 119, 194–5, 199–200, 204, 244–5, 285, 288; sustainability of, 4, 73, 140–1, 147–51; universal, 125, 128, 142, 155, 171, 281
health outcomes, 9, 52, 55, 58–9, 67, 88, 138, 142, 149–51, 164, 172, 199, 217, 228, 233–8, 284, 296–7; across scales, 31–2, 35–44, 49–50, 70–1, 83, 221; of care farming, 99–100, 102, 105, 109, 115–16; effect of modernization on, 10, 12, 26; effect of political economy on, 117, 123–6, 128, 133; individual, 10, 32; paradoxical, 21, 27–9, 279; planetary, 117, 166, 279;

population-level, 10, 32, 134, 138, 279–8
health system, 3–14, 19, 40–1, 50, 52, 59, 67, 80, 125, 145–55, 176, 183–5, 194, 203, 214–15, 217–18, 224–6, 228, 235–46, 269, 278–94, 296–7; in high-income nations, 4, 123, 137, 141, 149; modern, 49, 69, 71, 122, 215, 271; for planetary health, 21, 33–4, 69, 81, 97; post-growth, 14, 123, 147–8, 151, 154, 160, 166, 200–1, 206, 270–1, 277–8, 280, 282–3; relationship to political economy, 121–3, 127–9, 131–3, 137–8, 141–2, 144–55, 160, 166, 201; sustainability of, 9, 14, 72–3, 115, 183, 187, 225, 237–8, 271, 282–4, 292
herbalism, 148, 178, 183–6, 204, 214, 270–8, 282, 290
high-income nations, 3–4, 7–8, 23, 33, 36–8, 42, 45–6, 123, 130–1, 134, 137–9, 141–2, 144–5, 149–53, 162, 166, 177, 219, 234, 272, 281, 283, 292–3
Holocene, 21, 25–8, 35, 57, 130
horticultural therapy, 89–94, 285
hospice, 187, 192–3, 226, 288
hunter-gatherer populations, 29, 46–8

Indigenous people, 40, 43, 173, 214, 241, 265, 277; foodways, 239–41; worldviews, 59, 222, 277
individualism, 43–5, 52, 57, 83, 128, 133–5, 144, 155, 157–8, 177, 206, 224, 227, 291
individualization, 39, 157, 214
industrial ecology, 149
Industrial Revolution, 25–6, 35–6, 38, 61, 162, 206, 216, 220
inequality, 41, 136, 139, 163, 233–4. *See also* equity; inequity
inequity, 27, 40–2, 64, 66–70, 128, 136, 138, 155, 159, 163, 167, 172, 175, 223, 233–5, 239, 277. *See also* equity; inequality
infectious diseases, 25–30, 35, 53–5, 58–9, 61–7, 70, 124, 180, 281
informal networks of care, 12, 70, 118, 121, 124, 129, 134, 160, 173–6, 186–90, 193, 201, 228, 237, 241–3, 282–4, 287–8, 296–7. *See also* community networks
intentional communities, 7, 118, 177–86, 287. *See also* ecovillages

justice: climate, 66–7, 234; environmental, 162; social, 36–7, 51, 144, 163, 177, 277

left-right political divides, 12, 144, 155–6, 161–6, 285. *See also* environmental politics
life expectancy, 27–8, 36–7, 41, 51, 62, 70–1, 124–7, 133, 138, 142, 281
limits to growth, 4, 11–12, 32, 81, 122, 130, 135, 140, 143–5, 148, 153, 155, 218–19, 221, 225
Listening Space garden, 22, 84–7, 230, 247, 252–3, 258, 280. *See also* gardens
livelihood, 18, 35, 66–7, 97, 155, 160, 162, 171, 173, 176, 186, 201, 275, 282–3, 285, 287
living systems, 22–3, 29, 31, 57, 73–5, 77–8, 80, 96, 238, 262, 289, 291, 294
long-term care, 90–1, 97–8, 285. *See also* elder care
low-income nations, 27, 36, 42, 56, 130, 153–4, 271, 292

medicine: allopathic, 184, 271–2, 275; alternative, 118; biomedicine, 10, 26, 33–4, 38–9, 44–5, 61–2, 73, 81, 118, 137, 215, 222, 260, 269, 271–2, 274, 278, 288–90, 292–3; complementary, 129, 271–2;

medicine (*cont.*)
  traditional, 59, 66, 70, 129, 148, 151–2, 222, 271
medicinal plants, 4, 59, 82–3, 97, 183, 270–8, 290
mental health, 5, 16–17, 22, 27, 29, 79, 88, 99–116, 119, 159, 165, 180–1, 193, 195, 199–200, 204, 215, 231, 241, 243–6, 253, 259–69, 282, 285–90; effect of climate crisis on, 53–4, 59, 70; effect of microbiome on, 45–6, 48; and gardening, 82–3, 90, 93, 99–116; relationship to political economy, 126, 128, 136, 140–1, 145–6
mental illness, 7, 11–12, 22, 36, 40, 45–6, 54, 59, 70, 79, 90, 93, 97, 99–116, 126, 148, 155, 159–60, 180–2, 214, 243–6, 252–3, 258, 280–3, 285; and community care, 118–19, 160, 194–201, 282, 288
microbiome, 10, 44–50, 60–1, 63, 70, 76, 231, 285; resilience of, 47–8, 52
Midnight Kitchen, 204, 214, 247–58, 289
modernity, 5, 8, 10, 12, 21, 23, 26–7, 39, 42, 44–9, 52, 57, 65, 69, 86, 100–1, 127, 133, 139, 144–5, 147, 156–60, 167, 179, 200, 213–15, 223–6, 236, 256, 281, 288, 291; alternative modernity, 153–5, 160–1, 213–15
modernization, 26–7, 42, 53, 100–1, 118, 123, 133–4, 137–9, 141, 159, 166, 199–200, 215, 278, 292
modern medicine, 4, 49, 59, 61–2, 69–71, 122, 134, 150, 153, 191, 271–2, 296
mortality rate: child, 27–8, 51, 124–5; infant, 70–1, 124–5, 133
mutual aid, 5, 7, 12, 118, 155, 160, 169, 173–6, 182–3, 186, 214, 232, 280, 282–3, 287
mutually beneficial solutions, 35, 38, 41, 56–7, 82, 115, 142, 200, 223, 295

nations: high-income, 3–4, 7–8, 23, 33, 36–8, 42, 45–6, 123, 130–1, 134, 137–9, 141–2, 144–5, 149–53, 162, 166, 177, 219, 234, 272, 281, 283, 292–3; low-income, 27, 36, 42, 56, 130, 153–4, 271, 292
nation state, 133–4, 155, 157
native plants, 82, 95–7, 271–5, 290
Netherlands, 7, 11, 22, 99–108, 110, 114
net zero emissions, 4, 53, 56
non-communicable diseases, 27, 30, 42, 45, 49, 54, 59–60, 70, 125, 131, 281
non-rational drivers of behaviour, 119, 201, 288
Nourish Healthcare, 239–41
nutrition, 17, 26, 29, 35, 37, 39, 45–6, 54–9, 65, 79–82, 123, 215, 239–41, 264, 271, 281, 290; malnutrition, 29, 55, 66, 70, 124–5

open-source production, 147
organic farming, 82, 100, 114–15, 164–5, 179, 185, 286–7

palliative care, 109, 187, 193, 226, 251, 288
paradox, 5, 14–15, 21, 27–8, 38, 51, 67, 70–1, 126, 133, 135, 137, 154–6, 200, 211, 279, 291; Easterlin paradox, 127
permaculture, 177, 270
physical health. *See* health: physical
place-bound societies, 12, 84, 115, 117, 133, 141–6, 153, 155–9, 161–2, 166, 194, 198, 227, 282
planetary boundaries, 13, 28–9, 32, 34–8, 51, 53, 57–8, 71, 122, 130, 132, 142, 154, 171, 206, 210, 218, 224, 285, 296
planetary health, 3–14, 21–2, 29–30, 50–1, 65, 69–71, 213–14, 272, 274, 277–80, 286, 288–9, 291–6; diet for, 59;

effect of soil health on, 80, 164; as field of research, 23, 32–8, 130, 234; and gardening, 94, 97–8, 100, 115; in Anthropocene, 6, 21, 76, 292; relation to political economy, 11–12, 81, 117–18, 121–3, 129–30, 136, 140–4, 156, 165–8, 172–3, 176, 224; systems change strategies for, 203–5, 210, 213–14, 216–18, 222–8, 232–4, 238–40, 245–6, 283–4, 286, 288–9, 291–6

Pleistocene epoch, 24–5, 28

political-economic transformation, 81, 117–19, 121–42, 148, 156, 210, 218–22, 279

political economy, 3, 12, 17, 19, 121–42, 147, 154, 167–73, 186, 201, 224, 274, 279, 296; and health, 11–12, 117–19, 170; post-growth, 11–12, 117–19, 121–3, 131, 133–8, 141–2, 144, 147–8, 153, 156–7, 160–1, 173, 176, 185, 193, 199, 201, 203–4, 270–3, 276–8, 280–1, 292–3, 296; regenerative, 116, 133, 167; sustainable, 168–9, 171

pollinators, 29, 59, 95–6, 233

population growth, 27, 34, 42, 58, 129

populism, 135–6

precautionary principle, 35

prefigurative alternatives, 7–9, 14, 44, 115, 123, 142, 177, 203, 206, 212–16, 283–92, 294

primary care, 125, 138, 151, 155, 188, 193, 204, 235, 247, 251, 257–8, 271–2, 275, 277, 281–2

Principles for a Just Recovery, 12, 67, 118, 168–73, 176, 176n, 214, 232, 279, 286

quality of life, 16–17, 34, 39, 60, 66, 118, 130, 188, 190–3, 213, 224, 243, 279, 288, 293

regenerative agriculture, 72–80, 164–5, 285

relationship building, 98, 104, 115, 147, 169–70, 176, 204, 228, 231–3, 256–8, 273, 277–8

relocalization, 12–13, 81, 117–18, 142–66, 186, 193, 209, 235, 273, 283, 296

resilience, 3, 8, 13, 18–19, 36, 56–7, 66, 78, 82, 106–7, 127, 139, 147, 163, 168–9, 178, 180, 200, 204, 209–10, 213–14, 216, 219, 228–38, 246, 282, 284, 286; community, 67, 77, 95, 176, 182; ecological, 30, 73, 77, 80, 169, 270; of microbiome, 47–8, 52; social-ecological, 32, 95, 162, 218, 228–38, 284, 295

ritual, 178, 223–4

self-organization, 13, 203–4, 207, 210–12, 218, 238–47, 256–8, 260, 279, 284, 291

slow medicine, 118, 187, 191, 288

social care, 11, 99–101, 135, 171

social determinants of health. *See* health: social determinants of

social distancing, 41, 67–8, 83

social-ecological regime, 4–5, 13–14, 167, 203–16, 218–20, 228, 235, 245, 276, 278, 281, 283, 291, 294, 297

social-ecological scales, 4–6, 9–11, 14, 19, 21–2, 29, 31–71, 76–7, 80, 82–3, 100, 122, 139, 163, 205, 208–10, 221–2, 228, 233, 270–1, 282, 284–91, 294–6

social-ecological systems, 5–7, 31–2, 38, 52, 101, 139, 141, 156–7, 162–3, 166, 203–18, 224, 232, 238, 260, 279, 283–4, 295; change in, 3, 6–9, 12–14, 33, 203–46, 280, 283–4, 291, 293

social economy, 117, 135–7, 142

social enterprises, 98, 148, 283

social inclusion, 3, 11, 84, 86–7, 91–4, 97–8, 102–16, 201, 285
social innovation, 3, 81, 101, 147, 203, 205, 213, 229, 231–3, 238, 245–6, 284
social innovators, 15, 19, 101, 238, 292. *See also* change makers
social justice, 36–7, 51, 144, 163, 177, 277. *See also* climate justice; environmental justice
social movements, 8, 206, 211, 213
social prescriptions, 241, 251
soil health, 5, 11, 22, 44, 50, 61, 64, 72–80, 164–5, 214, 280, 285
soil sponge, 22, 70, 74–5, 77–80, 82, 97
sufficiency, 38, 140, 151, 279
supply chains, 4, 54, 82, 140, 147–8, 157, 161, 163, 273
surgery, 44, 61, 63, 88, 149–50, 237, 281–2, 293
sustainability, 3–5, 12–13, 52, 63, 66, 96–8, 129, 131, 137, 157, 160, 162–5, 203–6, 212, 217, 219, 226–8, 231, 237–9, 257, 287, 289, 291, 296–7; agricultural, 57, 118; economic, 168–9, 171; environmental, 6, 122, 134, 136–7, 157, 171, 215; of diet, 38, 59, 118, 239; discourses of, 3–4, 166; and health, 9, 22, 94, 117, 164, 203, 205, 211–12, 222, 228, 245–6, 284, 291; of health systems, 9, 14, 72–3, 115, 183, 187, 225, 237–8, 271, 282–4, 292; mainstream, 4, 79, 144, 148, 165–6; social-ecological, 177, 204, 279–80; transitions, 35, 64, 100, 203, 205–6, 212–13, 219–21, 245–6, 293
sustainable development, 130, 137; goals of, 37
sustainable future, 4, 9, 49, 117–18, 143, 164, 218–19, 279, 291, 294
sustainable retreat, 137, 297

syndemic, 41, 55–7, 70
systems thinking, 73, 81, 211, 222–3, 231, 279

taxation, 11, 97, 133–5, 172
technology, 11, 25, 33–4, 42, 44, 47–8, 86, 117–18, 128, 130, 132–3, 137, 145–56, 160–2, 166, 168, 179, 206, 208, 211–12, 218, 223, 236–7, 293, 296; appropriate technology, 12, 145–54, 160, 285, 292; medical technology, 5, 40, 125, 128, 137–8, 145–54, 281–2, 292
therapeutic community, 12, 119, 194–201
Therapeutic Landscapes Network, 88, 90
throughput, 12, 129, 131, 137, 141, 153, 156–8, 160, 280
time banking, 5, 241–3
tipping points, 66, 168, 212, 231
traditional medicine, 59, 66, 70, 129, 148, 151–2, 222, 271. *See also* alternative medicine; complementary medicine
transition movement, 85, 158, 230

unintended consequences, 13, 22, 46, 51–3, 63–4, 130, 134, 136, 210, 223, 226–7, 235
universal basic income, 155, 282
urban agriculture, 82, 103–6, 125–6, 285

values, social, 85, 87, 89, 96, 111, 115, 127, 140, 158, 179, 182, 184, 206–8, 222, 226–8, 231, 242–3, 253, 258, 262, 264, 266–7, 283, 290, 297; alternative, 212–13, 236; collective, 8, 168; conservative, 162–6, 228; green, 162–3; modern, 4, 144, 156–9, 173, 215

water cycle, 11, 73–80, 82, 97, 285
welfare state, 11–12, 97–8, 117, 133–7, 139, 142, 160, 167, 173, 175, 200, 215, 281, 286
well-being, 12, 16–19, 31, 33–8, 40, 53, 56–7; 76, 101–2, 118, 189, 195, 203–4, 233–5, 240–1, 270, 273, 277, 279, 282, 285, 287–90, 295–7; of community, 43, 59, 125, 240, 287, 289; during COVID-19 pandemic, 83, 167, 172–3, 176, 247, 252, 254, 257–8; in ecovillages, 178–9, 185; effect of gardening on, 83, 94, 170; effect of nature on, 88; effect of relocalization on, 144–7; eudaemonic, 44, 146; of future generations, 33; hedonistic, 43, 146; human, 6, 22, 34, 36, 43–4, 52–3, 59, 70, 123, 127, 130–1, 141, 144, 154, 172, 216, 293; relationship to political economy, 122–7, 130–2, 138–42, 151, 159, 167–8, 172–3, 176; subjective, 126, 132, 159
whole-systems care, 31, 72, 75
wicked problems, 10–14, 21–2, 51–3, 57, 64, 70–1, 81–2, 117–18, 123, 133, 135, 137, 142, 144, 154–66, 173, 209, 222, 228, 284–91, 296
Wildlife Gardening, 95–7. *See also* gardens

Printed and bound by CPI Group (UK) Ltd, Croydon, CR0 4YY
31/08/2025

14727212-0004